Staging Contemplation

Staging Contemplation

Participatory Theology in Middle English Prose, Verse, and Drama

ELEANOR JOHNSON

The University of Chicago Press

CHICAGO AND LONDON

The University of Chicago Press, Chicago 60637
The University of Chicago Press, Ltd., London

Published 2018
Printed in the United States of America

27 26 25 24 23 22 21 20 19 18 1 2 3 4 5

ISBN-13: 978-0-226-57203-1 (cloth)
ISBN-13: 978-0-226-57217-8 (paper)
ISBN-13: 978-0-226-57220-8 (e-book)
DOI: https://doi.org/10.7208/chicago/9780226572208.001.0001

The University of Chicago Press expresses appreciation to the Schoff Fund at the University Seminars at Columbia University for their help in publication. Material in this work was presented to the University Seminar: Literary Theory.

An earlier and shorter version of chapter 1, "Feeling Time, Will, and Words in the *Cloud of Unknowing*," appeared in the *Journal of Medieval and Early Modern Studies* 4 (2011): 345–68.

Library of Congress Cataloging-in-Publication Data

Names: Johnson, Eleanor, 1979– author.
Title: Staging contemplation : participatory theology in Middle English prose, verse, and drama / Eleanor Johnson.
Description: Chicago ; London : The University of Chicago Press, 2018. | Includes bibliographical references and index.
Identifiers: LCCN 2017060711 | ISBN 9780226572031 (cloth : alk. paper) | ISBN 9780226572178 (pbk. : alk. paper) | ISBN 9780226572208 (e-book)
Subjects: LCSH: English literature—Middle English, 1100–1500—History and criticism. | Theology in literature.
Classification: LCC PR275.R4 J645 2018 | DDC 820.9/001—dc23
LC record available at https://lccn.loc.gov/2017060711

♾ This paper meets the requirements of ANSI/NISO Z39.48-1992 (Permanence of Paper).

Contents

Acknowledgments

This book owes its existence to many excellent interlocutors, readers, and friends. I would like first to thank Susan Crane, Chris Baswell, Julie Crawford, and Alan Stewart for their advice on early versions of the manuscript, as well as Sarah Beckwith for her willingness to read a revised version—midsemester, no less—and provide me with incisive comments from top to bottom. I would also like to thank Julie Peters for reading my chapter on *Wisdom* at a key moment in its formation, as well as the members and attendees of the Critical Theory Faculty Seminar—Bruce Robbins, Tricia Dailey, Paul Strohm, Jean Howard, and Susan Crane (again) in particular—for their perspectives and suggestions on a draft of the *Mary* chapter. Edward Mendelson, thank you, once again and always, for your generosity as a friend and adviser; your comments on my introduction were beyond helpful. For inspiring and provocative conversations about second books, I would also like to thank Sarah Cole, Jim Adams, Rachel Adams, Michael Golston, Nick Dames, Erik Gray, Branka Arsič, Sharon Marcus, and Jenny Davidson. For their unflagging support during my pregnancies, I would like to thank the entire Department of English and Comparative Literature at Columbia University, especially Jean Howard, Susan Crane, Sarah Cole, Sharon Marcus, and Jennifer Wenzel, who helped me realize that I should probably take as much maternity leave as I could get. For hearty laughter and insights of a thousand varieties, as well as a small rocking horse named Plutarch, I thank Elisabeth Ladenson.

Thanks also go to David Wallace, Rita Copeland, and Emily Steiner, as well as to Carolyn Dinshaw and Nicholas Watson, for their comments on my arguments about Julian of Norwich. I am grateful to Jessica Rosenfeld and, as always, to the inimitable Steven Justice for keeping me sharp in my thoughts on *Piers Plowman*. Maura Nolan, thank you for talking with me so enthusiastically and thoughtfully about "participation" early in the gestation of this project. Ingrid Nelson and Shannon Gayk, thank you for encouraging me to publish my article on *Croxton* and *Cleanness* in your special issue of *Exemplaria*. Thanks to Bobby Meyer-Lee and Cathy Sanok for urging me to present work on "Informalism in *Wisdom* and *Mankind*." I am also indebted to the medievalists and early modernists at Princeton University—including Vance Smith, Andrew Cole, Nigel Smith, and Russ Leo—for thinking so carefully through my *Wisdom* and *Piers* arguments with me at various points. I also thank Larry Scanlon, Stacy Klein, and Sarah Novacich for their energetic engagement with my work on contemplative drama, vernacularity, and comedy. Thank you, Matthew Fisher and the Medieval and Renaissance Studies faculty at the University of California–Los Angeles, for inviting me to be Distinguished Visiting Faculty in Medieval Studies in 2016; your invitation prompted me to rethink how the various chapters of the book linked to one another. To all the members of the Former Working Group, thanks for your inexhaustible energy for talking about form in the Middle Ages. I am deeply grateful to the medievalist graduate students at Harvard University and to James Simpson, Dan Donaghue, and Arthur Bahr for their phosphorescent suggestions about my *Wisdom* chapter. Undoubtedly not for the last time, I'd like to thank Bruce Holsinger for his enthusiasm, support, and insight. Finally, I humbly and deeply thank the two mysterious and generous readers who read this book for the press and gave excellent feedback, as well as the unknown colleague who, after writing a tenure letter for me, sent me a raft of brilliant suggestions anonymously in the mail.

As always, I owe a great debt of gratitude to my unstintingly supportive parents: thanks again for the college education—that was definitely a good call. Thanks to my beloved friends Ellen, Emily, Sarah H., Beth, Erin, Marie, Catherine, Lara, Sarah I., and Mark "Memi" H. There is no way I would have made it this far without each one of you; I love you all. With all my heart, I thank my husband, Jonathan Owen, whose unshakable belief in me and in the importance of my work and career makes everything seem infinitely more possible, as well as much more delightful. Finally, I thank my son, Emlyn, my bright, bright star, for guiding my currach when the moon was new, and my sweet, tiny, wonderful daughter, Joan, for being with me so patiently and yet ferociously.

INTRODUCTION

Middle English Contemplation

Forming Vernacular Participation

This book studies original works of contemplative literature in Middle English between 1375 and 1475. The central works are *The Cloud of Unknowing*, *A Revelation of Love*, *Piers Plowman*, The N-Town *Mary* plays, *Wisdom*, and *Mankind*.[1] This is an unusual collection of works to group together under any single heading—much less under the traditionally fairly restrictive label of "contemplative" literature. For that reason, I will begin with a bit of definition and a good bit of redefinition. Traditionally, "contemplative" literature is taken to be the literature primarily about and for professional religious who are committed to living the "contemplative life."[2] There is good justification for this assumption, particularly in the study of medieval contemplative texts, since so many of them are epistles, dedicated or addressed to specific readers who are, in fact, contemplatives.[3] Thus, *contemplative literature* or *contemplative writing* normally denotes a genre that describes the practices to be undertaken as a primary lifework of these contemplative religious. Contemplation, as a primary lifework, is typically understood as the highest form of devotional prayer or attention that an individual person can address toward God. The definition put forth in the 2011 *Cambridge Companion to Medieval English Mysticism* is, however, instructive in how it begins to demarcate more capacious ideas about contemplation. *Contemplative* is defined there as follows: "A person or a state dedicated to a still and agenda-free receptiveness to whatever may be revealed in mystical experience. Often a monk, nun, or other religious person who has taken vows to dedicate their life to seeking to discern and respond to the presence of God . . . [i]n its fullest forms, always likely to assume or require a radical disengagement from the world through solitude, retreat from business and the cares of life, and a single-minded attentiveness holding the mind, body and soul in readiness to behold whatever God may show."[4] Though it is true that "later in the Middle Ages, [contemplation was] more widely available and practiced among lay people as part of a repertoire of devotional postures,"[5] contemplation is still largely conceptualized in scholarship as a rarefied behavior, in a rarefied context, for a rarefied slice of the general population, to be practiced on an individual basis.

One of the driving beliefs behind this book is that the practice and idea of "contemplation" are under an immense amount of cultural pressure in late medieval England—cultural pressure the extent of which has only been partially revealed in scholarship. This book defines *contemplative literature* as a subset of devotional literature, a subset that models for audiences a way of coming to know God as fully as possible, and of coming to understand their own relation to the divine *experientially*—a concept on which I will elaborate shortly. In its effort to make the relation of human to divine available experientially, contemplative literature seeks first to produce awareness that there is a specific relation between soul and God and then to embody that relation in poetic form and style. In the original vernacular works that I study, that relation between soul and God is conceived sometimes as a relation of time to eternity, sometimes as a relation of likeness or similarity between the self and God, and sometimes as a relation of man's sinful, doubting, and vulnerable nature to a God who is all-forgiving, all-knowing, and ever stable. Contemplative literature is often partially about prayer, but it is not simply a presentation of a strategy of contemplative prayer. Contemplation is, increasingly in the late English Middle Ages, a modeling of a practice of orienting oneself toward God, a practice that is open not just to dedicated religious in retreat from the world but instead to anyone who seeks a closer, more intimate mode of knowing the divine and, in particular, knowing the divine in and as his or her own soul.

This broadening of the definition of *contemplation* from the cultural context most usually associated with contemplative writings—namely, the contemplative life lived by monks in monastic settings—may strike some readers as anachronistic. Although it is unquestionably true that monastic settings continued to be a primary cultural center for the practice of the contemplative life, by the late fourteenth century, contemplation was not just for monks anymore. It was not just an overarching mode of life but also a quotidian practice or set of practices; it was not just a vocation but also an avocation, something done occasionally, sometimes seriously and sometimes playfully, sometimes in isolation and sometimes socially. One of my hopes for this book is that it will significantly expand what we as contemporary scholars take the notions of "contemplation" and "contemplative" to encompass; we have a tendency, looking backward, to presuppose more rigid boundaries between practices of contemplation and the rest of life than I think existed in the late Middle Ages. We have a tendency, in effect, to think about *the* contemplative life, constituted around *the* singular and all-encompassing practice of contemplation. What I want to reveal here is, first, that there were many ways of living *a* contemplative life, which is to say, a life in which multiple contemplative practices played a significant role.[6] Second, I will argue that the flourishing and evolution of late Middle English contemplative literature contributed significantly to the possibilities and practices of "contemplation" conceived far more broadly than we imagine when we think of "a contemplative" in radical withdrawal from the world, desperately attempting to banish all worldly concerns from his or her mind. In fact, one of the emergent properties of contemplative writing in the late fourteenth and fifteenth centuries is an investment in the idea that contemplation should not foreclose attention to earthly matters but instead should simply make that attention more focused on beneficent participation in the social world, the world of labor and other people. Put otherwise, late Middle English contemplative literature, far from existing in denial of or indifference to the social world, often has a politics to it, and that politics is oriented toward social parity, social participation, and social justice.

Given the amount of redefining I am doing here, why call these works "contemplative" in the first place? My justification for thinking of the works I study as "contemplative" literature is simple: each of the works in *Staging Contemplation* thematizes contemplation in its more traditional senses—as the defining prayerful practice of spiritual devotion or as a mode of life—precisely to put pressure on those traditional senses. *The Cloud of Unknowing* thematizes contemplation explicitly and early, but it makes clear—as I will elaborate shortly—that its particular treatment of contemplation as a practice and as a mode of life is radically different from what is usually understood by "contemplation." Contemplation is, for the *Cloud*, not just a type of prayer but also a type of attention and intention that one directs toward God. Julian's *Revelation of Love* speaks openly about contemplation and represents Julian's own prayerful interactions with Jesus, but it understands contemplation as a practice open to anyone, whether in retreat from the world or not, and further understands contemplation not just as a type of prayer but also, again, as a category and quality of attention and intention toward God. *Piers Plowman* also thematizes the contemplative life, as well as its notional opposite, the active life, as a template against which to develop a contemplative practice. But in *Piers*, the boundary between active and contemplative breaks down, and, as in *Cloud* and *Revelation*, the end of contemplative practice is a particular kind of attention, a practice of mind, but also a particular orientation toward the social world. The N-Town *Mary* play cycle is, in some ways, the most explicitly contemplative work I study, because it is superintended by an emcee character named Contemplacio.[7] But the play's dramatic treatment of contemplation, like those we will have seen in the prose works and in *Piers*, proves broader and more inclusive than what we generally expect of contemplative literature, or of a life lived in contemplation. In *Wisdom*, the signal that the play understands itself as a contemplative work inheres in its robustly articulated vocabulary about the likeness between self and God, as well as in the play's overt references to Augustine's contemplative magnum opus, *De Trinitate*. Finally, *Mankind*'s investments in contemplation and in being a contemplative work emerge in its signposting of itself as being about "participation," a key concept in late Antique theories of contemplation, as I will discuss presently, and in their realization in late Middle English contemplative literary works, though *Mankind* aggressively troubles what participation can mean and what kinds of participation can be good for the soul.

PARTICIPATION AND/AS CONTEMPLATION

This idea of "participation" is the most central element in my understanding of contemplative literature. The works studied in this book are all deeply invested in thinking through, staging, and revising what one can mean by "contemplation" and how one gets to that state through a participatory encounter with contemplative literature. Fully to understand what I mean by "a participatory encounter" or "participation," it is necessary to review the contemplative theology that precedes and informs medieval contemplative literature. Augustine's seminal contemplative treatise, *De Trinitate*, insists that those who practice contemplation remember that they are truly made in God's image (cf. Gen 1:27)[8] and that they therefore participate in God by their very nature.[9] Participation, originally a Platonic concept, means that all things—be they material or abstract—have a "form," a perfect and quintessential instantiation in the realm of ideas. In this form, all derived, real-time, material particulars of a given thing participate, as an image of that original form.[10] "Goodness," for instance, exists "formally"—there is an absolute "goodness" in the universe, which gives rise to all other goodnesses, such as civic virtue, kindness, or generosity.[11] All lesser goodnesses participate in—literally, they take *part* in—the primary and eternal goodness that is formal goodness. As the sixth-century Neoplatonic contemplative philosopher Boethius explains in his *Consolation of Philosophy*, "all which is good is good by participation in goodness."[12] In Christian Neoplatonic thought, when people are good, they are good because they participate in the supreme good that is God.

In *Staging Contemplation*, this idea of participation is central to a working understanding of the practice of contemplation in the late English Middle Ages, though I also mean participation, throughout, in a second sense. When I say that I am examining how these literary works enable audiences "to understand their own relation to the divine experientially," I mean that they invite readers and viewers to participate in literary sensation as a preliminary way of recognizing their participation in the divine. Participation in the literary field facilitates and enables an experience (or at least the beginnings of one) of one's supervening, ever-present, but often difficult-to-perceive participation in God. In arguing for this two-tiered participation, first in literature and then and thereby in God, *Staging Contemplation* takes these works seriously and on their own terms to elaborate how they literally and literarily initiate and enact contemplative states in and for the soul, by allowing the soul to perceive, through the literary encounter, that it partakes of the divine.

Building on the essential notion of participation, Augustine believes that man is able to participate in God even more fully than he could through his having been created in God's image because Christ, by taking on mortal flesh as Jesus, chooses to participate in humanity. In so doing and in sacrificing himself, he purges some of mankind's accrued sinfulness and restores them to a purer, more godlike state. Thus, Augustine construes participation, in postincarnational history, as a bidirectional phenomenon: man has, since Eden, been created in the image of God, but because Jesus also participates in humanity, mankind is even better and more fully able to participate in godliness.[13] This dual idea of participation—of man in godliness and God in humanness—is a foundational idea of Neoplatonic Christian contemplation, and its consequences reverberate in contemplative history throughout the Latin West.[14] In late antiquity and in the medieval vernacular works I will examine, the goal of contemplation—to bring the human soul into a more experiential understanding of its relation to God—fundamentally entails raising one's awareness of one's own always already present participation in God himself and, simultaneously, of God's historical choice to participate in humanity as the incarnated Jesus.[15] Contemplation does not necessarily result in radical fusion or union with God, but with an awareness that one's own nature is similar to God's, by virtue of mutual participation.

Staging Contemplation examines how medieval English works adopt this understanding of contemplation as a cultivation of a sense of participation between oneself and God and how these works attempt not only to express that experiential sense of participation discursively but also and more crucially to initiate it through literary and, increasingly, dramatic form. *The Cloud of Unknowing*, Julian of Norwich's *Revelation*, *Piers Plowman*, the N-Town cycle's *Mary* sequence, the play *Wisdom*, and the play *Mankind* each construe contemplation as the cultivation of self-conscious participation in God and of awareness of God's participation in man, and they also all seek in part to perform that contemplation in the formal apparatuses of the literary field. So, what makes contemplative literature "contemplative" is that it stages participation for its audience, creating literary experiences that initiate work of spiritual contemplation. The lion's share of the argument of this book will consist in teasing out just how that staging happens.

By saying that contemplative literature "stages" participation, I mean, first, to evoke the idea of gradualness, or proceeding through stages. The relationship between contemplative participation in literary works and contemplative participation in God is not a complete one but rather a *stage* of the larger work that is divine contemplation. The contemplative works I study in this book do not, that is, seek to perform in full the work of spiritual contemplation. This is why Julian of Norwich says of her own writings, "This boke is begonne by Goddes gifte and his grace, but it is not yet performed, as to my sight. For charite pray we alle togeder, with Goddes wurking: thanking, trusting, enjoyeng."[16] "Performed," in opposition to "begonne," means completed.[17] Julian suggests here that her book begins or initiates the true work of contemplation but that the full attainment of contemplative understanding requires a process of prayer, thanks, trust, and enjoyment that exceed the book itself. The same will be true of many of the other contemplative works in *Staging Contemplation:* they seek to initiate the true performance of divine contemplation by inviting readers and viewers to participate in the sensory space of literary form. These works are, in effect, primers for contemplation, which operate by devising and deploying participatory sensory proxies for the work of contemplating God. Thus, the contemplative works I study operate in a manner similar to what Jennifer Herdt describes in her book *Putting on Virtue*. For Herdt, the key to acquiring virtues is practicing at having them; one becomes virtuous by "putting on" (or practicing with) virtuous behaviors and ideas until one acquires them through habitual familiarization. In the contemplative works I study, the works themselves are designed to provide this kind of experience of rehearsal, practice, or the "putting on" of contemplative ideas and behaviors, which should eventually lead the spiritual worker to true contemplation.[18] They use the participatory forms of literature to stage a partial experience of the participation in God that is contemplation's goal. So, although it is not a complete performance of contemplation, contemplative literature is nevertheless performative, in that it stages a part of contemplation itself. Through the sensory experiences of literary form, the works I will study stage part of contemplation, laying the groundwork for what is yet to come and providing a distillation or sensory rendering of the full and satisfying work of contemplation that comes later. The second reason I say that contemplative literature stages contemplation is that, as I will detail, contemplative literature comes, more and more toward the end of the English Middle Ages, to take place in dramatic forms, to be *staged* before an audience.

CONTEMPLATIVE FORMS, CONTEMPLATIVE UNDERSTANDING

By invoking literary and dramatic "form" as keys to understanding the contemplative efficacy of these works, I do not mean to stipulate a singular, totalizing notion of "form." Quite the contrary, it will be the very pliancy and variability of formal construction, poetic device, dramatic device, tone, and discursive register that the contemplative works in this book will avail themselves of. The consistent element across all of these writings and their various deployments of literary forms is that they will all engage with and rely on the sensory experiences provided by the formal structures of literary works in order to stage contemplation. Thus, by literary "form" I mean simply to invoke those elements of the literary that are sensory—the things readers or viewers can feel. By focusing on how form conduces to sensation, I mean to invoke an idea of contemplative literature as experiential, creating initial contemplative experience by virtue of its sensory elements.

The role played by sense-experience in devotional literature writ large—not just in contemplative literature—has been a scholarly focus since the 1980s. Shannon Gayk's work has demonstrated the crucial role played by visual experience in devotional writings of the period. In her view, the reliance on imagery as a sense-perceptible cornerstone of spiritual devotion reaches an apex in the fourteenth century, when theologians and writers alike seem to converge on the realization that visuality conduces to affective experience, and that affective experience is indispensable to devotional practice.[19] Gail McMurray Gibson's study of East Anglian religious cultures makes clear that images, icons, and visuality in general were central to the cultivation of affective devotion in the late English Middle Ages.[20] Sarah McNamer has shown that the Pseudo-Bonaventurian *Meditationes vitae Christi*—one of the most widely disseminated texts of Christian devotion in the Middle Ages—is a key text for inspiring affective identification with Christ and Mary, and that it relies heavily on imagery and on the language of beauty and sweetness to achieve that identification.[21] Nicholas Watson's *Richard Rolle and the Invention of Authority* demonstrates Rolle's commitment to alliteration in the production of salvific and contemplative affect in readers.[22]

Most of the studies on the role of sense-perception and sense-experience in late medieval devotional writing have been geared toward affectivity—how sensory dynamics in a text produce devotional affect.[23] Although the role of affect and affectivity in late medieval religious culture can scarcely be overstated, *Staging Contemplation* focuses on the kinds of *cognitive* work that can be achieved through the experience of formal, sensory elements in a literary text. In saying this, I do not wish to drive a wedge between cognitive and affective work in medieval literary history; the boundary between them is often thin. But this book does not center on how sensory feeling makes one feel emotionally—though that will sometimes come up, especially in my discussions of comedy and empathy. Instead, the book centers on how sensory experience can produce certain desirable types of contemplative understanding. It focuses on how literary form produces what James Simpson has called "modes of knowing."[24] In particular, it focuses on how participatory contemplative literature helps readers and hearers understand-by-sensing their own participatory likeness to God.

Closely associating sense-experience with cognition rather than with affect may seem counterintuitive to modern readers, but it reflects classical and medieval theories of knowledge acquisition: sense-perception is theorized, going back to Aristotle, as a form of cognition.[25] Picking up on this idea, medieval philosophers construed sensation as the foundational form of cognitive activity.[26] Following sensation, one would hope to scale the cognitive ladder to imagination, then reason, and finally intellection.[27] What is significant about the late medieval English contemplative works in this book is that they all register the role of sensation in spiritual practice not as a weak or lowly mode of understanding, to be escaped from as soon as possible, but instead as a powerful tool of contemplation. They all register sense-experience, conveyed through literary form, as a cornerstone of the initial performance of contemplative understanding itself.

Several twenty-first-century writings have paved the way for this kind of analysis. Sarah Beckwith's work on drama has demonstrated that the experience of seeing drama enacted—whether in the a cycle drama's casting of one's neighbors as players in the life of Christ or in a miracle play's staging of parodic transubstantial rituals—produces devotional understanding for late medieval English audiences.[28] Jessica Brantley's *Reading in the Wilderness* reveals that visual engagement with the imagery and material textuality of devotional books prompts cognitive experiences of their teachings.[29] Michelle Karnes has shown that visuality is central to cognitive experience in late medieval devotional writings.[30] Denise Despres reminds us that image-based mental work is necessary in the spiritual transition from lower to higher levels of contemplative understanding.[31] Suzannah Biernoff's work situates sight as the primary cognitive sense; according to medieval cognitive philosophers, it is through that sense that most knowledge is produced.[32] Barbara Newman has proven the centrality of exportable visual experience in contemplative writings, particularly those composed by mystical women writers.[33]

Staging Contemplation continues in this validation of sense-experience in the cognitive work of contemplation in particular, but it shifts focus from visuality, imagery, and sight to aurality: the sounds, rhythms, syntaxes, puns, rhymes, dialects, alliterations, registers, and rhymes of contemplative works. Indeed, the Middle English works I examine in this book all take two interconnected ideas—about formal participation in literature through aural experience and the initiation of formal participation in God—as the sine qua non of late medieval English vernacular contemplative writing. Each work seeks to produce, primarily through aural experience, a feelable and therefore cognizable awareness of the soul's participation in God. Each does so by creating a partial experiential participation in an aspect of the divine. That is, these contemplative literary works all invite the participation of readers in their sensible, and particularly aural, workings as a preliminary enactment of the work of contemplation itself. In all of the works examined in this book, the audience's participation in the literary field—and specifically its participation in the aurality of form and style that literature affords—is designed to bring about a sense of one's own participation in the divine nature.

Although these works all register the importance of experientially instilling a sense of participation in God as a step toward contemplative understanding, each of them understands the particular quiddity of contemplation in its own way. *The Cloud of Unknowing* construes a fleeting experience of union with God as a primary goal of participatory contemplation. Julian of Norwich's *Revelation of Love* construes a feelable literary experience of how God can participate in both temporality and eternity as a contemplative goal. The N-Town *Mary* plays construe a miraculous sense of how Mary could hold the eternal God in her time-bound womb as a goal. *Piers Plowman* and *Wisdom* construe a sensible experience of man's likeness to and participation in the Trinity as a goal, and they construe a renewed and deepened sense of participation in the Christian community as a correlative goal. *Mankind* turns away from Trinitarian contemplation to revel in the pleasures of sin and to remind audiences that participation in a Christian community has its dangers and downsides, even though those dangers can, themselves, be avenues toward a deeper and fuller contemplative experience. Despite their differences, all these works share an awareness of the importance of literature's sensible, and especially aural, forms in staging participatory contemplation.

PARTICIPATION IN THE VERNACULAR

That preliminary sense of participation in God inheres in readers' and hearers' participation not just in literary forms but specifically in how such forms can work in the English vernacular. *Staging Contemplation* suggests that vernacular English has formal properties—originating in the aurality of English grammar, syntax, word meanings, paronomasias, insular poetic styles and strategies, as well as in English's discursive status as the language of the everyday, the language of slang and profanity, and the "kynde" or "natural" language—that enable particular sensory effects for contemplative audiences in England. These Middle English works all explore and exploit the formal, sensory facets of English as resources for contemplating God. For all of the works I examine, the impulse to make participation in God *feelable*, sensible in literary form, whether as an eternal being, an incarnated being, or a guardian and guarantor of the Christian social world, is the primary impulse, and it has consequences not only in local poetic forms but also in primary linguistic choice.

In demonstrating the formal salience of English, *Staging Contemplation* reassesses "vernacularity" as an impulse among contemplative writers in

England. Although the turn to English certainly has to do with a desire to provide wider demographic access to contemplative writings, I will suggest that the choice to compose in English and thereby to avail oneself of the formal particularities of a vernacular language is also about a different kind of access—namely, cognitive access, born of sense experience.[34] To explain what I mean, I will briefly turn to cognitive linguistics. Contemporary cognitive linguists call reading and learning situations in which readers or learners encounter a language in which they are fluent and in which that language behaves in standard ways, "fluent" situations. Readers tend to like these fluent situations and to process easily information conveyed fluently. But, in more recent years, cognitive linguists have begun to discover that "disfluent" situations, those in which native speakers' expectations of how their native language functions are frustrated, can produce a deeper cognitive access to information.[35] The reason why is simple: when readers or hearers encounter a language in which they are fluent, any aberrant, atypical, complex, or layered usage of that language will be striking, because they will sense an asymmetry between their reflexive expectations about how the language works and what is presented to them. Native speakers of a language, that is, are intuitively sensitive to its rules and registers, its forms, its denotative and connotative values, and its limits, so that they respond to divergences from those norms in ways that promote attentiveness and understanding. In the contemplative works studied in this book, the choice to compose in a vernacular language has to do with the kind of sense-based cognitive access readers can have to a language in which they are natively fluent, when that fluency is activated only shortly to be frustrated through disfluent usage.[36] As we will see, in the medieval contemplative context, there is a dynamic tension between fluent and disfluent learning situations—a tension that many contemplative writers try to get at by working with and through the idea of "kyndely" learning, language, and literary form. Indeed, the idea of leveraging disfluency to prompt deeper learning is a close analogue for what Langland does in his paradoxical evocation of the ever-elusive "kynde knowynge"—a mode of knowing that is born of familiarity—when that familiarity is staged only to be traduced by something nonstandard, unfamiliar, or unkind.

In the Middle English contemplative writings in this book, readers' and hearers' expectations of how Middle English works and how it sounds will be productively frustrated by strained syntax or aberrant grammar, odd rhythmical patterns, atypical semantic ranges, puns, interlinguistic shifting, slippage among registers of meaning, and the introduction of slang or profanity into otherwise high-style poetics. This sensory knowing of the norms and bounds of English, a sensory knowing born of fluency, is at work in Julian's *Revelation* when she conveys how Christ speaks to her in English. It is at work in *The Cloud of Unknowing* in the *Cloud*-author's percussive monosyllabic rhythms. It is at work in the N-Town *Mary*'s bilingual wordplay, where English is made to seem both familiar and strange through its vexed association with Latin. It is at work in *Piers Plowman* when Latin and English near-synonyms are brought into vertiginous proximity with each other, so that their likenesses and unlikenesses are simultaneously visible. This sensory knowing is what is going on in *Wisdom* and *Mankind* with Lucifer's and Titivillus's wobbly Latinity and their introduction of slang and hobbled rhyme as a sense-perceptible correlative for decay. In all of the works in this book, the sensible frisson between a fluent expectation of a language and the disfluent complicating of that expectation in formal practice is central to participatory contemplative experience in literature.

Thus, this book will reveal a different strain of thinking about and using English than what Vincent Gillespie has noted in the medieval theologians William Butler, Thomas Palmer, and Richard Ullerston. Butler, Palmer, and Ullerston viewed English as "linguistically, lexically, and syntactically inadequate to render the complexity and sophistication of the word of God" and as "a language of limited flexibility and responsiveness," whereas the works I will examine see English in quite another light.[37] In these works, English is staged as linguistically, lexically, and syntactically optimal, a language of maximal flexibility and suppleness in rendering contemplative truths about God available to native speakers of English precisely because of its ability to toggle between fluent and disfluent registers. Because of English's ability to flex and morph in the minds of native readers and hearers, when I talk about vernacularity in this book, I am actually talking about multiple and internally various Englishes, characterized not only by being recognizable as forms of English but also by their divergent discursive registers, their degrees of colloquialism, the presence or absence of slang, their susceptibility to perforation by other inset vernaculars (such as French or mock Latin), and their lexical and grammatical flexibility.

Staging Contemplation focuses on the English of late medieval England in particular because, in the late Middle Ages, the social parameters of contemplation are changing so rapidly there. The trend I have already in part addressed, in which contemplation is increasingly a practice urged on all Christians,[38] is happening on the continent already in the thirteenth century[39] but happens with perhaps greater force in England in the late fourteenth and fifteenth centuries, no doubt in part because of the surge of interest in vernacularization that accompanies Wycliffism and because of the pressures that Wycliffite ideologies of translation and spirituality place on more institutionally mainstream religion.[40] As is well known, one of Wyliffism's core tenets is a radical commitment to English as a legitimate and indeed necessary language into which biblical and theological texts should be translated so as to promote access to Christian knowledge.[41] This commitment to vernacularization is associated in the minds of medieval politicians and clergy with such turbulent events as the Peasants' Rebellion of 1381—so much so that the Blackfriars Council of 1382 suppresses Wycliffite writings and condemns those who preach them.[42] By 1389, owners of vernacular theological books are being harassed, and their books are subject to confiscation and burning.[43] As a result of these pressures, over the course of the 1390s, vernacular theological books are increasingly written anonymously, and translations and compilations begin to replace original works as the main mode of vernacular theological expression.[44] A few monastic houses seem to escape censure for owning vernacular theological texts,[45] but the 1401 *De Haeretico Comburendo* and Arundel's *Constitutions* of 1409 make the "simple ownership of vernacular theological writings prima facie evidence of heretical leanings."[46] At this time, Wycliffite preachers largely go underground, though the movement does not die;[47] quite the contrary, the attempt to stamp out Wycliffism and its shape-shifting avatar Lollardy eventually results in an increase in extrainstitutional theology in the period.[48]

The contemplative works I study in this book both reflect and contribute to this theological culture in the Middle English vernacular. This culture of political and religious unrest surrounding Wycliffism and its ideological stance toward English is part of why England of the late fourteenth and fifteenth centuries becomes a crucible within which to view self-conscious literary explorations of how to prompt and initiate contemplation in a vernacular language.[49] I do not mean to say that the Wycliffites directly spurred the literary stagings of contemplation that I will describe in this book, but rather that Wycliffite writings and activities are symptomatic of the cultural electricity around the issues and Englishes that animate the works I study.

STAGING CONTEMPLATION

Looking for the literary heirs to the innovativeness of the prose and poetic contemplative works I will discuss in the first three chapters of this book—*The Cloud of Unknowing*, *A Revelation of Love*, and *Piers Plowman*—Barry

Windeatt is right to point out the striking "lack of successors" in the fifteenth century for the high contemplative writings of the fourteenth, noting that the contemplative writings that newly circulate in the fifteenth century are translations from Continental works rather than original compositions.[50] Vincent Gillespie notes that "Arundel's decrees cast a long shadow" producing "a sense that the role of the vernacular in innovatory religious writing was diminished, its advocates cowed and anxious."[51] And it is true: the flowering of original Middle English contemplative prose and long-form narrative verse that exists in the fourteenth and very early fifteenth century in England, including *The Cloud of Unknowing*, Julian's *Revelation of Love*, Langland's *Piers Plowman*, and Rolle's *Form of Living*, withers in the wake of Arundel's *Constitutions*. To be sure, there are some original vernacular works written that are recognizably in conversation with contemplative writings—such as Margery Kempe's *Book*—and there are numerous translated works from other European languages, as well as some aureate, English theological treatises, as well as English poems that take on religious subjects, but not many original, vernacular English prose works of contemplation.[52] That does not mean, however, that original contemplative literature has died by the middle of the fifteenth century in England. Quite the contrary, it has merely changed form. The form of original Middle English contemplative literature in the very late English Middle Ages is drama. The N-Town cycle's *Mary* sequence and the morality plays *Wisdom* and *Mankind* are all high-order, original contemplative works, and they are the successors of the fourteenth-century works of contemplation in prose and poetry.

There has not been a full study of the relationship between Middle English contemplative prose or poetic works and dramatic ones as such. Instead, with the exception of a small number of pioneering studies, Middle English drama has traditionally been held apart from other kinds of devotional works—and from contemplative works in particular.[53] This scholarly bias does not reflect the reality of late Middle English literary production and ideology but instead occludes a fascinating and crucial evolutionary trajectory in Middle English contemplative writing, a trajectory that begins with Middle English prose contemplative treatises and ends with contemplative dramas. Middle English contemplative prose, poetic, and dramatic works coexist along a spectrum, innovating together toward an ever more participatory contemplative experience. So, finally, this book suggests reasons for the decline of original Middle English prose and poetic contemplative literature and the rise of dramas of contemplation in context of the political and religious climate of fifteenth-century England.

One reason for this surprising succession is necessarily conjectural and lies in cultural reactions to the religious conservatism of the late fourteenth century, coupled with the relative reformism of the fifteenth. After Archbishop Arundel's aggressive paradigms for enforcing orthodoxy and suppressing heterodoxy in the very early fifteenth century, there arises a surge of disappointment with his style of religio-political control. This surge results in a new era of reformist English religious culture.[54] Archbishop Chichele paves the way for a new English orthodoxy, and he sets about encouraging prayer and contemplation, urging monastics to serve as a "fountainhead" for the broader church reforms he sought to enact, as well as to inspire prayer and contemplation in society more broadly.[55] By 1450, the institutional church grants that the practice of contemplation should be as available to a merchant as to a monk,[56] and certain venerable religious institutions—most notably the Charterhouse of Sheen and Syon Abbey[57]—devote a great deal of attention to the production and circulation of vernacular theological works, including contemplative treatises.[58] Thus, the middle of the fifteenth century constitutes a pressure point for contemplative practice and contemplative writing: in the first half of the century, contemplation was restricted and regulated, in part through the prohibitions on original English contemplative texts; in the second half, monks and high-level religious officials encourage broader contemplative participation among all strata of society. The dramatic mode partially supplies the need that emerges for an increasingly public and increasingly collective contemplative culture, and it does so by obviating the concerns about vernacular theological literary production that kept an earlier generation of ecclesiarchs in a state of vigilant agitation.

The reasons I believe drama was able to supply this need so efficiently are many. First, although one might assume that the Lollard espousal of the English vernacular as a language of spiritual thinking, reading, and knowing would make Lollards sympathetic to vernacular drama as a mode of disseminating religious truth, since the dramas were both in English and notionally able to reach a wide audience, the opposite seems to have been true. The Lollard *Tretise of Miraclis Pleyinge* makes clear that plays are spiritually dangerous because they invite viewers to identify too closely with the action on stage qua the action on stage, rather than encouraging them to think beyond, to the divine truths represented in the plays. Drama is all the more dangerous because it is a game—something done "in pley and bourde"—rather than a matter of "ernestful" devotion.[59] Weeping on Jesus's behalf is a good thing; weeping on behalf of a local townsperson who masquerades as Jesus, on the other hand, is not. Indeed, thinking that such plays could conduce to correct spiritual practice is "maumetrie," mere idol making.[60] The treatise writer is aware that some dramaphiles might say that "recreacion is leeveful" but points out that the sportive, playful fun of miracle plays and other forms of religious drama is "fals and worldly."[61] Drama is then contrary to at least to some Lollard ideology, counterintuitively, in part *because of* its vernacularity—its comedic vernacularity in particular, its playful, "bourding" nature. I believe that in part because of its incompatibility with Lollard doctrine, drama becomes a mode of cultural expression that has some degree of freedom to experiment with contemplative ideas without raising the church's hackles about Lollardy. Dramas' partial immunity to charges of Lollard sympathies is evident in East Anglia of the 1460s, where Lollard men are burned alive for their critiques of Eucharistic devotion, but, for instance, the *Croxton Play of the Sacrament* gets away with torturing and disfiguring the body of God on stage—and urging viewers to laugh at the ridiculousness of it all.[62] Dramas are pulling off political and religious critiques that are not tolerated so well in other forms—at least until the sixteenth century shuts down religious drama as a threat to the Anglican reforms. Second, the dramatic mode is both powerful and nonthreatening simply because, through cycle dramas, it has been a mainstay of orthodox public spirituality in England for the better part of a century; if we reach back to the liturgical and paraliturgical dramas that give rise to the cycle dramas, drama has been an established part of ungainsayably orthodox public spirituality for more than two hundred years by the middle of the fifteenth century.

Third, because of their inevitable reliance on imagery, dramas have a concrete claim to being ideologically incompatible with Lollardy. The Lollard aversion to the reliance on imagery in devotional practice is well known in the English Middle Ages[63] and, indeed, partially inspires the aforementioned *Tretis on Miraclis Pleyinge.*[64] Dramas are prima facie un-Lollard since they rely on the very visuality that Lollards so stoutly condemned.[65]

Fourth and finally, texturing these historical and cultural reasons, there are formal and stylistic reasons that the dramatic mode becomes the main arena of action for participatory contemplative literature in the late English Middle Ages. Those formal and stylistic elements leverage the particular formal resources of vernacularity, much as do the earlier prose and poetic works I focus on in my first two chapters, but with a slightly different focus. Chief among the formal and stylistic affordances of drama is a participatory dynamic of comedy that contemplative drama creates while the contemplative prose and verse in the period do not. "Religious laughter" has been recognized as an important element of medieval vernacular drama since the mid-twentieth century. Examining cycle dramas, V. A. Kolve has suggested that this laughter comes in two types: salubrious laughter we experience at malefactors and laughter that has a concretely referential didactic purpose.[66] This religious laughter must have a certain "propriety," which is to say relevance to or support of the main narrative of the life of Christ, as well as "necessity," which is to say that the plays need this comedy to make their points: as Kolve elegantly puts it, "however funny, bumptious, coarse, or improvisatory these comic actions may seem, they have their roots in serious earth; they are intimately and intricately involved in their play's deepest meanings."[67] Kolve's assessment of how the comedic moments work in the devotional Corpus Christi plays (he focuses on York, Towneley, and Chester) is unexceptionable, but the comedy in the contemplative dramas I will examine—in the N-Town *Mary* plays and in the morality plays of *Wisdom* and *Mankind*—works a bit differently. It is more acutely participatory than what Kolve finds in the Corpus Christi plays, in three ways. First, it is more participatory in that the laughter is not meant to distance a viewer from a malefactor but to make viewers realize their vertiginous proximity to that malefactor. Second, laughter is, in these plays, part of participatory contemplation; it is not a device that points toward or anticipates a paraphrasable lesson but rather is an end unto itself, meant to produce specific contemplative experiences for audiences. Third, the dramatic comedy in these plays is often deployed in a way that imagines Christian practices of contemplation not just as social but indeed as collective.

Dramatic comedy makes contemplation collective by deploying particular formal resources of the English vernacular—whether in the form of Middle English puns, code-switching between English and French, code-switching between Latin and English, the introduction of slang, or sonic play—in a manner that sense-perceptibly calls viewers' cognitive attention at once to their collective participation in the drama enacted onstage and their distance from it, and, thus, their ability to observe it critically and reflectively. Comedic vernacularity points up what is strange and incongruous in Christian contemplative practice—the strangeness of Joseph's role in the story of *Mary*, the uncomfortable tension between action and contemplation in the play of *Wisdom*, the uncanny temptingness of the devil in his various linguistic guises in *Mankind*—in a way that is at once normalizing and accentuating of that strangeness. Comedy is the pinnacle of contemplative participatory technique in drama, but it relies, as we will see, for its particular efficacy on the deployment of defamiliarized English or other languages embedded within English, so that viewers can recognize the weird duality that is contemplation: at the same time, we well and truly do participate in God and are well and truly separate from him, alienated from his mystery and thus in need of constant contemplative refinement.

In focusing on dramatic form as a key to understanding the contemplative meaning and efficacy of these plays, this book speaks to performance studies and theater history from a period in which that conversation is necessarily fragmentary and speculative.[68] There are no extant records of actual performance in the Middle Ages of any of the plays that I study, no documents about actors, no decisive indication of how stagings would have worked in the fifteenth century. The N-Town *Mary* sequence exists in one manuscript, seemingly written by one author who tipped his or her works into a much larger set of plays. We do not know for certain where the *Mary* sequence is written—beyond that it is written in East Anglia—nor with certainty by whom it is performed, nor how. *Wisdom*, also East Anglian, exists in its complete form in only one manuscript, and it is not clear where or by whom the play would be performed, nor is it clear for how long the play is actively being staged. *Mankind* exists in the same manuscript that contains *Wisdom*, and, again, there are no extrinsic surviving records describing the circumstances of its performance; scholars have suggested groups as diverse as inn dwellers, tavern frequenters, aristocrats, clergy, and academics.[69]

Rather than hampering the effort to analyze the dramatic functionality of these plays, though, the relative dearth of information about their performance history simply invites a more immanently poetic and formal approach.[70] Using the formal properties of the dramatic works as they are recorded either in the play script itself or in the margins as stage directions is the best option for reconstructing something like a theory and history of how and why these plays were performed. Put otherwise, getting deep into the page of these plays' poetic and textual instantiations in manuscripts is our best way of getting onto the stage with them—particularly getting onto the stage with them as works designed to prompt participatory contemplative experiences of God. After all, in medieval England, writers of dramas are also, always, poets; there are no prose Middle English plays, undoubtedly in part for reasons of poetry's relative mnemonic availability to performers and audiences. But I will argue in this book that the Middle English contemplative playwrights and composers of the plays are not just following conventions in versifying their dramas but are in fact serious, careful, and skilled poets, invested in and capable of manipulating poetic forms to great contemplative effect. Leaning hard on poetics in these plays, though very rarely done as a fundamental methodological orientation in scholarship, produces real hermeneutic profit.

Still, because I do not want to elide completely elements of performance, I will here set up my coming analyses with some theoretical frameworks about spectatorship. There is a difficulty here, too, which is that most theater historians who work on spectatorship focus on periods during which treatises about theater spectatorship were written.[71] Because of the scarcity of medieval dramatic theory, one angle I will take now is to adduce what might be an average playgoer's experience of witnessing a play.[72] The composition of an audience of medieval plays is notoriously hard to pinpoint; scholars examining a single play will alternately assert that it was written for aristocrats or monks, educated people or the general population. This unclarity would have been in play in the Middle Ages as well: a play, once written and in some kind of circulation, could easily have come to be performed for any number of audiences, and, for that reason, it is my belief that, as early modernists have suggested about later dramas, medieval plays were written to have real appeal to a diverse audience, comprising elites as well as peasants, notionally secular people and notionally clerical ones.[73] Or, to be more precise, the plays leverage audience unpredictability as a compositional felicity: these are plays aimed not at a single, specific viewer or type of viewer but instead at a kind of spectatorial everyman, hovering between high and low, lay and religious. Throughout this book, when I talk about how an audience member might or would react, I am talking about this everyman figure. This everyman is fluent in English, has some recognition of Latin, has some working knowledge of French, and is at least somewhat familiar not only with orthodox Christian doctrine but also with orthodox Christian texts.

The fundamental tack I will take in adducing this everyman's response to medieval plays has to do with exportability. It is my contention that the plays I study are all designed to make the contemplative experiences of its players exportable to audiences. Allison Hobgood's book on early modern spectatorship urges us to be aware that, in the early modern period, the emotions were held to be "catchable," or contagious.[74] Although I am far less focused on affects—"passions," as Hobgood calls them—such as joy, fear, love, sorrow, and anger, and more focused on states of understanding and cognitive processing that plays can induce as a part of contemplation, I believe that contemplative states are "catchable" on the stages of the English Middle Ages.

They are catchable not just between players and audience members, however, but also between and among audience members. The contagiousness or exportability of contemplative understanding between audience members constitutes the final element of what dramatic staging does to and with participatory contemplation in literature: as we will see with increasing force in the latter, dramatic works I examine, the contemplative culture of late medieval England increasingly emphasizes the contemplative experience as something intersubjective, collective, and social.[75] As Eamon Duffy has shown, the baseline nature of religious and devotional experience across the various socioeconomic strata throughout the Middle Ages in England was collective, communal, and at least semipublic.[76] Laypeople did much of their spiritual devotion in church, surrounded by all their neighbors and friends; monks and nuns, of course, did their spiritual devotion in communities.[77] So, on the one hand, to suggest that any type of spiritual practice became more social and more collective over the course of the Middle Ages may seem otiose. But contemplation is a special and in some ways a privileged form of spiritual devotion, even though it is being more widely practiced by the early fifteenth century. It is "a rational reflection on incorporeal things which the philosopher, living in retirement from the active life of the world, has a duty to perfect, recognizing and uniting with uncreated truth through the cultivation of inner sight and the exclusion, so far as possible, of distracting bodily or 'corporeal' vision."[78] The contemplative subject is one who chooses isolation, the better to strip away the superficialities of human life and thereby to access higher truths about God—this is true for the *Cloud*-author and for Julian. *Staging Contemplation* shows that there is, however, an emergent thread of contemplative practice in late medieval England that hones in on and amplifies the social implications and possibilities of contemplation. Increasingly, in the vernacular contemplative works that appear in this book, the relationship between individual contemplation and social action and social responsibility is a *primary* concern. In particular, the more dramatic works—*Mary*, *Wisdom*, and *Mankind*—are keen to remind their readers sensually that the work of individual contemplation is inseparable from the work of social participation and social responsibility, though we will see that seed initially germinate in *Piers Plowman*. Indeed, these works will seek to engage the contemplative participation of their readers precisely toward an understanding that any act of contemplation that neglects the demands of the social world is not a true act of contemplation at all. That lesson, although fully present and perhaps even founded in *Piers*, is driven home by the dramatic works of contemplation in the fifteenth century.

PART I

Participating in Time and Eternity

CHAPTER ONE

Feeling Time, Will, and Words

Vernacular Devotion in The Cloud of Unknowing

Scholarship on *The Cloud of Unknowing* falls into two main camps, one of which focuses on the *Cloud*'s contribution to early English prose, while the other examines its theory of spiritual practice.[1] This bifurcation of critical attention manifests a crux in the *Cloud* itself—namely, how its intricate prose stylistics embody its equally intricate ideation.[2] As I will show, assessing the *Cloud*-author's style in direct relation to his theory of spiritual practice gets at the very core of his project: to design a work that teaches its devotional practice via a participatory sense-experience of literature. In evoking the discourse of participation, I do not mean to undercut the *Cloud*'s own explicit and recurrent focus on attaining union ("onhede") with the divine as the ultimate goal of contemplative practice. Quite the contrary, in *The Cloud of Unknowing*, the sensory cultivation of a contemplative's awareness of his participation in God is instrumental in his being able eventually to approach that union with God.

On its surface, *The Cloud of Unknowing* seems a fairly straightforward text. It is an apophatic treatise, composed around 1390. Its announced project is to explore and explain how, exactly, contemplatives can and should contemplate a God who is, by his very nature, unknowable. Indeed, the *Cloud*-author quickly and pervasively makes clear that the actual contemplation of God is not cognitive—in the sense of intellectually or rationally knowable—hence the work's governing image of a cloud of "unknowing." The *Cloud*-author also makes clear that, although loving affect is involved in the work of contemplation, contemplation is not *purely* affective. He tells us that in the highest states of contemplation, we neither know God rationally nor feel him affectively: "thou maist not see him cleerly by light of vnderstonding in thi reson, ne fele him in swetnes of loue in thin affeccion."[3] But if God is not to be fathomed rationally or felt affectively, what can we say about how we *are* meant to fathom God?

To get at the particular path to fathoming God, the *Cloud* deploys two key terms, each of which reaches toward a mode of knowing that is not quite rational, not quite affective, but something decidedly sensory. One of them, which arises in the ninth chapter, is "grope." When talking about the nature of "contemplacion" (*CU*, 9.34.12), the *Cloud*-author says, "& loke thou have no wonder of this; for mightest thou ones se it as cleerly as thou maist bi grace com to for to grope it & feele it in this liif, thou woldest think as I say" (*CU*, 9.34.15–16).[4] In this passage, the *Cloud*-author establishes something extremely important about the experiential nature of contemplation. By juxtaposing the terms "grope" and "feele," the *Cloud*-author disambiguates the multivalent and oft-used term "feele," indicating that he is not talking about an affective state of "feeling" but rather about a form of feeling that is, in some ineradicable way, sensory. We are not simply meant to feel an affective emotion of love for God; we are meant to "grope" toward God, to reach out toward him and grab onto him in a palpable way. Simultaneously, by saying "grope" rather than, for instance, "touch," the *Cloud*-author calls attention to a certain sensory strain in the act of contemplation: when we need to grope for things, we need to do so because our other senses—sight, hearing, even touch itself—are in some way impaired or inadequate. We do not grope for things in bright light; we grope for them in the dark. Thus, even as the *Cloud*-author seems to authorize some kind of sensory, physical metaphor for understanding the nature of contemplation, he reminds his readers that the nature of sensory feeling itself in the work of contemplation is far from self-evident. Contemplation is not about seeing, hearing, touching, smelling, or tasting God in any kind of unmediated way; instead, it is about the blind and deaf reaching toward him, desperate, directionless, but whole-intentioned.

Accentuating this image of the blind contemplative groping after God, the *Cloud* deploys a much fuller and more pervasive set of phrases for how one contemplates God, each of which denotes a compromised kind of sensation: "nakid entent," "blynde beholding," "blynde steryng," and just plain "blynde." Very early on, then, the *Cloud* indicates that the effort to contemplate God does not involve *seeing* but rather a kind of *un*seeing, and that that unseeing has to do with an intention that is stripped down to its essential character: "For at the first tyme when thou dost it, thou fyndest bot a derknes, & as it were a cloude of unknowyng, thou wost never what, savyng that thou felist in thi wille a nakid entent vnto God" (*CU*, 3.16–17.19–20, 1–2). This naked intention toward God, much like the image of blind groping, is a state that is not quite affective but is instead a kind of sensation that is determined and delimited by *will*, by the feelable intention of the contemplative to strain and reach toward God, however blindly and unsurely. Indeed, according to the *Cloud*, "the substaunce of this werke is not elles bot a nakid entente directe unto God for him-self" (*CU*, 24.58.15–16); thus, the would-be contemplative is advised, "Be blynde in this tyme, & schere awey covetyse of knowyng, for it wil more let thee than help thee. It suffisith inowgh unto thee that thou fele thee steryd likyngly with a thing thou wost never what, ellys that in thi steryng thou have no specyal thought of any thing under God, & that thin entent be nakidly directe unto God" (*CU*, 34.70.17–22). Thus, the *Cloud* correlates the idea of blindness—of attenuated bodily sensation—with the feeling of being stirred toward the contemplation of God, and it correlates that paradoxical state of stirring sensation with the idea of directed, naked intention.

Going further, lest we think that the striving, groping, naked reaching toward God is entirely unphysical, the *Cloud* later uses an image of wrestling to characterize it: "For I telle thee trewly that I had lever be so nowhere bodely, wrastlyng with that blynde nought, than to be so grete a lorde" (*CU*, 68.122.2–4). Despite its expressed aversion to physicality in the work of spiritual contemplation, in *The Cloud of Unknowing*, as in the actual cloud of unknowing that it imagines, the metaphorics of contemplation remain physical, sensory: contemplation denotes a groping, grasping, blind, desperate *wrestle* with the "blynde nought" that encases and constitutes true understanding. Despite the text's explicit warnings against bodiliness, against reliance on sight, there remains an acknowledgement that contemplation seems to require some kind of sensory engagement, a sensation that is not one of the bodily senses in its normal application but instead a feeling that calls the contemplative to reach out toward God blindly and nakedly, groping and wrestling with only his bare intention. The *Cloud*'s paradoxical theory seems to be that contemplation requires at once an annihilation of the standard bodily senses of sight, hearing, touch, taste, and smell, but that it also engenders or requires some emergent new sense, capable of groping and wrestling blindly toward God.[5] This sense is what *The Cloud of Unknowing* aims to cultivate in its readership.

After all, the *Cloud*-author is careful to remind his readers time and again that the text of the *Cloud* itself is geared not only to explain but also actually to enact some small part of the work of contemplation itself. He tells his audience that he presents his book to them, "So that thou mayst conceyve here by theese wordes sumwhat . . . that in this werk men schul use no menes, ne yit men mowe not com therto with menes" (*CU*, 34.71.6–8). There is no "mene," no intermediary or middleman, in the work of contemplation; and *yet*, the *Cloud* itself is somehow designed to help the reader "conceyve" the work of contemplation. Toward the end of the book, the *Cloud*-author returns to this theme of textual embodiment, saying, "Alle thoo that redyn or heren the mater of this book be red or spokin, & in this redyng or hering think it good & likyng thing, ben never the rather clepid of God to worche in this werk, only for this likyng steryng that thei fele in the tyme of this redyng" (*CU*, 75.130–31.24, 1–3). The "tyme of this redyng" is meant to convey to a reader a desire to "worche in this werk" of groping toward God. The book itself, as this chapter will detail further, is designed and styled to invite a reader into the contemplative act, to inspire an initiatory "steryng" in them that will help awaken them to the "blynde steryng" they are ultimately meant to feel toward God. Indeed, through its artful prose style, the *Cloud* creates for its readership a sensory simulacrum of the experience of spiritual contemplation itself, so that the work becomes not only a macrocosmic description but also a microcosmic initiation of spiritual work. As will become clear, the *Cloud*-author finds in the particular formal properties of his contemplative prose style a sensory experience that is uniquely appropriate to the work of contemplative devotion—a sensory experience that cognitively conveys the "groping" toward an understanding of God. Indeed, even though the actual work of contemplation—the striving toward and into the cloud of unknowing itself—is, as its name implies, non- or even anticognitive, the enacting of that work in the literary field of the text is decidedly cognitive, because it is decidedly sensory.

AUGUSTINE'S CHALLENGE AND THE *CLOUD*-AUTHOR'S RESPONSE

Since the *Cloud*-author's technique of spiritual practice is central to my argument, I will review how it works. As is widely known, the *Cloud* teaches a practice of prayer and meditation through which a spiritual practitioner can achieve union, or "onhede," with God (*CU*, 8.32.15). As in many devotional works, love is the primary unitive force the *Cloud* describes and seeks to cultivate in its readership. This "love" entails the exertion of will—what the *Cloud* calls "nakid entente"—toward God.[6] The *Cloud*-author figures this "nakid entente" as "a sharp dart of longing love," with which one must repeatedly strike or "smyte" the "cloud of unknowing" that separates one from God.[7] This "smiting" is the central activity of spiritual practice; devout "smiting" enables the spiritual practitioner to penetrate into the cloud and be absorbed up into it and into "onhede" with the divine.

The *Cloud*-author recognizes that the darts of "nakid entente" might prove hard to "grope," both conceptually and in practice, so he offers up a relatively concrete meditative tactic: to "have betir holde ther-apon," he explains, his readers should use language as a vehicle for loving will, so that the "entente" is "lappid and foulden in o worde"—namely, the word of prayer (*CU*, 7.28.8, 11, 10).[8] It seems natural enough that readers should fold their will into prayer, but exactly how the word of prayer is rendered a suitable vehicle for their "nakid entente" is of particular significance in the *Cloud*. The *Cloud*-author urges his readers not just to pray, but specifically to "take bot a litil worde of o silable" during the time of prayer, recommending the monosyllables "God" and "love": "& soche a worde is this worde GOD or this worde LOVE" (*CU*, 7.28.13–14). Readers are urged not just to utter this short word once but rather to repeat it over and over again: "fasten this worde to thin herte, so that it never go thens for thing that bifalleth. . . . With this worde thou schalt bete on this cloude & this derknes aboven thee" (*CU*, 7.28.15–16, 18–19). Prayer, for the *Cloud*-author, is neither narrative nor syntactic; instead, it is recursive and asyntactic. It is nothing more or less than the steady repetition of a single word that embodies the loving "nakid entente" that its utterer bears toward God. This mode of repetitive, self-identical, short prayer is meant to embody the "sharp darts of longing love" with which the spiritual practitioner must "smyte" and "bete" the cloud of unknowing: like tiny spearpoints of loving will, short words are sent to pierce into the cloud and produce the beginnings of a "onheed" or union between the contemplative and God.

But the connection between monosyllabic prayer and the work of spiritual devotion extends to a far deeper level of the *Cloud*-author's theory, having roots in his understanding of the difference and relationship between time and eternity. That understanding, in turn, underpins his theory of how one achieves true union with God by cultivating an awareness of one's ever-present participation in him. The *Cloud*-author's understanding of time and eternity reflects his engagement with earlier theorists, and particularly with Augustine, who understands time and eternity as fundamentally different dimensions, which structure fundamentally different modes of willing, loving, and using language.

In Augustine's view, divine eternity is uniform and unchanging, an ever-present and self-similar presence:

> All your years stand together, since they endure, and your past years do not exclude the coming years, because your years do not pass away: however, all these, our years, shall be, when all of them have passed. Your years are but a day, and your day is not daily changing, but always today, because your today does not yield to tomorrow; and thus it does not succeed a yesterday. Your "today" is eternity.[9]

By contrast with this unchanging divine presence, human experience is fragmentary and changeful, divided into past, present, and future. Moreover, since the past has passed, and the future has not yet arrived, Augustine suggests that only the present moment of time can be said truly to exist. When he goes on to explore the nature of that "present," he eventually concludes that the actual present moment is so fleeting that it effectively is of no duration whatsoever.[10] While God's eternal present is infinite, spanning all conceivable pasts, presents and futures, humanity's temporal present is infinitesimal, compressed on either side by the "past" and "future," reduced to a span too tiny to be conceived by the mind.

Despite the elusiveness of the temporal present, Augustine does recognize that time can be perceived in some manner, since the mind is able to experience duration. Augustine illustrates how the mind captures an impression of duration by recourse to another structure, more readily perceptible to the senses and thus more intuitively measurable: language.

> A stanza is long because it consists of so many verses; verses are long because they consist of so many feet; feet are long because they encompass so many syllables; a syllable is long because it is twice as long as a short one . . . *Deus creator omnium:* this verse of eight syllables alternates between short and long syllables. Four are short, the first, third, fifth, and seventh; they are single compared to the four long ones, the second, fourth, sixth, and eighth. These long ones are double the time of the short ones. I pronounce this and assert that this is so, as common sense perceives. As common sense makes manifest, I measure a long syllable by a short, and I find that it is twice as long. [11]

Using the phrase "Deus creator omnium" as a temporal ruler, Augustine demonstrates that different lengths of time can be sensibly measured and compared with one another. To make his point, he relies on the sensible sounds and rhythms of language, implicitly recognizing language as the vessel that makes time sensible and, because sensible, measurable and comprehensible.

This linguistic method of making time sensible and, hence, cognitively comprehensible, however, is limited. Since it defines time by comparison to different lengths of speech, this rendering of time is both relative and malleable: "But, thus, no certain measure of time is comprehended, since it is possible that it may take up an ampler time if a shorter verse is pronounced slowly, than a longer one, quickly. Thus also for a stanza, a foot, a syllable."[12] Thus, the linguistic method of rendering time still does not offer a final definition of what the present moment actually is: "From this it seems to me that time is nothing other than distension: but of what thing, I do not know, and I wonder if it is not my mind itself."[13] Despite his searching, Augustine can find no fundamental unit of time; for this reason, temporal "presence" remains defined only negatively, by its fleetingness, its lack of substance.

Having registered the limitations of language to help humanity grasp the nature of temporal presence, Augustine turns to consider God's eternal presence and how that presence informs the nature of his divine Word. Augustine understands God's Word as the eternal embodiment of his will, eternal and unchanging. "You call us, then, to understand the Word, the God who is God with you, which is said eternally and by which all things are said eternally.... For otherwise would be time and change and not a true eternity, nor a true immortality . . . therefore there is nothing in your Word that falls away or retreats, since truly it is immortal and eternal."[14] By contrast, as Augustine has just shown, human language is uttered in time and therefore bound to be comprehended in time. Because of this disparity, is not possible for humanity fully to fathom the true, eternal nature of the Word, nor of the ever-present divine will that the Word embodies. Augustine expresses this impossibility in a rhetorical question that laments the difficulty of understanding God's eternal presence: "quis tenebit cor hominis, ut stet et uideat, quomodo stans dictet futura et praeterita tempora nec futura nec praeterita aeternitas?" (Who will hold the heart of man, so that it may stand and see, how eternity, standing, is neither future nor past, but may speak in times future and times past? *Confessions*, 11.11.14). This rhetorical question reveals two interrelated challenges to humanity's comprehension of eternity: first, people are locked into the ever-moving circuit of time and, thus, cannot "hold still" in the present to consider God's changelessness. The second challenge is one of cognition and sensation: because people cannot "see" God's eternity, they cannot know it; to know God's eternity, one must be able, in some way, to feel it, to sense it. Because they are locked in time, humans cannot fully sense the nature of God's changeless eternity.[15] Or, in other words, because of humanity's full and complete participation in time, people cannot participate in eternity.

Even so, responding to his own rhetorical question precisely as a challenge, Augustine famously tries to "hold the heart of man still" and produce a sense of eternity for his readers by recourse to another linguistic structure: this time, an entire psalm. He points out that, before one recites a psalm, one's attention holds the entire psalm—the utterance of which lies in the future—in mind. As the psalm is recited, one continues to hold the words, sounds, and rhythms yet to come in one's mind, but one now also holds the already-uttered parts in mind, as well as the part one utters in a particular moment of speech. Thus, the psalm becomes a figure for how one can conceive past, present, and future simultaneously (*Confessions*, 11.28). God's eternally present Word likewise conceives of past, present, and future in one present sweep of consciousness, so Augustine suggests this psalm recitation as a possible model for understanding the eternity of divine presence. He understands human participation in the sensory and cognitive experience of the written word, the literary word, as a proxy for participation in divine eternity.[16]

He immediately admits, however, that there is still something about the eternity of the divine Word that the psalm model cannot embody: God's attention is undivided in his simultaneous awareness of all times as present time, whereas man's consciousness, in reciting the psalm, is divided (*Confessions*, 11.31). Thus, a chasm still gapes between human language and divine, making manifest the more fundamental chasm that separates the human experience of temporality from the divine experience of eternity. As I will reveal, this chasm lies at the heart of *The Cloud of Unknowing*, inspiring and structuring the *Cloud*-author's participatory staging of contemplation. Indeed, the *Cloud*-author seeks to bridge this experiential chasm between time and eternity through his theory and practice of monosyllabic prayer, which offers up a second means of "holding still the heart of man" by making God's eternal presence comprehensible to his readers. The theory makes divine eternity comprehensible by actualizing time as a sensible structure, though it does so in a radically different manner from what Augustine attempts in his psalm model. Monosyllabic prayer and the *Cloud*'s representation of it, as I will reveal, are designed to render time sensible in a way that enables readers to fathom cognitively and sensorily some simulacrum of the unknowable eternity of God's Word and will. Monosyllabic prayer enables contemplatives to feel their own likeness to God—and specifically to God's ever-presence—despite their status as time-bound beings.

ATOMIC ACCORDING IN *THE CLOUD OF UNKNOWING*

The *Cloud*-author begins this process by undercutting the assumption that the present moment of time has no duration and therefore cannot truly be sensed by the mind. As readers of the *Cloud* will recall, the *Cloud*-author understands time as "atomic." In this assertion, the *Cloud*-author situates himself in a significant theological and philosophical movement. Many medieval theologians dispute the Augustinian figuration of the present moment as too small to comprehend, instead asserting that time is constituted by tiny, indivisible units, called "atoms." As early as the eighth century in England, Bede, in his *De temporum ratione*, defines time based on an analysis of these tiny constituent parts: "The least time of all and that which in no way can be divided, are named 'atom' in Greek, that is, 'indivisible and inseparable.'"[17] In the thirteenth and fourteenth centuries, atomism gained a great deal of intellectual and theological currency, particularly in England and France. This period was indeed characterized by a profound and driving interest in measurement: the Oxford "calculators" and their counterparts in Paris were obsessed with a drive to measure and account for the physical world according to Aristotelian physics and, in many cases, atomism.[18] The *Cloud*-author affiliates himself with this Aristotelianizing group of theologians when he asserts that "atoms" are the basic units of time and that they are so tiny that they are "indivisible" and "undepartable" (*CU*, 4.17.19). Atoms are, in his view, "the leest partie of tyme," so small as to be "neighhonde incomprehensible" (*CU*, 4.17.18–19). "Neighhonde," however, is very different from "entirely," and it is in that difference that the *Cloud*-author bases his theory of spiritual practice. Atoms of time, for him, are of critical importance precisely because they are perceptible to the senses and, hence, comprehensible. As I will reveal, in his atomic theory of time lies his answer to Augustine's question of how God's eternity can be made sensible to a time-bound humanity, as well as the question of how humanity can be helped to participate cognitively in that eternity.

Once the *Cloud*-author has defined temporal atoms, he proceeds to map them onto human will. The atom of time, it turns out, "is neither lenger ne schorter, bot even according to one only steryng that is withinne the principal worching might of thi soul, the whiche is thi wille. For even so many willinges or desiringes—and no mo ne no fewer—mai be and aren in one oure in thi wille, as aren athomus in one oure" (*CU*, 4.18.2–7). The contemplative will and the hour are created alike in being atomic. Thus, they exist in what the *Cloud*-author calls "accord." This concept of "accord" suggests that there is not just a likeness but specifically a harmonious likeness that exists between time and one's loving will, something innately positive.[19] That "nakid entente" "accords" with time signifies that there exists a harmony of measurement and meetness between them, what I will call an *atomic according*.

This atomic according of will with time has immediate and fundamental consequences for the *Cloud*-author's theory of spiritual practice. Because the contemplative's will is atomic, and because spiritual work, performed by time-bound human beings, necessarily takes place in atomic time, time provides a scaffold within which spiritual work can and must take place. For the *Cloud*-author, spiritual practice consists in stretching out toward God with one's atomic, loving will, and then matching each unit of will to an atom of time, "so that [no atom of time] yede forby, bot alle thei schulde streche into the soverein desirable & into the heighest wilnable thing, the whiche is God" (*CU*, 4.18.10–12).

This modified characterization of how will is created "according" to time reveals a central tenet of the *Cloud*-author's theory of spiritual practice. Will can be brought into contemplative harmony because God has created will and time alike in being atomic. However, the structural parity of time and will does not mean automatically that a person necessarily lives in according harmony with God's intention. Quite the contrary, human will is something that must be realized and brought into synchronous fulfillment by the constant striving and moment-to-moment exertion. The "according" of time and will is a harmony in potential; that potential must be realized by constant exertion.

Given this theory of spiritual practice, it becomes clear why the *Cloud*-author favors monosyllabic prayer, why "o sillable . . . is betir then of two" (*CU*, 7.28.12). The shortest unit of audible language that carries meaning or, in the *Cloud*-author's terminology, can carry "entente"—the syllable—is an atomic structure.[20] The monosyllabic word, then, is literally the embodiment of an atom of present will, a temporal moment of "nakid entente." If atomic time is the container into which atomic will must be measured in every present moment, the atomic word of prayer is the measuring device. This is why "ever the schorter [the word of prayer] is, the betir it accordeth with the werk of the spirite" (*CU*, 7.28.12–13). Atomic prayer offers a sensible vehicle for the single atom of present will-in-time, an aural and rhythmical structure that accords with the atomic work of the spirit, so that one can feel one's atomic will align with atomic time. Through atomic prayer, the *Cloud*-author does Augustine one better; he makes the insensibly tiny present sensible to his readers, and he makes it sensible as the basic tool of spiritual practice.

The *Cloud*-author is not alone in mapping atomic language onto time; Bede also associates atomic time with the measurement of language into single syllables. In Bede's view, indeed, the grammarian will find it easier to sense atoms than the mathematician will, since grammarians are accustomed to feeling their way through syllables: "This is more visible to grammar teachers than teachers of arithmetic. And since they divide a verse into words, words into feet, feet into syllables, syllables into quantities, and moreover assign two quantities to a long [syllable] and one to a short [syllable], it is right that, not having anything into which they can further divide, they call this an atom."[21] Then in his *De metrica*, Bede returns to the relationship between time and language, but he makes more explicit that both of them are atomic in nature. He refers to syllables, indeed, as "atoms," the basic units of the verbal measurement of time, "because a syllable is briefest of all, and receives one time, which metricists call an atom."[22] For Bede, as for the *Cloud*-author, time and language are mutually atomic quantities, the former taking sensible form in part through its presence in the latter. For Bede, as for the *Cloud*-author, syllables are the fundamental, atomic units of language-in-time. But, as we will see, the *Cloud*-author goes far beyond Bede both in theorizing the significance of the atomic harmony between time and words and in how he encapsulates that harmoniousness stylistically in his vernacular work.

Indeed, by devising this now triune system of harmonious likenesses, which maps words onto will and will onto time, the *Cloud*-author lays the groundwork for the most important "according" that his work imagines. He claims that the reason one should stretch one's atomic will in every atom of time toward the "highest wilnable thing, the which is God" is that "[God] is even mete to oure soule by measuring of his Godhede; & oure soule even mete unto him bi worthines of oure creacion to his ymage & to his licnes" (*CU*, 4.18.11–15). Having asserted that the soul can mobilize its love in tiny units of atomic will and that atomic prayer is thus the vehicle most "accorded to" human will-in-time, he now suggests that atomic prayer makes the atomic will "meet" to God, "measured" to him.[23] This should be a somewhat startling suggestion, in context of the imaginative universe that the *Cloud* has created to this point. Since God, apophatically figured in the cloud of unknowing itself, is whole, unified, unbroken, seamless, and eternal, it seems counterintuitive that atomic prayer, which works precisely by its discrete and fragmentary synergy with the atomic will, would actualize the soul in its fullest likeness to him—that is, would enable the soul to recognize its own participation in God.

But this startling suggestion of a measured likeness between the atomic human will and God's unbroken eternity is central to *Cloud*-author's theory of practice. Underlying it is the *Cloud*-author's belief that the atom, the infinitesimal present moment of time, is paradoxically the nearest likeness of eternal presence: "In this [atom of] tyme it is that a soule hath comprehended, after the lesson of Seynte Poule, with alle seyntes—not fully bot in maner & in partye, as it is acordyng unto this werk, whiche is the lengthe & the breed, the height & the depnes of Everlastyng & Al-lovely, Almighty & Alle-witty God" (*CU*, 38.75.6, 13–16). According to the *Cloud*-author, the atom of time and "this werk" of monosyllabic prayer that takes place within that atom of time are "the lengthe & the breed, the height & the depnes of Everlastyng & Al-lovely, Almighty & Alle-witty God." To set out what he means by this mystifying statement, I will refer to a related treatment of time's relation to eternity, articulated centuries earlier by Boethius.

In the final prose section of the final book of the *Consolation of Philosophy*, Philosophy explains that God does not experience anything past or future, but only an ever-present and self-similar presence: "Eternity therefore is the whole and perfect possession of unending life."[24] For Philosophy, as for Augustine, eternity means the total possession of all times at once, as an infinite, unbroken presence. She further explains that human temporality, although modeled on eternity, can never equal divine eternity.[25] Even so, she emphasizes, hereby marking her difference from Augustine, there exists an essential likeness between the present moment of time and God's divine eternity. Indeed, it is in the tiniest of all present moments, the fleeting present instant of time in which all of human life transpires, that time most closely resembles the unchanging presence of eternity:

> And since this temporal state cannot possess its life completely and simultaneously, but it does in the same manner exist for ever without ceasing, it therefore seems to try in some degree to rival that which it cannot fulfill or represent, for it binds itself to some sort of present time out of this small and fleeting moment; inasmuch as this temporal present bears a certain appearance of that abiding present, it somehow makes those, to whom it comes, seem to be in truth what they imitate.[26]

In this passage, Philosophy's consolation inheres in the notion of presence: she asserts that the exiguous temporal moment is an image of eternity because it, although fleeting, is truly present. Thus, the closest that human beings can come to participating in the eternity of God is precisely in their participatory experience of the ever-fleeting present moment.

The *Cloud*'s theory and practice of prayer constitute a Boethian response to an Augustinian problem, with an atomic twist. This theory and practice of prayer realize that combining the idea that the present moment, albeit tiny and fleeting, offers the best likeness of God's eternal essence with his theory of atomic prayer can offer a means of making eternity comprehensible to a time-bound humanity. In the fleeting instant of atomic prayer, spiritual practitioners align their atomic will with atomic time. In so doing, they become fully present, their will perfectly actualized in time for that briefest of moments. Although this atomic accord between will, words, and time is instantaneous and fleeting by its very nature, the *Cloud*-author devises a method for making the experience of accord among them last longer by insisting that his readers repeat the atomic words on which they pray. Through the constant repetition of a single word, they exert a steady stream of self-identical will-in-time. That is, by aligning as many atoms of will with atoms of time as they can, spiritual practitioners create a concatenated simulacrum of eternity, a particulate stream of time and will that, because each particle is as small as can be imagined, approximates the seamless wholeness of eternal presence. Indeed, praying "Love, love, love," "God, God, God," is as close to a participatory emulation of God's eternally present being as a time-bound spiritual practitioner can attain.

At times, the *Cloud*-author's insistence on monosyllabic prayer seems to diverge from this focus on God and his eternal love, but that divergence sheds brighter light on his theory of spiritual practice. At certain points, the *Cloud*-author recommends the word *sin* as an appropriate prayerful monosyllable: "soche as thou mayst have in this worde SYNNE" (*CU*, 37.73.10). This recommendation, though it seems a bizarre choice as a vehicle for one's loving intention toward God, actually manifests a deeper truth about the *Cloud*-author's contemplative practice. As he himself specifies more than once, it does not matter much what words one chooses to pray with, so long as those words are short and repetitious: "& soche a worde is this worde GOD or this worde Love. Cheese thee whether thou whether thou wilt, or another as the list: whiche that thee liketh best of o silable" (*CU*, 7.28.13–15).[27] *God* and *love* may be easier for most people, but *sin* is no worse: indeed, if that word "thee liketh" best, if it accords better with the will of the contemplative, it is a better word to use. Prayer, for the *Cloud*-author, is not about absolute semantic meaning of a prayer word so much as how the sensory experience of language can capture intention in atomic time. In repeatedly praying on the word *sin*, the contemplative creates an experience for himself wherein, crucially, there is no past, nor future, of speech. In repeating *God*, *love*, *sin*, or any other short word, all willing experience becomes the selfsame infinitesimal present of atomic will-in-time directed toward God.[28]

Or, more precisely, toward an asymptotic approximation of God's eternity, a forging of a temporal likeness of God's unchanging being and intention.

By forging a serial likeness of eternal presence, atomic prayer enables practitioners to unite "in goostly onheed & acordyng of wille" with him, because will, through atomic prayer, is made atomically ever-present and thus made to simulate God's eternally present will (*CU*, 47.88.17–18). Because of that atomic simulation of eternal presence, practitioners can achieve "in maner and in partye" a likeness to or "accord" with the divine. They can achieve an awareness of their temporal participation in God's eternal being through a temporal simulacrum that, although imperfect in its simulation of the eternal divine, nevertheless provides a partial sense of ever-present presence. Thus, the *Cloud* offers atomic time to its readers as a sensory tool through which they can begin to experience their participation in divine eternity. Thereby, the *Cloud*-author bridges the Augustinian gulf between human existence and divine: through atomic prayer, one's "nakid entente" becomes unchangingly present, heart held still in sensible meditation on the divine.

ATOMIC STYLE AND LANGUAGE IN *THE CLOUD OF UNKNOWING*

The *Cloud*-author is not content simply to present his theory of spiritual contemplation discursively; like the others writers in *Staging Contemplation,* he seeks to embody it in literary form and style. Just as Augustine sought to create some participatory reflex of God's eternity in his literary representation of the psalm, so the *Cloud*-author seeks to create an experiential analogue of participation in God's eternity through his own prose style. He intimates as much when he says, "Ye! and it semith inpossible to myn understonding that any soule that is disposid to this werk schuld rede [this book], or speke it, or elles here it red or spoken, bot yif that same soule schuld fele for that tyme a verrey acordaunce to the effecte of this werk" (*CU,* 74.129.22–25). In promising that his reader will feel "a verrey acordaunce to the effecte of this werk" of spiritual practice "for that tyme" that he reads the *Cloud,* he casts his writing not just as a how-to manual on spiritual practice but also as a preliminary performance of that practice—as a means of participating in the work of contemplation through the work of literature. He achieves that preliminary performance by stylistically rendering the experience of atomic prayer through a carefully designed system of sensible effects in rhythm and sound. In combination, these effects create an atomic prose style.

Atomic style exists in the *Cloud,* in part, simply through its representation of prayer. By praying "love, love, love," a practitioner can feel his atomic accord with God's eternity; by reading "love, love, love," a practitioner can sense a measure of what he should experience in the work of prayer: the according of intention—this time, a readerly intention, rather than a prayerful intention—with a single, repeated monosyllable. By reading or speaking the words of the *Cloud,* one can hear the rhythmically and sonically self-similar monosyllable echo in one's ears. This echo sensibly embodies atomic time. Thus, as one focuses on each word in the monosyllabic string through the act of reading, one activates one's will as atomically present; reading through each monosyllable the *Cloud*-author writes, the reader serially refocuses intention, whether on *love,* on *God,* or on some other word. In his textual representations of atomic prayer, then, the *Cloud*-author enables readers to participate in atomic prayer by creating a microcosmic enactment of contemplative prayer in the text itself. In turn, that written simulation of atomic prayer is designed to create a sensible impression of how "atomic accord" between words, will, time, and, ideally, God's eternal love would feel. By reading or hearing read these striking monosyllabic prayers, and feeling how they use sound and rhythm to align one's words with one's will, and one's will with time, one will "fele for that tyme a verrey acordaunce to the effecte of this work" of spiritual practice (*CU,* 74.129.24–25). The *Cloud*-author helps his reader feel the beginnings of union with God through the act of reading. He allows them to participate in a preliminary way in God's eternity through their participation in his contemplative treatise.

Although the examples of atomic prayer are the most conspicuous instances of atomic language in the book, the *Cloud*-author infuses a feeling of atomic accord more diffusely as well, further to embody the "atomic accord" that constitutes spiritual practice. He does so by two means. The first is his hyperreliance on monosyllabic words throughout his work.[29] This tendency toward monosyllables arises especially when he directly addresses his reader, in imperative exhortations on how to do spiritual work: in his seventh chapter, he says, "lift than up thin herte unto God with a meek steryng of love. & mene God love that maad thee, & bought thee" (*CU,* 7.28.4–5). Later, he urges readers, "Be thou bot the tre, & lat it be the wright; be thou bot the hous," and "Prove thou, & do betir yif thou betir maist. Do that in thee is to lat as thou wist not that thei prees so fast apon thee, bitwix thee & thi God" (*CU,* 32.66.13–15, 34.70.15–17).[30] These strings of words create an atomic style in a given passage, sensibly preparing the reader for the actual work of spiritual devotion by deploying concatenated spondaic rhythms. By reading these monosyllabic strings, the reader participates sonically and rhythmically in the work of atomic contemplation of God.

The second stylistic means by which the *Cloud*-author embodies spiritual practice in his writing is his reliance on exclamations, such as "lo!" "ye!" "ne!" and "right nought!" He splices these expressions into his writing frequently, to convey aurally and rhythmically the atomic feeling of spiritual work through his writing, the "smytyng" of darts of intention against the cloud of unknowing itself.[31] Their piercing, staccato rhythm engages with readers' senses, thereby gathering and refocusing their intention squarely on the words they are reading. Through these monosyllabic exclamations, then, the *Cloud*-author again allows the feeling of atomic language to suffuse his writing, accomplishing a participatory simulation of the atomic presence that is the goal of devotional work. Through this atomic prose style, the *Cloud* is designed to produce a sensory experience that accords with the actual contemplative work of the spirit. Not just in its representations of prayer but also in its overall, monosyllabic style, reading the *Cloud* allows would-be contemplatives to experience some scintilla of participation in God.

Admittedly, the *Cloud*-author's deployment of stylistic devices designed to render "atomic accord" sensible is not equally dense at all points throughout his work. Instead, monosyllabic strings and exclamations tend to gather in moments of particular expository intensity. As a result, a reader's sensory experience of "atomic accord" is intermittent and irregular. The intermittency of atomic style, however, is crucial to its functionality, as well as to the *Cloud*-author's theory of spiritual contemplation. First, by writing most of the *Cloud* in somewhat more standard rhythms, and only periodically studding it with monosyllabic chains and phatic exclamations, the *Cloud*-author creates what we might call an experiential baseline: a fluent reading situation that his readers encounter as normal. When that baseline, fluent situation is punctured by monosyllabic cascades, readerly disfluency is created: the reader slows down, experiences the language as nonstandard, difficult, somewhat jarring. Thus, the intermittency of atomic style accentuates its effect, by allowing it to stand out more sharply against a sensory background that is relatively parseable and familiar. This dynamic, in which a baseline, normative, fluent style is created for a work only to be violated by occasional, aberrant, disfluent styles is one we will see in all of the subsequent works studied in this book as well.

Second, the intermittency of atomic style constitutes a microcosm of the phenomenology of contemplative participation in God. As the *Cloud* repeatedly reminds readers, the experience of being absorbed up into the divine cloud of unknowing is fleeting, brief, striking. It can happen suddenly, without any warning, to a neophyte as easily as to a well-practiced contemplative.

Atomic style functions that way within *The Cloud of Unknowing:* it is brief, fleeting, striking; and it occurs at any point during the experience of reading, without becoming more common or more lasting toward the end of the work. Thus, the *Cloud*'s lack of consistency in its stylistic staging of contemplation through atomic style is part and parcel of how that atomic style works to encapsulate, embody, and export the experience of participatory contemplation to a reader.

Third, the intermittency is of the utmost importance to the *Cloud*-author's expressed attitude toward physical sensation in the work of spiritual devotion. I will spend a good deal of time on this issue, since anyone familiar with the *Cloud* knows that the use of sensation in the work of spiritual contemplation is something the *Cloud*-author is quite exercised about. Indeed, as I intimated earlier, the *Cloud*-author is famously and overtly hostile toward the bodily senses, seeing them as detriments to the work of spiritual practice. He satirizes the use of the physical senses rather brutally, when he explains how some people, on hearing that the work of the spirit consists in denying the "outward wits" or outward senses, understand that injunction simply to mean that they should turn their bodily senses inward: "And thus they reverse hem agens the cours of kynde. . . . And than as fast the devil hath power for to feyne sum fals light or sounes, swete smelles in theire noses, wonderful taastes in their mowthes, and many queynte hetes and brennynges in their bodily brestes or in their bowelles, in theire backes and in theire reynes, and in their prive members" (*CU*, 52.96.22, 24–26). Although these wrongheaded spiritual workers believe that, in this state of ingrown sensation, "thei have a restful mynde of theire God," they in fact do violence to their souls and prevent the real work of spiritual union from taking place (*CU*, 52.97.5–6). The *Cloud*-author's critique of the sensorium continues and gains momentum in the work's next chapter, when he describes spiritual feigners, who sit wide-eyed "as thei were wode" and "as thei sawe the devil" (*CU*, 53.97.19–20).[32] "Som sette theire eighen in theire hedes as thei were sturdy scheep beten in the heed. . . . Some hangen here hedes on syde, as a worme were in theire eres. Som pipyn when thei schuld speke. . . . Som crien and whinene in theire throte . . . this is the condicion of heretikes" (*CU*, 53.97–98.21–5). For the *Cloud*-author, excessive immersion in the sensorium is a sign of falseness, an overemphasis on the body, to the detriment of the spirit. It seems problematic, then, to assert that he devises a prose style intended to convey sensation to his readers.[33] To explain how the *Cloud*-author could be opposed to sensation as a basic spiritual tool yet could use aural and rhythmical effects in atomic English prose to create sensation as an entrée to contemplative experience, I will look more deeply into what troubles him about sensation in the first place.

The *Cloud*-author's pervasive hostility toward the sensorium originates in his awareness that God, the ultimate source and end of spiritual practice, is not perceptible in strictly physical terms. As a result, the five senses, which engage with what is physically perceptible, are not useful in the work of spiritual devotion.

> For by thin ighen thou maist not conceive of any thing, bot yif it be by the lengthe and the breed, the smalnes & the gretnes, the roundness & the squarenes, the ferns & the neernes, & the colour of it. & by thin eren, not bot noise or sum maner of soun. By thin nose, not bot either stynche or savour. & by thi taast, not bot either soure or swete, sale or fresche, bittyr or likyng. & bi thi feling, not bot outher hote or colde, hard or tendre, soft or scharpe. & trewely neither hath God ne goostly thinges none of thees qualities ne quantitees. & therefore leve thin outward wittes, & worche not with hem, either with-inne ne with-outen. (*CU*, 70.124.6–13)

Since God, in his essence, has no bodily traits, one should not seek to experience him through the senses. Physical sensation in spiritual practice is dangerous, then, because it is misleading, taking one away from God, rather than toward him.

In this belief, the *Cloud*-author opposes theories of spiritual practice such as those of Richard Rolle, for whom physical sensation is part and parcel of the work of spiritual devotion, since physical sensation, in his view, conduces to affective experiences.[34] Reflecting his commitment to the sensorium as a tool of spiritual practice, Rolle actively seeks to incite physical feelings in his readers through his writing style, which tends noticeably toward the poetic.[35] The most illuminating analysis of how Rolle's writing style is designed to encapsulate the feeling of spiritual devotion that he describes is Nicholas Watson's, which argues that the sensory effects of song, which map onto the highest stage of spiritual development, called *canor*, are the organizing principles behind Rolle's style. In his analysis of the Latin work *Melos Amoris*, Watson argues that there is "a fusion of mystical theory with rhetoric, in which the passionate words to which Love inspires the saint in his praise of the joy of continual canor cease merely to represent mystical experience, and instead actually become it."[36] Later he concludes, "as a written representation of an oral activity (praise) the poem continuously comments on what it is doing, indeed, it consists of such comments . . . [and] translates every aspect of Rolle's spiritual experience of canor into a literary construct, in order to provide the reader with a rhetorical version or simulacrum of that experience."[37] Though perhaps most conspicuous in his Latin works, famously, Rolle deploys highly rhythmical, alliterative language frequently in his vernacular writings as well, most notably whenever he represents prayer or meditation, which he calls "sange" or "affeccion."[38]

> When will thow com to comforth me, and bryng me owt of care,
> And gyf me the, that I may se, havand evermare?
> Thi lufe es ay swettest of al that ever war.
> My hert, when sal it brest for lufe?
> Than languyst I namare . . .
> it drawes me til my day,
> The band of swete byrnyng, for it haldes me ay
> Fra place & fra plaiyng, til that I get may
> the syght of my swetyng, that wendes never away.[39]

Studded with alliterations, isocolonic clauses, isorhythmic clauses, and rhymes, this passage is designed to cultivate a reader's "affeccion" toward God by relying on its sonic and rhythmical intricacy to incite physical responses in its audience. Rolle states this explicitly after a "sange" or prayer he recommends in another work, *Ego dormio*. He says to his reader, "If thou wil thynk this ilk day, thou sal fynde swetnes that sal draw thi hert up, that sal gar the fal in gretyng, and in grete langyng til Jhesu; and thi thoght sal al be on Jhesu, and so be receyved aboven all erthly thyng, aboven the firmament and the sternes, so that the egh of thi hert mai loke intil heuen."[40] Through praying and reading, readers are meant to feel sweetness; their hearts are meant to "brest"; they should languish; they will feel "sweet burning"; they hope to gain "syght" of their "swetyng." This is the kind of spiritual practice—physical, fetishizing the sensorium—that the *Cloud*-author utterly scorns as a detriment to real closeness with and participation in God.

Correlatively, Rolle's florid prose style, designed to elicit and sustain a broad and variegated sensual response in its audience, is a strategy that the *Cloud*-author shuns. Instead, in his atomic prose style, he cultivates a sense-perceptible reflex only of the particular feelings he wishes to promote in his readership: first, the feeling of atomic accord of time with will, and will with words, and second, the feeling of participatory likeness between the atomic soul and the eternal God. Atomic prayer and atomic prose, although sensory, are not dangerous, because they allow one to feel a true preliminary sense of the divine—a sense of oneness, unity, and presence—rather than a deceptive one.

They do so using a strategy of ornamentation that differs radically from Rolle's. The intermittent ornamentation of the *Cloud*, designed to produce "in maner and partye" the feeling of divine likeness that is the goal and reward of full contemplation, but to do so without immersing a practitioner into inappropriate physicality, bespeaks one of the great formal strengths of prose composition. As Rolle himself notes, Rolle's highly rhythmical passages are "sanges," hyperstylized interpolations into an otherwise prose epistle. As "sanges," they manifest a level of rhythmical and sonic regularity that readers are meant to experience as lyrical. The *Cloud*-author, by contrast, never breaks into "sange" in his writing. Instead, he remains in the looser and more rhythmically irregular form of prose, which enables him to ornament his writing as much or as little as he likes.[41] Free from the highly regular formal strictures of song, he can cultivate an "affeccion" in his readership that is, in his words, "ordained and mesurid to God" (*CU*, 12.39.17), restrained and deliberate, rather than passionate and poetic, hence physical and false.[42] It is prose form and atomic style, precisely by virtue of their less regular ornamentation, that enable the *Cloud*-author to provide readers with a sense of spiritual meditation, but without causing them to "streyne" their hearts "in [their] brests over-rudely" (*CU*, 46.87.5–7). In his mandate on atomic prayer and in his echoic realization of it in his intermittent atomic style of prose, the *Cloud*-author avoids the pitfalls of hypersensuality, while he simultaneously creates an aural and rhythmical experience in his writing. Thus, the *Cloud* bodies forth a formal and stylistic reason why atomic prose might offer a better formal choice than Rollean "sange" in representing and indeed embodying spiritual work.

PARTICIPATORY CONTEMPLATION, THE PROBLEM OF TEMPORALITY, AND VERNACULAR RHYTHMS

The Cloud of Unknowing thus embodies four underexplored realities of late Middle English literary and contemplative culture. First, it cultivates and deploys an innovative practice of prose ornamentation by which a participatory experience of contemplative practice is made sensibly available to readers. Second, by doing so, the *Cloud* suggests new ways of thinking about Middle English "vernacular theological" prose writings, as deliberately crafted formal objects, designed not only to describe but indeed to initiate the contemplative work of the spirit. The *Cloud* is not simply a book from which to glean an explanation of a spiritual practice; it is a part of that practice, a literary enactment of the work of the spirit that promotes participatory union with the divine. It is thus a work of participatory contemplation, and it operates by devising an atomic, feelable likeness between the soul and God. The third aspect of late medieval English literary and contemplative culture that the *Cloud* embodies is the problem of temporality and human likeness to God—how we, as time-bound beings, could possibly hope to fathom the eternal God, how our temporal minds and temporal modes of knowing could possibly stretch to at least participate in a mode of knowing and mode of being that is defined by its lack of subjection to time, change, or decay. As I have shown in this chapter, *The Cloud of Unknowing* devises a prose style that embodies its intricate answer to these questions. For the *Cloud,* Middle English literary language can be made to enact the asymptotic approach of the human's temporal and atomic will to God's unchanging, seamless, and unbroken one.

And thus, fourth, the *Cloud* slyly bodies forth a reason for being composed in Middle English that has to do with sensory and formal effects. As with other writers of vernacular contemplative works, it has long been assumed that the *Cloud*-author writes in English because he seeks to make his work more accessible to a broad English audience, in a way that a Latin text could not have been. But the idea that the *Cloud* is a work meant for wide circulation seems prima facie untenable, given how self-consciously difficult and abstruse it is, both stylistically and conceptually. Indeed, it seems from his own statements that the *Cloud*-author knows he has composed a work for an extremely learned, extremely restricted group of spiritual devotees, and not at all for the masses. He says as much both at the beginning and toward the end of the *Cloud* itself, thus framing his work with rather stern warnings against the wrong kinds of readers:

> Fleschely janglers, opyn preisers & blamers of hemself or of any other, tithing tellers, rouners & tutilers of tales, & alle maner of pinchers: kept I never that thei sawe this book. For myn entent was never to write soche thing unto hem. & therfore I wolde that thei medel not ther-with, neither thei ne any of thees corious lettred or lewed men. Ye, though al that thei be ful good men of active levyng, yit this mater acordeth nothing to hem; but yif it be to thoo men the whiche, though al thei stoned in actyvete bi outward forme of levyng, nevertheles yit bi inward stering after the prive sperit of God, whos domes ben hid, thei ben ful graciously disposid, not contynowely as it is propre to verrey contemplatyves, bot than & than to be parceners in the hieghst pointe of this contemplative acte: yif soche men might se it, thei schuld by the grace of God be greetly counforted therby. (*CU,* prologue, pp. 2–3, lines 19–24, 1–8)

On one level, the *Cloud*-author's initial injunction seems simply to ward off immoral or spiritually problematic readers: janglers, tale-tellers, misanthropes. But, as he goes on, he disavows interest in any kind of "curious" persons, be they learned or unlearned. His book, he tells us, is only intended for the truehearted contemplative, not those who live the active life. His book is, quite simply, not for just anyone; it is only for those who want to be "parceners," or sharers, participants in God. He returns to this assertion at the end of his work: "& I prey thee for Godes love that thou late none see this book, bot if it be soche one that thee think is liche to the book; after that thou fyndest wreten in the book before, where it tellith what men & when thei schuld worche in this werk" (*CU*, 74.130.3–6). This book is intended for an elite group of people who are "liche to the book." Reflecting that textual assertion in material culture, fewer than twenty copies of the text survive, and two copies are retranslations into Latin, indicating that, if anything, the text's early readers recognized that it was intended for an elite audience of literati and sought to keep it that way.

Adding to the sense that the *Cloud* was neither written for nor indeed received by a large and Latin-unlearned body of readers, the *Cloud*-author composed a later work, the *Book of Privy Counselling*, aimed at familiarizing and simplifying the ideas of the earlier book. He admits of the vexed reception of his first work early on in the *Book of Privy Counselling*: "I merveyle me somtyme whan I here sum men sey (I mene not simple lewid men & wommen, bot clerkes [& men] of grete kunnyng) that my writing to thee & to other is so harde & so heigh, & so curious & so queinte, that unnethes it may be conceivid of the sotelist clerk or wittid man or womman in this liif, as they seyn."[43] On the surface, this justification for undertaking the *Book of Privy Counselling* seems to affirm the notion that the *Cloud*-author seeks to reach a wide audience—he specifically singles out "simple lewid men & wommen" as those who do *not* protest the difficulty of his first work. Instead, he tells us, the problems of comprehension lie with "clerkes" and men of "grete kunnyng." But this insistence reads as a "methinks the lady doth protest too much" moment: if clerks and learned men and women respond to the *Cloud* as if it is a difficult, "heigh" and "curious" text, that signals, at the very least, that the work was *not* received as easy, clear, or accessible. Responding to the apparent pressures to revisit the ideas of the *Cloud* in a less "harde," "heigh", "curious," and "queinte" manner, the *Cloud*-author composes the *Book of Privy Counselling* as a simplified, digest version of his original contemplative theory.

But this breaking down of ideas into a digest version is quickly made problematic: at one point the *Cloud*-author seeks to break his ideas down into simpler terms. This effort comes in his metaphor of God as a "plastre," or medical poultice, that one can apply to the soul.

> Take good gracyous God as he is, plat & pleyn as a plastre, & legge it to thi seek self as thou arte. Or, yif I other-wise schal sey, bere up thi seek self as thou arte & fonde for to touche bi desire good gracious God as he is, the touching of whome is eendeles helthe by witness of the womman in the gospel: Si titigero vel fimbriam vestimenti eius, salua ero. 'If I touche bot the hemme of his clothing, I schal be saaf.'[44]

This highly alliterative and highly quotidian metaphor—"plat & pleyn as a plastre"—seems designed to simplify and domesticate a reader's understanding of the transcendent God, to bring him imagistically into the realm of the everyday, and to bring him sonically into the realm of recognizably insular literary conventionality. But, simultaneously, even at this moment in which the *Cloud*-author seems keen to break down his abstruse and difficult theory of contemplation, he undertakes two formal choices that militate against the logic of simplification that seems to suffuse this passage. First, by comparing God to a plaster, or poultice, that can be placed on the sick soul, he makes oblique metaphorical contact with Boethius' *Consolation of Philosophy*, in which Philosophy tells Boethius that she must apply a poultice to the hardened cyst on his soul if she is truly to heal him: "But since this multiplicity of tumultuous affects overwhelms you—sorrow, ire, and mourning tear you up—since you are now weak of spirit, stronger remedies cannot yet touch you. So let us use gentler medicines, so that these affects that have hardened in you into a cyst may be softened, until it will bear a harsher remedy."[45] Even as he seems to offer his lessons up in a more familiar, more domesticated context, the *Cloud*-author situates them ever more firmly in the tradition of Latinate contemplation. Second, shortly thereafter, the *Cloud*-author makes a formal move that he does not make at all in his *Cloud of Unknowing* but that he will make repeatedly in the *Book of Privy Counselling*: he switches from English into Latin. By introducing Latin into the notionally simplified revision of his formerly all-English project, the *Cloud*-author suggests that having some Latin in his work may actually make it easier and more accessible to readers, thus problematizing retroactively any notion that Englishness was entirely about ease or access in *The Cloud of Unknowing* itself. It seems that *The Cloud of Unknowing* cannot have been written in English simply because of the author's wish to reach a wider, less educated audience.[46]

Instead, the choice to write in the vernacular is motivated by a particular mode of contemplative participation that English makes sensible and hence cognitively available—and that Latin could not. The *Cloud*'s motive for being composed in the vernacular has to do with its theological investment in the atomic language of contemplation and in its concomitant investment in rendering that theory of contemplation in language. Indeed, *The Cloud of Unknowing* could not have been composed in Latin because, as an inflected language, Latin contains a paucity of monosyllabic nouns and verbs. English, by contrast, with its relative wealth of monosyllabic words, is more innately suited to atomic language. If it were composed in Latin, even the *Cloud*'s representations of atomic prayer would be ruined: "Deus, Deus, Deus," and "amor, amor, amor" can neither represent nor perform the atomic accord between time, intention, and words that "God, God, God" and "love, love, love" are designed precisely to achieve.[47] Not only are the atomic prayers that the *Cloud* recommends difficult to render atomically in Latin, but the overall atomic style of the *Cloud* simply cannot be reproduced in Latin. In short, English is better able to embody the atomic accord between time, words, and will than is Latin. *The Cloud of Unknowing*, then, bodies forth a rationale for vernacularity that does not originate in concerns about access. Instead, in the *Cloud*, vernacular prose is first and foremost a formal choice, motivated by a deeply held sensitivity to the particular formal possibilities available in Middle English.[48]

And indeed, the *Cloud*-author's choice to compose in English has to do not only with the high density of available monosyllabic words but also with the fact that hearing a series of monosyllabic words strung together in a chain—although infinitely more possible in English than in Latin—is nonetheless a relatively uncommon linguistic experience. That is, the *Cloud*'s monosyllabic style gains some of its contemplative effect from its strangeness—a strangeness that is only plain to speakers and readers of English whose habits for reading and hearing it are so fully developed that the strangeness of a monosyllabic string can be fully parsed. The *Cloud*-author's atomic style, then, relies not only on the availability of monosyllabic words in Middle English but also on the fluent expectations of his readers for how Middle English normally behaves; it is in contradistinction to normative syntactic patterns that the *Cloud*'s atomic prayer chains and atomic prose style overall have their greatest sensory and, therefore, contemplative impact. Writing in Middle English gains the *Cloud*-author not only his best tool for embodying atomic prayer but also a level of audience familiarity with the normal sounds and patterns of English that will enable his stylistic innovativeness to scan as salient, and worth unpacking slowly and carefully. Atomic style, by its exploitation of the heavy load of monosyllabic words in the English language, bodies forth a new reason to compose in a vernacular language—a reason not based on access so much as on sensation, not based on democratization so much as the participatory power of agitating an audience's fluent expectations of a language only to frustrate those expectations with dense clouds of monosyllabic words. Atomic style, in *The Cloud of Unknowing*, is a nonnormative but parseable—at once familiar and unfamiliar, fluent and disfluent—linguistic situation, one that enables preliminary participation in God by exploiting a sensory facet of the English language in participatory contemplative writing. Atomic style enables a preliminary and preparatory feeling of time and eternity, which in turn enables greater understanding both of God and of the nature of spiritual contemplation.

The rest of the Middle English literary works of contemplation that I will study in this book will likewise recognize a particular capacity in Middle English to initiate the work of divine contemplation. Like the *Cloud,* each text will use its readers' participation in the formal field of the literary work as a partial enactment of their participation in God; each will use the literary work, that is, as a way of creating a feeling or sense of participation between the reading contemplative and the ever-present God. The particular cast of that participation will shift and slip greatly, arcing, with time, toward a cast more public, social, and intersubjective. Indeed, the next contemplative work I will examine, Julian of Norwich's *Revelation of Love,* does not seek radically to restrict its own audience, nor does it envision spiritual devotion as a process of stripping one's individual, isolated will down to atoms, which can be used to approximate divine presence. Instead, Julian's work envisions a more generous kind of contemplation, one for every Christian man and woman, one that seeks to promote an awareness of a dyadic relationship between contemplative and Jesus, as well as an awareness of what it means that Jesus participated so willingly, fully, and lovingly in humanity.

CHAPTER TWO

Julian of Norwich and the Comfort of Eternity

To understand the place of Julian of Norwich's writings in the corpus of Middle English contemplative literature, it is critical to understand her in her immediate cultural and historical context. In the last quarter of the fourteenth century, she sequesters herself in an anchorhold and begins to contemplate and record a series of visions she had during an illness in 1373. In a myriad of ways from then on, Julian's life is remarkable. Not only is she the first named female writer in England known to literary history, but her *Revelation of Love* has also been read, studied, and admired for its innovative theology of love and comfort since the early fifteenth century at least; Margery Kempe makes a pilgrimage to consult with Julian about visionary experiences at that time, indicating the respect and renown that Julian and her works already possess.[1] Moreover, Julian is evidently a respected and trusted figure in her town; she is made beneficiary of a significant number of wills, including that of a priest, a merchant, and the daughter of a local earl.[2] Theologically, socially, and literarily, Julian is unquestionably unusual.

At the same time, she is undeniably a product of her larger historical and cultural context. Meditating on and recording her visionary experiences during the upsurge of academic Wycliffism in and around Oxford in the 1380s and during the larger surge of Lollardy and its various manifestations and repressions from the 1380s through the 1410s, Julian lives during a time of great theological diversity and change. In fact, living and writing in East Anglia, Julian partakes of one of the most concentrated and innovative theological and devotional climates in medieval England. As Gail McMurray Gibson's work has shown, medieval East Anglia—of which Norwich was the mercantile capital—produces a culture of unusually profound devotion to the incarnation and humanity of Christ.[3] The surrounding counties of Norfolk and Suffolk, moreover, are centers of nonconformist religious practice, as well as centers of strict orthodoxy, so that Julian's region boasts a diverse array of Christian ideas and perspectives.[4]

By and large, whether orthodox or heterodox, the devotional practices and patterns that animate medieval East Anglian religious culture center on affective devotion to the Son's incarnation, and particularly his incarnation in the body of Mary, so therefore often on *imitationes* of Christ and Mary. This rich tradition of affective piety and *imitatio* is anchored in part by the rapid and pervasive penetration of the Pseudo-Bonaventurian *Meditationes Vitae Christi* into English religious culture in the fourteenth and fifteenth centuries.[5] This text, eventually translated into an immensely popular and canonical English version in the first decade of the fifteenth century by Nicholas Love, is invested in the cultivation of empathy and compassion for Christ and Mary as cornerstones of devotional practice, and this cultivation works in part by emphasizing the sensory and affective experience of the Passion.[6] As such, the *Meditationes* focuses far more on Christ's humanity than on his divinity,[7] delivering to its readers richly detailed images of Jesus and his suffering, which become cornerstones of their individual devotional practices. Indeed, many manuscripts of the *Meditationes* are illustrated, actively encouraging image-based engagement with the life of Christ.[8]

Famous for its extended and vivid depictions of Christ's Passion, which describe the changing colors of Christ's drying flesh and blood on his face and body, Julian's *Revelation* likewise manifests the affective and imitative religious practices and incarnational focus that typify East Anglia.[9] Her work's emphasis on the sweetness and innocence of Mary before the birth of Christ is consistent with the East Anglian emphasis on apocryphal gospel stories about Mary's youth.[10] The frame of Julian's entire visionary experience—namely, that she wished for and was granted an illness during which she would experience a simulacrum of the suffering of Christ—resonates with the imitative devotional culture of her locale.[11] However astonishing Julian herself may be as a female writer and historical actor, *A Revelation of Love* is, from a certain distance, quite typical of its period, region, and devotional culture.

But, as numerous scholars have shown, on closer inspection, Julian's theology is far from strictly orthodox.[12] Her writing makes daring and innovative claims about the nature of the relationship between mankind—whom Julian calls her "evencristene," or even-Christians—and Christ.[13] Her insistence that Jesus loves people down to "the lowest part of their need"—acknowledging even the scatological as part of what God loves in man—is equally innovative.[14] Her extended meditation on her lord-and-servant vision, included only in the longer version of her work, is theologically radical, refusing concretely and decisively to establish boundary lines separating Jesus from Adam, Adam from the rest of mankind, or Jesus from mankind.[15] Julian's theology of love envisions a God who is nonjudging and nonpunitive, maternal and vulnerable, domestic and familiar.[16] Rather than fixating on human sin as a primary obstacle to contemplation and spiritual perfection, she views sin as nothing or even as "behovely" for the sinner (*Rev.*, 209.27.9–10)—a point I will return to in my sixth chapter. Hers is a God whose ungainsayable might and power never detract from his ultimate intention: as she puts it at the end of her longer work, love was always his meaning.[17] However much Julian's theology may have emerged from her historical moment and cultural context, she was very much a theologian of her own stripe.

Some of Julian's most innovative and least examined theology, however, comes not just in her depictions of the Son as Jesus, the mortal, suffering human, but also in how she understands the Son in his perpetuity, as well as in his eternal self-sameness. The *Revelation* enacts a sophisticated meditation on the three temporalities of the Son—his participation in time as the embodied and historical Jesus, his status as perpetual as the historically born but now ever-living and ever-dying Christ, and his eternal status as the divine Son of God.[18] Julian sensorily explores the nature not only of the incarnated and temporal Jesus, but also of the sempiternal, unchanging Godhead that exists from all time within the Son and of the perpetual Christ, as well as how we, as mere humans, might begin to fathom our participation in him and in his three timescales.

She does this through the structures, styles, and forms of the *Revelation*. For Julian, the central experiential challenge of staging contemplation of the divine temporalities in literary writing lies in how to make the Son's eternity and perpetuity—what she will call his "everlasting" or "ever ylike" and "continuel" natures (*Rev.*,135.4.9; *Vis.*,105.4.55; *Vis.*,77.8.3)—felt, and to do so without erasing or denying the equally comforting truth of temporal experience itself. Where *The Cloud of Unknowing* sought to convey a sensory and asymptotic approach to God's ever-present being for the time-bound atomic contemplative, the *Revelation* will emphasize the porosity of the boundary that separates eternity from time but that also joins them together through the incarnated Christ. It will do so by devising three intersecting prose modalities, each designed to help readers participate in a sensory simulacrum of Jesus's temporality, his eternity, or his perpetuity.

To focus on the *Revelation* for its forms and styles is not unprecedented. Recent scholarship has analyzed Julian of Norwich's work not just as a sophisticated theological treatise in terms of its content but as a shining example of Middle English prose style, literary construction, and authorial self-positioning.[19] Although Julian calls herself unlearned, "a simple creature unletterde" (*Rev.*, 125.2.1), scholars have shown that she engages her literary and conceptual forebears in ways both innovative and challenging.[20] Julian herself urges her readers to understand her books as part of a tradition of contemplative writings, instructing them explicitly in how "to lyeve contemplatifelye" (*Vis.*, 71.4.38). As part of the burgeoning late Middle English corpus of vernacular contemplative writings—along with the contemporary *Cloud of Unknowing* and the earlier writings of Richard Rolle—Julian's work bodies forth a programmatic and sustained attention to how language and style can be used to convey contemplative experience to a readership.[21]

Julian's articulation of the idea that the written contemplative work can enable a reader to participate in the work of spiritual contemplation is less overt than what we find in the *Cloud* but nonetheless central to her project. The *Revelation* does not use terms like "grope" or "wrastlyng," but it does set out how it is meant to work—how it promotes an audience's participation in Julian's visions. This theory emerges in two interrelated ways: the first comes in a particular phrase by which Julian describes the efficacy of her visions; the second in how Julian understands her visions to apply to other people. In the first chapter of the short version of her work, Julian's text announces that it contains "fulle many comfortabille wordes and gretly stirrande to alle thaye that desires to be Cristes loverse."[22] From this announcement, readers are meant to understand that Julian's book will bring about comfort for her readers by stirring them to love of God. Indeed, the *Revelation* repeatedly uses the word *comfort*, or its derived forms, to express how it is meant to work on the minds and hearts of readers. In the short version of her work, Julian describes how, in one of her visions, Jesus speaks to her "fulle comfortabelye" (*Vis.*, 95.15.2.).[23] Looping this description of how Jesus speaks to her back into conversation with her statement that her own writings contain "comfortabille wordes," it seems that the logic of Julian's writings rests on her sense that the comfort of Jesus's utterances, in which Julian participates directly in her own visions, is exportable to her readers via the written instrument of her text. The *Revelation*, that is, is a participatory work through which the "comfortabille" experience of Jesus's revelations can be brought to the reader sensibly, not just by the action of exposition but by participation in the literary field. The doubly participatory nature of Julian's vision—her visionary participation in Jesus's comfort and her audience's participation in her visionary experience through her writing—has its clearest and most explicit articulation in the sixth chapter of her short version, when she says, "Alle that I saye of myselfe, I meene in the persone of alle mine evencristene, for I am lernede in the gastelye schewinge of oure lorde that he meenes so" (*Vis.*, 73.6.1–2). Toward the end of her short text, she further insists that "the luff of God es so mekille that he haldes us partiners of his goode deede" (*Vis.*, 103.19.39). When she asserts that we—all of her even-Christians—are "partiners," or partners, in God's goodness, she Englishes the Latinate idea of participation.[24] Her *Revelation* will thus remind readers of that participation in God, in his "good deede," but like the other Middle English works in this book, the *Revelation* will seek not just to explain but also to initiate partipatory contemplation of God through participation in the literary work.

When considering Julian's work in apposition with other contemplative writings in vernacular prose, such as *The Cloud of Unknowing* or the works of Rolle, it is essential to remember that hers differs from theirs in how it represents divine contemplation and exports it to a readership. Whereas the *Cloud*-author and Rolle describe discursively and didactically how the work of contemplation is done, Julian recounts her own contemplative experience for her readership as a personal narrative. Whatever interpretive and exegetical work she does in addition to that recounting, she does around the narrative core of the sixteen sequential visions she had during her illness. Her contemplative "treatise," then, is built not as a manual but as a memoir of gradually acquired, comforting knowledge.[25]

Though Julian parts ways with many other writers of Middle English contemplative prose in this choice, she riffs on another contemplative tradition: the *consolatio*—though, as we will see, this riffing is always reinventive.[26] Indeed, when Julian describes her writings as "comfortabille," as she repeatedly does, she takes a first step in designating them not just as contemplative works but specifically as vernacular *consolationes*. In this vernacularizing designation, however, she signals not that she will obediently and humbly follow the precise patterns and contours of *consolatio* but rather that her visions will represent a process of spiritual fortification and learning that will engage with but reinvent the conventions of the *consolatio* genre in order to export them to her own Middle English readership.[27]

ETERNITY AND ITS CONSOLATIONS

The *Revelation*'s relation to *consolatio* centers on an organizing thematic from Boethius's *Consolation of Philosophy*, one that that Julian will both deploy and aggressively modify: the idea of divine eternity as a source of consolation or comfort. According to Boethius, God's eternity enables him to be just toward mankind because it allows him to see the past, present, and future and to know the intentions of the good and the deeds of the bad.

> For God always remains the constant, foreknowing watcher, and his eternally present vision runs forth with the future quality of our actions, dispensing boons to the good, punishments to the bad. Not in vain are hopes and prayers placed in God; when these are rightful, they cannot but be efficacious. Avoid therefore vices, collect virtues, lift up your soul to righteous hopes, give your humble prayers on high. If you do not choose to lie, a great charge of probity is yours, for you act before the eyes of an all-seeing judge.[28]

For Boethius, God's eternity signals the certainty of salvation for the virtuous, but also the certainty of punishment for the wicked. His eternity is specifically cast as the source of his unfailing justice. Because God's justice is necessary to Philosophy's consoling message that Fortune is a false construct, his eternal knowing becomes a source of consolation for Boethius.

Julian, too, sees eternity as central to her message of comfort, but her understanding of how and why God's eternity matters to her message of comfort is pointedly different from what we find in Boethius's *Consolation*. For Julian, God's eternity is not a proof of his justice; it is a proof of his love. She describes God as a being "that ever was and es and ever shall be: alle mighty, alle wisdom, and alle love" (*Vis.*, 71.5.7). For Julian, God's eternity enables him to love mankind, as she puts it, "endelesslye." The words "endelesslye" and "endeless" recur throughout her work; these words characterize God's love, his comfort, or his ability or will to hold mankind "sekerlye."[29] In the short version of her work, Julian develops her theory of God's eternal love in her imperative: "Thinke also wiselye of the gretnesse of this worde: 'That ever I suffred passion for the.' For in that worde was a hye knawinge of luffe and of likinge that he hadde in our salvation" (*Vis.*, 89.12.41–43). The referent of "this worde" is Jesus's whole utterance, encompassing his Passion as a source of eternal consolation—though it happened in historical time, Jesus's Passion is, for the *Revelation*, a source of salvation that has "ever" existed.[30] According to Julian, "he has made alle thinge that is made for love. And thorowe the same love it is kepede and ever shalle be withouten ende"; because of Jesus's ever-extant love of mankind, mankind shall be held and protected perpetually—"withouten ende"—going into the future (*Vis.*, 73.5.14–16). Moreover, Jesus's eternal love is self-identical: "he is ever ylike in love" (*Vis.*, 105.19.55). This unchanging, eternal love enables him to "kepe us fulle sekerlye."[31] His ability to love man "sekerlye" is at the heart of Julian's comfort.[32]

In the later, longer version of her work, Julian further emphasizes the loving comfort found in divine eternity. When she returns to the "think on this word" passage, the "word" is no longer Jesus's entire utterance but the single word "ever": "Think also wisely of the gretnes of this word: 'Ever.' For in that was shewed an high knowing of love that he hath in our salvation" (*Rev.*, 201.23.35). By specifying the word "ever" unambiguously as the referent of "word," Julian nominates divine ever-presence itself as the center of spiritual comfort, the root of Christ's capacity to love mankind "endelesslye." She goes on to explain that the "ever" present nature of his love ensures that man will eventually join God-as-Jesus in "endlesse blisse" and will be saved "from endlesse paines of helle" (*Rev.*, 201.23.37–40).[33] Later, when she says, "For I saw that God began never to loven mankynd," she means that his love for mankind is infinite and uncreated, not bound by time or the existence of the created world (*Rev.*, 295.53.21). Since it exists outside of time, God's love never actually "began": as she puts it, before he made us, he loved us.[34] Because of God's ever-present love, humanity is held in "everlasting sekerness" (*Rev.*, 175.15.2). In the long version, understanding and feeling God's eternity become central comforts of Julian's vision.[35] In this insistence on divine ever-presence as a source of comfort, Julian concurs with Boethian consolation. But, by dispensing with the idea of eternal justice, and instead focusing solely on God's *love* as eternal and ever-present, she revises the canonical Latinate *consolatio*, which understands divine eternity as an element of a consoling theodicy, into a comforting vernacular theology of love.[36]

Julian's theorizing of divine eternity as a source of consolation gains momentum in the long version of her work. In her short version, Julian uses the term "pointe" as a metaphor for the temporal brevity of human life: "this langoure that we hafe here is bot a pointe, and when we ere takene sodaynly oute of paine into blisse it shalle be nought" (*Vis.*, 107.20.20–21).[37] Here, Julian's idea is that human life, which is "paine," is so brief, in comparison with the "blisse" of the afterlife as to be, in effect, "nought." In the long version, Julian shifts the valence of this metaphor of how the "pointe" can be used to figure the nature of human life. She now says God is "in the mid point of all thinges," including human life (*Rev.*, 163.11.1, 163.11.16). In this metaphoric rendering of the relation between human life and God life on earth becomes "the temporal counterpart to the eternal 'myd poynt' that is God."[38]

In choosing thus to elaborate on the "point" metaphor in her longer version, Julian signals her theological tangency with the *Consolation*, since the same metaphor appears there: "Time is to eternity as a circle to its middle point . . . right so is the order of changeful fate bound to the stable simplicity of providence."[39] God's eternity makes him like a "punctus" in the middle of a circle. Through its stability, unchangeability, and centrality, his "punctus" constrains human life into order—the implied circle around the midpoint of his unchanging eternity. Thus, when Julian describes not just human life as a single point but also God as a midpoint to which the points of human life are fixed as the perimeter of a circle, she evokes the metaphorics of the *Consolation*.

The *Revelation*'s echoes with the *Consolation*'s treatment of time and eternity resonate more loudly as Julian's autoexegesis progresses. After his explanation of God's eternity by recourse to the point image, Boethius explains how this image helps clarify the problem of chance in human life. Referring to how human life is fettered always to a steady midpoint, he says, "this same order constrains the fortunes and deeds of men by an indissoluble linkage of causes."[40] Similarly, Julian adds to her longer redaction a discussion of how God's eternity and eternal providence can coexist with the human perception of chance.[41] As does Boethius's Latin *consolatio*, Julian's Middle English work of comfort denies the absolute existence of chance, explaining that "nothing is done by happe ne by aventure, but alle by the foreseing wisdom of God" (*Rev.*, 163.11.5–6).[42] Conceding that human beings nevertheless *perceive* chance and happenstance, Julian blames this perception on an incapacity in human vision: "If it be hap or aventure in the sight of man, our blindhede and our unforsight is the cause" (*Rev.*, 163.11.6–7). God's eternal vision, which sees all causes, guarantees by its very nature that chance does not exist:

> For tho thinges that be in the foreseing wisdom of God bene fro without beginning, which rightfully and worshipfully and continually he ledeth to the best ende as it cometh aboute, falling to us sodeynly, ourselfe unweting. And thus, by our blindhede and our unforsighte, we say these thinges be by happes and aventure. Thus I understonde in this shewing of love, for wel I wot in the sight of our lord God is no happe ne aventure. (*Rev.*, 163.11.7–13)

In this argument, Julian mounts a critique of chance that is based upon the fundamental difference between human perspective, which is bound by temporality, and divine, which is eternally present and unchanging. In pinning the human misapprehension of chance to temporality, Julian again foregrounds her work's tangency with the *Consolation*: in Philosophy's formulation, fortune "truly is of nothing" [verum non de nihilo est]; everything humans perceive to happen by chance "has causes" [causas habet]. It is only because humans do not see causes in advance—they are "unforeseen" [inprouisus]—that they believe fortune exists.[43] Julian shares this perspective; in her formulation, the human perception of chance is contingent upon the "unforesight" of man, while divine foresight sees all, securing mankind against the vagaries of fortune: "in our lorde God is no happe ne aventure."[44]

The Boethian inflection of Julian's logic becomes yet stronger when she shifts focus from the limitations of human understanding to the protection of God's providence:

> Our lorde hath it ordeynit to fro withoute beginning. For there is no doer but he. I saw fulle sekerly that he changeth never his purpose in no manner of thing, ne never shalle without end. For ther was nothing unknowen to him in his rightfulle ordenance fro without beginning. And therefore all thinge was set in order, or anything was made, as it should stand without ende. (*Rev.*, 165.11.35–39)

This argument recalls the sixth prose section of book 4 in the *Consolation*, in which Philosophy explains that "the order of fate proceeds from the simplicity of providence" and that "therefore God disposes what happens singly and stably by providence."[45] In its increasing foregrounding of the comforting nature of the eternity of the divine, Julian's *Revelation* is a full-fledged consolation of eternity.

To this point, I have stressed the *Revelation*'s thematic reliance on eternity as the conceptual basis of its consoling theology of love. But the thematic emphasis on eternity's consolations has striking formal and stylistic consequences. Julian creates programs of stylistic variation in her writing that are designed to encourage the reader to *sense* the all-important relationship between time and eternity that she thematizes as a source of comfort and consolation. She creates, through stylistic and formal variation, a sensory correlative for the idea of eternity that she describes discursively. Before she deploys her sensory correlative for eternity, however, she establishes the feeling of temporality in her writing that will give context to that infinitely consoling feeling of eternity.

COMFORTABLE STYLE I: TEMPORAL PROSE

Julian's normative style for her work, the initial style, the baseline, is what I call "temporal prose." It occurs in Julian's work when she narrates what is outside the visionary experience itself, as when she explains the real, earthly, and temporal circumstances in which her visionary experience took place:

> Ande *when* I was *thrittye wyntere alde* and a halfe, God sente a bodelye syekenes in the whilke I laye *thre dayes and thre nightes,* and *on the ferthe night* I toke alle my rightinges of haly kyrke, and wened nought tille have liffede *tille daye.* (*Vis.*, 65.2.1–4; italics mine)

Here, at the very beginning of her narrative, Julian uses temporal style to contextualize her visions, establishing the real-life circumstances into which her decidedly suprareal and supratemporal visions will intrude. Temporal prose contains no alliteration, no rhyme, and no rhythmical regularity. It thus seems natural, unartificed, and spontaneous.[46] But the seeming lack of rhetorical intricacy is a feint. This prose style, for all its apparent naturalness, is far from artless. In this passage, Julian uses temporal operators and phrases to reveal her own age and the amount of time that her visionary experience lasted: "when," "thrittye wyntere alde," "thre dayes and thre nightes," "on the ferthe night," and "tille daye." In her use of temporal markers, she establishes a chronological sequence for the events she will describe. The temporal prose of the narrative that encases her visionary experiences makes temporality itself sensible. Thereby, this prose makes readers aware that they—like Julian—participate in time.

This chronological sequencing recurs throughout Julian's narrative of her illness and life outside of the visions. She frequently begins clauses with *when*, *then*, *after*, *until*, and *before*, not only confirming the temporal sequence of her visionary experience but also synthesizing her sixteen discrete visions into a unified, linear narrative. These sequencing effects occur in the second chapter of the short vision, when she describes the trajectory of her illness:

> Ande *when* I was thrittye wyntere alde and a halfe, God sente me a bodelye syekenes in the whilke I laye thre dayes and thre nightes. . . . And *after* this I langourede *furthe two dayes and two nightes,* and on the *thirde night* I wenede ofte times to hafe passede. . . . Thus I endured *tille* daye, and *by then* was my bodye dede fra the middes downwarde. (*Vis.*, 65.2.1–17)

In her recurrent use of temporal markers, Julian creates the experience of a time-bound and continuous narrative, which, in turn, renders the continuity and temporal verisimilitude of her visionary experience sensible to her readers in the experiential time of their reading. Julian's temporal prose also renders a sense of chronological continuity within her illness narrative—a continuity that emerges through her anatomization of her pain and suffering.

> *After* this the overe partye of my bodye *begane* to die, as to my felinge. Mine handes felle downe on aythere side, and also for unpowere my hede satylde downe on side. . . . *Than* wende I sothelye to hafe bene atte the pointe of dede. (*Vis.*, 67.2.33–36)

Through this sequential description, Julian makes her reader imagine the "dede" rolling its way gradually over her body, moving through her in what she believes will be the final moments of her life. She uses her temporal style to locate her sickness unto death concretely in time.

But this intensive temporalization of her failing body serves as a foil. As Julian continues with her sickroom narrative, she emphasizes that her anticipated death will finally take her out of time and out of the world.

> Than saide I to the folke that were with me: "It es todaye domesdaye with me." And this I saide for I wenede to hafe died. For that daye that man or woman dies is he demed as he shalle be withouten ende. This I saide for I walde thaye loved God mare and sette the lesse prise be the vanite of the worlde, for to make thame to hafe minde that this life es shorte, as thaye might se in ensampille be me. For in alle this tyme I wenede to hafe died. (*Vis.*, 77.7.14–19)

Existence in time, Julian reminds us, is finite. Life can end at any given moment, in any "todaye." But, as she goes on to note, though "this life es shorte," the end of existence in time means the beginning of existence in life "withouten ende." Thus, for her, the end of life-in-time entails immediate comfort in an unending existence beyond time. The careful situating of her sickroom narrative in time serves to set up the eventual release from time that comes with death.[47]

She wishes her insights about the brevity and vulnerability of existence in time to be exportable to her immediate audience—"the folke that were with [her]"—but, by extension, also to her readers. For Julian, this sickroom moment renders not only the finitude of her own life in time but also, by her "ensampille," the temporal finitude within which her readers live. When Julian carefully situates her dying experience in time, her readers are reminded of their own participation in temporality. When Julian says that she "wenede" to die, readers feel their own shimmering expectation of death, their own awareness that "this life es shorte," and that the next life, the life beyond time, is the one "withouten ende." Indeed, Julian's repetition of the verb "wenede" itself highlights humanity's bondage by and to time: one can only expect things when one exists in time, since expectation itself bespeaks a present consciousness that looks forward in time to a certain future. Being alive in time is to expect to die. To read Julian's temporal prose style, in turn, is to participate sensibly—through the literary field—in mortality, impermanence, space, and contingency. To read her prose is to be reminded of our shared participation in humanity, in vulnerability, in subjection to death, in time.

COMFORTABLE STYLE II: "EVER YLIKE" PROSE

This darkly participatory teleology, however, is not the ultimate point of Julian's stylistic rendering of time. Quite the contrary, Julian's rendering of time and mortality underpins her central rendering of comfort. Rupturing the decidedly mortal order of her baseline temporal style, Julian develops another style, which I call "ever ylike" prose. This second style comes into play in her verbal revelations—what she calls, "worde formede in [her] understonding" (*Rev.*, 157.9.24–25). In these verbal visions, Julian presents the voice of Jesus speaking directly to her. When Jesus speaks, he speaks with conspicuous and emphatic rhythm. The outstanding such passage is the famous "I it am" revelation, in which Jesus says, "I it am that is hiaste. I it am that thowe luffes. I it am that thowe likes. I it am that thowe serves. I it am that thowe longes. I it am that thowe desires. I it am that thowe menes. I it am that is alle" (*Vis.*, 91.13.26–28). Unlike the temporal prose that surrounds it, this verbal showing consists of a series of short clauses, replete with sonic and rhythmical likeness. The clauses are anaphoric, each beginning with the phrase "I it am." They are also, for the most part, isosyllabic: "I it am that is hiaste" contains seven syllables, as do the second, third, and fourth clauses, as well as the sixth and seventh. Moreover, the clauses are nearly perfectly isorhythmic: they contain a series of identical words ("I it am that thowe"), and then one word that changes in each clause—"luffes," "likes," "serves," "longes," "desires," and "menes." All of these words but "desire" are disyllables stressed on the first syllable, which is also thus the penultimate syllable of the clause; "desires" and "is alle" are also stressed on the penultimate syllable, even though the words are trisyllabic. As a result, every clause has an identical, or nearly identical, stress pattern. In their sonic parities, these rhythmical lines create a sense of unchanging self-similarity; these lines create a correlative, then, of how Julian understands the nature of divine presence. Julian uses poetic likeness (anaphora and regular clausal rhythm) to make a series of complex ideas available to her readers' senses; she uses ornamentation to create a sensory mode of knowing God's eternity—his "ever ylike" (*Vis.*, 105.19.55) and "everlasting seker" (*Rev.*, 175.15.2) being—in her work.

In addition to her rhythmical renderings of God's "ever ylike" nature, Julian also renders it syntactically in this verbal vision. At first, the "I" of "I it am" exists in relation simply to the idea of highness, asserting its own identity as that which is "hiaste": "I it am that is hiaste." But the subsequent clause redefines the "I" by placing it in relation to a "thowe": "I it am that thowe luffes." The idea, repeated again and again after the introduction of the "thowe," is that God is whatever human beings ("thowe") act toward, whether through affect (love, like, long for), intention (desire, mean) or deed (serve). But, no matter what action the "thowe" undertakes, God is always the subject of the sentence and the intended object of the subordinate clause, the being that receives that loving, liking, serving, desiring, or meaning. The cognitive effect of the passage is thus to render sensible how God exists stably in an always self-similar essential state of pure being; this lesson is encapsulated in the repeated and unchanging phrase "I it am." But the passage also renders sensible how man exists unstably in an always changing state; this idea is encapsulated in the subordinate clauses. Syntactically, this passage encourages readers to participate dually and knowingly in humanity's changeful time-boundness and simultaneously in Jesus's ever-similar eternity, his unchanging "sekerness."[48]

Later, in the long version, Julian deploys a rhythmical passage with a repetition, but the repetition shifts slightly each time. The first instance of the repetition reads, "Now sitteth nott the lorde on erth in wildernesse, but he sitteth on his riche and nobil seet." The second and third read, "Now stondeth not the son before the fader." The fourth one reads, "Now is the spouse, Goddes son, in pees with his loved wife." The fifth one reads, "Now sitteth the son, very god and very man, in his citte in rest and in pees, whych his fader hath dyght to hym of endlesse purpose, and the fader in the son, and the holy gost in the fader and in the sone" (*Rev.*, 287–89.51.265–78). In this cascade of rhythmical language, Julian again deploys sonic likeness, the anaphoric word "now," to convey her larger message: that God, whether as father, son, lover, master, or servant, is ever constant in his "endlesse purpose," stable and self-similar in his ever-present love toward man. He is the ever-present, unchanging, loving "now," no matter whether human beings understand him as father or son, standing or sitting. Julian uses repetition and likeness, again, in combination with unlikeness in successive clauses to formally embody God's unchanging love as something that, although changing in how it is perceived by man, nevertheless suffuses the "now" of man's experience. Through poetic ornamentation and rigid syntactic framing, Julian's language becomes a structure that can embody and enact a reader's participation in God. Through poetic ornamentation and rigid syntactic framing, Julian shifts her discourse from the fluent ease of temporal style to the disfluent challenge of eternal prose.

Julian's rhythmical rendering of God's ever-present love emerges in perhaps its most pointedly *vernacular* formulation when she claims that the Lord will make "all things well," in the following passage: "And thus oure good Lord answerde to alle the questions and doubtes that I might make, sayande fulle comfortabelye on this wise: 'I maye make alle thinge wele, I can make alle thinge wele, I wille make alle thinge wele, and I shalle make alle thynge wele. And thowe shalle se it thyselfe that alle thinge shalle be wele'" (*Vis.*, 95.15.1–4). Like the earlier "I it am" passage, this passage is rich with anaphora, isorhythm, and isosyllable, creating a structure of sonic and rhythmic likenesses from clause to clause. The idea evoked by the repetition of the formula "I [modal verb] make alle thing wele" is simple: God, the "I" subject, is an ever-present and recurrent agent who makes "all thing wele." But the architecture of rhythmical and grammatical likeness in this contemplative passage also serves to highlight *differences* between clauses. In this case, the rhythmic parity of the clauses highlights the play of modal verbs: Julian moves from "maye" to "can" to "wille" to "shalle." Because these are the only terms that shift among the lines, there is a great deal of interpretive pressure on them, a pressure to which Julian herself responds in the next section of her work.[49]

For Julian, this modal triptych becomes an aural figure for the Trinity. She explains that "I maye" denotes the Father, "I can" denotes the Son, "I wille" denotes the Holy Spirit, and "I shalle" denotes the unity of the Trinity (*Vis.*, 95.15.5–8). By associating the modal verb *may* with God the Father, Julian etymologically associates him with strength or "might," from which *may* derives. By associating the Son with the verb *can*, Julian again uses English etymology to make certain very subtle claims, because *can* derives from the same Old English root as "ken"; thus, in differentiating the power of the Father (might) from the power of the Son (knowledge), Julian, like Jerome, Augustine, and many others, calls attention to the Son's incarnate wisdom, his living knowledge, in apposition with the Father's divine "might" and the Holy Ghost's loving "will."

Rather than arguing from point to point that God the Father represents or performs "might," that the Son represents or performs "knowing," and that the Holy Ghost represents or performs the divine loving will, Julian embeds these ideas in a sophisticated grammatical meditation, a meditation carried by modal verbs. Like the "I it am" passage, this isorhythmic, isosyllabic, and programmatically modal passage creates a formal structure in which God's unity of essence and multiplicity of action are rendered sense-perceptible and therefore comprehensible. But by using different variations on a single grammatical class—here, modal verbs—Julian linguistically enacts an awareness of God as both various and unified, as plural, yet coincident. She also makes God's essence sensible as stable—he is that which makes all things well—by substituting a different auxiliary verb with each iteration while keeping the same subject among clauses. Neither "wille" nor "shalle" nor "can" nor "maye" can alter the first person singular pronoun "I": it anchors every sentence and controls every verb. In devising this anaphoric and incantatory passage, Julian has again rendered eternal stability in form; she has performed a sophisticated grammatical contemplation of the Trinity, and one in which the specific semantic meanings of each modal verb map onto a Person of the Trinity. But, whichever Person of the Trinity he may act as, God always holds the same intention toward us—to make all things well; and his fundamental being, embodied in the unchanging "I," holds steady. Because the rhythmical passages are anaphoric catalogues, there are no hypotactic structures linking the sentences together, no temporal markers—no "whens," "thens," or "afters," no time, no expectations of death. Thus, Julian creates not a narrative or argument about God's eternal love but a participatory contemplation on it, a collocation of phrases that begin to make God sensible as eternal, "ever ylike," and "everlasting." In reading this passage, readers' contemplative awarenesses of God's mind-bending temporalities are staged poetically, through literary form. They are staged by the swerve from easy, fluent English into complex, nonstandard, disfluent English.

In creating this grammatical Trinity to enable her readers to participate linguistically in the supralogical truth of the three-Personed God, Julian's work comes into close contact with Augustine's *De Trinitate*. In book 14, Augustine articulates his principle of contemplative participation by urging on his readers the idea that the human mind is the best means of coming to know the Trinity, since it is made to participate in the Trinity by a logic of likeness:

> The mind must be considered as it is in itself before it participates in God, and his image must be found in it. For, as we have said, even though wearied and deformed by giving up direct participation in God [i.e, in Eden], nevertheless the image of God remains. For it is his image in this, that participation in him

> is possible, that we can participate in him; which so great good would not be possible without our being made in his image. Thus, then, the mind remembers itself, understands itself, delights in itself; if we discern this, we discern a trinity; not yet quite God in himself, but now at last an image of God.[50]

For Augustine, the likeness between our mind and the divine Trinity enables us to become aware of our supervening participation in God, our being created in his image and likeness. As he goes on to elaborate this theory, Augustine will famously assert that the three cardinal functions of the mind—memory, understanding, and will—embody on the human scale the Persons of Father, Son, and Holy Ghost, respectively. Thus, for him, contemplating the nature and structure of the triune but unified human mind enables a deeper, fuller understanding of God by a logic of participatory likeness. What Julian does in her modal meditation on the Trinity is not to suggest that the human *mind* can participate as an analogue of the divine Trinity but rather to suggest that human *language* can do that, and specifically the vernacular language in which we all participate every day of our lives, and in which we actively and directly participate in the reading of Julian's text.[51] She demonstrates how participation in language enacts some part of contemplative participation in the divine.

Thus, in her mixed style of prose, Julian devises a system that renders temporality and eternity equally sensible, and that enables her readers to begin to fathom their own participation in God via their participation in language. On the one hand, her sequential prose makes time sensible through her careful insistence on chronological and spatial continuity within her narrative and in her life. On the other hand, in her verbal visions of Jesus, the voice of the divine intrudes into her narrative from eternity, from outside of time, in the form of incantatory and echoic passages that formally render the nature of divine eternity itself as that ever-steady being that exists outside of time. The stylistic difference between her temporally sequential narrative and her "ever ylike" incantations provides a stylistic framework within which the taking of spiritual comfort in God's ever-loving self-similarity can occur: as the reader experiences temporality in parallel with Julian, expects death in parallel with Julian, and then transitions into a feeling of divine everlastingness, that reader feels the full and ever-present love that God bears toward her as the ultimate consolation in the face of temporal human suffering. Julian devises a twin strategy of writing that renders God comprehensible both through linear, temporally continuous narrative and through poetic devices that capitalize on the particularities of English grammar. She devises her own vernacular, stylistic, and formal vehicle to embody the "comfortabille" contemplative message that she seeks to convey: that we all participate everlastingly in the unchanging love of God, even though we exist in time.

COMFORTABLE STYLE III: CONTINUAL PROSE

Julian augments her stylistic renderings of human time and the eternal, "ever ylike" love and being of God with a third style. This style appears in what Julian calls her "bodily sights." These are usually visions of Jesus's Passion, but they also include visions of the pregnant Mary and images that are more quotidian, including hazelnuts, herring scales, and droplets of water. These visual experiences, like the "ever ylike" speeches of Jesus, intrude into her narrative frame of the temporal sickroom. Julian registers this intrusiveness of "bodily sight" by her repeated use of the word "sodaynlye" to characterize her experience of them:

> And in this, *sodaynlye* I sawe the rede blode trekille downe fro under the garlande alle hate, freshlye, plentefully and livelye, right as methought that it was in that time that the garlonde of thornes was thyrstede on his blessede hede. (*Vis.*, 67.3.10–12)

Evidently, suddenness is a key characteristic of "bodily sight." She describes these sudden visions as ruptures into the bodily experience of sickness: "Than wende I sothelye to hafe bene atte the pointe of dede. And in this, *sodeynlye* alle my paine was awaye fro me" (*Vis.*, 67.2.36–37). After her pain is gone, Julian reveals that "*sodeynlye* come into my minde that I shulde desire the seconde wounde . . . And in this *sodaynlye* I sawe the rede bloode" (*Vis.*, 67.3.1, 10). Julian disrupts the experience of linear, continuous, earthly temporality—developed in her temporal accounts of her sickroom—with these sudden, piercing accounts of her bodily visions. Through these sudden interruptions of the temporal narrative of illness, readers are thrust into a new kind of narration and a very different style from either temporal or "ever ylike" prose. In this interruptivity, readers are urged to become aware of their contemplative participation in a third kind of time. "Sodaynlye" is, for Julian, not a mere word, but a stylistic device with which she pierces the continuity of her narrative, to suggest that her visionary experiences lie somehow athwart the ongoing "real time" of the sickroom and somehow separate from Jesus' eternal self-sameness.

As in her temporal prose, in the prose style that delivers her bodily sights, Julian deploys a great deal of temporal language—adverbs of time, for instance—as well as a great deal of spatial language—prepositions of position, direction, or motion. Returning to the passage about the thrusting of the crown of thorns:

> And *in* this *sodaynlye* I sawe the rede blode trekille *downe fro under* the garlande, alle hate, freshlye, plentefully and livelye, right as me thought that it was *in that time* that the garlonde of thornes was thyrstede *on* his blessede hede. (*Vis.*, 67.3.10–12)

In her usage of prepositions and temporal markers ("in," "downe fro under," "sodaynlye," and "in that tyme") Julian insists on the spatial and temporal particularity of the scene she describes. In this insistence, her prose style formally renders temporal and spatial order sensible as constraints placed upon the divine.

But introducing an eternal being into time and space is no mean feat; this is why, in her long version, Julian introduces additional means of rendering the mystery of divine incarnation yet more sensible and, thereby, more comprehensible.

> The gret droppes of blode felle downe fro under the garlonde like pelottes, seming as it had comen oute of the veines . . . The plentuoushede is like to the droppes of water that falle off the evesing of an house after a grete shower of raine . . . And for the roundhede, they were like to the scale of hering in the spreding of the forhede. (*Rev.*, 147.7.10–12, 17–20)

Here, Julian invents a system of domestic, quotidian imagery—the droplets falling of the eaves of a house, the pellets, and the herring scales—to familiarize the mystery of the incarnate God. Working in tandem with the prepositional form of her spatial language—"downe fro under," "oute of," "falle off"—this system of domestic analogies enables Julian to render sensibly available the truth that God lived and died on earth, in time and in space. It also reminds readers that they, through Julian's vernacular vision, can participate at once in their own familiar day-to-day world of herring scales and eaves *and* the more wondrous and terrible world of Christ's incarnation and death. Her style is designed to create a feeling of empathy with Jesus' sufferings by producing the vivid impression that he suddenly appeared to her—and that, in all his majesty and horror—he has suddenly become present to the reader—in the real, daily world of time and space.

This sudden presence of the Passion in the world of daily things, however, does not mean that Jesus' self-sacrifice is in some way fleeting or transitory. Quite the contrary, as Julian says more than once, the vision of the bleeding Jesus goes on "continuely," "lastande" in time:

> And *in that time* that oure lorde shewed this that I have *nowe* saide in gastelye sight, I saw the bodilye sight *lastande* of the plentyouse bledinge of the hede . . . (*Vis.*, 71.5.1–2)

> And *after* this, I sawe with bodely sight the face of the crucifixe that hange before me, in whilke I behelde *continuely* a party of his passion. (*Vis.*, 77.8.1–3)

These visions are "continuel" and "lastande" and filled with a suffering that collapses distinctions among past ("in that time"), present ("nowe"), and future ("after"), yet encompasses all of them. Thus, these visions emerge through a prose style that can both convey continuity and distinguish that continuity from the everyday progression of moments and lived events into which these visions suddenly penetrate. "Continuel" prose insists at once on its temporality and its supratemporality—on its suddenness and its lastingness.

Julian's "continuel" prose sensibly renders a kind of temporality with particular significance to incarnational theology: perpetuity. Perpetuity is that which exists in time, but is not subject to cessation; it is thus the conceptual middle ground between eternity and time. A prime example of perpetuity is the world: it is created in time, but will never cease to be.[52] By this definition, Julian's understanding of Jesus's Passion is perpetual: because Jesus was born and crucified in time, the Passion is "temporal," but because it goes on "continuely" and offers consolation to mankind throughout all time going forward, it is beyond cessation.[53] Julian grasps the importance of perpetuity to her overall "comfortabille" project, accentuating it in her "continuel" style, which makes Jesus's Passion imaginable as something "lastande" in perpetuity while it also locates that Passion securely in time and space. By encapsulating the perpetuity of the Crucifixion through her style, Julian helps her audience experience sensorily the miraculousness of Christ's simultaneous temporality and supratemporality, his being both mortal and deathless.

To familiarize this idea of perpetuity to her audience, Julian introduces a metaphor—her vision of the world as a hazelnut: "And in this, he shewed me a litille thinge the quantite of a haselle nutte, lygande in the palme of my hande, and, to my understandinge, that it was as rounde as any balle. I lokede theropon, and thought: 'Whate maye this be?' And I was answered generally thus: 'It is alle that is made. . . . It lastes and ever shalle, for God loves it'" (*Vis.*, 69.4.7–12). The hazelnut has "quantite," and is thus spatially finite; it is "made," and thus necessarily temporal. But it also "lastes and ever shalle," and is thus deathless, "lastande," and "continuel." Like the world that it is meant to represent, the hazelnut is perpetual. Julian apposes this perpetual hazelnut with a vision of Mary, "in bodilye lyekenes, a simpille maidene and a meeke, yonge of age, in the stature that sho was when sho conceivede" (*Vis.*, 69.4.21–23). By apposing the image of Mary with the perpetual world-hazelnut, Julian analogically and appositively reminds us how Jesus exists perpetually in Mary. Mary's time-bound ("yonge") body will contain the eternity of God, once she has "conceivede" Jesus. In holding the infant Jesus in her womb, Mary literally embodies perpetuity: she contains within herself a child who is created in time but endures forever as a "lastande" comfort to humanity. Julian is keenly invested not only in juxtaposing the temporality of the sickroom with the eternity of God but also in making sensory Jesus's perpetual incarnation of his own eternal being into a body that suffers the constraints of time and space. Her embodiment of perpetuity in "continuel" prose enables her to render that mystery sense-perceptible to her readers. The *Revelation*'s stylistic reflexes of the three times of God—temporality, eternity, and perpetuity—create a feelable, sense-perceptible simulacrum of the multiple temporalities of divinity itself.

By participating in Julian's language, thereby experiencing a linguistic simulacrum of the three divine times, readers are made aware of their own capacity to cultivate their own participation in the divine being through the work of contemplation. Thus, Julian's text shares the *Cloud*'s apparent conviction that a primary drive of a participatory contemplative work should be to address the temporality/eternity incompatibility. Also like the *Cloud*, the *Revelation* seeks to bring readers to some kind of "gropable" understanding—via the sensible action of the literary field itself—of their own likeness to God not in spite of but indeed *because of* that seeming chasm that separates temporality from eternity. In the *Cloud*, it is the embodiment of atomic time in the prose stylistics of the work itself that facilitates a reader's awareness that she, although bound in time, can nevertheless asymptotically approach identity with the ever-presence of God, through the deployment of atomic prayer. Atomic prayer and its intratextual reflex, atomic style, facilitate the perception of likeness between reader-contemplative and God. In the *Revelation*, the likening between time-bound, mortal human existence and God's "ever ylike" sameness and security occurs not asymptotically but appositively. Rather than suggesting that living the world of atomic moments can approach the nature of eternal life, Julian's writings suggest instead, by interweaving temporal, "ever ylike," and "continuel" prose with one another, that all of these modes of temporal experience can coexist side by side—that the eternal world of God, the continual world of Christ's self-sacrifice, and the temporal world of Julian and her sickness are all part of the same multitemporal story. As readers move through her narrative, they are made to feel—through the action of Julian's triune prose style—a sense of what it is to inhabit time, to inhabit eternity, and to inhabit perpetuity, and to feel how porous the boundaries are between those states. The end of this trinity of styles is to enable readers to understand how very possible and, indeed, how very easy it was for Christ to enter into time and into human form, while holding his eternal love for humanity always in the realm of "everlasting sekernesse," and being "continuely" recrucified for man's transgressions. Through her prose stylistics, readers are helped to participate in what it is to live equally in time, eternity, and perpetuity. As I will explain presently, they are helped to contemplate God's temporalities by their immersion in the forms of the English vernacular.

VERNACULARITY IN *A REVELATION OF LOVE*

The default scholarly ascription of motivation for Julian's writing in the vernacular is simply that, as she says early on in her text, she was not lettered and could not read Latin.[54] Thus, English was the only choice for her. However true her assertion of her Latin illiteracy may be, her choice to compose in the vernacular also originates in sensory and stylistic motivations. Julian's usage of the modal verbs as a grammatical reflex of the Trinity bodies forth the possibility that the particular formal and structural capacities of Middle English lend themselves more readily to divine contemplation than those found in Latin. Latin does not have modal verbs, so the specific kind of grammatical meditation on the nature of the Trinity that Julian enacted with her "I may make all things well, I can make all things well, I will make all things well" refrain would not be possible in Latin. Julian's grammatical play in her Trinitarian meditation is key to the participation that her text generates. Similarly, Julian's "I it am" aria, which Englishes the Hebrew name of God—Yahweh—works by exploiting audience fluency in English: native readers will immediately grasp the meaning of the phrase, but they will also recognize the inversion of object and verb as somewhat unusual, and they will recognize that this phrase is marked by anaphoric repetition. Having marked the disfluent strangeness both of the phrasing and the emphatic repetition, the reader is all the more likely to slow down and process the phrase itself as a set piece—eventually perhaps registering it as a proxy for the name of God, symbolizing through its repetition his invariance, his stability, his "everlastande sekernesse" (*Vis.*, 81.9.15). Middle English becomes a formal structure in which the contemplative can perceive sensibly and thereby participate in the comforting and ever-present nature of God. Thus, although the *Revelation* may be written in English in part because Julian wished to reach the widest possible audience, or it may be written in English because Julian knew no Latin, it is nevertheless true that part of Julian's contemplative agenda—embodying the ever-stable truth of Christ's loving orientation toward mankind and embodying the logic of the Trinity in literary language—could not have been achieved in the same way in Latin. For Julian, as for the *Cloud*-author, Middle English is a choice with powerful sensory possibilities for producing active textual participation, and it is thus a choice that can initiate participatory contemplation of the divine.

Although it, like the *Cloud*, avails itself of the formal particulars of English, the *Revelation* makes a telling shift away from the *Cloud* in terms of how it imagines its readership. Whereas the *Cloud* insists on a small readership of devout, strictly contemplative people, Julian envisions for her text a theoretically unlimited readership: her "evencristene." Whereas the *Cloud* directs itself toward what we might call a vernacular contemplative elite, Julian directs her text toward anyone who seeks to understand Christ and feel their participation in him burgeoning in their hearts.[55] In directing her work to her "evencristene," Julian also flags up the particular centrality of likeness to her sense of participation in the larger Christian community to which she belongs. She does not refer to her fellow Christians as "other Christians," nor in fact as "fellow Christians." Instead, she refers to them with an adjectival construction that signals likeness, parity, and equality: "*even*cristene." Her sense of the community in which she lives and works, then, is as a nonhierarchized group of contemplatives-in-potential, all of whom are like one another in their fundamental constitution as Christians. Thus, Julian's *Revelation* is designed, in the end, not only to help readers linguistically feel their own participation in God but also to feel their own comforting coparticipation in the church, along with everyone else in their Christian community—a community that, itself, exists in time, in perpetuity, and eternally in God's love: as Julian puts it, "or [before] God made us he loved us," not "or [before] God made me he loved me" (*Rev.*, 379.86.18).

In my next chapter, I will examine how *Piers Plowman* picks up a theological and formal impulse very much akin to what we find in *A Revelation of Love*. Like the *Revelation*, *Piers* will use narrative form to generate a sophisticated formal meditation on the nature of God and man's participation in him. But, rather than approaching that problem through an exploration of prose stylistics, *Piers* will approach the problem through a multipronged analysis of modes of gaining knowledge, culminating in a formal, poetic staging of how self-knowledge and knowledge of God interrelate. *Piers* will seek to promote—through vernacular literary language and form—an audience's ability to sense one's own fundamental kinship with God. And, in a manner far more explicit and sustained even than what we find in the *Revelation*, *Piers* will take pains to show the pervasive interpenetration of the world of contemplation and the social world. *Piers* will take pains, that is, to show how the eternal things of God and Christ and the temporal things of man can and indeed must coincide.

PART II

"Kyndely" Participation

CHAPTER THREE

Piers Plowman and Social Likeness

How to Know God "Kyndely"

Although the Middle English works I have examined so far have engaged with the Latin contemplative tradition, none of them has had much to say about one prominent branch of contemplative theory—namely, the difference between the contemplative life and its nearly omnipresent other, the active life.[1] Although many late antique Christian theologians held the contemplative life in higher regard than the active,[2] as early as the writings of Gregory the Great, some recognized that the life of contemplation cannot and should not be sustained in its purest state of withdrawal from the world throughout someone's life. Instead, it is sometimes advisable or necessary, even for a cloistered monk, to break away from contemplation and to manage the details of the active life. As evidence, Gregory points out that Christ himself lived the "mixed life" of both contemplation and action.[3] What this signifies, for Gregory, is that even the most devout contemplatives must undertake works of charity and compassion toward their neighbors if they wish to follow the example of Jesus. Later medieval theologians, notably the Victorines, go one step further, to insist that contemplation must lead toward charity, which they understand to encompass "love, service to others, social justice, liberation, healing, and compassion."[4] For them, the imitation of Christ involves a willingness to walk away from the life of pure, isolated contemplation from time to time and instead to devote oneself to the service of mankind.

Even though the Middle English contemplative works I have studied so far remain focused on the nature and process of contemplation itself, rather than on exploring the relationship between the active and contemplative lives, there are Middle English contemplative works that take the relationship between active and contemplative life as their motivating force—owing perhaps to the increasing awareness in the late Middle Ages that all people, not just clergy, anchorites, or anchoresses, could participate in the contemplative life, to one degree or another.[5] The most notable and influential among them in England is William Langland's *Piers Plowman*.[6] As will become clear, *Piers* advocates for a new version of the mixed life in the way it stages a new kind of participatory contemplation for its audiences. That new version will erode the conceptual barrier that notionally separates an "active" from a "contemplative" life in the first place.

To argue that *Piers* stages the active and contemplative lives ultimately to support the mixed life is not, in itself, new. Scholars of the 1930s through 1950s saw *Piers*'s focus on the relation of the active with the contemplative life as a central feature of Langland's design. For these scholars, one of the primary interventions of Langland's writings into contemporary theology was to approve and, indeed, magnify the excellence of the mixed life and suggest that a life of pure contemplation was not the highest attainment of the Christian soul.[7] My analysis will return to and validate some of these out-of-fashion engagements with the poem but will do so to suggest not simply that *Piers* advocates the mixed life as a standby of holy living. As will become clear, the poem retheorizes exactly what the mixed life is, how it works, and why it matters. *Piers* insists that active labor and spiritual contemplation are, in the end, inextricable from each other; it does so by showing how social engagement is not separable from one's engagement with God. In this emphasis on social engagement, the poem appears as a kind of fulcrum between the prose contemplative works I have examined so far, which focus squarely on the contemplative practice of learning to sense one's relation to God, and the dramatic works yet to come, which will focus more on social engagement *as* contemplative participation.

Staging contemplation is, for *Piers* as for *A Revelation of Love* and *The Cloud of Unknowing*, very much a matter of sensory experience and literary form. This staging is also, for *Piers*, very much *not* a didactic experience, in a strict sense, corroborating Mark Miller's recent argument that the poem is not pedagogical, in the sense of seeking to impart concrete, particular packets of knowledge expositionally and/or discursively.[8] Instead, in *Piers*, the literary rendering of participatory contemplation is an *experience*, a zone of sensory complexities to be wandered through, as a means for grasping abstract truths about God that remain, always, slightly beyond discursive, rational access.[9] In this emphasis on the nondidacticism and deliberate difficulty of the poem, my work will be more aligned with Anne Middleton's study of *Piers*'s generic affiliations, which demonstrates that Langland imports recognizable literary structures—such as the opening gambits of *chansons d'aventure*—into his poem; this importation is designed, in Middleton's view, to resist any immediately graspable didactic trajectory.[10] Maureen Quilligan, likewise, has called attention to how *Piers* uses allegory to create complexly intersecting and highly unstable webs of meaning, rather than readily exportable discursive content.[11] Like theirs, my method will be focused on the formal workings of the poem, but my focus on the formal will also seek to explicate how distinctly English poetic forms bear on distinctly medieval theological principles and practices of participatory contemplation.

CONTEMPLATION AND "KYNDE KNOWYNGE"

Like the *Cloud* and the *Revelation*, *Piers* signals contemplation as a primary concern very early on, when the main character (not yet named as Will) asks his interlocutor (not yet named as Holy Church), "kenne me kyndely on Crist to believe" (*PP*, A.1.79; B.1.81; C.1.78). I construe Will's wish to "believe" "on Crist" as a request for contemplative understanding, in part because of that wish's association with the phrase "kenne me kyndely." This phrasing—"kenne me kyndely"—has received a good deal of critical unpacking, as it comes up more than once in the poem and seems central to how we understand the protagonist's emergent quest. The Middle English "kenne" means "teach" or "make known."[12] "Kyndely," however, commands a wider semantic range—and one that the poem will continue to reshape over the course of its narrative.[13] Deriving from *kind*, denoting birth, nature, naturalness, property, sex, gender, proper manner, type, class, or group,[14] "kyndely" can mean according to nature, innately, according to natural moral law, by instinct, by birth or descent, properly, truly, rightly, justly, appropriately, gladly, courteously, and nobly.[15] In simplest terms, then, the phrase "kenne me kyndely" can mean that the main character asks to be taught "kindly," or naturally, how to believe in Christ.[16] But, because of the semantic plasticity of "kyndely," the phrase contains more generative ambiguity than can be fully accounted for by that translation. It can mean "teach me naturally to believe in Christ," "teach me innately to believe in Christ," "teach me by birth and descent to believe in Christ," "teach me properly to believe in Christ," "teach me familiarly to believe in Christ," or "teach me nobly to believe in Christ." Moreover, because of its embrace of the concept of kinship, the phrase can also mean "teach me by family kinship to believe in Christ." Building on this last sense, what the narrator asks for, then, is participatory understanding of God—a contemplative understanding based on an awareness of an always already present kinship with him.[17]

Complicating the already layered semantic value of its adverb, the phrase "kenne me kyndely on Crist to believe" introduces a two-part conceptual paradox. First, to anyone fluent in Middle English, it would be apparent that to be "kenned" any "kynde" understanding is logically contradictory. How is it possible to be *taught* knowledge that, by definition, is natural, inborn, and familiar? How is it possible to learn something that you already have within you? Langland highlights this paradox aurally, by creating alliteration between "kenne" and "kyndely," thus making sense-perceptible the connectedness between the two concepts and thereby following a long-standing insular practice of using alliteration to emphasize relationships between words.[18] Both etymologically and alliteratively, this line calls attention to its own central idea—how to teach innate knowing of Christ—as a difficult and important one.[19] Second, because "kyndely" is positioned between "kenne" and "to bileue," the adverb can apply to either verb; that is, we can take Will's request to mean not only "in a natural way, teach me to believe in Christ," but also "teach me to believe in Christ naturally." That is, Will's request for "kyndely" knowledge can be taken to apply dually to how the lesson is taught and to the nature of the belief itself. He is asking for native, natural, inborn knowledge, which can somehow be naturally taught.

Reemphasizing the difficulty of how to teach a person to "know" Christ "kyndely," Will more directly requests "kynde knowynge" soon thereafter, when he complains to his teacher, "Yet haue I no kynde knowynge . . . yet mote ye kenne me better/ By what craft in my cors it comseth, and where" (*PP*, A.I.127–28; B.I.138–39).[20] Through an extension of the alliterative "k" sound, now in the *c* of "craft" and "cors," "kynde knowing," as a mode of understanding religious truth, is explicitly associated with natural physicality—with one's "cors," or body. But it is simultaneously sonically associated with acquired "craft." Thus, bearing out its conceptual assertion in its own poetic practice, the poem uses the insular "craft" of alliteration to intimate that "kynde knowing" is a knowing born of bodily understanding, a cognitive experience born of corporeal, sensory experience. Thus, the poem's alliteration asserts that that understanding can be facilitated by craft, or art.

In this insistence on art's facilitation of contemplative understanding, the passage intimates something about the poem's overall agenda. The challenge that the poem lays out for itself is not just to think about contemplation but also to enact it poetically—through "craft"—thereby to produce not only for the protagonist but also for its reading audience a "kynde knowynge" of God. The ethos the poem pushes toward, then, is the dual ethos of participation itself—the ethos that animates the other Middle English works I have examined so far. *Piers Plowman* is concerned, as will become clear, to make its narrator and readers feel the inescapable truth of their always already present participation in God, their kinship to him, their "kynde" knowing of him, and to do so through the field of formally wrought Middle English—Middle English poetic styles and strategies as well as Middle English etymologies, puns, and morphologies. The poem's alliterative mining of "kynde knowynge" as a touchstone for its emergent contemplative practice is just the beginning.[21]

En route to these English contemplations, the poem undertakes a sweeping assay of epistemologies—of how we learn through our cognitive faculties—and thus an assay of what one might assume are the key faculties in the work of gaining "kynde knowynge." As Michelle Karnes, Steven Kruger, and Nicolette Zeeman have shown, this assay, which takes place largely between the eighth and thirteenth passus of the B-text, offers a critique of the very idea that we might come to know spiritual truths wholly through our most elemental cognitive capacities, such as Thought and Wit, or through the behaviors, people, or textual resources we rely on cognitively, such as Study, Clergy, or Scripture.[22] Through its sprawling epistemological critique, the poem destabilizes readers' senses that they know how to do contemplation in the first place; it destabilizes their sense that it is even possible to contemplate God through cognitive means.[23]

That destabilization serves a crucially important participatory purpose for the poem. It draws readers deeper into the complexities of "kynde knowynge," teaches them to be suspicious of the notionally higher cognitive faculties, and sets them up to experience the more basic sensory renderings of likeness between the soul and God that the poem will pursue in its later passus.[24] That is, the middle section of the poem does not simply stage the exhaustion of the mind's individual cognitive capacities; it also, and perhaps more so, stages how a different mode of knowing—as we will see, one based on analogy and synthesis, rather than distinction or analysis—underpins any effort to know God "kyndely."

HOW NOT TO KNOW GOD "KYNDELY"

When Will meets Thought, a dynamic of likeness between them is immediately in play, as the protagonist informs us that a man "lik to myselue,/ Cam and called me by my kynde name" (*PP*, B.8.70–71). Will, however, does not immediately recognize Thought as his own and asks his identity. Thought replies that he is, "That thow woost wel . . . and no wight bettre" (B.8.73) before he reveals his identity. In this cagey response, Thought is reenacting but also recasting the central paradox of "kynde knowynge": how is it possible for you to gain knowledge of something you already possess innately, as a part of your own self? But now there is a twist: by using the word "kynde" in the reflexive phrase "by my kynde name," the poem quickens a reader's awareness that "kynde knowynge" is also always and decisively *self*-knowing.[25] The fact that Will initially is unable to recognize Thought as his *own* thought indicates that he still lacks "kynde knowynge," not just about the Dos or about God, but also, and most disablingly, of himself.[26] To be sure, as many scholars have noted, Thought seems to fail to convey to Will what he seeks to know,[27] but there is another dynamic in play: Will's failure to grasp that this seeming stranger Thought is in fact his very own thought, his "kynde" thought, signals that self-knowledge is precisely what Will needs, yet precisely what he most lacks.[28] If Will cannot recognize Thought as a part of himself, the poem suggests, he cannot possibly begin to contemplate God by thinking.[29]

Having revealed that the failure of Thought in contemplating God is first a failure of self-knowledge, the poem moves to anchor that revelation in the forms of Middle English morphology and insular poetics. This occurs when Thought and Will encounter Wit, and Thought says, "Wher Dowel and Dobet and Dobest ben in londe/ Here is Wil wolde wite if Wit koude teche" (*PP*, B.8.126–27). When Thought says that "Wil wolde wite if Wit koude teche" where the three Dos are, he couples each noun—Wil and Wit—with its derivative verb form—"wolde" and "wite." By extending the *w*-alliteration from "Wil" and "wolde" to "wite," the poem suggests that "Will" resonates poetically with and thus resembles "Wit." Thus, through the insular poetic technique of creating alliterations between semantically connected terms,[30] the poem suggests that not just Thought, but Wit, too, is a "kynde" version of our protagonist, "Wil."[31] Thus, a complex logic of participation emerges in this scene of the poem: by talking with him, Will participates in Thought, but Thought simultaneously participates in Will because he is Will's own Thought. Similarly, Will participates in Wit through their interaction, but Wit also always already participates in Will. He is, after all, Will's own Wit.

This dynamic reminds readers that they themselves participate in Will, too, because he is not simply a character named William but also a personification of the basic human power of desire.[32] This revelation is sonically anchored by the association of the proper name "Wil" immediately and alliteratively with its common verbal definition: to want, to will, to desire.[33] Through this morphological pun on William and the human faculty of will—a pun only available in English—Will becomes a proxy for the reader's will in reading the poem, in questing for his or her own "kynde knowynge." Through its alliterative punning on Will's name, the poem amasses a concatenation of participations between narrator, his interlocutors, and his readers. This concatenation sensorily renders that it is only by self-examination and self-knowledge that one can acquire contemplative "kynde knowynge" of God.

Will now begins to direct his questions more to the nature of Kynde itself, when he asks the pointedly paronomastic question, "What kynnes thing is Kynde?" (*PP*, B.9.25). Wit responds, "Kynde . . . is creatour of all kynnes thynges,/ Fader and formour of al that euere was maked—/ And that is grete God that gynnyng hadde neuere/ Lord of lif and of light, of lisse and of peyne" (*PP*, B.9.26–29). Thus, Wit makes explicit what has been implied throughout the poem: Will's effort to understand things "kyndely" or naturally is an effort to contemplate God himself. But that effort, as we should now realize from Will's alliterative encounters, hinges upon a more basic effort to understand oneself, to see one's self as "kynne" of the divine "Kynde." From his encounter with Wit, Will goes on to meet with Studie, Clergie, Scripture, and Ymaginatif, always failing to register the possibility that these personifications might indeed be aspects of his own soul, his own self, and therefore that self-study is one's best and only avenue toward "kynde knowynge."

The scenes in which Will meets, interrogates, and exhausts the various doppelgangers for the cognitive powers of his own soul constitute a prompt to understand participatory contemplation in a specific way. Each of these cognitive methods, taken on its own, is doomed to fail. But taken in the aggregate, they begin to articulate an overarching principle of contemplation: it is in the assembling of all the parts of oneself that one begins the work of coming to a "kynde knowing" of God.[34] Will must become aware that these many forms and figures of knowing are part of him. He must engage, that is, in synthetic self-knowing.[35] For as long as Will seeks out the magic bullet of contemplation in a single cognitive mode, conceived as something external to himself, he is doomed to confusion. As we will see, Will's eventual obtaining of some degree of "kynde" knowing of God will hinge on his eventual ability to abandon analysis and division and instead to focus on synthesis and cohesion within himself, thereby discovering "kyndely" likeness between himself and God.[36]

HOW TO KNOW GOD "KYNDELY" I: SYNERGY AND SYNTHESIS

Personifying this lesson that Will must gather his faculties together and recognize that they are all parts of his soul, Anima soon appears. Anima represents not any one single power of the soul but the whole soul, gathered together in its many manifestations. Rather than hiving off parts of himself, Anima begins by showing how he encompasses each of those notionally other faculties.

> The whiles I quykke the cors . . . called am I Anima;
> And whan I wilne and wolde, Animus ich hatte;
> And for that I kan and knowe, called am I Mens, "thought";
> And whan I make mone to God, Memoria is my name;
> And whan I deme domes and do as truthe techeth,
> Thanne is Racio my righte name, "Reson" on Englissh;
> And whan I feele that folk telleth, my firste name is Sensus—
> And that is wit and wisdom, the welle of alle craftes—
> And whan I chalange or chalange noght, chepe or refuse,
> Thanne am I Conscience ycalled, Goddes clerk and his notarie;
> And whan I loue leelly Oure Lord and all othere,
> Thanne is "Lele loue" my name, and in Latyn Amor;
> And whan I flee fro the flesh and forsake the careyne,
> Thanne am I spirit spechelees, and Spiritus thanne ich hatte.
> (*PP*, B.15.22–36)

Anima is not simply Anima: he encompasses mind, reason, memory, love, sense, wit, wisdom, and thought, depending on his functionality in any given moment. Through this passage, Anima urges Will to understand that the proliferation of terms for a single referent—Anima himself—is a means for gaining the "kynde knowynge" that he seeks, recognizing one's internal faculties not as separate from oneself but rather as manifestations of oneself that arise to accomplish the contemplative tasks of the soul that occur in any given situation.

In keeping with the poem's drive to use "craft" to quicken contemplative "kynde knowynge" in Will's "cors," Anima activates the particularities of Middle English—here, in conversation with Latin—to render his lesson concretely sense-perceptible, and not just abstractly intellective. After all, the ontological synthesis that Anima enacts for Will's edification takes place across two linguistic planes. First, he stages his various avatars within a single language—Reason, Mind, Sense, Spirit, and so forth—all in Middle English. In so doing, he reminds Will to be aware of the parts that exist within his own soul, different in behavior but all fundamentally participating in the same soul. Second, in switching to the biblical language of Latin and showing its compatibility with the "kynde," or familiar, language of the everyday, he reminds Will that his contemplative focus on his own internal self must always stretch toward a contemplation of God. Through Anima's translational monologue on his internal manifestations, Mind is shown to be a coparticipant in Anima, along with Soul, Spirit, Love, and Reason; through this aria, participation is made sensible both in terms of the participation of the parts of the soul in the whole soul and in terms of the mutual participation of English in Latin and of Latin in the English poem that contains it. In a sensible way, translation itself, both between Latin and English and within English through synonymy, formally performs the kind of synthesis to which the contemplative must attain. It is a synthesis that shows how one's everyday self, registered by the presence of English, has a perfected referent, in which it participates as a worldly synonym, in the Word of God, registered by the presence of Latin.

Cognitively, through these intra- and interlingual collocations, the reader of the poem is made to slow down, to consider the semantic field that each term imports, and to dwell in the hyperabundance of signification that the poem deploys. Although Anima introduces these terms as versions of himself, at the same time, the fact that each word, though subsumable under the large referent "Anima," does indeed mean something slightly different reminds the audience that the proliferation of participating parts of the soul does not bespeak radical identity but instead admits of some internal difference and variability. Anima's bilingual monologue ends up demonstrating the possibility of diversity in unification, difference in similarity. This possibility anticipates the Trinitarian similes that will appear in the poem's Trinitarian meditations in passus 16 and 17.

Despite Anima's best efforts to urge Will to grasp this differentiated union as a primary element of contemplative awareness, he still struggles. Immediately after this passage, he complains, again, that he wants "kynde knowyng" of the truths that Anima has both spoken and enacted sensorily: "I wolde I knewe and kouthe kyndely in my herte!" (*PP*, B.15.49) Anima responds by chastening Will, calling him "inparfit" (*PP*, B.15.50). The reason for Anima's exasperation is that he had only just finished providing Will with a formal and sensible path toward kind knowing: the knowing based on a differentiated likeness of terms within a language and kinship of terms between languages. He had just modeled for him a way of "kynde" knowing that relies on the "kyndely" participation of multiple terms within a language in a single referent and on the "kyndely" likeness among terms across two languages, showing how English can participate in Latin, and Latin in English. He has provided Will with a formal means for feeling how it is possible for things to participate in other things, while also maintaining distinctions from each other. He has just provided, that is, a lexical means for sensing the nature of participation: all of Anima's manifestations are derived from Anima and are similar to him, though Anima somehow exceeds them all—just as all people participate in God and are similar to him, though he exceeds them all.

But Anima's linguistic enactment of participatory contemplation does seem at last to penetrate into Will. In response to Anima's demonstrations, Will reminds us of his own name: "I haue lyued in lond . . . my name is Long Wille" (*PP*, B.15.152).[37] He then quickly moves on to make a statement that theorizes participatory contemplation: "Clerkes kenne me that Crist is in all places;/ Ac I seigh hym neuere smoothly but as myself in a mirour" (*PP*, B.15.161–62). Our narrator, having just reminded us that his name is "Will"—both the name William and the faculty that maps, for Augustine, onto the Holy Ghost in the divine Trinity—channels Paul's and Augustine's formulation of the fundamental nature of contemplation.[38] Contemplation during life is to look into a mirror, therein to see oneself as a participant in God's goodness, as a shadowy reflection of him. In Will's affirmation of this theory of contemplation and near-simultaneous deployment of his own paronomastic name, the poem suggests that he has begun to internalize Anima's lessons—that he has begun to see that synthetic self-examination is the most essential tool in producing "kynde" knowing of God.

With Will's awareness of the centrality of participation to the process of spiritual contemplation at last established, Anima turns to the most substantial similetic revelation of the poem so far—a revelation that again relies on proliferation within a single language and translation across languages. He tells Will that Piers the Plowman knows more about God and about charity than do priests (*PP*, B.15.200–201), because he labors and suffers, whereas they simply move words around proudly and flaunt their supposed knowledge.

> Therfore by colour ne by clergie knowe shaltow hym neuere,
> Neither thorugh words ne werkes, but thorugh wil oone,

And that knoweth no clerk ne creature on erthe
But Piers the Plowman—Petrus, id est, Christus.
(*PP*, B.15.209–12)

Taking the first two lines on their own, Anima seems to be saying that will alone is required for one to attain understanding of God and of charity. Given, however, that we have just been reminded that our narrator's name is Will, this simple assertion seems particularly loaded: Anima suggests that no amount of study, rhetoric, words, or works will bring our narrator to contemplation, but only an immersion in himself alone, in his identity with the willful desire for God.[39] Will must do what he himself has already said; he must look to himself as a mirror for the divine.[40]

As the passage continues, the second set of two lines both complete and complicate the sense of the first two, taking the poem's theory of contemplation out of the individual sphere and into a more social sphere. We read that only Piers Plowman—alone of all the earth—can do this work of relying on his "wil oone" to understand God. This assertion is unpacked only when Anima switches from English into Latin, and reveals that Petrus—translating into English as Peter, or Piers himself—is Christ. It is only through Christ's will, the will of the Holy Spirit, *as embodied by Piers the Plowman,* that one can hope to attain a contemplative understanding of God and charity. By itself, that is a theologically unexceptionable point: it is only with Christ's willing grace that we can approach him contemplatively. So, the association between Christ and "will" makes sense; but what of the mediating role of Piers between Christ and will? As will become clear, in associating Christ so closely with Piers, this passage is not merely an instance of slippery allegoresis, in which Piers's precise ontological meaning in the poem radically shifts over the course of the narrative. Instead, this insistence on the identity of Piers with Christ evokes all the other instances in which Piers has appeared in the poem, and it forces the audience to try to make sense of this assertion that he is synonymous with Petrus and thereby with Christ in those scenes as well.[41] Moving backward in the poem, what we have seen of Piers so far is that he is a laborer who enforces strict adherence to the Ten Commandments as the only path to truth (*PP*, B.5.557–600) and that he demands constant, honest labor from all of his followers if they are to undertake the spiritual pilgrimage to Truth with him (B.6.130–38). Now we learn that Piers is Petrus, who is Christ. In Piers himself, an ever-shifting vernacular signifier—now a poor laborer, now a pilgrim, now Christ himself—begins to crystallize the ultimate point of all this attention to participatory contemplation in the poem, a point which only becomes clear in the Easter Passus.

HOW TO KNOW GOD "KYNDELY" II: TRINITARIAN SIMILETICS

Piers's theological and formal investment in participation, as well as its insistence that Piers is Petrus, who is Christ, are somewhat clarified in the B-text's passus 16, when Will encounters the Tree of Charity. This tree has mercy and truth as its trunks, loyal words as its leaves, buxom speech and demure looks as its blossoms, and charity itself as its fruit. Will is meant to cultivate this fruit of charity under the tutelage of Piers the Plowman. At the delightful mention of Piers's name, which now also evokes the name of Christ, the narrating Will swoons into a deeper dream and finds himself examining the Tree of Charity with Piers Plowman as his guide. Piers quickly discloses to Will that the tree represents the Trinity (*PP*, B.16.63) and that the three types of fruit on the tree signify marriage, maidenhood, and widowhood (B.16.68, 71, 76).[42] These three virtuous forms of sexual living become an interpersonal analogy for the holy Trinity.[43]

In this correlation between the Trinity and the three virtuous forms of sexual life, there is something else at work, not just on the level of the poem's theory about virtuous living but also on the level of form—something fundamental to the poem's staging of contemplation through the "craft" that will quicken kind knowing in its readers' "cors." The fruit metaphor comparing human sexual life with the Trinity is both extraordinarily economical and extraordinarily complex.[44] The relation of fruit to tree, in nature, is a relation of participation: the fruit is born of the tree and thus participates in treeness, much as human beings are born ultimately of God's design and thus participate in godliness. More specifically, the fruit are fundamentally connected with the tree by a relation of kinship—the tree is parent to the fruit. The fruit is, thus, a "kynde"—both natural and familial—manifestation of the tree itself. What the image of the tree of charity implicitly encourages Will to do, then, is to develop a "kynde knowynge" of the closeness of his own relationship with the divine Trinity through the analogy of the sociosexual trinity that the poem imagines of marriage, virginity, and widowhood.[45]

Even so, the precise significance of this Trinitarian analogy remains unclear. Are we meant to understand that matrimony somehow directly represents God the Father, widowhood the Son, and virginity the Holy Ghost? Are we meant, that is, to understand this relation of kindness as a tight ontological mapping?[46] To help resolve this contemplative confusion, the poem introduces Abraham, also called Faith, to serve as a temporary exegete for Will's dreams and for the theological concepts that they enact. According to Abraham,

> Might is in matrimoyne, that multiplieth the erthe,
> And bitokeneth trewely, telle if I dorste,
> He that first formed al, the Fader of heuene.
> The Sone, if I it dorste seye, resembleth wel the widewe:
> *Deus meus, Deus meus, vt quid dereliquisti me?*
> That is, creatour weex creature to knowe what was both.
> As widewe withouten muliere is noght muche to preise:
> *Maledictus homo qui non reliquit semen in Israel . . .*
> Thus in thre persones is parfitliche pure manhede—
> That is, man and his make and mulliere hir children,
> And is noght but gendre of a generacion, bifore Iesu Crist in heuene;
> So is the Fader forth with the Sone and Fre Wille of bothe—
> *Spiritus procedens a Patro et Filio—*
> Which is the Holy Goost of alle, and alle is but o God.
>
> (*PP*, B.16.212–25)

Abraham begins by ironing out the metaphorics of the previous presentation of the Tree of Charity. Might, which betokens the Father, is embodied by the fruit of matrimony. Widowhood then maps onto the Son.[47] We are then led to expect that he will finish his remapping of the divine Trinity onto a sociosexual Trinity by suggesting that maidenhood corresponds with the Holy Ghost. But, having engaged our expectations by going two-thirds of the way through an explication of the Trinity, he instead veers off course, leaving the Holy Ghost as yet unaccounted for and abandoning the third part of the foregoing sociosexual trinity in favor of a new sociospiritual Trinitarian formation: the family—"man and his make and mulliere hir children" (*PP*, B.16.222). As this new exegetical turn continues, the poem suggests that Free Will—the *spiritus* that proceeds from Father and Son—is equivalent to the child of God and Christ. Abraham thus uses the family as a triune likeness for the Holy Trinity. The family represents the idea of multiplicity in unity and difference in similarity that are central to contemplative "kynde knowynge."

But Abraham's simile is problematic because "family" bespeaks hierarchy, with the parents occupying a higher position of power than the children.[48] This kind of hierarchy does not sit well with orthodox Trinitarianism, in which each Person of the Trinity is meant to be coequal with the other two. Registering this issue, the poem quickly moves to refine the likenesses it endorses as a sensory mode of "kyndely knowynge" the Trinity. Will next encounters the Samaritan, who presents two new similes for the nature of the Trinity. The first simile compares the Trinity with a human hand, thus programmatically aligning the Trinity with tangible human experience. It describes God the Father as "a fust with o fynger folden" (*PP*, B.17.139), the Holy Spirit as the "pawme" that "profreth forth the fyngres" (B.17.142), and the Son as "the fyngres that fre ben to folde and to serue" (B.17.147). Each of these parts of the hand participates in the totality of the hand, yet each has its own functionality. Each is its own recognizable structure, yet each depends on the others: the fingers, for instance, touch "at techynge of the pawme" (B.17.149). Through this similetic demonstration of multiplicity in unity, the passage demonstrates that "thus are thei alle but oon, as it an hand weere,/ And thre sondry sightes in oon shewynge" (B.17.153–54). Joined together inseparably ("asondry were thei neuere" [B.17.166]), the three participating parts of the hand "halt al the wide world withinne hem thre" (B.17.161). As "fust," God the Father is "formour and shappere" (B.17.169), who has "al the might . . . in makynge of thynges" (B.17.170); the Son, however, is the one who actually interacts closely with the created world: "the fyngres formen a ful hand to portryee or peynten; / Keruynge and compasynge is craft of the fyngres" (B.17.171–72). In his hands-on interaction with the world, the Son is "the science of the Fader" (B.17.173), his incarnated, worldly knowing, derived through his "werkmanshipe" (B.17.176). In his mediating and joining role, the Holy Ghost–palm receives "that the fust and the fyngres wille" (B.17.180). Coequal and balanced in a way that Abraham's familial trinity was not, the hand simile urges Will to a fuller and more "parfit" contemplative understanding of God.[49]

This elaborate hand simile works in several interconnected ways to make the truth of the divine Trinity kindly knowable. First, this carefully designed—borrowing the poem's own language—carved and compassed simile deploys English translations for the Latin words that are most closely associated with each of the Persons of the Trinity: God the Father is "might" or power; God the Son is "science" or knowing; the Holy Ghost is "wille." Just as Julian of Norwich had done in her own Trinitarian meditation, Langland here spools out an embedded and decidedly English meditation on the nature of the Trinity. Thus, the poetically articulated truths about the Trinity ring true not only in how they are discursively explicated but also in the reader's "kynde knowynge" of the meanings of each of the words associated with each of its three Persons. Second, in unfurling so slowly and so recursively, going through the functionality of the fist, the palm, the fingers back and forth, and demonstrating their separate yet equal action, the simile forces a reader to engage actively and imaginatively with the simile, truly feeling how his or her own hand works according to the description. The reader is made to feel—tangibly, sensibly, "kyndely"—the theological truths embodied by the passage. Third, having sensorily realized the truth of the Trinity, the passage ends by introducing a flurry of first person possessive pronouns to insist even more closely on the reader's own participation in the Trinity: "And alle are thei but o God, as is myn hand and my fyngres;/ Vnfolden or folden, my fust and my pawme—/ Al is but an hand, howso I turne it" (*PP*, B.17.138–84). No longer is the Trinity some structure wholly outside of the self; here, it is mirrored in the Samaritan's human hand, which in turn functions as a proxy for that of the reader. Whereas Abraham analogized the Trinity with sexual choices and with the family, the Samaritan compares the Trinity with something more immediate, more concrete, more inescapably and universally proximal to one's experience of self, and less hierarchical. The Samaritan brings the Trinity, as it were, ever closer to home. Thus, the hand simile serves to remind Will and the reader of something about the human condition—namely, that man is created in the likeness of God and that, therefore, we participate in him, just as our own hands participate in our bodies. In this move, the poem reminds Will and the reader, on a very local, very physical, very "kynde" scale, of the supervening truth of humanity's participation in the divine.

In making this analogy between a part of an individual human person and the Trinity, this passage reinvents the kind of contemplative work that Augustine models in his *De Trinitate*,[50] when Augustine's attempts to understand the nature of the Trinity lead him to the awareness that there exists in the human soul an analogous trinity, one that participates in and reflects the nature of the holy Trinity.[51] For Augustine, the structure of the human self that bears closest resemblance to God is the mind, in its constitutive powers of memory, knowledge, and will. For Augustine, the human mental trinity, although a "kynde" analogy for the divine Trinity, is still somewhat ineffable, and certainly not concretely physical; this, indeed, is part of what makes the mental trinity such an apt comparator for the divine Trinity. *Piers* seems to do something similar, by localizing, embodying, and indeed humanizing the Trinity, and thus formally rendering the likeness that exists between man and God.[52] But in its hand simile, Langland's poem radically reimagines the contemplative paradigm that Augustine inaugurates. In *Piers*, the structure of the human self that bears closest analogical resemblance to the Trinity is not the mind but the hand—the part of the body that, as we see in the poem's elaborate analysis of it, does work in the world: it makes things, paints things, ministers to others, touches, feels, and holds onto the real world, in all its temporality and changefulness. The fingers carve and compass the real, physical, tangible world; they and the palm and the fist synergize to produce "workmanship." Thus, *Piers*'s chiral reinvention of the Augustinian mental trinity suggests that human beings best actualize their likeness to God not just by abstract meditation in the mind but indeed by interacting with the temporal world through labor, through touch, through artistic craft, and through workmanship. Langland's human trinity is a laboring trinity, an artistic trinity, a temporal trinity, and an *active* trinity, making its way through the social world as an agent of labor and production.[53]

Thus, this new representation of the divine Trinity reinforces what Abraham began to do with his comparisons to marriage and family: it makes clear that humanity's participation in the eternal divine *entails* humanity's participation in the temporal world, the world of active labor in society. All these similes, then, drive home the point that contemplation, although valuable, has as its end and purpose a return to participation in the world, a return to the active life of touching, feeling, making, working, ministering, and interacting with other people.[54] "Kynde" knowing is starting to seem to mean a knowing not just of oneself, as an isolated and atomistic individual, but also and perhaps more specifically knowing of oneself in social and material relation to the rest of man*kind*.[55] Participation, for Langland, is not just about how we relate to God in his eternity; it is also about how we relate to each other in the temporal, social world.[56]

From this simile, the Samaritan immediately turns to another, which seems on first blush decidedly less human, less physical, less bodily, and less implicitly social than the hand. He "likens" the Trinity to a "torche" or "tapur" (*PP*, B.17.204).

> As wex and a weke were twyned togideres,
> And thanne a fir flawmynge forth out of bothe.
> And as wex and weke and warm fir togideres
> Fostren forth a flawmbe and a fair leye
> So dooth the Sire and the Sone and also *Spiritus Sanctus*
> Fostren forth amonges folk loue and bileue.
> (*PP*, B.17, 205–10)

Now, rather than with a fist, the Father is equated with wax; rather than with fingers, Christ is equated with a wick; rather than a palm, the Holy Ghost becomes a flame. The human element thus seems to evaporate from the poem's contemplative similetics. But that human element quickly returns, though in a revised form. We learn that this flame—the flame that is like the Holy Ghost—can wax and wane, according to the level of spiritual devotion and right living in the heart of man (*PP*, B.17.215–17). And with this insistence, the Samaritan quickly brings his taper simile back to the realm of the human, and specifically to the realm of human labor:

> And as glowynge gledes gladeth noght thise workmen
> That werchen and waken in wyntres nyghtes,
> As dooth a kex or a candle that caught hath fir and blaseth,
> Namoore dooth Sire ne Sone ne Seint Spirit togideres
> Graunte no grace ne forgifnesse of synnes
> Til the Holy Goost gynne to glowe and to blase.
> (*PP*, B.17.219–23)

With this image, the taper Trinity suddenly is shown to be coterminous with the temporal world of labor; indeed, it is shown quite directly to illuminate that world.

As the passage goes on, it becomes clearer that the Holy Ghost—the flame of the candle—is associated not just with work but also with the level of charity that powerful people display to their "euenecristene," or their "kynde":

> Be unkynde to thyn euenecristene, and al that thow kanst bidde—
> Delen and do penaunce day and nyght euere,
> And purchase al the pardon of Pampilon and Rome,
> And indulgences ynowe, and be *ingratus* to thi kynde,
> The Holy Goost hereth thee noght, ne helpe may thee by reson;
> Ne brenne ne blase clere, for blowynge of vnkyndenesse
> . . .
> Forthi beth war, ye wise men that with the world deleth,
> That riche ben and reson knoweth—ruleth wel youre soule;
> Beth noght vnkynde, I conseille yow, to youre euenechristene;
> For manye of yow riche men, by my soule, men telleth,
> Ye brenne, but ye blase noght, and that is a blynd bekene!
> (*PP*, B.17.251–57, 260–64)

In this extended exhortation to the powerful to take care of their fellow man if they wish to have the support of the Holy Ghost, the most salient line is the final one: "Ye brenne, but ye blase not, and that is a blynd bekene." With the combination of the second person pronoun and the imagery of burning and blazing, we are encouraged to see the "wise men" whom the passage addresses as the candles themselves—the vehicles-in-potential for the salvific and warming flame of the Holy Spirit. The "wise man" thus participates directly in the candle simile of the Trinity. Through him, all readers are reminded that the Holy Spirit will only animate their hearts if they avoid being "unkynde" to their fellow, "kynde" Christians; no amount of penance, no amount of indulgence purchasing, no amount of self-interested piety will bring the light of the Holy Ghost into their hearts without loving kindness toward others. It is thus through the active life—the live of "leel labour" undertaken in the temporal world—that man becomes his fullest realization of his participation in God. It is through "kyndely" labor toward others that one attains a fully participatory "kynde knowynge" of God, becoming a luminous taper in oneself.[57] Put otherwise, this passage adds a final definition of "kynde" to the idea of "kynde knowynge": here, "kynde" signals good conduct toward man*kind;* it signals sociality and, in particular, prosocial labor, as a key to contemplative "kynde knowynge."[58] For Langland, the active life really *is* active: it is a life of labor, of active social engagement, and not simply of compassion for others. And that active life of labor is wholly compatible with the life of contemplation.

The Trinitarian section of the poem, encompassing the Tree of Charity, the simile of the hand, and the simile of the taper, domesticates and naturalizes the highly abstract problem of Trinitarian contemplation—much as Julian does in her modal trinity in the *Revelation*. *Piers* makes the eternal Trinity available through a series of similes that analogize the Trinity with the "kyndely" world of bodies, relationships, domestic objects, labor, and time. But *Piers* goes further and specifically uses simile to remind its readers that they are like God primarily by their "kyndely" relationships with other people and in how they labor in the world for the good of others. The similes create an awareness of the fundamental likeness between man and God as one both inborn ("kynde" in that sense) and acquired through "kyndely" labor directed toward others. For *Piers*, "kynde" knowing of God originates in "kynde" social behavior, which is central to the poem's revision to the idea of the mixed life: here, the mixed life does not entail a switch between action and contemplation but instead a recognition that "kynde" social behavior is key to participatory contemplation of God at every moment. More so than they were for either the *Cloud* or the *Revelation*, contemplative practice and contemplative knowing are, for *Piers*, contingent upon kindly participation not just in God but also and perhaps primarily in mankind.

HOW TO KNOW GOD "KYNDELY" III: CHRIST AS EVERYMAN, THE SAMARITAN, OR PIERS PLOWMAN

The "kynde" similes that Langland has deployed in his analogies for the Trinity set up the participatory contemplations of the next passus. In this passus, Jesus appears. But, rather than identify him immediately and explicitly as Jesus, the poem first forces readers to dwell in an uncertain simile: "Oon semblable to the Samaritan, and somdeel to Piers the Plowman/ Barefoot on an asse bak bootles cam prikye" (*PP*, B.18.9–10). Someone appears who at once bears a likeness to the Samaritan and to Piers Plowman, but we do not know for certain the identity of that "semblable" person until the famous image of the ass emerges. Making explicit the ontological disorientation that this similetic diptych produces, Will quickly asks Faith what the meaning of the procession before them is and "who sholde iuste in Ierusalem" (B.18.19). Faith's response is, "'Iesus,' he seide,/ 'And feeche that the fend claymeth, Piers fruyt the Plowman'" (B.18.19–20). Thus, Will has learned that the man riding the ass, who looks like both Piers and the Samaritan, who will joust in Jerusalem, is none other than Jesus himself. Will comes to register, through the literary forms of character and allegoresis, that Jesus is transtemporal and transhistorical: he is the Samaritan in the imagined past of the Bible, he is the historical Jesus, and he is the Piers Plowman of Will's present-day dreamscape, all at once.

Rather than seeking to know more about how exactly Jesus, the Samaritan, and Piers correspond, and rather than going forth to see more of what Jesus is about to do, Will asks simply, "Is Piers in this place?" (*PP*, B.18.21), indicating that he, Will, is more acutely interested in the movements of Piers Plowman even than of Jesus himself. So deeply, it seems, has Will internalized the centrality of labor and socially beneficent conduct in the seeking of contemplative "kynde" knowing that he is distracted from his immanent vision of Christ qua Christ by his passionate love of Piers, the laborer, the virtuous active man. Yet Will's question reveals a lingering lacuna in his understanding; namely, he still fails fully to understand how intimately linked Piers is with Christ, how linked the active life is with the life of spiritual contemplation.

Faith responds to Will's question with a fascinating metaphor for the incarnation, based on the idea of Piers the laborer as a kind of everyman, whose armor Jesus will borrow for his fight:

> This Iesus of his gentries wol iuste in Piers armes,
> In his helm and in his haubergeon, *humana natura*.
> That Crist be noght biknowe here for *consummatus Deus*,
> In Piers paltok the Plowman this prikiere shal ryde;
> For no dynt shal hym here as *in deitate Patris*.
>
> (*PP*, B.18.22–26)

By taking on the armor of Piers, Jesus presents himself not only in the likeness of man but specifically in the likeness of a *laborer*. It is not in a knight's armor that Jesus appears but in the armor of a simple man, a plowman, a field worker. And yet, despite the nonnoble rank of the figure whose clothing Jesus takes on, the clothing nevertheless apparently constitutes an appropriate and useful armor for Jesus. Thus, the passage seems to suggest that when Jesus takes on Piers's clothes, he is enabled to be a warrior against Satan precisely because of Piers's status as a laborer. The willingness of mankind to work, to labor for the good of all, is the habit of "*humana natura*" that Jesus chooses to don as he moves toward his self-sacrifice.

All of this similetic overlay—Jesus resembles Piers the laborer, but he also resembles the Samaritan; the Trinity is like a hand but also like a candle; the Trinity is like a family but also like the poem's offered range of sexual lives—has two interrelated effects. First, the proliferation of similes throughout the poem, but particularly in the final third, makes it impossible to create hard-and-fast, rigid correspondences between ontological entities. In so doing, the similes do not call attention to contemplative answers but rather to the means by which a contemplative person should ask questions, the formal and sensory means by which it is possible to attain an increasing understanding of and sense of intimacy with the divine. Namely, the accretion of similetic discourse calls attention to likeness itself, as a sense-experience that can be directly mined for its power to provoke participatory understanding. Likeness itself becomes a primary mode of knowing that readers are meant to take away from the poem. All of the similes and likenesses in the poem, then, are not simply about the things under comparison; they are also, and primarily, about the nature of simile itself. Just when the poem seems to land on a particular simile as the most appropriate way of understanding a particular contemplative problem, it will either switch similes or complicate the simile, so that readers are left pondering a proliferation of likenesses, rather than a single, stable one.

Correlatively, since these similes for the nature of the relationship between man and God refuse to sit still and signify in a totalizing, one-to-one correspondence between ontological entities, they cause a reader to meditate more deeply on the nature of the relationship between God and humanity *and* between the world of contemplation and the world of action. What we learn about Jesus is that he is a laborer, a healer who ministers to the sick, a knight, a king, a conqueror; he participates in a wide array of male subject positions in the medieval English social world. This proliferation of roles suggests, particularly in association with the insistence that the Trinity is a hand, that all human beings, whatever their job or role in society, are in a position either to shore up and uphold Christian values of kindness to others or to fail to do so. Put otherwise, the notoriously slippery allegoresis that structures the poem—in which Piers is at once just a laborer and sometimes seemingly Jesus himself, or in which the Trinity is both a hand and a candle, as well as a family—serves a fundamentally contemplative purpose throughout.[59] Namely, this slippery allegoresis allows readers not to understand discursively but to perceive sensorily the porosity of ontological boundaries that separate people from each other as well as from God. Through this similetic apposition, the audience can realize that the boundaries between self and God are bidirectional constructions that, in practice, begin to soften as soon as we realize that all human beings participate in the Trinity, that the Trinity is social, that Christ is a laborer, that all laborers are Christly, and that all humans should thus participate lovingly and actively in society as their primary means of participating in God. Contemplative "kynde knowynge," then, entails labor on behalf of "mankynde," and the awareness that "kynde knowynge" means not just the knowing of God but also the knowing of oneself as a participant in the human social world.

HOW TO KNOW GOD "KYNDELY" IV: LATIN AND ENGLISH

The fact that in *Piers Plowman* participation in the social world *is* contemplative participation in God is undergirded by another kind of participation—namely, participation in Middle English. Returning to the phrase "kynde knowynge," by relying specifically on the word "kynde" to ground its meditations on the nature of humanity's connection with God, *Piers* makes a quiet claim for the salience of the vernacular as a mode of doing the feelable, sensible, formal contemplative work that it outlines for its own protagonist, and that it recommends to readers. First, the semantic richness of the word "kynde"—denoting at once nature, genre, kindliness, family, reflexivity, likeness, and nativeness—is not available in any single Latin word. Second, the term "kyndely," precisely because, in denoting nativeness, naturalness, and familiarity, it describes the vernacular, the "mother tongue" of Langland's readers. Thus, by pinning his poem's theological quest, from the outset, to the alliterative concept of "kynde knowynge," Langland quietly makes claims for the centrality of English as a familiar, natural, indeed *kindly* mode of doing the work of contemplative theology. When he asks for "kynde knowynge" of Christ, Will implicitly asks to receive his knowledge via the English vernacular.[60]

This linguistic investment in the "kyndely" acquisition of knowledge is borne out in the formal strategies of the poem, which leverage English—often in generative friction with Latin—for its ability to provoke participatory reading experiences. In *Piers,* there is a powerful plenitude in the vernacular, particularly when the poem stages English's translatability into Latin, and Latin's translatability back into English. The translation between languages serves a crucial theological end, which is to create a feelable demonstration of the compatibility between the eternal Word of the Bible and the temporal word of man. The translatability of English words into Latin and vice versa—of Petrus into Piers and Piers into Christ, or of Anima's many manifestations—harmonizes the everyday, temporal language of man and the supratemporal, eternal, unchanging language of God.

In making this assertion, I do not wish to essentialize Latin as God's own tongue, or even to suggest that medieval theologians or readers thought of Latin in those terms. Instead, I mean simply to invoke the cultural status held by Latin in the period, in that it was the language of the Vulgate Bible and was not the language of everyday social exchange in England. As Nicholas Watson puts it, "because of its lucidity, its distance from ordinary speakers, and the way it had to be acquired through formal study aided by grace . . . the Latin language is closer to heaven than the vernacular."[61] Latin, that is, has a certain gestural value, inhering in its seeming to step away from the worldly, temporal, quotidian concerns that readers would routinely accomplish in their "mother tongue" and in its seeming to step toward the Bible and the world of sacred things. When Langland makes his bilingual puns on Petrus/Piers and Christ or on Anima's many incarnations in both Latin and English, however, he does not eject his writings from the everyday and catapult them decisively into the eternal. Rather, Langland's deployment of the heavenly language of God in synergy with the putatively "kyndely" language of the everyday is not concerned to overwrite English, nor indeed the everyday world it embodies; instead, Langland's synergistic code-switching makes the compatibility between God's eternal Word and man's temporal words available to the senses. It performs a potential for harmonious likeness between the supernal and the here and now. But it does so in part by making "kyndely" English itself suddenly strange, unfamiliar, un-"kyndely," or what I called in my introduction "disfluent." Going back now to Anima's bilingual monologue, the native reader of English must reexamine what he or she knows about the meanings of these familiar, common, "kyndely" words based not only on their apposition with other words in English but also on their apposition with their cognates in Latin. A reader must think about how it makes sense for Anima and Reason, Mens and Spirit, Conscience and Love to coparticipate in a single entity; a reader must slow down in his or her reading to parse out the translations between Latin and English, to see how the Latin inflects and complicates the meaning of the "kyndely" English tongue. Moreover, throughout Anima's monologue, Langland integrates the Latin into his English alliterative pattern with variable emphases, to underscore both the likeness and the difference between words: "Racio" alliterates with "Reson," "spirit" and "spiritus" obviously alliterate, but "Sensus" only *almost* alliterates with "feele," and "lele love" does not alliterate with "Amor." Thus, as the reader of this passage attempts to map English and Latin meanings onto each other, the poetic form of the passage will sometimes urge a greater perception of likeness and will sometimes urge a sense of dissimilarity. Through this poetic form, the poem forces its readers to feel the simultaneous compatibility and dissonance that can exist between the language of the everyday and the language of the Bible. It stages harmony between English and Latin while maintaining some degree of difference and strangeness between them.

But there is a context in which the poem edges much closer toward a full likening between Latin and English, toward a staging of full compatibility between the Bible and "kyndely" life in medieval England. In the Piers/Petrus/Christus scene, it is not merely through the juxtaposition of the lexemes Piers, Petrus, and Christ that Langland urges an awareness of the compatibility of eternal, biblical Latin and temporal, "kyndely" English. He also modifies his poetic habits in that scene. At numerous points in the poem, Langland's Latin occurs outside of the metrical logic of the English; the Latin, that is, frequently does not work into the alliterative long-line patterns of the Middle English but rather interrupts it, sometimes in prose.[62] In the Piers/Petrus and Anima passages, however, the Latin completes the alliterative patterns of the English lines in which it appears. *Consummatus* alliterates with "Crist" and "knowe"; *humana* alliterates with "haubergeon" and "helm;" *deitate* alliterates with "dynt" and "dere." The two languages are thus alliteratively shown to be compatible with each other; indeed, they are shown to have enough formal likeness to fit together into the supervening alliterative scheme of the poem, each language completing the alliterative patterning of the other. Thus, in the Easter passus, the language of the Bible is made to harmonize metrically with and participate in the quotidian language of English, and so the forms of the poem embody the theological content of the scene: Christ, the eternal Wisdom of the Trinity, has well and truly come into history and into the world. Langland's poetics seem thus simultaneously to take literally Augustine's statement,

"He is called God. For He is not actually known in the sound of these two syllables, but still everyone who knows the Latin language, when this very sound touches their ears, moves to think about a certain nature, most excellent and immortal,"[63] and also to register that English, by its "kynde" worldliness and familiarity, can be a profound formal resource for making God's incarnate presence on earth felt and understood. That is, through the conjoining of Latin and vernacular into a single alliterative scheme, the poem performs the interpenetration of the eternal Word with the temporal words of everyday English, and it does so, in the "Petrus, id est Christus" scene, while telling the story of Christ's incarnation in time and in the flesh, and of his wearing the armor of a laborer. Since the alliterative patterning of the poem takes place primarily in English, here, the poem's formal point is that Latin can be made to participate in Englishness, that the supernal can be made to participate in "kyndeliness." To gain a fuller "kynde knowynge" about Christ, it seems one must find a way to understand the eternal language of the Bible as a participant in the "kynde" English of the everyday world of labor and social relations.

THE DARK SIDE OF "KNOWYNGE" ONESELF AND THE SOCIAL WORLD "KYNDELY"

In the final sections of the B-text, the emphasis on labor increases dramatically. When Will finds himself holed up in the Church of Unity, he learns that the entire Christian social world can be figured as a system of agrarian labor. Allegorically, the oxen of the true church are gospels; their yokes, which keep them plowing straight and true, are the four great patriarchs; and the seeds that are planted in the resultant furrows are the sacred virtues (*PP*, B.19.264–311). But a somewhat more literal unpacking of the images at work here is called for. The poem seems to be suggesting not just that the gospels can be thought of metaphorically as the oxen that plow the fields of the soul, but also, and perhaps rather, that religious labor and physical labor are radically, ontologically, and temporally coincident—that the labor you do in the fields really is the labor that you do on your soul, every time you do it.

> And sente the sonne to saue a cursed mannes tilthe
> As brighte as to the beste man or to the beste womman.
> Right so Piers the Plowman peyneth hym to tilye
> As wel for a wastour and wenches of the stewes
> As for himself and hise seruantz, saue he is first yserued.
> (*PP*, B.19.436–40)

What the poem is getting at, finally, is not simply a defense of the mixed life, as earlier scholars suggested, but rather an insistence that the entire notion of separating the spiritual or contemplative life from the active life is prima facie wrongheaded and impossible.[64] Labor is contemplation; contemplation is labor. Thus, Piers goes beyond other contemporary ideas that nonmonastics could practice contemplation. Piers suggests that labor *is* contemplation, not simply that all people could undertake contemplation if they so chose.[65] The poem envisions a world in which the ontological and phenomenological boundary between work and contemplation is entirely broken down. All that we do as "lele" laborers in the present day pays dividends in the economy of Christian salvation.

Once Langland has established this equivalence between labor and contemplation, he quickly turns to demonstrate the potential dark side of the overlapping worlds of contemplation and action. Antichrist appears, and his first action is to render the tillable land, which we have just learned coincides with the spiritual domain, untillable: he overturns the soil to root out what lives there (*PP*, B.20.54); he makes falsehood spring out and spread across everyone's lands (B.20.55); he cuts down truth and plants guile in its place (B.20.56–57). After the landscape of contemplative labor has been rendered unusable, Antichrist amasses an army, forcing Conscience and Truth to take up arms in order to defend themselves and their church. The battle does not go well for Conscience and his army of righteousness; instead, the righteous are gradually beaten down by the sins and by Antichrist, and they eventually retreat into the Barn/Church of Unity (B.20.298). The danger of participating in a world in which the spiritual world coincides with the world of labor is that when people cease to labor, their spiritual safety decays. This is why Wasters—lazy, nonlaboring slugabeds—are the archvillains throughout much of the poem: their refusal to work will have spiritual consequences not only for them but for other people as well. Soon thereafter, Conscience abdicates his place as head of the Church of Unity and vows to head out into the world as a pilgrim until he can find Piers Plowman (B.20.381–86).

This vow leaves the poem on extremely unstable ground. On the one hand, there can be few images darker or more ominous than that of Conscience leaving his post as guardian of righteousness in the Church of Unity. But, on the other hand, for Conscience to have at last fully realized the centrality of Piers Plowman, and of the practice of socioeconomically and spiritually salvific labor that he represents, to the project of collective salvation seems a decidedly positive ending. In the end, the poem's moral undecidability is perhaps the high-water mark of its contemplative form: rather than deciding for the reader how he or she is meant to feel about the "conclusion" of the poem, it ends simply with the line, "And sitthe he gradde after Grace, til I gan awake" (*PP*, B.20.387). We learn nothing about what Will feels emotionally, nothing about what he will do, except that he will be "awake"—he will emerge from the poem with a heightened mental attention, a heightened contemplative capacity, in the world. He makes no effort to interpret his final dream, no moves toward a rhetorical conclusion, nor toward prognostications about the fate of man. Instead, the poem ends in such a way that the reader is forced, in effect, to continue the project of contemplation that has been encouraged throughout: the reader must return to his or her daily, "kynde" life, among his or her larger community, and figure out how to participate *there* en route to participating in God.

REVISIONARY CONTEMPLATION: PARTICIPATION IN THE C-VERSION OF *PIERS PLOWMAN*

Regarding the idea that participatory contemplation of God and social participation are and must be coterminous, the C-text becomes yet more outspoken than the B-text. Examining the C-text for its own investments in the ideas of contemplation and labor that emerge in B suggests that, between his penultimate and ultimate versions of his poem, Langland becomes more invested in how to urge people to labor, how to urge them to work as part and parcel of their spiritual practice.[66] Put otherwise, C's theory of contemplation is yet more based in the real, material world of labor and economics even than B's was, and is based in that world from a much earlier moment in the poem. The first major instance of C's reinvestigation of the problem of labor comes in its fifth passus, the oft-cited "autobiographical" interlude of the final version of the poem. As Anne Middleton and J. A. Burrow have shown, this passus works over the issue of whether or not poetry-writing constitutes a good use of time, and an appropriate labor as a part of the larger moral and socioeconomic economy of Christian England.[67] Throughout the passus, Reason and Conscience dispute with Will about whether he is "an ydel man" (*PP*, C.5.27) who merely spends time and resources without ever contributing anything good to the world. They call this life a "lollarne lyf" (C.5.31), riffing at once on the idea of laziness and on the Lollard movement of religious reform that was still wreaking havoc in England. Will's initial response to these charges is to fall back on the law—both the Statutes of Laborers that were current in English legal discourse and the Hebrew

Bible—to show that someone who lives his life in prayer and contemplation is under no obligation to work (C.5.35–62).[68] His defense culminates with charges against people who live the active life, and the insistence that Will knows what Christ wants him to do (C.5.83) since, "Preyers of a parfit man and penaunce discrete/ Is the leuest labour that Oure Lorde pleseth" (C.5.84–85). To this massive statement on the value and indeed moral sufficiency of prayer, Conscience replies quite simply that he does not accept Will's rationale and that it seems more appropriate for a contemplative to be a cloistered person, rather than someone who runs around begging in cities (C.5.89–91). Evidently, Will was ready and primed to have the edifice of his self-defense torn down: with only three lines of Conscience's rebuke articulated, Will admits to having wasted his time and failed to pull his weight for the common weal.

Although we do not immediately see Will, in his waking life, toddle off to the fields to do labor, this episode sets the tone for the rest of the poem. In the C-text, the plowing of the half acre, the punishment scene by Hunger, and the zealous advocacy of Piers Plowman for the life of labor are all set into the framework that the C-text autobiography has inaugurated, in which the idea of the contemplative life as something distinct from the life of labor is called into question. Moreover, in the C-version, Will, our poetic hero and guide, has been called out as a lazy time waster before he even arrives at the major contemplative episodes of the poem. The augmented emphasis on sloth and laziness that arises in passus 5 of the C-text is anchored in how Langland divides up his famous procession of sins in the C-text, as against the B-text. In the B-text, when Sloth appears, he comes just after Glutton, in the middle of a passus; in the C-text, Sloth's appearance correlates with the start of a new passus, passus 7, thus marking Sloth's appearance as particularly important. Sloth, in effect, gets his own passus and does not have to share that space with any of the other sins. In the C-text, then, more even than in the B-text, Sloth, laziness, the failure of the drive to labor, these are marked as archsins.[69]

This amplification of sloth is tied to contemplation in a passage in C-text passus 7 that does not appear in the B-text. In C-text passus 7, we encounter a character named Contemplacion, during a conversation about whether or not people will follow Piers on his pilgrimage to Truth. Contemplacion avers, "By Crist, thow Y care soffre,/ Famyne and defaute, folwen Y wol Peres./ Ac the way is wel wikked, but hoso hadde a gyde/ That myhte folowe vs vch a fote for drede of mysturnynge!'" (*PP*, C.7.304–7). These are the final lines of the seventh passus, and the eighth passus opens immediately with Piers shepherding his people to the half acre and asking them to labor for him.

Contemplacion, in seeking to follow Piers the Plowman, will end up doing hard labor. Contemplation is thus explicitly marked in the final version of the poem as a life path that is utterly compatible with the active life of participation in the land-based economy of medieval England. Thus, less than halfway through the poem, the C-text has distinguished itself from the B-text by claiming, first, that the life of contemplation, when lived in isolation from a monastery or from a labor economy, is a bad misuse of time, and, second, that the truest contemplatives—and indeed, contemplation itself—are defined by their zeal for work, following Piers enthusiastically into the active life of physical labor.

Next, from the eighth passus of the C-text, Langland removes a passage that is present in the B-text and in the A-text that compares the active and contemplative lives. The B-text reads, "Kynde Wit wolde that ech a wight wroghte,/ Or in dichynge or in deluynge or trauaillynge in preieres—/ Contemplatif life or actif lif, Crist wolde men wrought" (*PP*, B.6.246–51, cf. A.7.231–36). The earlier texts, then, at this relatively early moment in the poem, still set forth the legitimacy of two *different* lives: the active and the contemplative, working in ditches versus praying. Rather than discussing the relative merits of each life and acknowledging each as a justifiable way to please Christ, the C-text focuses exclusively on physical work:

> "And lo, what the Sauter sayth to swynkares with hands:
> 'Yblessed be al tho that here bylyue biswinketh
> Thorw eny lele labour, as thorw lymes and handes:'
> Labores manuum tuarum quia manducabis. . . .
> This aren euidences," quod Hunger, "for hem that wolle nat swynke,
> That here lyflode be lene and lyte worth here clothes."
>
> (*PP*, C.8.259–64)

This passage, spoken by Hunger to the wasters on Piers's half acre, makes no space for the living of the contemplative life that is lived *away* from physical labor. In the moral universe of the C-text, as articulated by Hunger, labor is the *only* path to salvation. Now, Hunger is a far from unproblematic figure in the poem: he traduces Piers's own power and authority, and he proves to be a punitive upholder of Old Testamental vengefulness rather than a forerunner or defender of Christ's infinitely just rule on earth. For that reason, we must take his injunctions against the nonlaboring life with some degree of skepticism; even so, the fact remains that the poem seems to present an even less dualistic theory of action and contemplation than earlier versions of the poem, and to present it earlier on than it appears in the B-text.

The starkest change between the B-text and the C-text in terms of their treatments of the active and contemplative lives, however, comes in B's presentation of Haukyn, the Active Man, as compared with C's presentation of the same material. After cycling through Thought, Wit, Study, Clergy, and Scripture, as if exasperated with the whole enterprise of contemplation, *Piers* B introduces Will to Haukyn, who personifies the Active Life. Initially, we are led to believe that the active life might be a legitimate way out of the epistemological bog that contemplation has led us into: Haukyn presents himself as a loyal, devoted worker—a truehearted follower of the Christian active life. He tells us that he hates idle people and that he identifies with the true laborers of the world (*PP*, B.13.239–40)—undoubtedly a good thing, given the poem's repeated and strenuous condemnation of "Wastours" who do not work. But after Haukyn's strenuous assertion of his devotion to righteous labor, Will begins more closely to examine his clothing only to find that Haukyn's habit (at once sartorial and moral) is full of holes and spattered with excrement and garbage—not at all what we would expect to see bedecking the righteous active laborer. The damage to Haukyn's clothing allegorically figures the sins he commits on a regular basis ("vnbuxom speche," for instance, as well as boasting, bragging, and being a bad neighbor) through his living of the active life (B.13.273–91). Apparently, the active life can be a dangerous life, one full of opportunities for sin, however much it may also parallel or complement to the effort to gain "kynde knowynge" by some form of contemplative exercise. In Will's and the readers' own shared quest for salvific understanding of God, we seem to be again left in an epistemological and moral wasteland—a wasteland that will persist until Haukyn's sins are at least provisionally purged by Conscience and Patience in the B-text. The C-text, by contrast, removes the vast majority of the B-text's condemnations of Haukyn, instead redistributing them among the seven deadly sins from the sin process in its sixth passus. Indeed, nearly four hundred lines of critique of the Active Man Haukyn from the B-text (B.13.272–460) are removed in the C-text. In addition to lightening the moral charges leveled against him, the C-text pointedly depersonalizes Haukyn, calling him not Haukyn, but simply Activa Vita. In so doing, the C-text makes ever clearer that the active life is more than just a choice that Haukyn makes; it is also a category of subject position to which any person could subscribe. The C-text is much keener to endorse an uncomplicated version of the active life as a legitimate option for anyone seeking to participate in God, much keener to recognize the importance and legitimacy of participating materially and physically in the world as a mode of contemplation. The C-text, then, is even more committed than is the B-text to the compatibility between worldly labor and moral virtue, and it is committed to that compatibility earlier on. Thus, the C-text sets up the eventual end of the poem, which manifests the radical compatibility and even coincidence of labor with contemplation, even more fully and decisively than does the B-text. As Langland revised his poem into its final version, he seems to have become more committed to outlining how and why the life of "kyndely" labor and the life of contemplative "kynde knowynge" not only are, descriptively, but also should be, normatively, practiced as coterminous.

LITERARY CONTEXTS AND CONSEQUENCES: LANGLANDIAN DRAMA

But why does this evolution across the versions of *Piers* matter, from a larger literary-historical standpoint? How does it dovetail with the overarching story of contemplative literature's own evolution and revision across the late English Middle Ages? From the late fourteenth and fifteenth centuries, sixteen manuscripts survive of the B-text[70] and more than twenty partial or whole copies of the C-text,[71] so that this poem, in its latter two versions, is one of the most frequently copied and widely disseminated Middle English poems. Unsurprisingly, given its wide dissemination, *Piers* spawned a tradition of copycat poems, beginning at the start of the fifteenth century and continuing well past 1450. These texts include *Pierce the Ploughman's Creed*, *The Plowman's Tale*, *Mum and the Sothsegger*, and later poems, all of which emphasize the importance of labor.[72] One of the most important claims that *Piers* makes for this tradition, both formally and thematically, is that there is no individual who can achieve salvation in isolation from his social responsibilities. And the later version of the poem makes this point more aggressively even than had the B-text.

Building on these ideas, I suggest that the amplified emphasis on labor informs not only the proto-Protestant Langlandian copycat poems but also the upsurge of contemplative dramas in the second half of the fifteenth century in England. As *Piers* is copied, collected, anthologized, excerpted, edited, and disseminated in its latter two versions throughout the fifteenth century, the dually social and contemplative energy of the poem goes rogue, helping to inspire some of the great contemplative works of late medieval England. By its titillating intertwining of literary contemplative forms, *Piers* manifests a way forward for contemplative literature at the end of the Middle Ages, a way that would seamlessly integrate action with living in the social world. Given the high concentration of contemplative dramas in East Anglia (*Mary* from the N-Town cycle, *Wisdom*, and *Mankind* all originate there), and given that eight manuscripts of *Piers Plowman* survive from East Anglia of the fifteenth century alone, it seems entirely plausible to posit a shaping impact of *Piers* on how contemplation goes on to be staged in dramatic literature.[73]

But to call *Piers* the literary point of *origin* for the emphasis on the social world in the late Middle English dramatic literature of contemplation would be misleading. In fact, this kind of emphasis is not original to *Piers:* scholars of the cycle dramas—particularly of the York Corpus Christi cycle—have long noted that, by articulating the life of Christ through the bodies of local guildsmen, these devotional plays promote sociality and theorize labor in relation to religious life. In Sarah Beckwith's formulation, the York plays pursue "social integration and unity in the name of a single administering body," where that body is the church.[74] But where Beckwith sees the York plays as a concerted way of enforcing specific mercantile roles and values and regulating labor and trade, making the plays "the aesthetic mirror for York and its ideal form,"[75] I would suggest that something slightly different is afoot in *Piers*, which resonates more loudly with what we will see in the *Mary* plays, the play of *Wisdom*, and *Mankind*. In these later plays, the overlay of contemplation on action—of the world of the spirit and the world of social interaction and interdependency—is not designed to reinforce trade or shore up mercantile social relations. Instead, in my view, the overlay is geared toward a more distinctly contemplative end. It seeks to urge all viewers to register that they, by participating in the social world positively and morally, are always already participating in contemplation, and that that participation in the social world achieves for their souls what concerted and even cloistered contemplative practice achieves for clergy. That participation does not consist in the viewers' acquiescence to economic relationality but rather points toward a more basic recognition that the promise of Christian salvation extends to and encompasses all Christians, and that their best mode of realizing and accessing that salvation is through their loving and generous participation in the earthly body of Christ—namely, the community of Christians all around them. In these emphases, the *Mary* plays, *Wisdom*, and *Mankind* all participate in the same literary and cultural moment that informs the contemplative forms of *Piers*. Thus, I mean not so much that the plays I will examine in my next chapters are in a *Piers Plowman* tradition but instead that they body forth a shift toward the increasingly social dimension of contemplative practice, a shift that *Piers Plowman* champions particularly loudly.

To say that *Piers* unidirectionally shapes late Middle English drama would be misleading for another reason, since *Piers* is itself deeply informed by the broader cultural context of mystery plays. In the Easter passus of both *Piers* B and C, the substitutability of Piers the laborer with Christ the Conqueror-King is, I believe, inspired by Langland's exposure to liturgical and early cycle dramas. To assert that Langland might well have been influenced by liturgical drama is relatively unproblematic: scenes from the Bible, notably scenes pertaining to the Nativity and the Passion, date back to the tenth and eleventh centuries.[76] Thus, it seems highly probable that Langland would have had—and would have expected his audience to have—familiarity with a certain performative iconography of the Passion. To assert an influence of the cycle dramas on Langland may seem, by contrast, somewhat problematic, given that the earliest dates for surviving play manuscripts reach back only to about 1370, and the earliest date for the earliest version of *Piers* is only a few years before that, in 1362. But some version of extraliturgical drama reaches back farther than that, as evidenced by Robert Mannyng's shrill admonishments in his 1303 work *Handlyng Synne*, which explicitly criticizes the enacting of religious dramas outside of church confines.[77] That Mannyng would decry such performances signals that they were already going on by the first decade of the fourteenth century, at least in some form, and were widespread enough to be a recognizable threat to whatever Mannyng though churchly worship was supposed to look like.[78]

So why would this matter, whether Langland might have seen, in some form, an extraliturgical performance of the Easter scenes from the Bible? As is well known, by the last quarter of the fourteenth century, these mystery plays cast local tradespeople in the roles of all of the biblical figures from the life of Christ. The man who would play Christ in one of these plays would be a neighbor, a familiar person with an English name, and likely a laborer of some kind. He would be a "Piers" in that sense, an everyday working Joe. Part of what the casting of the cycle plays achieves allegorically, of course, is to remind people that every laboring man they know is a potential "Christ," to remind them that their even-Christians literally share in the body of Christ. Langland's blurring of the identities of Piers and Christ in both the B-text and the C-text benefits from a similar logic, by which the laboring "Christ," aka. Piers, is indistinguishable from Christ. The substitutability between these figures is not simply another manifestation of the much-studied Langlandian allegorical impulse but also a manifestation of Langland's imbrication in his own immediate culture and, specifically, dramatic culture of contemplation.

With this in mind, I would further suggest that Will's swooning searching for Piers—asking feverishly where he is, where he can be found—constitutes a vernacular reenactment of the liturgical *Quem queritis* plays, staged in churches during the Easter plays that predate and likely inform the evolution of the mystery plays themselves.[79] In these plays, players would reenact the seeking after Christ by the Virgin Mary, Mary Magdalene, and Mary, sister of Lazarus, that supposedly followed his burial in the holy sepulcher. When Will demands of his various interlocutors where Piers can be found, it initially seems simply his desire to find his favored teacher and interlocutor; when Piers is revealed to be Christ, however, we are meant to understand retrospectively that Will has been enacting a vernacular *Quem queritis* for much of the poem—seeking out Christ-cum-Piers upon his various disappearances. So, the shaping influence of early medieval religious drama—both dramas that would take place within the sacrosanct confines of the church and those that would rely on the marketplace for some of their deeper Christological meanings—on Langland's poem appears throughout and underscores the poem's insistence on the compatibility of the working world with the contemplative world.

Piers recognizes that the dramatic staging and procession of the Passion enable the emergence of a different and more concretely coincident relation between self, other, social world, and Christ. The poem registers how the dramatic mode can be mined for its collective power, not just in terms of access but also and more profoundly in terms of how it demonstrates the perforation of the social here and now with the transcendent, biblical there and then. High medieval through fourteenth-century dramatic form is, I would suggest, a primary driver for *Piers*'s enactment of how contemplative life must be overlaid with the social world. Simultaneously, I would suggest that *Piers* functions as a quasi-dramatic fulcrum between earlier prose contemplative works and later, fifteenth-century dramatic ones.[80] Indeed, part of the reason for the supposed falling off of innovative and original contemplative writing in the fifteenth century is that we, as scholars, are not always looking in the right places: vernacular stages.[81]

CHAPTER FOUR

There's Something about Mary

Staging the Divine in "Kyndely" Language, Time, and the Social World

As its first witness to the emergent sociocultural phenomenon in which drama becomes a predominant cultural form of participatory contemplation, this chapter shows how a unified and probably single-author section of a cycle drama—the sequence of Marian plays from the East Anglian N-Town cycle (c. 1468), narrating Mary's own conception, childhood, marriage, and conception of Jesus—explores the Middle English vernacular as a resource for creating participatory contemplation for an audience.[1] Studying the N-Town *Mary* plays in their historical and cultural context presents challenges, since the cycle survives in one manuscript, BL Cotton MS Vespasian D VIII, and there are no records of the performance or early ownership of the plays.[2] Scholarly consensus, based on the internal stage directions of the plays, is that they were probably performed in a large, fixed, round play place, rather than on pageant wagons; N-Town probably did not process through a town, as the York cycle did.[3] Although many towns have been suggested as the possible home of the N-Town cycle, the preponderance of evidence points toward Bury St. Edmunds.[4]

Throughout the several plays that comprise it, the Marian sequence of the N-Town cycle shares in a robust late medieval devotional tradition focused on Mary, on her compassionate suffering, and on her status as mediatrix between God and mankind[5]—the woman whose body ushers God into the world as the human Jesus.[6] In this devotional tradition, the goal is often to promote audience members' feelings of being implicated in the events of Mary's life by an *imitatio Mariae,* in which the imitant seeks to align her emotions and physical sensations with Mary's own.[7] But the *Mary* sequence from N-Town does not sculpt an audience member's emotions into alignment with Mary's own per se. Instead, the play sequence strives to make Mary sensorily available as a cornerstone of contemplation, and specifically as a means of recognizing how a mortal human being might hold God within herself, how a mortal human being, although bound by time, might be able to bear the eternal Word in her heart, mind, and imagination.[8] In this emphasis on creating a sense experience of contemplation, the sequence resonates with the "sensory concreteness" that Gail McMurray Gibson ascribes to the incarnational devotion of the East Anglian region more broadly.[9] But, where Gibson finds this "sensory concreteness" generally in detailed visual artworks and visual representations, the *Mary* plays—while undeniably reliant on the visual for some of their effects—pursue this recognition in a pointedly auditory way—namely, by creating a series of formal poetic and linguistic meditations on the relationship between temporal existence and the unchanging presence of the divine.

Indeed, one of the claims this chapter makes is essentially a methodological one: although the great majority of excellent early drama scholarship since the late twentieth century has focused on getting scholars off the page and onto the stage, my reading of the N-Town *Mary* is essentially a poetic one, which I hope will demonstrate that, in this play, being on the page is an important part of being on the stage. That is, in order fully to grasp and experience the staged and participatory dynamics of contemplation in the play, one must think seriously and carefully about the play as a *poem*, keen to explore and exploit poetic effects *as* dramatic effects.

CONTEXTS FOR THE *MARY* PLAYS: EAST ANGLIA AND *THE MIRROUR OF THE BLESSED LYF OF JESU CHRIST*

To situate the *Mary* plays' particular brand of participatory contemplation, I will begin with two types of contextualization. First, I will review the devotional history of the geographic area that generated the N-Town cycle. Second, I will analyze the contemplative theory and prose stylistics of a particular work that is known to have had direct bearing on the composition of the *Mary* plays thematically, to suggest that it also has bearing on them aurally and, in particular, on how they deploy Middle English as a sensible, formal device for rendering contemplative understanding to their viewers.[10]

Medieval East Anglia—where the N-Town plays are composed as well as where Julian of Norwich records her visions—is a region of unusually intense worship of the Virgin Mary, both within England and in comparison with other regions, including Italy and Spain.[11] Gibson suggests that the focus on Mary originates in a regional interest in what she calls an "incarnational aesthetic": an intensive focus on representations of the mystery of the incarnation of the eternal Word in mortal flesh.[12] In point of fact, Gibson argues that the intensive incarnational emphasis in East Anglia makes Mary, in some ways, even more central than Christ himself as the "very emblem of Christian mystery."[13] At all turns, the N-Town's *Mary* sequence manifests its deep imbrication in this devotional culture; as Teresa Coletti puts it, "The Middle English N-Town cycle evinces an extraordinary consciousness of the motifs and interpretations that characterized late medieval devotion to the Virgin."[14] So prominent, indeed, is the Marian focus within the N-Town manuscript that Martin Stevens calls it an "under-plot" of the whole play cycle, a thread of narrative attention that is almost as important as the life of Jesus himself.[15] In being structured around Mary in this way, the N-Town cycle is a product of its larger cultural environment, obsessed with how Mary can be the vehicle for the incarnate Word, with how God enters into time and space as the mortal Jesus through her body.

Through their staging of the Virgin Mary and her life, the *Mary* plays encourage the audience to contemplate the mystery of the incarnation by participating in the paradoxical truth that Mary—a mortal human being—makes manifest in having been the mother of the eternal God in the bodily form of the mortal Jesus.[16] The *Mary* plays deploy formal devices to cultivate a sensory, contemplative understanding of her as the vessel through which an eternal God comes into the human world of time and space. Mary's theological status as the time-bound, human, mortal vehicle for God's entry into time and space as the time-bound, human, mortal Jesus is a key manifestation of her medieval status as the mediatrix par excellence,[17] mediating between God and man, as the means by which the divine comes to participate in the human, and the means by which the eternal enters into the temporal.[18] The plays' representations of Mary will seek to activate the audience's awareness of her status as vessel of the eternal Word, mediating divinity to humanity.

In representing Mary as *Maria mediatrix*, the plays' formal rendering of contemplation will deploy the Middle English vernacular as a central tool. The centrality of Middle English in the plays hinges on the plays' tangency with another vernacular, fifteenth-century text. Indeed, although the N-Town cycle derives its Marian focus from the larger theological environment of East Anglia, some of the particularities of this Marian underplot and how it is realized in and through the English vernacular derive from Nicholas

Love's *The Mirrour of the Blessed Lyf of Jesu Christ,* manuscripts of which were widely available in East Anglia, and which had not only survived the Arundelian crackdowns unscathed but had indeed been held up as a standard of orthodox, anti-Lollard, devotional writing, despite its being composed in English.[19] In addition to being a thematic touchstone for the *Mary* plays, Love's work bodies forth a theory of why the vernacular is not just a possible language for embodying contemplative truth but indeed a preferable language for it. That theory, modified through its realization in dramatic form (rather than in the prose of Love's *Mirrour*) will animate much of the formal contemplation of the *Mary* sequence as well.

From early on in his wildly popular fifteenth-century English translation and adaptation of Bonaventure's *Meditationes Vitae Christi,* Love makes a concrete connection between vernacularity and the work of spiritual contemplation—perhaps owing to his own exposure to the vernacular contemplative tradition that had begun to coalesce in England by the first years of the fifteenth century.[20] He tells his readers that texts are written more clearly nowadays in English than they were written before in Latin and that this clarity helps people have greater access to the teachings of the Bible: "Wherfore at the instaunce and the prayer of somme deuoute soules to edificacioun of suche men or wommen is this drawynge out of the forseide book of cristes lyf wryten in englisch."[21] He also tells his readers that he will add "certeyn parties" and will draw together "dyuerse auctoritees" that will be maximally edifying to his "symple" readers; that is, he will augment his Latin original text by adding extra English material and by interpolating auxiliary Latin sources translated into the vernacular. He will translate his main source into English "with more putte to in certeyn parties and also with drawynge of dyuerse auctoritees and materes as it semeth to the writere here of most spedeful and edifienge to hem that ben of symple vnderstondynge."[22] Without his translation of Bonaventure's text into English, avers Love, and without his own superadded explications, translations, and integrations of other authoritative Latinate texts, his simple readers would not have access to the life of Christ in the way that they now shall. In these assertions, Love's translational ethos seems to corroborate the traditional "access model" for the rise of the vernacular as a medium for religious writings: bringing texts into English brings them to a wider audience.[23]

Immediately after he claims English's utility to the conveying of religious knowledge to the "simple understanding" of devout "men or women," however, something more nuanced emerges in his theorizing of the utility of the vernacular to the work of spiritual contemplation. Love turns to talk about the contemplative contents of his book, and he informs his readers that it is more useful to contemplate the humanity of Jesus than the divinity of the Godhead: "To the whiche symple soules as seint Bernard seith contemplacioun of the manhede of criste is more lykynge more spedeful and more siker than is highe contemplacioun of the godhede."[24] Although Love does not stipulate a causal relation between this assertion—about the greater efficacy and "likingness" of contemplating the "manhede" of Jesus relative to contemplating the "godhede" of God the Father—and his previous defense of the project of translating devotional texts into English, the close apposition of these two claims suggests a correlation between them.[25] Love suggests appositively that vernacularity and contemplation of the humanity of Christ are connected.[26]

Love fleshes out his theory of the vernacular as better suited to incarnational contemplation when he tells his readers that contemplation works best when one uses "kyndely"—familiar or natural—things to get to the more abstract unknowables of divinity, thus manifesting an ethos of the vernacular as "kynde" that resonates with what we saw in *Piers Plowman*. Love suggests that the familiarity and naturalness of English are more suited to the contemplation of Christ's life than are the formality and complexity of Latin.[27]

> Wherfore it is to vndirstonde at the bygynnynge as for a principal and general rule of dyuers ymaginaciouns that folowen after in this book that the discryuynge or speches or dedes of god in heuene and angeles and other gostly substaunces ben only writen in this manere and to this entent that is to seie as deuoute ymaginaciouns and liknesses stirynge symple soules to the loue of god and desire of heuenly thinges. For as seint gregory seith therfore is the kyngdom of heuene lickened to erthely thinges: that by tho thinges that ben visible and that man kyndely knoweth he be stired and rauysched to loue and desire gostly invisible thinges that he kyndely knoweth not.[28]

For Love, the likening between earthly and heavenly things seems indeed to be coterminous with the creation of a feeling of "kyndeliness," of familiarity and naturalness. Thus, he will need to create and cultivate "kyndeliness" in his textual representation of the life of Christ. Put otherwise, since the fundamental work of contemplation is to cultivate one's awareness of the likeness between the kingdom of heaven and the kingdom of earth, that work should take place in a linguistic modality that is familiar and natural, rather than one that is alien and difficult, so as to bring the kingdom of heaven into familiar—that is, "kyndely"—territory. Fluent reading situations, those in which a reader does not have to struggle hard to decode meaning, promote contemplative understanding, in Love's theory.

In advocating the use of familiar, natural, "kyndely" tools in the work of spiritual contemplation, Love, like Langland, implicitly justifies his turn to English on grounds partially but not fully assimilable to the straightforward "access" model for vernacularization that he himself seems to endorse. Love's choice of the vernacular originates in his specific understanding of contemplation: in the *Mirrour*, English is a formal reflex of the familiarity and likeness that the text endorses as the affective and cognitive basis for contemplative practice itself.[29] In his reading of Love's vernacular representation of the life of Christ, Watson asserts that Love uses the vernacular as a way of keeping "symple" readers and contemplatives grounded, preventing them from an inappropriate reaching for knowledge that lies beyond their star.[30] From this viewpoint, Love's commitment to the vernacular as a vehicle for meditations on the life of Christ must indicate his perception of "only grossness of understanding" among his readers.[31] Although the political implications of such a scholarly claim are clear—namely, that Love sought to cater to a Latin-illiterate, "simple" readership—the sensory implications of Watson's insight invite some fleshing out.

By asserting that English makes the mysteries of God "visible" to contemplatives, Love's text suggests that vernacular meditations have a unique claim on a contemplative's *formal* understanding of the incarnation—his or her ability to *sense* the incarnation as something "kyndely." Love, that is, is keen to leverage the power of linguistic familiarity in making Christ's incarnation feel real, natural, and immediate.[32] Evidently, there is something more to the "kyndeliness" of the vernacular language than simply its simplicity. Its superiority as a language for Love's contemplations lies not just in its democratizing potential[33] but also in its very "kyndeliness" and in how "kyndely" language is a better vehicle for meditations on the life of Christ simply by virtue of its sensation, its feeling of familiarity, of knownness. Love, that is, offers up a theoretical justification for vernacularity that is based on how it feels, sensorily, to read or hear one's own native language—based, that is, on vernacular fluency and how it creates a feeling of familiarity that promotes understanding—which Love here figures as "visibility" or as "imaginability." For Love, "kyndely" recognizability is the key to a contemplative understanding of the incarnation, and it necessitates the use of vernacular Middle English.

In his insistence on simple, straightforward, familiar, "kyndely" reading experiences for his readers, Love seems to part ways with the other contemplative theorists I have examined in this book so far, each of whom is invested in exploring and exploiting the weirdness of Middle English—its availability for puns, its monosyllables, its modal verbs, its etymologies—and not just its familiarity and simplicity, openness, or clarity. He seems, that is, invested in what cognitive linguists call "fluency" rather than what they call "disfluency." But there is an area in which Love seems to diverge from his own stated program at least slightly, by making his "kyndely" English—like Langland's—a little more than kin and a little less than kind, which is to say, by taking that which is familiar and therefore easy and making it unfamiliar and therefore difficult by making it hyperornate. In doing so, he causes his readers to slow down, to attend fully to the meaning of what he expresses. He avails himself of the vernacular's capacities to create sensory learning situations for contemplative readers by shuttling them between easy, familiar, fluent reading situations and difficult, unfamiliar, disfluent ones. He does so particularly in his treatments of the Virgin Mary.

That Love places special emphasis on Mary is well known: he adds in a number of passages about the Virgin Mary that are not present in his Latin source, including an Ave Maria passage, which Marian Davis identifies an index of his intensive thematic focus on Mary.[34] Love's pronounced attention to Mary entails not just a thematic focus, however, but also, and perhaps more crucially for the *Mary* plays, a formal and sensory one. Because I believe it to be relevant not just to Love's formal commitments but also to some of the formal choices we will see in the N-Town *Mary*, I will include all of Love's Ave Maria passage, which Ian Johnson refers to as a "versified prayer."[35] I have accentuated certain words typographically, to highlight the sonic and rhythmical patterning that Love infuses into writing. Alliterating words within a line are italicized, similiters cadens are in boldface, and rhyming words within a line or across lines are underlined.

Heile *Marie mayden mekest*
gret of the aungel *gabriel* in Jesu *gracious* **conceyuynge**
Ful of grace as moder chast
with outen *sorwe* or peyne thi *sone* Jeſu **berynge.**
Oure lord is with the by trewe feith
and byleue at *Jeſu joyful* **vprisynge.**
Blessid be thou *souereinly* in wommen by *sadde* hope *seynge*
thy *sone* Jeſu to heuene myghtily vp *styenge.*
And *blessed be* the fruyte of thi wombe Jesu in euere lastynge *blisse*
thorw perfite charite the *quene* of heuene gloriously *crownynge.*
Gete vs thise vertues as for oure spede
to thy sone Jesu and thy **plesynge.**

> Be thou oure help in al oure nede
> and socoure at oure last endynge. Amen.[36]

Although Elizabeth Salter's thesis on the overall moderation of Love's prose style still holds true, there are passages in the *Mirrour*, such as this, where Love breaks into highly ornamented prose.[37] As Love dilates upon the traditional words of the Ave Maria, which he has already, in previous sentences, translated into fairly straightforward English prose, his language becomes extremely poetically wrought. First, he adds a great deal of alliteration into his explication of the Ave Maria: the first clause contains three *m*-alliterations; the second three *g*-alliterations. There are two alliterating elements in line 4, three in line 7, and two in line 10. To these alliterations, Love adds a rhyme scheme, based on the prose effect of similiters cadens: even-numbered lines 2, 4, 6, 8, 10, 12, and 14 all end with rhyming gerunds, as does line 7. Because of the replication of the gerund at my line 7, the prayer contains three consecutive *-ynge* end-words in a row, forging a trinity of similiters cadens at the center of the prayer. The sonic echoes in the odd-numbered lines are weaker, but still a discernible presence: "grace" and "chast" share a medial vowel; "spede" and "nede" rhyme fully.[38] As I hope my unpacking of Love's poem demonstrates, Love adds in a good deal of poetic artfulness: alliteration, repetition, and rhythmical patterning. Evidently, the meditative worship of the Virgin Mary in Love's vernacular requires not only focused thematic attention to Mary's virtues but also focused *sensory* attention.[39]

Love secures this attention by programming his text with complex rhythmical patterns, which cause an attentive reader to slow down if he or she is to take in the intricate sonic play that informs the passage. English may indeed be useful to Love because of its simplicity, its familiarity, its accessibility, and its "kyndeliness," but it is seemingly also useful for how that "kyndely" familiarity makes aberrantly hyperornamented usage all the more resonant and striking. It is useful, that is, for how familiarity and ease of lection overall in the text breed sensitivity to nonstandard, hyperornamented usage at local moments. Mary is ideally represented in English because she is a paradigmatic "kyndely" touchstone for meditations on the incarnation *and* because, for a "symple" English readership, English can make sense-perceptible that no matter how human and "kyndely" she may be, there is always some spiritual surplus in Mary that transcends discursive explication and must instead be rendered in complex sound, in rhythm, in sensation. Thus, Nicholas Love avails himself of his simple prose-style baseline precisely in order to violate that baseline for tremendous disfluent effects—much as did the author of *The*

Cloud of Unknowing. And much, as we will see, as does the playwright of the N-Town *Mary* plays.

Love's investment in making Mary sensible through highly wrought English phrasing, rhythms, rhymes, and poetic devices undergoes further investigation in the N-Town *Mary*. There, the Marian elements of the N-Town cycle, as inflected by Love's *Mirror*, constitute not only an "under-plot," but also an "under-form," a unifying principle that plays out not just in emplotment but in focused and concerted formal choices as well. But the "incarnational aesthetic" and the Marian "under-plot" that the N-Town cycle stages go far beyond what we find in Love's *Mirrour* and are underpinned by a unifying problem that is at once theological and sensory: how the conjoining of God's eternal divinity with temporal human form can be staged in vernacular literary language.[40] As we will see, for the sequence of *Mary* plays, expectations of Middle English are useful precisely in how they can be played with, recast, and violated to specific contemplative ends. The *Mary* plays, that is, adopt Love's idea that the "kyndely" language of quotidian vernacular English has particular potency in doing the work of contemplation because of its availability for nonstandard, hyperornamented, complex usage, but the plays apply that idea to Marian contemplation in yet more daring and certainly more dramatic ways, showing how much *more* there always is in Middle English than what one's quotidian, fluent expectations might make allowance for.

Many of the formal and stylistic choices I will examine in these plays will be familiar to anyone steeped in the broader tradition of Marian literature. But, what I want in particular to call attention to is how the *Mary* plays' representation of the miracle of the incarnation in Mary will be shaped by specifically *dramatic* choices that the play sequence makes about how to stage Marian poetics, choices that include the enactment of verbal puns, acrostics, and scenes of linguistic code-switching, all of which rely on the vernacular so as to resonate with a collective audience that is fluent in the "kyndely" tongue of Middle English. Throughout the *Mary* plays, staged poetic tropes combine to create a shared and communal Middle English drama of contemplation of God's incarnated temporality and nonincarnated eternity for its assembled viewers. Through the dramatic staging of carefully crafted Middle English poetics, the plays will allow audience members formally to contemplate how God can be both eternal and, in the incarnated Jesus, temporal. They will rely on drama to make that contemplation more fully participatory, I would argue, than it can be in unstaged Marian devotional texts. In this participatory contemplation, the *Mary* plays go further than had Love in his *Mirrour*; they create Mary not only as a sensory touchstone for the contemplation of God but also as a linguistic echo chamber in which audience members can aurally sense their own participation in Christian mystery.[41]

STAGING CONTEMPLATION: CONTEMPLACIO, THE EXPOSITOR

The earliest and most overt manifestation of the *Mary* plays' insistence that they will initiate participatory contemplative work comes in the plays' expositor figure.[42] At their start, the *Mary* plays introduce an emcee character named Contemplacio, who will shepherd the attention and understanding of the audience throughout.[43] This is certainly true, but the fact that it is *Contemplacio* who has the role of expositor also signposts the play sequence unmistakably and specifically as a contemplative work,[44] designed to create contemplative participation in God's mysteries for its audience.[45] The presence of an emcee figure to superintend the plays' devotional projects, coupled with the fact that it is Contemplacio who is that emcee, then, does the same kind of generic positioning as the *Cloud*'s thematizing of "groping," as the *Revelation*'s theorizing of Julian's work's "comfortable" language, or as *Piers Plowman*'s association of "kynde knowynge" with "craft" and the "cors": it signals to the audience that the play seeks not just to represent but indeed to enact some part of the work of spiritual contemplation, and that the audience, guided by Contemplacio himself, is meant to participate actively in that work. As will become clear, the true role of Contemplacio in this play sequence is to quicken the audience's awareness of the mysteriousness of the historical act of God's enfolding his eternal being into humanity's time-bound existence inside the body of Mary.[46] In particular, Contemplacio will prime the audience's sensitivity to the kinds of temporal paradoxes the play will go on to generate around the Virgin Mary—the human vessel that, through divine grace, carries God into time in his mortal form.

When Contemplacio appears, he immediately alerts viewers to the theme of temporality, asking Christ to save the assembled audience from "perellys past, present, and future" (*MP*, 2). In this temporal triptych, Contemplacio reminds viewers that although Christ is born into history, as a fully mortal human being, the salvific potential of that incarnation is not limited to any single historical moment but instead embraces all time. Christ's incarnation is, as Julian's "continuel" revelations also insist, perpetual: it is a historical event that, once initiated in time, stretches forward infinitely into the future.

At the same time, Christ's incarnation works backward, in that it retroactively provides salvation to sinners who lived before him: Adam and Eve, as well as the Old Testament patriarchs, are all retrieved from hell in the Harrowing of Hell, signaling unambiguously that Christ's incarnate protection embraces all of history. Like Julian, this playwright seeks to convey how, although Jesus's entry into the world occurs in history and therefore in time, his protection transcends his historical life, encompassing all time.

From there, Contemplacio carefully makes the audience aware of how Christ can protect humanity from all perils past, present, and future, as well as how the plays themselves can and will manipulate the audience's experience of temporality:

> Sovereynes, ye han sen shewyd yow before,
> Of Joachym and Anne, here botherys holy metynge.
> How Our Lady was conseyvid and how she was bore,
> We passe ovyr that, breffnes of tyme consyderynge;
> And how Our Lady in here tendyr age and yyng
> Into the temple was offryd, and so forth, proced.
> (*MP*, 254–59)

Contemplacio begins with a synoptic address, reminding the audience of "what [they] han sen shewyd" already, earlier in the play, as though they had witnessed the actual events themselves in real time. From there, Contemplacio's shepherding of the audience's attention shifts to highlight further how freely the play manipulates historical time as well as the time of performance. The third line of Contemplacio's first stanza informs the audience that the plays will "passe ovyr" how Mary was conceived and born, "breffnes of tyme consyderynge" (*MP*, 257), thus demonstrating to the audience that Contemplacio's dramatic representation can subject time itself to condensation.

In so doing, Contemplacio implicitly puts forth a theory of how and why dramatic enactment is a useful means for enacting contemplations on God's incarnated humanity: formally mimicking how the Son, by virtue of his dual nature as divine and human, exists in all times at once—past, present, and future—the plays show that they can render multiple temporalities formally available within a single dramatic narrative. As Contemplacio stages his ability to manipulate time through dramatic narration, viewers are reminded that, to the true contemplative, the "now" of Mary's historical life is still spiritually coterminous with the "now" of the enacted plays, and that, through dramatic contemplation, viewers can become aware of that temporal overlay and can participate in it imaginatively.[47] Indeed, at this moment, Contemplacio deploys a flurry of deictic language, underscoring grammatically the miraculous way in which the play can stage a collective contemplation that will make Mary's here and now contemporaneous and collocal with the here and now of fifteenth-century England: "as a childe of thre yere age here she xal appere/ To alle pepyl that ben here present" (*MP*, 262–63). By thus foregrounding the coincidence of the historical past and its present theatrical re-presentation, Contemplacio urges his viewers to meditate on how time is not always entirely linear, laminar, or singular. Contemplacio, then, models dramatically for his audience the kinds of temporal plasticities and overlaps that are involved in the divine incarnation, enabling the audience to feel through dramatic staging a simulacrum of what it is to be in many times at once—that is, a likeness of what it is to inhabit temporality the way that the Son can, as an eternal being who willingly comes into temporality but whose salvific protection stretches into the future perpetually.[48] This layered temporality is more participatory for the audience than it would be in an unstaged, nondramatic Marian work simply because deictic language in a written text resonates less loudly and less fully than deictic language in a staged text: the here and now in a read text can plausibly be construed simply to be the here and now of the writer and the text—not necessarily the here and now of the reader. By contrast, Contemplacio's staged here and how unequivocally embraces the here and now of the entire assembled audience. By inviting the assembled viewers to participate imaginatively in this layered dramatic temporality, the *Mary* invites them to perceive their own participation in God, their own ability imaginatively to experience multiple times simultaneously.

Critically important in how Contemplacio does this simultaneous work of sensitizing viewers to time as a theme and helping them feel Mary's and Jesus's particular relationships with temporality is Contemplacio's own dual temporal status within the play: he seems both to be part of the historical narratives the play tells and to be a member of the audience to whom the plays are performed in the present. His own here and now is clearly, at once, the here and now of the life of Mary *and* the here and now of the audience. Although he does not directly participate in the historical action of the play, he does identify with the "we" of the players of the play as the plays progress, highlighting that he is a participant in the play's action, or at least in collusion with their playing. When Mary will be presented at the Temple, Contemplacio says, "That holy matere we wole declare" (*MP*, 267), thus, by the "we," identifying himself as a player in, rather than simply a witness to, the unfolding Marian drama. Toward the end of the same play, he says to the assembled audience, "And we beseche yow of youre pacyens/ That we pace these materys so lythly away . . . Now xal we procede to her dissponsacyon" (*MP*, 581–82, 585), again indicating verbally by his use of "we" that he is a player, or at least in league with the players of the play. But, at the same time as he clearly identifies with the "we" of the players, he makes direct addresses and exhortations to his viewers as if he himself were among them, watching the theological drama of Christ's incarnation unfold before him as a spectator. At the beginning of the play of Mary's conceiving of Jesus, Contemplacio audibly identifies with the audience, crying out in desperation to God,

> Cum vesyte vs in this tyme of nede;
> Of thi careful creaturys, Lord, haue compassyon!
> . . .
> Man is comeryd in synne. I crye to thi syght:
> Gracyous Lord, gracyous Lord, gracyous Lord, come downe!
> (*MP*, 1074–75, 1090–91)

Here, Contemplacio hovers between the there and then of biblical time in the diegesis of the play and the extradiegetic here and now of medieval England, reminding viewers that they need God's presence in the world—the ongoing truth of his incarnation as Christ—in this very moment, in the here and now. In this toggling between identifying with the "we" of the players and the "we" of the audience that is begging God to come to them, Contemplacio forces the audience to remember that the distant historical life of Mary is, in fact, not distinct from but coterminous with the current day of medieval England. Contemplacio's address serves to alienate the audience from the experience of history as history in the modern sense, where that history is truly past and done with, and instead encourages them to experience history as simply a deeper layer of the here and now, past events whose meaning stretches onward in perpetuity.[49]

CASTING AND STAGING *MARY*: NEIGHBORS, WIVES, AND CHILDREN AS VESSELS OF THE WORD

The interpenetration of past and present that Contemplacio flags up verbally in the plays is underscored physically by casting choices. Although we know far less about the casting and staging of the *Mary* than we do, for instance, about the York *Corpus Christi* plays, Peter Meredith has proposed that the *Mary* sequence was designed to be played by a local guild or parish.[50] If, then, all of the actors onstage at any given time would then likely be members of a local guild or figures from within an East Anglian parish, viewers of the play would experience the shiver of recognition that their friends, neighbors, and local tradespeople are able, through their being cast in dramatic roles, to embody the historical figures from the life of Christ.[51] That is, watching one's neighbor impersonate the pregnant Mary reminds a viewer that all people can host the mystery of Christ's incarnation within themselves, at all times. One's neighbor's innate likeness to Mary—that neighbor's ability to host the presence of Christ within herself by loving and worshipping Christ—is made explicit, literal, and immediate. In watching the *Mary* plays, one witnesses how one's friends and neighbors, cast in the role of Mary herself, host Christ—the Word of God—within their time-bound hearts, minds, bodies, and voices. By seeing the plays performed live by one's neighbors, one would see a representation of how Mary and Christ are mysteriously present in and as all human beings who partake in the ongoing Christian drama of salvation. In the various plays of the Marian sequence, Mary would physically appear on stage in the form of familiar neighbors from everyday life.[52] In that staging of local denizens as figures from the gospels, the plays are deeply social in their participatory contemplation. The plays implicitly ask each viewer to recognize that everyone else in his or her town has the capacity to embody Mary by playing her onstage, and therefore also has the capacity dramatically to host the miraculous truth of the incarnation. The plays, then, make a sensible, perceptible, formal reality of what is a thematic insistence in Julian's work: those who participate in this kind of contemplation are "evencristene," all equally capable of coming to what Langland calls a "kynde knowynge" of God.

Deepening the plays' sensory rendering of contemplation, audience members would not only participate in the present moment of the dramatic spectacle, but—since the N-Town cycle plays were probably performed annually on the Feast Day of Saint Anne, and probably at or near Bury St. Edmunds[53]—they would also reexperience their own memories of past performances of the play on that day and in that place. As with liturgical and festival experience, the experience of this drama encodes a way of experiencing time itself as something other than strictly linear. This play sequence encodes a temporal experience that is cyclically self-reenacting and recursive across multiple performances; it encodes an experience of a layered present, in which the past and, indeed, future performances are all simultaneously held in the mind of a community of audience members.[54] The *Mary*, then, demonstrates the power of dramatic form to do the kind of contemplative work we have seen in prose treatises and poems—*The Cloud of Unknowing*, Rolle's *Form of Living*, Julian's own *Revelation of Love*, Langland's *Piers Plowman*, or Love's *The Mirrour of the Blessed Lyf of Jesu Christ*—but to do that contemplative work in a more fundamentally collective way.

Thus, the "kyndeliness" that Love leans on as a way of understanding the importance of the familiar in doing contemplation becomes an intersubjective "kyndeliness" in the *Mary*. The "kyndeliness" of these plays inheres not only in their being performed in the vernacular but also in their being performed by one's friends and neighbors, for one's friends and neighbors, year after year. Their "kyndeliness" inheres in their being about divinity but by and for man*kind* as a group, a collectivity. The plays register and amplify this shallowly buried metatheatrical valence semantically, by deploying the words "kynrede" (family), "kyndredys" (family members), "kynnysmen" (kinsmen), and "kynde" (offspring) numerous times, highlighting by that repetition that Mary's "kynrede" are in truth the "kynrede" of everyone in the audience (*MP*, 36, 83, 549, 719, 732, 736, 757, 780, 789, 1305, 1507). Mary is our "kynde," we are hers, and, ultimately, we are each other's.[55]

The "kyndely" familiarity of Mary, however, is always in productive contemplative tension with her depiction as slightly supernatural, slightly beyond "kynde": early on in the play sequence, Mary is established as a wise, old-souled little girl who encapsulates, at once, preternatural wisdom and youthful physicality. The audience meets her at the tender age of three.[56] Even at this young age, she seems to possess advanced spiritual awareness and an astonishing level of rhetorical polish. She tells her parents:

> Fadyr and modyr, if it plesynge to you be,
> Ye han mad your avow, so sothly wole I,
> To be Goddys wyff, I was nevyr worthy.
> I am the sympelest that evyr was born of body.
> I have herd yow sey, God xulde haue a modyr swete;
> That I may leve to se hire, God graunt me for his mercy,
> And abyl me to ley my handys vndyr hire fayr fete!
>
> (*MP*, 287–93)

Mary's meekness, her obedience, and her devoutness, joined with her self-possession and willingness to consecrate her body to God at a young age are designed to strike the audience as unusually mature. Flagging the surprise and admiration the audience is meant to feel, Mary's father, Joachym, responds to her proclamation, "Iwys, dowtere, it is wel seyd./ Ye answere and ye were twenty yere olde!" (*MP*, 295–96). Programmed into the play through its characters, then, are normative responses to the miraculous strangeness of Mary's situation. Those normative responses train the audience's attention on how Mary, though young, seems to violate standard understandings of wisdom as being acquired only over the course of time.

Following Joachym's protestations of Mary's unusual maturity, the play then takes pains to enact it, by showing Mary expound upon the fifteen degrees of holiness to a priest at the nearby temple—further embodying the preternatural extent and depth of her understanding. She goes through all fifteen of them without missing a beat, causing the priest, at the end, to echo Joachym's previous comment: "A, gracyous Lord, this is a merveylous thynge/ That we se here all in syght;/ A babe of thre yer age so yynge/ To come up these greycs so vpryght" (*MP*, 445–48). Joachym and the priest together cue the audience in how to understand Mary, highlighting her miraculous wisdom and maturity. The exclamations about Mary's maturity alert the audience to the paradoxical reality of her being physically youthful while also somehow possessing knowledge and understanding that seem to defy her chronological age. The onstage actors not only model an audience response to Mary—awe and amazement—but they also carefully focus the audience's attention on Mary's seemingly innate ability to hold Christ's supratemporal wisdom (the Word of God) in her time-bound, mortal body.[57] In being staged and diegetically witnessed by Joachym and Anne as preternaturally filled with biblical knowledge, Mary seems preternaturally able to host the Word, to hold God's wisdom within herself, even long before she becomes physically pregnant with Jesus.

It was likely a young child—as is known to have been the case in Philippe de Mézières's fourteenth-century French liturgical play *Presentation of the Blessed Virgin Mary in the Temple*—who played the role of the child Mary.[58] Casting a small child in the role of Mary would further force viewers to recognize and internalize that the wisdom of Mary and her being, as it were, pre-pregnant with the Word long before she is pregnant with Christ—miracles that constantly reenact themselves in the hearts and minds of faithful Christians. Any little child who was cast in the role of Mary, and who spouted the fifteen articles of faith as Mary, would have brought home for the audience the ever-present and astonishing truth of the Marian miracle; namely, that a mortal human being, innocent and young, should be able to hold the eternal Word of God incarnate within her. Thus, in their casting, the *Mary* plays afforded a physical and visual means of rendering not only the contemplative truth that God's eternal Word could be incarnated into a human being but also the truth that *any* human being, any woman, any child, could create in herself a likeness to Mary, could model in herself and for the good of her townspeople the ongoing mystery of the divine incarnation, conceived as the ability to hold the Word inside oneself.

MARIA: THE DRAMATIC POETRY OF MARY

Enriching the contemplative functionality of its emcee figure and its casting choices, the *Mary* plays devise elaborate poetic engines for their participatory contemplations on the incarnation. Namely, they turn to explore poetically just how God—an eternal, ever-present, unchanging being—can become human, take shape, and be delivered into time through Mary's body. They do so through a set of interrelated poetic forms: acrostics, anaphora, and linguistic code-switching. Each of these forms allows the plays to render in form the complex temporality of the incarnation and to create a participatory enactment of it for its audience members, so that they feel, through the formal structure of literary language, the coexistence of time and eternity in themselves.

As Mary nears adulthood in the narrative, the plays present an acrostic on her name in Latin. This MARIA acrostic urges a participatory meditation on the nature of Christ's paradoxical temporality—eternal, yet mortal, and therefore decisively time-bound—in relation to Mary herself. It urges readers and viewers of the play to understand Mary's name not just as a static signifier but as a bearer of layered meaning that relates to her character's suitedness for being the vector of the eternal God into the mortal world. It does so by elaborating each letter of her name with one of a set of five alliterative phrases, each of which contains a description of some aspect of her moral character.

> M—mayde most mercyfull and mekest in mende;
> A—auerte of the anguysch that Adam began;
> R—regina of regyon, reyneng withowtyn ende;
> I—innocent be influens of Jesses kende;
> A—aduocat most autentyk, your antecer, Anna.
>
> (*MP*, 546–50)

In addition to their thematic specification of her moral character as being above reproach, these five phrasal descriptors place Mary at five distinct historical moments: the "current" moment of her maidenhood, the historical banishment of Adam and Eve from Eden, her eternal dominion over all things in heaven as its queen, her innocence at the moment of her birth that originates many generations back, and her role as a perpetual, transtemporal "aduocat" for all Christians living on earth at all times.[59] Through this acrostic, then, "Mary" becomes at once a reified, nearly allegorical, transhistorical being *and* a set of particular historical instantiations. The MARIA acrostic thus performs the work of exegetical reading, since the historical, allegorical, tropological, and anagogical levels of meaning are rendered available in one dramatic move. The acrostic simultaneously allows five separate significations to exist for Mary, five different modes of being and times of life that her name embodies, across the four different modes of contemplative reading. She is shown to be united, ever steady in being always "MARIA," but multiplicitous in her temporal instantiations. The acrostic shows in poetic form, that is, the possibility that she, though "meke" and "innocent," can contain a wealth of meaning and power because she exists across different times. In this verbal, poetic staging of Mary's multiplicitous temporalities, the acrostic prefigures the temporal plenitude that she will later host physically when she becomes pregnant with Jesus.[60]

Because Mary's acrostic determines her multiplicity-within-singleness through clausal exposition, the MARIA acrostic produces a feeling of multiple temporalities at the same time as it evokes them thematically. When thought of simply as "Maria," Mary's name seems fixed and relatively bounded, the term by which her particular personhood is signaled. But, when the play analyzes her name into a concatenation of five clauses, it reminds the audience that her name—the word itself—is not static but, rather, exists in time and is thus subject to change and variation. Each clause draws out from a single letter an alliterative idea, so that the individual letter is temporally dilated, extended through time by the action of syntactic elaboration. The MARIA acrostic is a rendering of "Mary" that shows—aurally and syntactically as well as thematically—her dilation in and across different times.

But, at the same time, the alliterativeness of each clause causes the ear to return repeatedly to a single sound—the *m*, the *a*, the *r*, the *i*, or the *a*—in each line. Thus, the MARIA acrostic allows an audience member to feel how MARIA is not a static signifier but a matrix of meanings and capacities, which are elaborated through syntax and through time, while simultaneously reminding that audience member sonically that, despite MARIA's incontestable existence in time, some essential aspect of her being is steady, invariant, and ever-present within the line of verse. The acrostic, that is, figures temporality through its syntactic elaboration of Mary's name while it figures selfsameness or perpetual presence through its use of alliteration. What the acrostic achieves, then, is a poetic meditation—a meditation born of sound and rhythm—on how temporal variation and ever-presence can coexist. The acrostic formally enables contemplation on how progressive motion through time can be compatible with a selfsameness, a full dwelling in a dilated present moment. In this duality of progress or change and steadiness or sameness, the acrostic figures the paradox of Jesus's incarnation into the body of Mary. Human beings and human language cannot fully access or represent eternity, but the acrostic seeks at least to represent how there can be a greater fullness to every moment, a plenitude, an excess, and a beyond-time that transcends the succession of individual moments from past to present and future. The acrostic becomes a powerful instantiation of the play's formal rendering of the mystery of God's more-than-"kynde" incarnation into time.

And indeed, of his incarnation into staged, performed English. Of course, Marian acrostics were not unique to the Marian play sequence; far from it, Marian acrostics are, in the genre of Marian lyrics, a highly familiar trope of devotion. The alliterative properties in this acrostic are also not unique to this drama. But there is something about the staged and performed setting of this drama that makes the troped and alliterative acrostic yet more compelling and effective than it would be in a text that was not meant for performance. In performance, this moment could have been spoken in one of two ways. It is conceivable that an actor would pronounce each letter of the Latin name before launching into the clausal exposition; it seems far likelier, however, that the MARIA spelling of Mary's name in Latin at the left-hand margin of the text was primarily designed for the text itself, as a reading aid, and that in performance, the actor who played Mary would simply have read out the alliterative clauses that follow each letter in the manuscript. This gradual reading through of the alliterative lines would not allow Mary's full Latin name to appear simultaneous and whole but would instead allow her Latin name, Maria, to emerge gradually, as the acrostic worked its way from Mary's meekness to her status as advocate for mankind. In performance, then, the audience would hear the *M* as a repeated element in the first line, then the *A* as a repeated element in the second, the *R*, the *I*, the *A*, so that only by reaching the end of the passage would they be in possession of Mary's full name, in Latin, the language of the Bible. In this way, the actor's articulation of these lines, while done in English, would gradually bring the readers into the Latin language of the Bible, the eternal language of the Bible, even though it would do so precisely by drawing that name out in narrative time, and in English. When read on a page, the full five-letter acrostic MARIA would be available at once, thus foreclosing on the temporal dilation that is made more available in oral performance.

Indeed, since the five-lettered version of Mary's name—MARIA—is Latin, but the glosses provided on each letter are exclusively in English, the passage enacts an interlinguistic contemplation on time and on the nature of eternity as well. In this contemplation, Latin is cast as the unchanging, permanent feature of the acrostic, while English is shown to be extensible into time. Latin, thus, is implicitly cast by the play as the linguistic embodiment of eternity, while the vernacular is cast as the embodiment of time. It is through the processing of biblical Latin into quotidian, temporal English that this acrostic subtly enacts that we begin to discern what will be a dominant formal dynamic toward the end of the play, when Latinity and vernacularity are shown at once to be different and similar, unique yet mutually translatable, the one representing the divine and eternal, the other representing the human and temporal. Thus, this local, poetic rendering of the compatibility between time and eternity creates a linguistic simulacrum of the paradox of the incarnation. Hearers' participation in the plays' poetic and linguistic acrobatics enables them to feel in themselves how eternity could be compressed into time. The plays' formal meditations on the relationality between time and eternity allow viewers to experience the miraculousness of their own eternal salvation, via the incarnation of Christ in MARIA. For the *Mary* playwright, Latin will be useful in part because it creates generative formal friction with English—making English, in all its "kyndeliness," *less* familiar, *less* readily comprehensible, and therefore more useful as a disfluent contemplative "dart" (borrowing the *Cloud*-author's phrasing) for piercing the cloud of eternal unknowability.

"HEYLING" MARY: THE AVE/EVA TROPE

The drive to stage poetically how Mary challenges the linear order of time changes form later in Gabriel's salutation, this time with a twist on a standard Marian trope that emphasizes recursivity, return, and renewal. Gabriel leverages a familiar pun on Eve's name to show how Mary comes to right the wrong that Eve's sin brought into the world:

> GABRIEL: "Heyl, ful of grace, God is with the!
> Amonge all women blyssyd art thu.
> Here this name, *Eva*, is turned *Aue*
> . . .
> I comende me onto yow, thu trone of the Triniyté!
> O, mekest mayde, now the modyr of Jhesu!

> Qwen of hefne, lady of erth, and empres of helle be ye;
> Socour to all sinful that wole to yow sew,
> Throu your body beryth the babe oure blysse xal renew
> . . .
> And as I began, I ende, with an Ave new.
> (*MP*, 1280–82, 1396–1400, 1402)

This nearly ubiquitous trope of reversing "Eva" to produce "Ave" showcases verbal recursivity as a way of understanding how Mary's pregnancy reverses historical time.[61] By showing how Mary's salutation—"ave"—is "Eva" inverted or "turned," Gabriel formally renders the idea that Mary turns time around, that she returns humanity to a lapsarian moment and heals the breach between man and God that Adam and Eve's sin created.

Capping off this familiar theological point, Gabriel himself performs a circularity in his narrative, saying in the final line of this section, "And as I began, I ende, with an Ave new." As he began, with "heyl," so he ends, with "Ave." Mary renews what Eve destroyed; the branch of humanity that Eve had made barren, Mary makes reflower. But there is a further slippage in Gabriel's insistence that he ends as he had begun: "heyl" and "ave," though they have the same meaning, are drawn from different languages. To grasp the recursiveness of Gabriel's utterance fully, then, an audience member must mentally overlay Latin on English, first recognizing that "heyl" and "ave" mean the same thing, and are thus substitutable terms, and second recognizing that Gabriel has shifted languages from the vernacular, everyday language of English—"heyl"—to the biblical language of God—"ave." Thus, even though the two words mean the same thing, they dial into the Mary narrative in significantly different ways: the first renders her participation in the temporal world; the second renders her participation in the heavenly world of salvation. Here, it is not simply the case that Mary's "ave" reverses Eve's sin but also that Mary's eternal "ave" shows itself compatible with the daily, English "heyl." Thus, the interplay between "kyndely" English and learned Latin augments the play sequence's sense that time and eternity are, through Mary, capable of interpenetration, of dialogue.

TALKING IN TIME, TALKING IN ETERNITY: THE MAGNIFICAT

This repeated, productive contact between English and Latin, figuring in this play the contact between the temporal world and the heavenly, sets up the dramatic climax of the *Mary* plays' formal contemplations of the nature of the divine incarnation into Mary's body and thereby into time. This climax arises during her dialogue with her cousin, Elizabeth, during their concurrent pregnancies, Mary's with Jesus and Elizabeth's with John. During their conversation, Mary speaks the truth of mankind's salvation by Jesus in Latin, and Elizabeth then speaks the same narrative, but in English.[62] The linguistic dialectic that the two women create demonstrates how two structures—one the biblical language, another a quotidian one—can be compatible, equivalent, and, most important, mutually comprehensible, while also remaining ontologically distinct.[63]

This linguistic exchange between Mary and Elizabeth begins with Mary's announcement that she will "begynne" a "holy psalme" (*MP*, 1492). She proclaims, following the words of the Magnificat: "Magnificat anima mea dominum / Ex exultauit spiritus meus: in deo salutari meo" (*MP*, 1493–44). To Mary's enactment of the Latin Magnificat, Elizabeth responds first by recognizing in Mary's switch into Latin that she is pregnant with God's son: "Be the Holy Gost, with joye, Goddys son is in the cum" (*MP*, 1495). That is, Mary's switch into Latin provokes Elizabeth to register and acknowledge the mystery of the incarnation. Once she has done so, she begins to translate Mary's Latin into English: "That thi spirite so injouyid the helth of thi God so" (*MP*, 1496). Elizabeth acts as a vernacularizing conduit for Mary's divinely inspired Latinity, rendering available in English what Mary utters in Latin to an English-speaking audience of the plays.

The Magnificat was one of the Latin texts that many Latin-illiterate playgoers would probably have understood and would certainly have recognized, but this familiarity does not by any means make Elizabeth's Englishings extraneous. Quite the contrary, that the intercharacter translations from English to Latin take place through a highly familiar canticle serves to draw the audience deeper into the participatory contemplation of the drama. It serves to situate them within a cascade of code-switching, to position them, as it were, on the threshold of the vernacular temporality of the "kynde" everyday and the Latinate supratemporality of biblical time. It positions them, that is, on the threshold that separates the quotidian, temporal world of Englishness from the Adamic, transhistorical world of Latinity, but that also simultaneously joins those two worlds together.[64] The code-switching, then, is another means by which the plays urge viewers to understand how Mary as mediatrix can mediate the supratemporal Word of God to them in their quotidian, mortal lives. Through Mary's and Elizabeth's bilingual contemplation, the audience is able to participate linguistically in the salvific truth that Latin and English, the language of God and the language of the everyday, are mutually compatible, mutually comprehensible, and mutually interpenetrating. I do not mean to suggest that English and Latin are held pervasively in the Middle Ages as a strict binary, nor do I mean to fetishize Latin as a monolithic language that normally stands removed from any vernacularity. Indeed, as David Townsend and others have shown, there are multiple Latins at play in the literary culture of the Middle Ages, to such an extent that even Latinity should be thought of as a mode of vernacularity in certain contexts.[65] What I do want to suggest is that, in this particular play, we are encouraged to encounter English and Latin as a sensory dyad, within whose aural bounds participatory contemplation can begin to take place.

Indeed, as they continue, Elizabeth's Englishings of Mary's Latin prove to be more than straightforward, word-by-word translations: her English renderings add important exegetical information to Mary's Latin utterances.[66] When Mary says, "Quia fecit mihi magna qui potens est/ Et sanctum nomen eius" (*MP*, 1501–2), Elizabeth answers, "For grett thyngyes he made and also myghtyest/ And right holy is the name of hym in vs" (*MP*, 1503–4). By switching from the first person singular "mihi" to the plural "us," Elizabeth performs substantial exegetical work on the meaning of Mary's pregnancy. She reminds her English-speaking audience that God, who makes great and mighty things, incarnates his name in both Mary and Elizabeth, the mothers of Jesus and John, respectively. But since Elizabeth and Mary are onstage before an audience—an audience that Contemplacio has already disabused of the idea that an ineradicable ontological wall separates the viewers from the characters of the play—the "us" again functions to remind the audience that they, too, contain God's name incarnated within them, both as the eternal Latin words of the Magnificat and as the deeply felt and quotidian English meaning of those words. Elizabeth's switch to the English first person plural, like Contemplacio's time-shepherding gestures, draws viewers into the action and implicates them in the mystery of divine incarnation. Because of the familiarity of the Latin Magnificat even to Latin-illiterate audiences, hearers of this scene, upon encountering the "us" of Elizabeth's vernacular rendering, would likely recognize that Elizabeth is not simply parroting Mary but is instead making a subtle interpretive commentary on her biblical words. Through Elizabeth's sensibly embellished Englishings of Mary's canonical Latin, the mysteries that seem to pertain only to Mary are made to extend, albeit less physically and less immediately, to all of mankind.

Through the formal and linguistic structures of the acrostic, the puns, and code-switching, the *Mary* plays stage how eternity relates to temporality, and how it is possible for temporal language to encapsulate eternal truths. They stage how—most crucially—it is possible for the Word to become flesh as the living human Jesus, and how the audience can and indeed does participate in that miracle. When we, as viewers of the Marian drama, hear the Latin Magnificat drawn into "kyndely" English and then elaborated upon in subtle ways by Elizabeth, we experience a linguistic reflex of Jesus's birth into time, and into the world.

The contemplative effect of this bilingual passage, however, is made not only so that the individual viewer can feel involved in bringing the eternal into the temporal but also so that the collectivity of viewers can feel so involved *together*. When medieval audience members hear the Magnificat uttered in both Latin and English, as I have mentioned, they hear something that they know reflexively, from liturgy, even if they do not understand the meanings of each individual word; they hear a text that resonates not only within the play but also with their past experiences of hearing the Magnificat sung. When the audience members witness Mary and Elizabeth talking to each other, easily and naturally forging the mutual translatability of Latin and English, they also simultaneously witness two local guildswomen speaking together. Because of the performance of this scene by local people before an audience that already knows all the words, and thus can participate concretely in the words themselves, perhaps even singing or speaking along in the very moments of their utterance, and can participate as a collectivity, as the assembled ecclesia that all Christians are supposed to be at all times, the contemplative message of Mary's encounter with Elizabeth signifies not just as a source of understanding to the individual person about his or her relationship with God but also as a source of understanding about that person's "evencristene"—his or her spiritual community—in relation both to self and to God. As they hear Elizabeth's drawing of Mary's Latin into English and expanding upon it, audience members are made to realize that they and all their neighbors similarly bring the Word of God into their daily lives and expand upon it as a community through their thoughts, words, and deeds. As they hear the enactments of contemplation in the plays, audience members are reminded that the liturgical rituals in which they all participate at church extend far beyond the church doors, out into the rest of the social world.

Through the very collectiveness of these dramatic modes of meditating on Mary's salvific relationship with time and eternity—the acrostic, the code-switching, the punning—the *Mary* sequence suggests how staged works of drama might be optimal vehicles for the kinds of "kyndely" contemplation that Nicholas Love endorses in his *Mirrour of the Blessed Lyf of Jesu Christ*. For Love, as I have argued, the experience of English's very familiarity conduces to a familiar understanding of Christ, an understanding appropriate to "symple" readers and aspiring contemplatives. In his representations of Marian devotion in particular, the simple familiarity of English begins to morph into complex, audible ornateness. For the playwright of the *Mary*, that morphing into complexity becomes a provocation to explore a wider range of means for infusing an experience of Marian contemplation into his work. In the *Mary*, the level of formal contemplation that we see in Love's use of alliteration in his translation of the Ave Maria is greatly augmented: the *Mary*-playwright urges his readers to experience Mary as a figure at once familiar and strange, to know her miraculous ability to hold eternity in her time-bound body through the sparklingly asymmetrical contact between the vernacular and Latin. As viewers wrestle with the play's complex, "kyndely" English, they wrestle more deeply with the saving truth of Mary's status not only as mediatrix but also as *translator*, the one who literally carries eternal salvation across to viewers, from her own Latin into Elizabeth's English, and thereby into the time-bound world of everyday life and the social world.

JOSEPH'S VERNACULAR ROLE IN THE CONTEMPLATIVE DRAMA: COMEDY AND DOUBT

Although it does rely on liturgical modes and forms—such as, on a small scale, the Magnificat inclusion and, on a larger scale, the feast day of Saint Anne, for which the plays were likely in part composed[67]—to stage dramatic contemplation of Mary, the performativity of the N-Town's overall Marian drama also distances itself from the performativity of the liturgy in its reliance on one additional form of vernacularity, a form that underpins and guarantees the high seriousness and formal rigor of the others. That form comes in the play that focuses on Joseph's doubts about Mary's pregnancy. This play is not one of the main *Mary* sequence plays; instead, it interrupts them by being added into their midst by a later compiler. Rather than being irrelevant to a historical reading of the *Mary* sequence because of its lateness and additiveness, however, this Joseph play constitutes evidence of a certain kind of reader response in that it evinces an effect that a later drama compiler deliberately tipped into the supervening Marian narrative. Specifically, the Joseph play suggests that a reader and copier of the original Marian sequence wanted to inject some comedy into the otherwise quite serious Marian drama—and wanted to do so for a specific and surprisingly contemplative reason. The form of contemplation that this play introduces to the larger, paraliturgical Marian drama is comedy.

The comedy inheres in a series of puns that Joseph makes. When he hears that Mary must be married off to someone and that he himself is in the running, he is exceedingly anxious, but he is soon convinced to make his way toward Mary and the bishop, over his protests: he wonders why the bishops insist "that every man xuld come and brynge with hym a whande" (*MP*, 750).[68] Here, the word "whande" encodes a pun, meaning both the tree branch that each of Mary's suitors is meant to bring to her and a phallus. The audience's mirth at Joseph's sexual innuendos would increase dramatically when he acquiesces to go, saying, "I xal take a wand in my hand and cast of my gowne" (*MP*, 758). He means, of course, that he will swap his at-home clothes for travel clothes and take a branch with him. But by overdetermining the carrying of the "whande" as being something he would do "in his hand," the passage strongly invites the audience to understand Joseph to be making a masturbation reference. Coupled with his assertion that he will doff his gown, the audience is invited to think of him masturbating. Joseph's sexualized grumbling continues with his lamenting the possibility that he may "falle" on the journey (*MP*, 759), a clear reference to losing an erection in context of all the other purple puns in this scene. To reduce the odds of his "falling," he vows that he will take as his foe anyone who should dare to "take away [his] staff" (*MP*, 760), meaning his walking stick, but also his penis. As he walks along, he calls attention again to his "staff," and to how he "holdes" it all the way (*MP*, 763). When he finally arrives before the bishops, Joseph panics, and he swears that he "kannot [his] rode fynde" (*MP*, 808); apparently, the little "whande" he brought "in his hand" all that way was too small, or too detachable, for him to keep track of. Through the vernacular puns available in this passage, Joseph is made to seem old, vulgar, impotent, onanistic, and, most important, risible.[69]

By making us laugh at Joseph's unenviable conjunction of impotence and onanism, the play achieves several interconnected goals. First, it suggests that Joseph will not—because he could not physically—impregnate Mary. Any child she has will indeed be the child of God, not the physical child of Joseph and his ever-falling "whande." Second, Joseph's skepticism about the bishop's insistence on his participation in the marriage selection process models skepticism anyone might have about any part of the Mary story: reading the passages on a literal level, Joseph rightly thinks he is too old to be a husband to Mary, rationally thinks he shouldn't have to go, and reasonably worries about his physical health on the journey to her. It is only on the allegorical level—in which audience viewers always already know that Joseph's sexual performance is not at all at issue in Mary's life, because she is the bride of God, and in which all his protestations about his old age read as proof of his sexual incapacity—that the audience can perceive Joseph as what he is: someone outside their own circle of faithful Christians. As a Jew, he prays to God, but he does not have any sense of the mystery of Christ that awaits him. The comedy surrounding his skepticism and nonknowledge serves as a way for audience members to experience their own doubts and disbeliefs about the Mary story but to recognize all the while that those doubts and disbeliefs are misplaced and laughable. The complexly "kyndely" vernacular of the *Mary* sequence's contemplative, participatory poetics is made more un-"kynde" by this added play; the fluency of the staging of Mary is becoming more disfluent. The interpretive intervention of this fifteenth-century compiler, scribe, and editor causes the high-style, formal Marian kindliness to instead slip into informality, sexual pun, and low style. That interpolated informality—here, in the form of encoded sexual puns—serves a crucial participatory purpose: the staging and encapsulation of doubt. This staging of doubt in turn serves the overall contemplative functionality of the *Mary* sequence.

Undoubtedly, this claim will strike some readers as implausible, since contemplation is supposed to be full of grace and gravitas; why call this ribald kind of participation "contemplative"? Why even include the Joseph play in an analysis of the *Mary* as contemplative? What I want to emphasize here, and in the coming two chapters, is that fifteenth-century dramatists recognize a particular participatory power in humor and comedy, a power that inheres primarily in comedy's ability to get an audience member to engage with and ultimately overcome his or her own doubtful resistance to divine contemplation. That movement of a viewer into doubt, into resistance, or into sin and only then into purification and contemplation is part and parcel of how late medieval English dramas stage participatory contemplation. The Joseph play that gets added into the original *Mary* sequence acts as a kind of poultice, to draw doubt out of the minds of viewers. It functions by staging doubt and skepticism directly and then deriding them. Moreover, as will also be true in the two plays yet to come, when one is standing in a crowd of viewers laughing at some "unkynde" contemplative element together, not only would one's own faith be reaffirmed, but so would one's own knowledge of one's supervening participation in the supervening community of Christian faithful. Thus, the low comedy of the contemplative dramas is central not only to an individual trajectory toward high contemplation but also in making that trajectory shared, collective, and communal.

This idea of communal devotion is key to participation in the drama of Christian practice more broadly, but by interrupting the high seriousness of the *Mary* sequence's contemplations on Mary with the low comedy of Joseph's sexual dysfunction, the N-Town drama shows where its own particular brand of sensible and participatory contemplation differs from and exceeds what is possible in liturgical contexts. Spooling out ribald puns on erectile dysfunction, gesturing masturbatorily upon approaching Mary, and mooning over one's withered rod have no place in the officially sanctioned and sanctified space of the church, and thus no place in official, formal liturgy. But the work that these comedic elements do for the overarching contemplative drama of the *Mary* plays is, itself, theologically salutary and important, precisely in airing and then shutting off any doubts by mocking and, indeed, castrating them. These extraecclesiastical, extraliturgical plays, then, are able to achieve a more nuanced mode of contemplation than that which could properly be sought after in church. The extraecclesiastical, dramatic mode so does by availing itself of doubt, of nonbelief, and of derision.

In its insistence on the collectivity, vernacularity, and comedy, the *Mary* sequence and the Joseph play anticipate what I will discuss in my next chapter. There, we will see that the morality play *Wisdom* continues in the Marian dramas' pursuit of a collectivized, vernacular, and specifically comedic contemplation, but it also returns to *Piers Plowman*'s heavy emphasis on labor and likeness to the Trinity as cornerstones of that collective contemplation. In that turn toward Trinitarian theology, *Wisdom* will make wholly explicit a logic of likeness that has run more obliquely through all of the previous works in this study. Where the *Cloud* talks about "meetness" and "accord"; where the *Revelation* creates the possibility for readers to feel their own linguistic likeness to Christ's multiplicitous temporalities through its variegated prose style; and where *Piers Plowman*, the *Mirrour*, and the *Mary* sequence, in different ways, riff on the idea of "kyndely" linguistic experience as a means of understanding likeness between self and God, as well as between self and other people, *Wisdom* will theorize likeness directly and explicitly, in its role in contemplation as well as its role in the social world. In aiming squarely at the role of an individual contemplative's participation in the social world, *Wisdom* will draw our attention back toward *Piers Plowman*, with its emphasis on labor and work. In doing so, it will retain and, in some instances, heighten the *Mary* plays' liturgical forms, interlinguistic play, poetic form, and comedy—though *Wisdom*'s comedy will be less purple but more interested in exploiting the outer linguistic limits of Middle English.

PART III

Vernacular Comedy and Collective Participation

CHAPTER FIVE

Likeness and Collectivity in the Play of *Wisdom*

The morality play *Wisdom* (c. 1460) thematizes contemplation early on, and it maintains that thematic emphasis throughout.[1] Undergirding this emphasis, like the other works studied in this book, the play deploys a series of interlocking formal choices, all of which combine to stage participatory contemplation through the sensible field of vernacular literary language. For *Wisdom,* the central challenge of contemplation is to feel the truth of man's being created in the image of God. Just after introducing its first two characters, Wisdom (Jesus) and Anima (the human soul), the play emphasizes that as a core contemplative principle. Anima asks Wisdom "how may [one] have knowynge/ Of [the] Godhede incomprehensible?"[2] To this request for contemplative knowing, Wisdom responds with a description of the nature of contemplation:

> By knowynge of yoursylff ye may have felynge
> Wat Gode ys in your soule sensible.
> The more knowynge of your self passyble,
> The more verily ye shall God knowe.
>
> (*W*, 95–98)

Wisdom is explicit in asserting that self-knowledge ("knowynge of yoursylff") is the key to contemplation and that this knowledge of self must be "sensible." In fact, so deep is the play's investment in sensibility that it redundantly refers to "sensible" learning and to "feeling," as if to underscore not just the value but indeed the *necessity* of sensory experience in doing the work of contemplation. In so doing, *Wisdom* makes explicit that feeling—the rendering sensible of—the likeness between man and God is of primary importance in achieving the work of contemplation. As will become clear, throughout its staging of contemplation, *Wisdom* solicits the active and self-conscious participation of its audience in sensing and feeling this likeness by exploiting the formal boundaries of stage and reality, performance and ritual, actors and viewers, social participation and participatory contemplation.

In this staging of participation, *Wisdom* deploys its own theatricality, its poetics, and the familiarity and pliancy of the English vernacular as powerful resources for participatory contemplation. In this play, however, the nature of the vernacularity will be different from what we have seen before. *Wisdom* will begin by creating a complex, multimodal set of interpretive expectations for its viewers—a jointly sensory and hermeneutic baseline for the play. These expectations will fit into several categories, three of which are aural, one visual: linguistic, discursive, poetic, and sartorial. Soon, however, the contemplative baseline the play has set up will be violated by Lucifer, whose familiarity with the contemplative norms established in the play makes him an ideal distorter, perverter, and reviser of those very norms. That is, his fluency in the play's normative contemplative vernacular makes him an ideal purveyor of disfluencies. When Lucifer creeps onto the scene, with all his disfluent contemplations to unleash on the play's protagonists, new modes of vernacularity creep onstage with him—modes that include slang, colloquialism, intervernacular code-switching, and the calling out of local place-names and proper names. Taken together, Lucifer's many brands of disfluent vernacularity will combine to serve as a formal, sensory correlative of the moral havoc he wreaks on the soul.

INITIAL CONTEMPLATION: ANIMA'S LIKENESS TO WISDOM

Wisdom's initial amatory dialogue between Anima and Wisdom deploys multiple formal modes of rendering a likeness between Anima and Wisdom sense-perceptible, of showing that they participate in a shared kind of selfhood. The first mode is sartorial. Wisdom immediately appears, according to the first stage direction, "in a Ryche purpull clothe of golde, wyth a mantyll of the same ermynnede wythin." He also wears, according to that same stage direction, a furred hood, a wig, and a "Ryche Imperyall Crown, sett wyth precyus stonys and perlys." Thus, sartorially, the play registers Wisdom's majesty, opulence, and formality.[3] Visually echoing the opulence of Wisdom's appearance, Anima appears dressed in white cloth bordered with gold and miniver. She also wears a mantle and a wig "lyke to Wysdom," according to the second stage direction, as well as a "ryche" crown with golden tassels. From this costuming, Anima's initial state—regal, stately, opulent—is visually represented to the audience as similar to Wisdom's. By presenting these characters in this sartorial likeness early on and showing them to be in harmony of thought as well, the play creates an expectation in its audience that outward appearance—the material clothing that the characters wear—is a reliable way to deduce internal, moral being, and, hence, moral relationality between characters. Anima matches Wisdom's level of sartorial opulence because she matches him in her behavior, attitude, and disposition.

Concomitant with the sartorial rendering of Anima's likeness to Wisdom, the play deploys a series of aural cues to deepen and nuance Anima's likeness to Wisdom. This aural cuing happens in three ways. First, the play creates a likeness between the two initial main characters that is based on shared poetic forms. When Anima speaks, she reproduces Wisdom's chosen verse form exactly: long-line stanzas of eight lines apiece, of the rhyme scheme *ababbcbc*. Thus the rhythms and rhymes of Anima echo those of Wisdom, so that the two characters seem to speak with a single voice, to share a common mode of self-expression, a common aural form, or a shared poetics. Second, Wisdom and Anima both deliver Latin biblical lines at the beginnings of their utterances and then comment on them in English. Anima emerges saying, "Hanc amavi et exquisivi" (*W*, 17), and then proceeds to dilate upon that notion in English. Echoing her, when Wisdom responds, he says, "Sapiencia specialior est sole," and then proceeds to dilate upon *that* notion in English. In paralleling their bilingual verbal strategies, the play formally demonstrates a likeness between Anima and Wisdom—a likeness that might best be termed a shared exegetical practice, in that both figures reveal their comfort and familiarity with the Latin text of the Bible, as well as with traditions of dilating upon it in commentaries. Third, in addition to poetic and exegetical echoing, the play cultivates a discursive likeness between the two initial main characters. As their amatory discourse moves forward, they each channel the Solomonic tradition: "Hanc amavi" and "Sapiencia specialior" are both from the Wisdom of Solomon.[4] Then, after Wisdom has exclaimed, "How lovely I am, how amiable/ To be halsyde and kyssyde of mankynde . . . I love my lovers wythoutyn ende," Anima cries out in response, "O worthy spouse and soveren father,/ O swet amyke, our joy, our blys!" (*W*, 43–44, 47, 69–70). Thus, the two figures are shown to share the same devotional tradition embodied by the highly amatory, lyrical, and sensual Song of Songs—a shared discursive mode. Anima and Wisdom are alike on many levels because they participate in a shared mode of being that is at once sartorial, poetic, exegetical, and discursive.

Having staged the shared multimodal selfhood that embraces Anima and Wisdom as at once sartorial, poetic, exegetical, and discursive, the play turns to explain how and why that multimodal likening matters theologically. Anima asks what the soul is, to which Wisdom responds as follows:

> Yt ys the ymage of Gode that all began,
> And not only ymage, but hys lyknes ye are.
> Of all creaturys the fayrest ye ware
> Into the tyme of Adamys offence.
>
> (*W*, 103–6)

Here, we find the explanation of how the human soul relates to God: we learn first that the soul is the "ymage" of God; second, we learn that it is his "lyknes" or similitude. The overdetermination of likeness in this passage signals that that concept—of likeness between self and God—is the goal of participatory contemplation.[5] This lexical overdetermination of likeness also retroactively accounts for the sartorial, poetic, exegetical, and discursive systems of likeness that the play has devised to this point: the play has been urging its audience to feel the likeness between the soul and God by enacting it formally through the devising of the multimodal shared self of the Soul and Wisdom. Likeness, that is, is the key to contemplation; it motivates the sensory, participatory forms of the play.

ENTER THE POWERS: THE DIFFERENTIATED POWERS OF THE SOUL IN LIKENESS TO WISDOM/GOD

This drive to create a participatory experience of contemplative likeness in the play becomes more nuanced when it is revealed that the Soul is not an undifferentiated entity but instead a delicately balanced amalgamation of mental Powers. In the second scene of the play, the audience encounters the Augustinian powers of the soul, harvested and vernacularized from *De Trinitate*'s *memoria*, *voluntas*, and *intellectus*: Mynde, Wyll, and Understondynge.[6] As they introduce themselves, the Powers further specify the nature of the likeness between the soul and God. We begin with Mynde, the Augustinian analogy of God the Father, who says, "I am Mynde, that in the soule ys/ The veray fygure of the Deyté" (*W*, 183–84), thus registering that the soul contains the image of God the father in the form ("fygure") of the mind. He goes on in a seemingly redundant phrase to affirm that "by mynde of me, Gode I kan know." On the one hand, this phrase simply articulates the truism that it is by self-examination that one comes to understand God. But for *Mynde* to say "by *mynde* of me, Gode I kan know"—to utter aloud his own name in his articulation of how contemplation works—overdetermines the idea of mindfulness and/as self-knowing in spiritual practice, thereby emphasizing it as a paradox along the lines of "kynde knowynge." Mynde can only know God by having "mynde" of itself, that is, by honoring its own true nature and being self-aware. For Mynde, the way to God is mind itself.

When Wyll speaks, the discourse that associates likeness to God with self-awareness increases in intensity and specificity:

> And I of the soul am the wyll.
> Of the Godhede lyknes and a fygure
> . . .
> Wan gode wyll resythe, God ys in us knett.
> (*W*, 214–15, 231)

Wyll is not only the "fygure" of God but also the "lyknes." In this reduplication of near synonyms, the play seems keener than ever to insist that likeness is the fundamental nature of man's relationship with God. When Wyll then insists that God is "knett" in those who live a life of good will, he suggests that the likeness between man and God creates a bond, or union, between the soul and the divinity. And when Wyll describes what knits God to man, he specifies that it is the working of "gode *wyll*," emphasizing that Wyll knows God by its own nature, by willing. As was the case with Mynde, it is self-knowing that constitutes the approach to God, but Wyll's staging of this fact becomes more insistent.

When Understondynge speaks, he enacts the most fully developed explication of how to contemplate God by contemplating the self that we have heard so far in the play.

> The thyrde parte of the soule ys understondynge.
> For by understondyng I beholde wat God ys
> In hymselff, begynnyng wythout bygynnynge,
> Ande ende wythout ende, that shall never mys.
> Incomprehensyble in hymselff he ys;
> Hys werkys in me I kan not comprehende,
> How shulde I holly hym than, that wrought all this?
> Thus, by knowynge of me, to knowynge of Gode I assende.
> (*W*, 245–52)

Initially, in the first four lines, Understondynge simply explains his role in the soul, and how, through self-beholding, he can come to behold God "in hymselff." But the play does something rather marked at that point: by enjambing line 2 into line 3, the phrase "in hymselff" takes on a great deal of metrical emphasis, so that the passage seems to insist not that by Understondynge's self-examination he comes close to a kind of mediated understanding of God, but rather that he comes to understand God *in himself*, as he truly is. The assertion that one could understand God "in hymselff" is rather bold, particularly given that most of the Latin contemplative writers—Saint Paul chief among them—insist that we can only see God in this life through a glass darkly, and that we must wait patiently for the afterlife before we are to see him face to face, as he truly is, in his essence.[7] But Understondynge quickly changes tack, from asserting his own power to understand God to staging what it is to try to understand something in the first place: he recognizes that God is "incomprehensible in himself," and that he cannot even fully comprehend God's works "in me." After all the bold assertions of understanding's powers, it seems that understanding itself quickly falls short of what is needed to comprehend God. It seems to fall short, that is, until the next line, when Understondynge poses the question, "How shulde I holly hym than, that wrought all this?" This desperate-seeming question, counterintuitively, is what leads directly to Understondynge's assertion that "Thus, by knowynge of me, to knowynge of Gode I assende." In this seemingly paradoxical pair of utterances—the one implying that Understondynge cannot grasp God, the other that he has already somehow grasped God—Understondynge enacts a fundamental idea about how contemplation works. When a contemplative reaches the limit of understanding, that is when the purest knowing of God is possible—when cognition has reached its limit but knows somehow that there is something more, something beyond itself, yet to be contemplated. When contemplatives see and know their own incapacities, they see a glimpse of what might lie beyond—as a parallel, we might think here of the image of the cloud of unknowing itself, when a contemplative's cognitive faculties shut down. When Understanding fails, and when it feels that failure, it gets closer to God.

After Understondynge's staging of how contemplation works, through a cultivated awareness of likeness between oneself and God, but a simultaneous awareness of the inadequacy of the self fully to fathom God, Wisdom reemerges, to reorient us in Trinitarian contemplation by mapping it securely and unmistakably onto the Powers of the soul:

> Lo, thes thre myghtes in on soule be:
> Mynde, Wyll, and Understondynge.
> By Mynde, of God the Fadyr knowyng have ye;
> By Understondynge, of God the Sone ye have knowynge;

By Wyll, wyche turnyt into love brennynge,
God the Holy Gost, that clepyde is Love,
Not thre Godys, but on Gode in beynge.
Thus eche clene soule ys symylytude of Gode above.
(*W*, 277–84)

Thus, Wisdom reminds the audience that when they view the interactions among these three Powers of the soul, they are seeing a likeness—a "symylytude"—of the divine Trinity. Through this emphasis on likeness, Wisdom creates, in effect, a shared contemplative vernacular for his audience, a zone of familiar forms, tropes, phrases, and ideas about the nature of contemplative participation in God. Through this passage, hearers are presented with the notion that man is like God through the very structure of the soul, and that contemplation consists in cultivating awareness of that fact.

Undergirding these thematic emphases on the likeness of the human mind to God, this introduction of the Powers of the soul replicates and reinforces the "feelable" likenesses that we have already seen at work between Anima and Wisdom through their shared modes of being. When the three Powers of the soul appear onstage, they deploy the long-line stanzas of eight lines apiece and the *ababbcbc* rhyme scheme of Anima and Wisdom, rhythmically staging the likeness between the Powers and God that the Powers articulate explicitly in the content of their speeches, and participating in the poetic vernacular the play had already performed through Anima and Wisdom. Again like both Anima and Wisdom, the Powers rely heavily on an amatory discourse, calling God, "fayere and fre" (*W*, 187), "desyderable" (*W*, 253), and the source and end of all the "love brennynge" of the Soul (*W*, 281). The fundamental kinship among the soul's Powers is thus rendered both in metrical likeness and in amatory likeness, in both a shared poetic mode and a shared discursive one. The discursive and poetic likenings among the parts of the soul and between those parts and Wisdom adds sensory depth to the emergent contemplative dynamics of the play: viewers learn to construe amatory discourse and Wisdom's regular meter as feelable formal signs of the affinities and likenesses between the soul and God, as the forms of participation. These formal signs combine to create the baseline vernacular for the play, its normative formal embodiment of contemplation.

The figuring of likeness between the soul's parts and the Trinity becomes subtler, however, once the three Powers of the soul begin to distinguish themselves. In a particularly elegant rhythmical display of the lessons of likeness that the play contains, Wisdom says, "Thre myghtys every Cresten soull has,/ Wyche bethe applyede to the Trinyté" (*W*, 177–78), and the three Powers reply as follows:

> MYNDE: All thre here, lo, byfor your face:
> Mynde,
> WYLL: Wyll,
> Understondynge: And Undyrstondynge, we thre!
> (*W*, 179–82)

Thus, immediately after Wisdom and Mynde have agreed that the human soul is constructed as a likeness-in-miniature of the divine Trinity, the final metrical line of the stanza, "Mynde, Wyll, and Undyrstondyge, we thre" (broken into three typographical lines at 180–82), poetically performs the central paradox of the Trinity—namely, that three Persons can exist in one, as one, and at one time—through metrical completion. That is, since Mynde, Wyll, and Understondynge all share the final metrical line of the stanza, their performance of it embodies the paradoxical possibility of multiplicity in unity, and unity in multiplicity. Each of the Powers keeps his own identity clearly defined—Mynde says "Mynde," Wyll says "Wyll," and Understondynge says "Undyrstondynge"—yet the articulation of the whole line embodies the truth that, while not entirely coincident, the three Powers are formally unified into a single unit. The ability of the Powers to share this single line poetically hammers home Wisdom's and Mynde's thematic point: the Powers of the Soul are created in the likeness of the divine Trinity.

To this point, the primary formal and thematic drives in the play have been toward likeness—toward the creation of a multimodal, shared vernacular of contemplation among diegetic characters. Wisdom and Anima are joined by likeness, in terms of sartorial appearance, poetic rhythm, exegetical behavior, and a shared immersion in the amatory discourse of the Song of Songs; the parts of the soul, Mynde, Wyll, and Understondynge, are all similarly likened to each other and to Wisdom. What we will now begin to see, with the emergence of Lucifer, is the undoing of all these modes of likeness, through Lucifer's distorted vernacular. Indeed, Lucifer's lurching poetics, distortionary exegetical practices, and even his unstable costuming, by leveraging the play's established contemplative forms only to violate them, lay bare the precarious balance of power that exists in the human mental trinity, as well as that trinity's collective susceptibility to forms and ideas less salvific than those of Wisdom.

DANGEROUS LIKENESS: LUCIFER'S SEDUCTION OF THE POWERS OF THE SOUL

When Lucifer appears, he is clad "in a develys aray wythout, and within as a prowde galonte," as described in a stage direction at line 324, thus not only differing sartorially from the protagonists of the play but also, and perhaps more troublingly, differing from *himself*—his exterior manifestation and his interior one clash. For Lucifer, costuming becomes not a site of parity and compatibility but a site of difference and incompatibility. Visually, Lucifer creates a disorienting experience for an audience: viewing him, the audience sees him engage vaguely with the sartorial conventions of the play—he is, after all, a "galonte" figure—but in a manner that is decidedly distorted and debased, encased as it is in a diabolical outer coat. As we will shortly see, Lucifer's incoherence is contagious, his internal discord and differentiation spilling over into and corrupting the soul and its Powers.

Lucifer's sartorially staged incoherence is reinforced rhythmically in his versification. The long lines of the eight-line stanzas that the play has deployed up until this point essentially break in half: Lucifer's lines are short and choppy, few containing more than two beats. Meter, until now something streamlined, coherent, and harmonious in Wisdom's, Anima's, and the Powers' poetic forms, gets chopped up, made palpable as something nonunified, unstable, and inconstant. Lucifer's poetics break the smooth and balanced verse forms that the play had generated thus far. Further eroding the play's poetic vernacular, Lucifer's rhyme scheme switches from the balanced *ababbcbc* to the lurching and repetitious *aaabaaab*. Lucifer's opening lines follow:

> Out, harow, I rore!
> For envy I lore.
> My place to restore,
> God hath made man!
> All cum thei not thore,
> Woode and they wore,
> I shall tempte hem so sorre,
> For I am he that syn begane!
> (*W*, 325–32)

Having already established—both sartorially and metrically—that he is a being divided and disjointed, rather than unified and whole, Lucifer now reveals that his plan is specifically to pervert the soul of man and "to tempte man in [his] lyknes" (*W*, 373), since, as he well recognizes, "Of Gode, man ys the figure/ Hys symylytude, hys pyctoure" (*W*, 349–50). Where Lucifer sees man's likeness and unity with God, he seeks to promote dissimilarity and disunity; where he sees man's coherence and wholeness, he provokes dissolution and fracture; where he sees balance, he provokes imbalance. The play registers these provocations in its diabolically decayed verse form.

Lucifer is, as we already know, a chameleon, capable of presenting himself either as a gallant or as a horrible fiend, and that chameleonic ability manifests itself in his rhetoric as well. He adopts his most dazzling and confusing rhetorical strategy when he first encounters the Powers of the soul. His first gambit in their seduction is a bastardized presentation of familiar theological concepts through pirated biblical citations. Upon encountering the powers of the soul, rhythmically unified in their virtuous contemplation of the divine, Lucifer chastens them: "Ye fonnede fathers, founders of foly,/ *Vt quid hic statis tota die ociosi?*" (*W*, 393–94). Here, Lucifer pirates a Latin biblical injunction against idleness from Matthew 20 but then grossly misinterprets it as a critique of the contemplative life. By inserting this familiar biblical Latin into an inappropriate context, he grossly distorts the nature of what the Powers are doing and how they live their lives—casting their contemplative withdrawal from worldly things as a moral failure, a manifestation of sinful sloth. Nota bene, audience: Lucifer is dangerous because he knows the Bible well enough to pervert it, all the while making it sound familiar and plausible. Lucifer is dangerous because he knows how to activate familiar and orthodox texts, such as Matthew, but to sinful ends. Lucifer is never going to show up and sound like a devil, at least not in this play. Instead, he's going to sound like a knockoff Wisdom. Put otherwise, Lucifer is dangerous because he takes the baseline contemplative vernacular of the play, in which the audience has become fluent, and redeploys it disfluently, unfamiliarly. Indeed, in creating his decontextualized deployment of biblical Latin, Lucifer revisits and perverts Wisdom and Anima's initial code-switching strategies. For both Wisdom and Anima, quoting Latin biblical lines and glossing them righteously constituted an opportunity for creating a shared exegetical mode of being. For Lucifer, the inclusion of biblical Latin serves instead a mystifying purpose, allowing him to misinterpret and obfuscate the meaning of the Bible as he translates his Latin into English. Where Wisdom's code-switching promoted the perception of interlinguistic likeness and symmetry, Lucifer's promotes unlikeness and asymmetry; where Wisdom's promoted understanding and contemplation, Lucifer's will promote misunderstanding and the corruption of the Soul's "symylytude" to God. Thus, where Wisdom's code-switching bridged the eternal truths of the Latin Bible with the day-to-day world of spoken English, Lucifer's merely highlights the unbridgeable temporal gulf between the eternal Word of God and man's half-cocked temporal interpretations of it.

Although the Powers seem initially to respond stoutly to this critique—Mynde protests, in defense of the contemplative life, "He ys not ydyll that wyth Gode ys" (*W*, 398)—the play's versification indicates to us that Lucifer's damage to the Powers' cohesion and moral righteousness has already begun: the Powers have already started to participate in Luciferian form. Mynde's initial defense against Lucifer's corrupted and corrupting exegesis proceeds as follows:

> MYNDE: My mynde ys ever on Jhesu
> That enduyde us wyth vertu;
> Hys doctrine to sue
> Ever I purpose.
> (*W*, 381–84)

Despite his insistence on his continuing devotion to Christ, Mynde's rhyme scheme has shifted—and the same will soon be true for Understondynge and Wyll—from the balanced and elegant *ababbcbc* rhyme scheme of Wisdom to the lurching *aaabaaab* of Lucifer. Compounding this metrical corruption, there is an attrition in the length of Mynde's lines, so that they begin to be as choppy and percussive as Lucifer's. Through the overwriting of the Powers' initial poetic modes by Lucifer's, we begin to perceive in form the inevitable dissolution of the soul's mental trinity.

Sensing the soul's vulnerability, Lucifer's logic becomes yet more insidious. He falls back on seemingly orthodox logic that affirms the importance of maintaining attention to one's worldly obligations even when one seeks contemplative understanding. But Lucifer activates this mixed-life logic with a diabolical twist, though that twist is not immediately discernible. He begins by suggesting that "All thynge hat dew tymes—/ Prayer, fastynge, labour—al thes;/ Wan tyme ys not kept, that dede is amys./ The more pleynerly to your informacyon" (*W*, 401–5). So far, Lucifer's logic seems perfectly reasonable—echoing, as it does, Ecclesiastes 3:1–8.[8] By borrowing language from the Bible, Lucifer acts as if he provides this perspective as a spiritually salutary service to Mynde—truly for Mynde's "informacyon"—rather than as a self-interested bit of coercion. What the Powers of the soul fail to notice, of course, is that Lucifer is again decontextualizing biblical ideas, rather than situating them in their proper interpretive frameworks. Here, he uses Eclesiasties to urge the Powers toward corrupt and morally dangerous temporal pursuits—not at all the intention of the biblical passage he cites. He corrupts the eternal Word of the Bible by putting it into whatever context he chooses.

Lucifer's pattern of hijacking and decontextualizing biblical ideas continues when he tells the Powers that Martha, who represents the active life, was pleasing to God (*W*, 413). Mynde responds by recontextualizing this assertion, reminding Lucifer that, although it's true that the active Martha pleased God, the contemplative "Maria plesyde hymm moche more!" (*W*, 414). Thus, where Lucifer tries to tear theological ideas about contemplation from their narrative context, to unsettle their relation to the contemplative tradition, Mynde struggles to remain rooted in the context from which these ideas are derived. But Lucifer, more than ready for this protestation, performs his greatest act of rhetorical distortion—one based, again, on a decontextualized, disfluent deployment of a familiar biblical truth. He reminds the Powers of the soul that Christ himself lived the mixed life, and not the life of contemplation.

> And all hys lyff was informacyon
> And example to man!
> Sumtyme wyth synners he had conversacyon,
> Sumtyme with holy also comunycacyon,
> Sumtyme he laboryde, preyde; sumtyme tribulacyon.
> Thys was *vita mixta,* that Gode here began.
>
> (*W*, 423–28)

Here, Lucifer takes a fundamental tenet of the contemplative tradition—one examined and embodied by the writings of Julian of Norwich, William Langland, and others (namely, that the contemplative life is one lived by participating imaginatively in the life of Christ), but he mobilizes that tenet as a way of pushing the Powers of the soul away from contemplation and toward action.[9] He does so by deploying biblical discourse in a decontextualized way, pushing the Powers away from virtue and toward sin precisely by echoing familiar biblical knowledge while in fact distorting it. He makes hearers who are fluent in or at least familiar with biblical discourse suddenly struggle with disfluent, unfamiliar ideas based in distortionary misreadings of the Bible.

In making this argument—namely, that disfluency is the domain of the devil—I seem to part ways with the arguments I have made so far in this book, in which the experience of disfluency is contemplatively salutary because it is highly participatory, drawing readers and viewers into the dynamics of a contemplative work more deeply and enabling them experientially to access the truth of divine participation. But, as will become clearer in this chapter and will be a major focus of the next, one of the things we see in dramatic works of contemplation is their eagerness to create disfluent situations that draw the audience toward a contemplation not directly of God but of sin, dissipation, and wrongdoing as intermediate stages en route to the full and satisfying contemplation of God that is yet to come. In *Wisdom*, Lucifer must disfluently disassemble the salutary contemplative vernacular of Wisdom and Anima precisely so that the audience can feel, toward the end of the play, that salutary vernacular's recoalescence.

As his assault on contemplative theory and practice continues, it becomes more overtly distortionary: Lucifer exhorts the Powers of the soul to "be in the worlde! Use thyngys necesse!" (*W*, 442). The association of this urging to be in the world and use needful things with the urging to follow in the mixed-life footsteps of Jesus distorts canonical theories about the mixed life, in which living the mixed life entails breaking away from contemplation simply to serve others, not to indulge in one's own desires and to use the needful things of the world. Lucifer's garbled logic, like his vexed sartorial trappings and twisted verse, creates a distorted simulacrum of the real truth of Christian contemplation. Like all distortions, this one is dangerous precisely because it seems, on the surface, so like the truth.[10] Indeed, Lucifer's allusion to the Christic example of the active life succeeds in pulling the Powers into his clutches.

Having thus corrupted the Powers, Lucifer's discursive distortions quickly evolve into yet another kind of distortion. This new form of diabolical distortion depends for its efficacy on the audience's fluency in Middle English. This form is slang. Slang is noticeable for what it is—common, low-register usage, usage based on idiomatic speech rather than more regular forms of language production—when a person is fluent enough in a language to be struck by an introduction of slang as a marked code-switch. In the otherwise mostly high-flown language of the play, the introduction of slang is designed to be sonically striking and jarring to a listening audience. It arises in two ways. First, when the Powers have become corrupted, they begin to interlard their English with French slang ejaculations and references to Frenchness:

> UNDYRSTONGYNGE: We woll be fresche, and it hap *La plu joly!*
> Farwell, penance!
> MYNDE: To worschyppys I wyll my mynde aplye!
> Undyrstondynge: Myn undyrstondynge in worschyppys and glory!
> WYLLE: And I in lustys of lechery,
> As was sumtyme gyse of Fraunce!
>
> (*W*, 512–17)

Here, Frenchness and the French language are associated not just with being in the world but with being in the world in a corrupt, debased, and morally unstable way. This slippery slope of interlinguistic play—in which French is cast as a low, lusty argot—correlates with how the play allows language to become corrupted *intra*linguistically. The introduction of French accompanies a second slang: an informal, slangy, and poetically depraved English. In this depraved English, the lexicon that the Powers deploy, which has been formal and elevated until this point, following the diction of Wisdom, becomes idiomatic, colloquial, and debased. It overflows with profane language and the swearing of oaths. The tone of their speech, formerly balanced and calm, becomes reactive and excitable.

> LUCYFER: Geve to your body that ys nede,
> Ande ever be mery! Let revell route!
> MYNDE: Ya, ellys I beschrew my snoute!
> Understondynge: And yff I care, cache I the goute!
> WYLL: And yff I spare, the Devyll me spede!
> (*W*, 504–8)

> LUCYFER: Go your wey than, and do wysly. . . .
> MYNDE: I yt defye!
> . . .
> With "Wy, wyppe!
> Farewell," quod I, "the Devyll is uppe!"
> (*W*, 509, 511, 516–17)

In this passage, the audience experiences diabolically slangy form in the Powers themselves. Lucifer, through his broken, lurchy verse and his distorted language use, has remade the powers of the mind in his own image—exactly as he said he would. Through their immersion in Lucifer's disfluent vernacular, the Powers of the soul lose their previous mode of speech, informed by high biblical discourse and by Wisdom's steady, balanced poetics; in its place, they now speak with all the tics of a life lived decisively in the "active" world of temporal concerns. Where they spoke in an orderly, unified, elegant, balanced, and dignified way, they now speak in a manner that is excitable, fractured, worldly, colloquial, idiomatic, and temporal, in the sense of being concerned with debased worldly pursuits, such as lechery, merriment, and a focus on the needs of the body, rather than on the needs of the soul. As such, the Powers' new argot becomes a formal embodiment of the cloyingness of temporal concerns, their power over human consciousness, and their ability to make one forget oneself and one's connection with God. The soul's Powers, formerly possessed of high-style language, now seem capable of dwelling only in linguistic gutters.

In perverting their language and bringing it down from the heavens to the temporal muck of worldly concerns, Lucifer brings the Powers into an ever-greater likeness, as he has said he would, with himself and with his own twisted modes of thought, speech, and behavior. Quickly, the Powers become corrupters of the law, they become seducers, and they become hoarders of wealth:

> MYNDE: Wronge ys born upe boldly,
> Thow all the worlde know yt opynly;
> Mayntnance ys now so mighty,
> Ande all is for mede!
> UNDYRSTONDYNGE: The lawe ys so coloryde falsly
> By sleyttys and by perjury,
> Brybys be so gredy,
> That to the pore trouth is take ryght non hede!
>
> WYLL: Wo gett or loose, ye be ay wynnande!
> Mayntnance and perjury now stande:
> Thei wer never so moche reynande
> Seth Gode was bore!
> MYNDE: Ande lechery was never more usande
> Of lernynde and lewyde in this lande!
> UNDYRSTONDYNGE: So we thre be now in hande!
> WYLL: Ya, and most usyde everywere!
> (*W*, 668–83)

The Powers of the soul are united not in virtue, but in dissipation, not in their likeness to God, but in their likeness to Lucifer. The Powers are now so preoccupied with temporal concerns that they can no longer access the truth of their essential, inborn likeness to the eternal God.

The eventual consequence of all this temporal worldliness is to tear the Powers of the soul away not only from God but also from one another. Indeed, the trinitarian unity of spirit that we saw early in the play among the Powers begins rapidly to unravel when Lucifer introduces his temporal temptations. This process of unravelling is signaled to the audience first when Mynde claims that he feels a "synglere solace" (*W*, 573). The TEAMS edition glosses this phrase as "particular pleasures," but the word choice of "synglere" conveys to the audience that Mynde is now no longer acting as an agent of good for the soul, in concert with Wyll and Understondynge, and also with God, but now as a free and pointedly individual agent. He acts now only for his own individual, separate, and isolated benefit and pleasure. This collapsing into separateness and isolation is part of how the play constructs its vision of the sinful self, the self estranged from God, from its compatriots, and from virtue.

Registering this emergent spiritual separateness sonically, the parts of the soul begin to sing a song together—a three-part motet, comprised of a tenor, a middle, and a treble, and they announce it as such:

> MYNDE: A tenour to you bothe I brynge.
> UNDYRSTONDYNGE: And I a mene for ony kynge!
> WYLL: And but a trebull I outwrynge,
> The Devell hym spede that myrth exyled!
> (*W*, 616–19)

Formerly united in praising Wisdom and able even to share a single metrical line among them, the Powers of the soul are now fractured into different parts—literally, into three different musical parts.[11] Formerly steeped in a formal, balanced, and unified solemnity, the Powers are now engaged in the devil's divisive "myrth." As the Powers descend into diabolical behaviors, they shift from oneness with each other to difference from each other.[12]

Kinetically underscoring this newfound sonic separateness and singularity of each part of the soul, the play enacts a series of dances, in which six mute dancers emerge with each of the Powers of the soul. Mynde is now accompanied in his revels by Indignation, Stubbornness, Malice, Discord, Haste, and Vengeance; Undyrstondynge is joined by Wrong, Trickery, Duplicity, Falseness, Plunder, and Deceit; Wyll is joined by Wrecklessness, Idleness, Surfeit, Greed, Adultery, and Mistress.[13] Thus, the three Powers of the soul have been subdivided and tarred with the brush of worldliness and temporality. None is a pure agent of the love of God anymore; instead, each has minions, servants, and submanifestations. What had been a staging of contemplative unity has become a staging of separateness and dissimilarity. With all twenty-one actors on stage, in what must have been a cacophonous and chaotic scene of mayhem, a dance begins.

Although we do not know what exactly the dance looked like, there is something decisive we can say about the philosophical and theological impact that the introduction of any group dance would have had in this particular play. As scholars of dance and music history have shown, group dances like *caroles* and other round dances in the fourteenth century had become something of a craze, which resulted in stout condemnation of this kind of dancing by clergy.[14] Clerics condemn participation in round dances as diabolical, motion in the direct and unabashed service of the devil.[15] The reasons for the clerical condemnation of this dance craze were simple: caroles are round dances, performed in mixed-gender groups, which require that people touch each other and respond to each other's calls.[16] They are seen, thus, as kinetic conduits for debauchery. Unlike processional movement, which is linear, orderly, and regulated by sacred song, caroles are irregular, circular, high-contact, and governed by contemporary secular music.[17] These are the kinds of dance that the plays would stage: the stage directions note that, with these splinterings off from the Powers, a bagpiper and a minstrel appear on the stage, suggesting further that some sort of carole dance, and certainly some sort of nonsacred dance, is taking place (*W*, stage direction after 724).[18] The goal of the play's staged dance, then, is to bring its characters closer to one another, in a chaotic, repetitious, circular way, not to bring them closer to approach God.[19] Indeed, as Mynde puts it, "Thys ys the Devllys dance!" (*W*, 699). The fact that caroles are regularly held in public squares and plateas—the very locations that likely host morality dramas as well—would make the play's enacted dance eerily resonant with viewers' memories of having danced in that very place themselves.[20] Through the music and dance, viewers are sonically and kinetically urged to feel implicated in the diablerie on stage. Through the music and dance onstage, the play is able to go one step further than prose or poetic works of participatory contemplation could go, literally getting into the ears of its audience, getting into their bodies, making them participate in diablerie by being sonically penetrated by it.

As the diabolical dance scene concludes, the Powers compete with one another to establish who is the most important and powerful, since they are no longer working for the shared goal of being close to God.

> MYNDE: Ye may not endure wythout my meyntenance.
> UNDYRSTONDYNGE: That ys bought wyth a brybe of our substance.
> WYLL: Whow, breydest thou us of thin acqueyntance?
> I sett thee at nought!
> MYNDE: On that worde I woll tak vengeaunce!
> Wer vycys be gederyde, ever ys sum myschaunce.
> Hurle hens thes harlottys! Here gyse ys of Fraunce.
> They shall abey bytterly, by hym that all wrought!
>
> (*W*, 760–67)

At this point, all the extraneous dancers leave the stage, and the Powers of the soul begin to assault each other verbally—insulting each other and threatening each other with lawsuits and false imprisonment. From unity, harmony, and oneness in their likeness to Wisdom, the Powers have utterly disintegrated into chaos and cacophony. Where they once shared a sartorial, discursive, and poetic habit with Wisdom's orderly and eternal mode of being, they now share a habit with Lucifer and his chaotic, changeful, and temporal mode of being. Through dramatic performance, *Wisdom* has enacted the perilousness of the soul's likeness to the divine and its susceptibility to diabolical disintegration into a broken and unredeemed world—a place of cacophony, of physical and verbal debasement, and of sin.

SALVIFIC LIKENESS: THE SOUL, THE POWERS, WISDOM, AND THE SOCIAL WORLD

Just in time to save the Powers of the soul onstage, Wisdom reemerges. With him returns the discursive, rhetorical, and metrical order to which the play initially habituated its audience. The play's original *ababbcbc* rhyme scheme returns; the inundation of colloquialism ebbs from the play; and the explicit discourse of likeness to God returns with added vehemence. Wisdom chastens the Powers of the soul for their misconduct, calling out, "O thou Mynde, remembyr thee!" (*W*, 872) To this paronomastic injunction—meaning at once "recall your true nature" and "re-member yourself," as in "put yourself back together"—each of the Powers responds by quickly falling back on the ideas of likeness and participation in God that had animated the beginning of the play. Mynde says, "I se how I have defoulyde the noble kynde/ That was lyke to thee by intellygens" (*W*, 926–27). To this nudging by Mynde, Undyrstondynge replies, "By you, Mynde, I have very knowenge/ That grettly God we have offendyde . . . Therfor to hym let us resort" (*W*, 932–33, 937). Finally, Wyll announces, "I wyll retorne to Gode and new begynne/ Ande in hym gronde my wyll stable" (*W*, 942–43). In their newly formalized discourse, their regular versification, and their chaste tone, the Powers demonstrate that they have begun to cast out the Luciferian likeness they had allowed to invade them and that they have cast out the temporal concerns and temporal discourse he brought with him. With those castings out, the play's initial formal norms and modes, its fluent vernacular, based on likeness with Wisdom, come surging back.

Poetically anchoring this return to the discourse of stability and divine likeness is perhaps the high point of rhythmical invention in the play. The stanza that follows Wisdom's return is the only stanza in the play that contains twelve lines. Of those twelve, four are spoken by Mynde, four by Undyrstondynge, and four by Wyll, so that the total number of lines is evenly balanced among them. Moreover, Wisdom's *ababbcbc* rhyme scheme returns, though with a superadded quatrain, *cdcd*, at the end.

> MYNDE: To my mynde yt cummyth from farre
> That doutles man shall dey!

> Ande thes weys we go, we erre.
> Undyrstondynge, wat do ye sey?
> UNDYRSTONDYNGE: I sey, man, holde forthe thi wey!
> The lyff we lede ys sekyr ynowe.
> I wyll no undyrstondynge shall lett my pley.
> Wyll, frende, how seyst thou?
> WYLL: I wyll not thynke theron, to Gode a vowe!
> We be yit but tender of age.
> Schulde we leve this lyve? Ya whowe?
> We may amende wen we be sage.
>
> (*W*, 880–91)

Although the Powers are not yet fully reunified in their thinking—Undyrstondynge and Wyll both at this point think Mynde's newfound moral concerns are unnecessary—they are already reunified in their poetic form. In this one twelve-line stanza, we have another figuration of the mental trinity in poetic form: each of the Powers utters four of the twelve lines, so that each Power is responsible for exactly a third of the whole. Together, the three quatrains function as a unified totality, the three pieces joined together by the two inset couplets—*bb* between Mynde and Understondynge and *cc* between Understondynge and Wyll—which, in themselves, highlight the likeness and connectedness between the parts of the soul that share them. The twelve-line stanza—unified by couplets, but constituted by three discernible quatrains—metrically mimics the Trinitarian logic of Augustinian psychology. Their Trinitarian reunification in poetic form has a spillover effect into their interactional style. Indeed, the formal repairing of the verse produces the correlative effect of making each of them value and solicit the opinions of each of the others: Mynde asks Undyrstondynge what he thinks and Undyrstondynge asks Wyll what he thinks. The discord and hostility among the Powers has already been partially healed, simply by the return of Wisdom and his likeness-producing verse form, even though the latter two Powers are still attracted to sin as a concept.

Realizing the depth of Undyrstondynge's and Wyll's corruption, Wisdom turns from rhythmical aids to visual ones: he reintroduces Anima (who has been offstage during most of the play) to the Powers, and he shows sartorially how she is now, because of the Powers' failures, entirely degraded. According to the stage direction after line 902, Anima "apperythe in the most horrybull wyse, foulere than a fende." Wisdom chastens the powers for allowing Anima to be so defouled by telling them, "As many dedly synnys as ye have usyde,/ So many devyllys in your soule be./ Beholde wat ys therin reclusyde!" (*W*, 908–10). Leveraging the participatory and performative power of the dramatic form to enact this point kinetically, the stage direction at line 912 indicates that at this moment, "six small boys in the lyknes of devyllys" run out from under the skirt of Anima, in a horrific enactment of the chaotic, fractured, spatiotemporally disunified sinful soul, the soul who has been too long aligned with Lucifer. Moreover, that each part of the soul is subdivided into seven—six emergent devilkins and the part of the soul itself—signals numerically the soul's having fallen into the seven deadly sins. This kinetic demonstration of the soul's dissolution and dire immersion in the sins of the temporal world is, at last, enough to call both Understondynge and Wyll back from the brink of sin and to reunite them in their intention to return to the contemplation of God. As with the dancing of the Powers' minions, the insistence on temporality via the movement of bodies through space drives home the point that, for this play, living too much in the temporal world is a danger to contemplative understanding and an undermining of the soul's likeness to God.

But there *is* a way of living in the world that the play codes—both formally and theologically—as contemplative and salvific. The lexical, rhythmical, visual, and kinetic modes of disunity are eventually redeemed as sacred song—indeed, as liturgy. As soon as the Powers have reunited in their intention to return to God, all the demons recede from the stage (as indicated in the stage direction at line 977), and the Soul begins to sing Passion Week songs "in the most lamentabull wyse, wyth drawte notys" (according to the stage direction at line 995). In this singing of the Passion Week songs, which was almost certainly performed as plainsong,[21] the play reclaims music from the domain of mirth, pleasure, and temporal dissipation that it has occupied in the play until this point—during the scenes when the corrupted Powers caroused with their henchmen—and recasts music instead as somber and unifying meditation on the Passion. Formally, the play uses musical unity to signal moral unity. In so doing, the play finally resituates its players in sobriety, somberness, and shared devotion to Christ. It resituates them in Wisdom's original vernacular. Now that Wisdom has returned and the breaches among the Powers of the soul have healed, a new music can ring out, a music both somber and devotional, a music of one voice, a music utterly devoid of slang or low style, articulating the need for sorrowful penance and the mindfulness of Christ's self-sacrifice for all mankind. Wisdom, Anima, and the Powers sing about breaches of faith and the difficulty of coming to consolation: "Magna velud contricio, contricio tua: quis consoletur tui? Plorans ploravit in nocte, et lacrime ejus in maxillis ejus" (*W*, 998).[22] With this monovocal singing of the Passion lamentation, the Powers of the soul are once again unified with each other through the supervening order of liturgical observance; they are no longer the cacophonous, slangy noisemakers they had been during the reign of Lucifer.

Indeed, the singing of the music of the Passion seems actually to redeem time and space, and to do so by reminding the Powers and the audience that the everyday here and now of medieval England is coterminous with the salvation history of Christ's Passion. Concomitant with this salvific music, ordered motion returns to the play as well: the Powers, together with Anima and Wisdom, enact a processional[23]—the very kind of linear, regular, and regulated motion that the spastic dancing of the corrupted Powers had undone.[24] In their processional movement off the stage, the Powers, Anima, and Wisdom physically enact a restoration and reformation of divine order, likeness, and similitude in the play: the Powers literally follow in the footsteps of Wisdom. Thus, whereas singing cacophonous music and doing chaotic dance, earlier on, merely reinforced the Powers' descents into colloquialism and corruption, here, the singing of the archetypical Christian anthem has the opposite effect, reinforcing the ongoing contemplative truth that Christ's self-sacrifice is a constantly self-reenacting, suptratemporal reality, which offers comfort and spiritual cohesion to all who sing or hear it and who follow in the footsteps of Christ, who is Wisdom. The play drags us through the chaos and disorder of a temporal life precisely in order to make the participation in danced, sung, and spoken contemplation all the sweeter in the end. This dynamic of sin as a prelude to or precondition of higher eventual contemplative understanding is one we will see played out more fully in *Mankind*.

CONTAGIOUS LIKENESS: ANIMA AND AUDIENCE

If *Wisdom* were, at bottom, a play defending the contemplative life and critiquing the active life, as many scholars have contended,[25] it would end at this point, with a radical rejection of the temporal concerns and distortions that Lucifer had brought and with an affirmation of contemplative Christian devotion. But it does not end. Instead, we immediately encounter a nine-stanza monologue delivered by Wisdom on the points of virtue. Most of these points make reference to social justice, social virtue, labor, charity, and other components of the active life. The first point of virtue argues for generously distributing one's wealth to those in need (*W*, 998–1005). In the third point, Wisdom tells us that we please God better when we suffer patiently a word of reproof from a neighbor than when we scourge ourselves with rods;

thus, the third point advocates the deliberate maintaining of social peace (an active-life virtue) and valorizes it more highly than the mortification of the body (a contemplative behavior). The fifth urges pity and compassion on one's neighbor who is "seke and nedy" (*W*, 1031) and insists that this is more valuable to God than if one were to fast for forty years: "Lo, pyte God plesyth grettly,/ Ande yt ys a vertu soveren, as clerkys rede" (*W*, 1036–37). Sixth, we are told to restrain our tongues from ill speech about other people; again, this virtue points toward the cohesion and health of the social world as a primary drive. The seventh mandates that we not stir our neighbors to evil; this refusal to corrupt other people, we are told, pleases God more than a thousand lashings of the body with thorny branches. Thus, once again, the life of social virtue is valued more highly than the life of highly ascetic and deeply individual contemplation. The passage culminates with the urging, "Lo, Gode ys plesyde more wyth the dedys of charyte/ Than all the peynys man may suffer iwys" (*W*, 1063–64). Thus, the ultimate virtue to which Wisdom urges the soul is charity, which seems to encompass, at once, contemplative love of God and active love of one's neighbors. Contemplation and love of God, Wisdom hereby suggests, are inseparable from the active life of loving one's neighbors as oneself. Anima and her parts, newly made resonant with Wisdom through the singing of the Passion song and the united procession, it seems, must now learn to resonate with their fellow Christians. They must learn to resonate with and as a community.[26] As they are in *Piers Plowman*, in *Wisdom*, the social world and the world of contemplative likeness to God are, in the end, one world.[27]

Formally underscoring this idea about the dual nature of charity as simultaneously and inextricably both contemplative and active, at this point Anima and the five senses reappear, along with the Powers of the soul. According to the stage direction at line 1065, all are dressed in the same costumes, and all sing the same song; the shared visual and musical language among them has been redeemed. Thus, they perform both visually and aurally a demonstration of collective unity, oneness, and solidarity, after a long while of dissipation, disintegration, and asynchrony. Contemplation, according to *Wisdom*, is about collectivity, togetherness, and socialization, not just solitary devotion to God.[28] Indeed, the play's final stanza, spoken by Wisdom, asserts just that:

> Ande so to ende wyth perfeccyon,
> That the doctrine of Wysdom we may sew:
> *Sapiencia Patris*, gruant that for hys passyon!
> (*W*, 1163–65)

The crucial word here is the first person plural pronoun, "we." Through it, the play signals decisively to its audience that the actions depicted in the play have not been abstract meditations on the problem of contemplation but instead have performed some part of the work of contemplation itself and have solicited and attained the contemplative participation of the audience through its staging and performance. Through its staging, initially, of the practices of Wisdom and later of the practices of Lucifer, the play awakens its audience's sensitivity to the dynamics of contemplation that would be the eventual goal of the play; it activates the sensitivity to Wisdom's ultimate return and restoration of the sounds of somber, liturgical contemplation of the likeness between the soul and Christ. When Wisdom returns and restores contemplative balance to the play, reminding viewers and players alike that they well and truly do participate in Christ, the play of *Wisdom* becomes a self-consciously participatory performance of contemplation, a staged and participatory exploration, in particular, of how to understand and cultivate one's own likeness to Jesus. But, like *Piers Plowman*, the play insists that the social world is the final arena in which the conflicts of the soul play out,[29] so that true contemplatives must define their likeness to Christ by their ability to serve and care for the larger Christian community.

This reading begs the question of audience. In part because of its intertextuality, W. A. Davenport suggests that the play could have been written for an aristocratic house, or even a university setting.[30] Milla Cozart Riggio comes down more decisively on the side of an aristocratic household as the play's intended audience.[31] By contrast, Gail McMurray Gibson inclines toward a more monastic setting.[32] What I hope is borne out by my reading is that the reason for these long-standing arguments about audience is that the play is designed to dwell in the ambiguous region between the Good Life of the active layperson and the Good Life of the contemplative monk—indeed, it is designed to have immediate application to both types of audience and to recognize the high probability of overlap between those two types of audience. In *Wisdom*, virtuous participation in the real social world is crucial to the state of the contemplative soul, whether that contemplative is a monk or a layperson.[33] The play's ambiguity about its own audience is thus pointed, underlining the play's larger investment in the centrality of the active life to the well-lived contemplative life.[34]

Indeed, the poem's catholic conception of its audience—its sense that *all* Christians are implicated all together in the struggle for dominance between Lucifer and Wisdom—is something that the play itself repeatedly stages by reminding its viewers of its own central conceit: it is a psychomachia, showing the soul at war internally. As such, it is not simply a made-up play about abstract or fictitious characters living in a faraway land and distant time, nor is it a play with specific relevance only to certain members of the social world. Quite the contrary, *Wisdom* is an enactment of the battle between Jesus Christ (Wisdom) and Lucifer for the control of the human soul that is going on at all times, in all places, and in all people. The viewers of the play, then, must be reminded—and frequently—not to allow themselves to witness the action passively but to feel how the war they witness among the Powers and the war between Wisdom, Anima, and Lucifer are quite literally always already going on inside themselves, both as individuals and as a collectivity. Put otherwise, the audience members, in watching the play, must realize that they are looking inward toward the contents of their own souls, as well as out and onto the stage; they must realize that they are looking at the present moment of their own lives, even as they look at the abstract zone in which the three powers of the mind interact. Witnessing the onstage drama makes the audience aware of the dangers they face when they fail to cultivate their own likeness to Christ and the rewards that follow if they do cultivate that likeness.

The play produces this awareness not only, as I previously suggested, by including music and dance as inducements to the audience's sonic and rhythmical participation in the drama but also by breaking the fourth wall that separates players from audience.[35] Now, to assert that there is a fourth wall in the first place in a medieval drama is not unproblematic: about *Wisdom* itself, Milla Cozart Riggio has asserted that "such a barrier does not essentially exist."[36] While it is true that there is far more porosity between the audience and the players of medieval drama than there is between players and audiences in some more modern periods, the assertion that "such a barrier does not essentially exist" is overstated, and it occludes some of the most powerful formal and sensory effects of morality drama as a mode. Albeit there is "no inherent, independent stage for acting,"[37] medieval dramas—cycle dramas and moralities alike—do nevertheless for long stretches of time energize the idea that the action on the stage is somehow distinct from the rest of the world, although they do so often precisely to rupture that created distinction for theological reasons. That rupturing function is, in fact, critical to the participatory efficacy of this contemplative play in particular: if audience members truly and consistently felt part of the action—if they felt as if there were no separation of them from the action—there would be no shock when Lucifer interacted with them, or when any other character did. But that shock is central to the psychological and contemplative dynamics of the play, as I will elaborate shortly. It is true, then, that the fourth wall is generally more porous in medieval plays than in later ones, and that it is not physically reified by architectural structures, but that does not mean it does not exist—simply that its existence serves to highlight its own createdness, its perforability, and the recurrent vulnerability of the audience to whatever action is going on before them.[38]

The play stages that vulnerability of the audience to Lucifer's machinations when Lucifer, having just seduced the onstage Powers, selects a "schrewede boy" from the audience and carries him, crying, off into the distance (as described in stage direction at line 549).[39] In this carrying off, all members of the audience are again made to feel vulnerable to Lucifer's machinations, and in two ways. First, of course, they are made to realize, through their identification with the boy simply as another member of the audience, that Lucifer can snatch people up, whenever he wishes. But second, they are made to feel vulnerable because they are urged to feel complicit in Lucifer's wickedness. Since "schrewede" in Middle English denotes wickedness, evil, depravity, malice, poor behavior, or unruliness, we must imagine the scene as one in which a boy in the audience, probably a plant from the group of actors, behaves in an obnoxious, distracting manner. Very likely, the audience members around the boy, who is doubtless whining, fidgeting, and generally being disruptive, would become increasingly annoyed with him during the staged action. They, in all likelihood, would wish the "schrewede" boy to disappear. At that very moment, of course, when Lucifer whisks him away, the annoyed and somewhat relieved audience is made to feel complicit in Lucifer's action, as though they invited him to run off with the child. In this moment, then, the dramaturgy of the scene insists that the psychomachic world of the stage is coterminous with the world of the viewers: as participants in the world of time and space, everyone is equally subject to the temptations and powers of Lucifer, not just the actors. In this moment, Lucifer reminds the audience that they participate in the drama of the play not just as representational theater but as a dramatic literalization of an ongoing spiritual reality: the powers of the mind are not, that is, simply onstage; they are within all of us, all the time. We are all, always, interacting at dangerous proximities with Lucifer, always inviting him to participate in our lives in ways we can neither predict nor control. Lucifer's assault on the boy is a figure for the assault on all members of the audience by sinful temptation that goes on every day. Through this assault the play forces viewers to recognize that they truly—not just theatrically—do participate in the drama of this narrative. Viewers are reminded that the action depicted onstage is not separate from the real world of the audience but is instead a hyperreal, distilled figuration of it, in which the struggle that exists within the soul of every viewer—to turn away from temporal diablerie and toward Godly virtue—is enacted.

Further activating the audience's awareness that it is implicated in this cacophonous disintegration of the immortal soul into temporality, fracture, and discord, the actors who play the Powers also rupture the fourth wall, though in subtler ways than Lucifer does. First, Wyll swears "by Sent Audre of Ely" that he will be seen as noble (*W*, 831). In referring to this saint—the patron saint of the cathedral at Ely—the play likely was making a local reference; indeed, it has been suggested that the play may well have been crafted and performed near Bury St. Edmunds.[40] Thus, the reference to the patron saint of Ely would strike a chord with the audience as a reminder that they—their own immediate, local concerns, both as individuals and as a community—are directly implicated in the action of the play.[41] Anchoring the immediacy of the play yet more securely, two lines later, Wyll refers to his "cosyn Jenet N" (*W*, 833). This reference to a "Jenet" could simply be a recognizably common English name, a quotidian name that anyone in the audience would be likely to know someone by; when the audience hears this name, they would experience the recognition that this "Jenet" is not simply a figure in the play but also a generalized representation of any woman in their own lives. A second interpretive possibility is that "Jenet N" might be a textual placeholder and that the actors in the play, during real performances, might indeed substitute in a name of someone well known in the household or town in which the play was then being performed. In so doing, the plays would create the shiver of recognition that the world of the stage and the world of the audience overlap in uncomfortable and uncanny ways. Whether referring to a common woman's name or to a specific woman in the audience, the shout-out to "Jenet N" would make the audience uncomfortable by driving home the point that the personified figures Wyll, Mynde, and Understondynge are *not* simply abstractions, but instead embedded members of an interconnected and vulnerable community.

The collective vulnerability of the community gains specificity soon thereafter, when Wyll, who has become a force of unchecked sexual desire in the play, says of this poor Jenet that she "mornyth wyth a chorle" (*W*, 834), meaning that she is in an unfortunate marriage. Wyll goes on to say that he plays with her sexually "wen [he] lyst rave" (*W*, 836); this Jenet, then, stands accused of committing adultery with Wyll before the entire community of viewers. But *Wisdom* does not stop there: Jenet's churlish husband scorns and slanders her for her sexual misconduct (*W*, 837), and Wyll wishes to know how he might unjustly punish this husband legally, to exact revenge for his sexual meddling. Mynde responds to Wyll's plea for counsel, vowing to "rebuk [the husband] thus so dyspytuusly/ That of hys lyff he shall wery/ And quak for very fere" (*W*, 841–43). So our Jenet is slandered by Wyll to the audience, named as an adulteress, and *then* implicated in a collusive scheme to terrorize and punish her own husband. The depraved Powers of the soul, then, in the particular contents of their call to "Jenet N," remind the audience of multiple kinds of vulnerabilities that an unchecked, depraved Mynde and Wyll can unleash on a community. Not only can they corrupt a Jenet, but they can bring down her husband with her; a depraved Mynde and Wyll endanger not just the individual, but the relational, intersubjective fabric of society.

In staging the audience's vulnerability, both as individuals and as a community—through the kidnapping of the "schrewede" boy and the calling out of poor Jenet—to sin and to Lucifer, *Wisdom* also makes quite plain why and how drama can be a more directly, concretely, interpersonally, and physically participatory mode of staging contemplation than could the prose and poetic works I examined in the first half of this book. The kidnapping and calling out make palpable to everyone assembled that no one is safe from Lucifer, that anyone can be whisked away or called out and shamed by him at any time. Indeed, so directly participatory is *Wisdom*'s staging of audience vulnerability to sin and temptation that it enacts that contemplation nearly fully. The contemplation it performs so fully, though, is not its main and salvific contemplation on man's likeness to God; instead, it is a secondary contemplation on man's susceptibility to sin, to becoming all too much like Lucifer. In that emphasis on staging sin, *Wisdom* anticipates what I will turn to focus on in my analyses of *Mankind*.

CONTEMPLATIVE VERNACULARITY

For its jointly individual and communal efficacy in staging contemplation both of the divine and of our susceptibility to Lucifer, the play's participatory dynamics depend not only on the dramatic possibilities inherent in staging but also on the sensory experience of hearing and participating in one's own native language. *Wisdom* relies on Middle English through its deployment of the proper names of Ely and Jenet, as well as through Lucifer's and the Powers' jarring deployment of slang and embedded lines of French. The references to Ely and Jenet usher into the play a particular form of vernacularity, which has to do with localness: audience members would hear the reference to Ely and the shout-out to Jenet and recognize that those words constitute an immediate, concrete frame of reference for the play. Place-names and proper names are familiar lexemes that necessarily strike a native speaker as salient, marked, different from what lies around them in the normative discourses of the play. They are, borrowing from Nicholas Love and *Piers Plowman*, "kyndely" words that bring about "kyndely" modes of knowing—modes that are immediate, physical, and reflexive. They constitute swerves into the real temporal world from the high-flown, abstract reaches of much of the rest of the play.

The play's exploitation of a native English speaker's sensitivity to colloquialism, to slang, and to the introduction of French as an alien tongue enables another sensory dynamic, one that reinforces the play's broadest contemplative goals. By introducing low-style speech, utterly incongruous with the high-style speech that the play had established as its initial norm, the play creates a comedic frisson of disfluency—a verbal experience that has its effect precisely in gumming up normative expectations about language and discourse. That frisson would allow all the members of a viewing audience to laugh together, in registering the introduction of slang and French as linguistic correlatives for the moral decay the Powers undergo. The exploitation, then, of a native-English sensitivity to the boundaries of a particular language—native speakers *know* when they are hearing code-switching—produces a sudden awareness not only of collective in-group participation but also of a sharp change in tone, from the heavy sobriety of much of the play to mirth, joviality, levity, and fun. That shift from sobriety to mirth is underpinned by the dramatic form of the work: in seeing one's friends, neighbors, and fellow clergy around oneself burst into laughter, one's own laughter would both be urged forth and also implicitly legitimized, so that the collective experience of laughing at the Luciferian slang and Luciferian French would reinforce one's sense of being part of an in-group, reminding all present that the words of contemplation must not be argot and helping everyone feel the lowness and dangerousness of the failure to cultivate one's own likeness both to God and to one's fellow (English) contemplatives.

At the same time, a surprised-by-sin dynamic is immediately at work when the audience members share their laughter at the sudden explosion of slang and code-switching that is, in effect, the discourse of the devil.[42] As the audience bursts into laughter at the sight and sound of these diabolically debauched mental faculties, they sensibly experience how diabolical frolicking in these low and alternative tongues is pleasurable, enjoyable, titillating, and seductive. From the standpoint of virtue, we are not supposed to chuckle along with Lucifer; we are supposed to fear him, as we learned with the thieving of the "schrewede" child. And yet the play urges viewers to laugh at the Powers of the soul and, therefore, to laugh along *with* Lucifer. Thereby, the play introduces that uncomfortable tension of recognizing sin and yet gravitating toward it through its exploitation of slang vernacularity. In that exploitation, hearers are reminded not only that they always already participate in the very language that Lucifer drags the powers of the soul down into, but also that they enjoy it. The play's disfluent frissons are pleasurable, and that pleasure embodies the dangerousness of sin.

Thus, through the contemplative power of shared laughter, once again, the players remind the audience that these abstractions—the Powers of the soul—have intimate connections with the immediate temporal world of quotidian medieval England. This is a play in which we all participate, every day, not only as individuals but also as a community. When we witness and laugh at the corruption of the Powers' likenesses to God, we feel a reflex of that corruption within our worldly, temporal, vulnerable selves and our worldly, temporal, vulnerable community. Through their comedic staging and rupturing of the fourth wall, the scenes of the play are designed to drive home the perilous coterminousness of the time of the soul-on-stage and the souls in the audience.

In its enactment of the inextricability of the social world from the world of contemplation, the play of *Wisdom* makes oblique contact with the contemplative tradition that *Piers Plowman* manifests, if not immediately with the poem itself. Like *Piers*, *Wisdom* insists on the inseparability of the active life from the contemplative. Like *Piers*, *Wisdom* is pervasively concerned to remind its audience members that they are not passive witnesses to the action of the work but instead are actively implicated in it at every possible moment. Like *Piers*, *Wisdom* avails itself of literary language and literary style to make sense-perceptible the supervening truth of man's likeness to Jesus. But, whereas *Piers* is designed as an exploration of the power of written narrative to produce contemplative understanding, *Wisdom* is somewhat less concerned with narrative per se and significantly more concerned with how the staging and performance of vernacular temptation might stage and indeed perform the work of contemplation for a diverse group of viewers. For the *Wisdom*-playwright, the dramatic form is the ideal arena in which to explore how contemplation, though often conceptualized as a solitary practice, is actually inevitably and pervasively shared among all participants in a Christian community. Dramatic form becomes that ideal arena through its capacity to create ritual participation in virtue through sensory experience.

But it is also an arena within which to explore the role of laughter, the role that shared pleasure can take in helping viewers sense the chaos of sin. In my next chapter, I will move deeper into an exploration of how the dramatic form works to make sin and the pleasures of laughing at and even indulging in sin legitimate and efficacious avenues toward contemplative participation in Middle English.

CHAPTER SIX

Laughing Our Way toward God; or, Dramatic Comedy and Vernacular Contemplation

Mankind is the least obviously "contemplative" work taken up in this book. Indeed, although it is one of the most widely taught plays of the medieval dramatic canon, it is the play that has received the least attention for the seriousness of its theological and contemplative workings—undoubtedly because those workings are often rather uncomfortably smeared over with fecal matter.[1] But the defecatory action of the play is inextricable from its staging of participatory contemplation.[2] In its scatology and in its comedy more broadly, *Mankind* capitalizes on the same thing as do the N-Town depiction of Joseph amid its *Mary* plays and *Wisdom*'s depiction of the fall of the Powers of the Soul: the contemplative power of laughter. Through laughter, *Mankind* enacts its participatory contemplation on the seductions of sin in a manner far more risqué, profane, and potentially politically reformist than any of the other works I have examined so far. Through the rowdy, bawdy, raunchy, and excremental *Mankind*, we will get deeper into what makes comedy such a powerful tool for participatory contemplation and how that comedic contemplation plays out on the stages of late medieval England.

In its heavy reliance on gross, physical comedy, this play offers up an important corrective to how we, as modern scholars, understand the literature and cultural reality of contemplation, in part by showing at a greater level of granularity and grittiness contemplation's compatibility with and even reliance on comedy. Comedy is the tool by which the play draws audience members into a participatory contemplation not on God or Jesus per se, but instead on their own sinfulness. For *Mankind*, the darkness of sin will not be shown as something to conquer, revile, and reject without contemplation; instead, the state of extreme and excremental sin in this play is shown to be a necessary part of the process of contemplative arrival. The audience's comedic contemplative participation in sin functions as a necessary initial phase in the devout contemplation of the true nature of the soul its participation in God's mercy.[3]

As did the laughter in *Wisdom* and the Joseph play, the laughter that this play invites as a cornerstone of its dramatic contemplations depends heavily on vernacularity. Like *Wisdom* and the Joseph play, *Mankind* relies on English's familiarity, quotidianness, and malleability for its comedic efficacy. English, by virtue of its fluent "kyndeliness," also has the capacity to behave in the most disfluent and unkindly of ways—sometimes on its own, and sometimes when put into frictive contact with Latin. As will become clear, English's capacity to stage unkindly experience facilitates the play's participatory contemplation of sin.

Mankind makes explicit its investment in the idea of participation very early on. In its second stanza, Mercy addresses the audience, adopting an emcee role analogous to what we saw Contemplacio perform in the N-Town *Mary* plays. In *Mankind*, Mercy reminds his audience that "mankynde was dere bought" (*M*, 9) through "the pytuose deth of Jhesu" (10); from there, Mercy beseeches the gathered "soverence" of the audience to "rectyfye" their lives (13), so that all "may be partycypable of Hys retribucyon" (16).[4] In context, "partycypable" seems to mean something slightly different than it has meant in my analysis to this point; here, "participation" denotes not the contemplative self-identification directly with the divine, but rather the right to participate in his forgiveness, in his salvific rewards, in Mercy itself. To be "partycypable" of Christ's "retribucyon" is to share in Christ's merciful salvation, to take part in it.[5] Later, when the titular character Mankind has appeared, he addresses the audience members, reminding them that they take their very being from divine providence (*M*, 187) and stating his hope that all the gathered audience is predestined for God's mercy (189). Recapitulating the logic and phrasing of Mercy, he goes on to say, "Every man for his degré I trust shall be partycypatt" (*M*, 190), to the extent that he "mortyfye" his "carnall condycyon" (191). Participation, in this play, appears to denote a sharing in the comforts of mercy, contingent on a willingness to humble oneself and expurgate one's carnal sins. Soon thereafter, Mankind slightly retextures how we understand participation in this play. Hailing Mercy as "father," Mankind asserts that "Of the very wysdam ye [Mercy] have partycypacyon" (*M*, 210). This usage of participation implicitly sets up Mercy as a kind of contemplative mediator between Mankind and the "wysdam" of God. Mankind can participate in Mercy, as we already learned, and Mercy participates in God's wisdom. The repetition of "participation" in different contexts and grammatical forms, as well as by different characters, signals that it is a keyword for the play, and a concept that will be under pressure throughout: how Mankind can "participate" in God's mercy and salvation and how Mercy entails a "participation" in divine wisdom will be the contemplative foci of the play.

It quickly becomes clear that contemplative participation in divine Mercy has an active component: Mercy requires labor. Participation is not the abstract contemplation of the Trinity and its reflection in the human mind, nor even the virtuous active life of *caritas,* as it was in *Wisdom,* nor is it a cultivation of an awareness of the mystery of divine eternity's incarnation in the flesh, as it was in the *Mary* sequence. Instead, initially, participation has to do with working the field. We see this dynamic clearly enacted early in the play, when Mankind works away with his spade, immune to sin and temptation precisely because he is preoccupied with his labor. As Mercy puts it to the audience, laboring in "good workys" will not let the "gostly enmy" "interrupte" the blessed condition of the soul (*M,* 25–28). Later, addressing Mankind, Mercy hones his theory of labor's centrality to participatory salvation: "Yf ye dysples Gode, aske mercy anon,/ Ellys Myscheff wyll be redy to brace yow in hys brydyll./ Kysse me now, my dere darlynge. Gode schelde yow from yowr fon!/ Do truly yowr labure and be never ydyll" (*M,* 305–8). On one level, Mercy simply reemphasizes the importance of avoiding idleness, and thereby not letting temptation interrupt the good work of the soul. But, through the image of Mischief yoking Mankind in a "brydyll," Mercy metaphorically reminds Mankind that he can—and must—choose to be the one who drives the plow by engaging in virtuous labor, or else he runs the risk of becoming the devil's workhorse. In this emphasis on physical, and specifically agrarian, labor as an alternative to perdition, *Mankind* declares its conceptual and theological affinities with *Piers Plowman* and its agrarian staging of contemplation in the final passus.[6] But, whereas *Piers* stages the agrarian battle for the soul in the most direly apocalyptic of terms, *Mankind* will stage it through mock-Latinate English and scatology. Moreover, whereas *Piers* stages labor *as* contemplation, *Mankind* will stage labor as a way of avoiding sin, although, as we will see, the avoidance of sin by labor will not be the ultimate contemplative point of the play.

UNKINDLY LATIN; OR, THE PROBLEM WITH MERCY

The efficacy of the mock-Latin English and scatology of the play is set into sharp relief by the play's initial poetic mode, which comes in Mercy's opening salvo:

The fownder and begynner of owr fyrst creacyon
Amonge us synfull wrechys He oweth to be magnyfyde,
That for owr dysobedyenc He hade non indygnacyon
To sende Hys own son to be torn and crucyfyede.
Owr obsequyouse service to Hym shulde be aplyede,
Where He was Lorde of all and made all thynge of nought,
For the synfull synnere to had hym revyvyde
And for hys redempcyon sett Hys own son at nought.

Yt may be seyde and veryfyede, mankynde was dere bought.
By the pytuose deth of Jhesu he hade hys remedye.
He was purgyde of hys defawte that wrechydly hade wrought
By Hys gloryus passyon, that blyssyde lavatorye.
O soverence, I beseche yow yowr condycyons to rectyfye
Ande wyth humylité and reverence to have a remocyon
To this blyssyde prynce that owr nature doth gloryfye,
That ye may be be partycypable of Hys retribucyon.
. . .

O ye soverens that sytt and ye brothern that stonde ryght uppe,
Pryke not yowr felycytes in thyngys transytorye.
Beholde not the erth, but lyfe yowr ey uppe.
Se how the hede the members dayly do magnyfye.
Who ys the hede forsoth I shall yow certyfye:
I mene Owr Savyowr, that was lykynnyde to a lambe;
Ande Hys sayntys be the members that dayly He doth satysfye
Wyth the precyose rever that runnyth from Hys wombe.
(*M*, 1–16, 29–36)

When Mercy talks, his lexicon is heavily Latinate, relying on English translations of recognizably Latin words, frequently nouns that end in *-cyon* or verbs that end in *-yfye*. As a result, he sounds inkhorn and churchily pedagogical. Augmenting that churchy tone, Mercy's versification is meticulously tidy: every line neatly embraces a clause or, in many cases, an entire sentence. Thus, he uses his syntactically tidy poetics to reinforce and punctuate the substance of his thought. Augmenting his churchy formality further, Mercy speaks alternately in the first person singular and plural, in effect creating the audience as his congregation—the "we" and "owr" becoming signs and signals of the audience's collective participation in Christian mercy. Mercy's poetics, much like the poetics of Wisdom and Anima in *Wisdom*, are designed to allow his moral order and virtue to suffuse his speech, as well as to attempt to embrace the audience in that virtue. But there is a real problem with Mercy's tidily churchy poetics. He goes too far: Mercy's inkhorn lexicon, coupled with his almost slavishly consistent versification, his pedantic tone, and the sheer length of his opening remarks make his poetry sound tired, boring, stiff, and uninviting. Mercy is so suffused with divine order, divine power, and divine goodness that he seems inhuman, distant, removed from the concerns of everyday life, even as he addresses the plays' audience members and talks repeatedly about their "dayly" duties toward God. The problem with Mercy is that he is too far removed from real life, so that he is no fun.

Mercy's overdetermined lexical, rhythmic, and tonal rigidity calls its opposite into being, in the form of Mischief. Mischief immediately registers and mocks Mercy's inkhorn tone:

> MISCHIEF: I beseche you hertyly, leve yowr calcacyon.
> Leve yowr chaffe, leve yowr corn, leve yowr dalyacyon.
> Yowr wytt ys lytyll, yowr hede ys mekyll, ye are full of predycacyon.
> But, ser, I preye this to claryfye:
> Mysse-mache, dryff-draff,
> Sume was corn and sume was chaffe,
> My dame seyde my name was Raffe;
> Onschett yowr lokke and take an halpenye.
>
> (*M*, 45–52)

Beginning with his scornful demystification of the familiar opposition of chaff and wheat (here, corn), usually deployed to remind students that there was a sweet kernel of truth in a lesson, which they had to penetrate through chaff to attain, Mischief makes light of Mercy's didactic posture, casting him as a rigid pedant rather than a servant of God. His clangily rhyming *-cyon* triplet, tied to an equally clangy *-ye*, *-affe*, *-affe*, *-affe*, *-ye* quintet, mocks Mercy's previous and much more balanced alternating *ababbcbc* rhyme scheme, making the Latinity of Mercy's poetry into "mysse-mache."

When Mischief goes on making mock of Mercy, he launches into a hybrid combination of English and Latin, in which English words are given recognizably Latin endings: "Corn servit bredibus, chaffe horsibus, straw fyrybusque" (*M*, 57). Mischief's "mysse-mache" discourse highlights the unnaturalness and fungibility of language itself, so as to demonstrate that, however churchy it may be in Mercy's mouth, Latin is not beyond spoofing.[7] One can make basic English words with basic meanings—corn, horses, bread, and fire—behave formally like Latin, though Latin's very formality introduces its opposite: absurdity.[8] It does so by demonstrating that Latin's formal structure is just that—formal structure—and has no intrinsic sanctity or meaning. Latin and Latinity, it seems, are not sacrosanct for Mischief, who sees them not as the signs of divine authority, as they were for Mercy, but instead as linguistic structures like any other, subject to re- and misappropriation. The reappropriation and misappropriation of Latinity removes the play's tone from one of inkhorn seriousness and into one of debased, comedic amusement.

This amusement is central to the contemplative logic of the play. Anyone in the audience of this play would know that he or she was supposed to side with Mercy, supposed to like Mercy, or, at the very least, supposed to heed Mercy. But Mercy is stiff and difficult to relate to, as Mischief's interlinguistic argot makes plain. Moreover, like *Wisdom*'s Lucifer, Mischief is the character in the play that is the most dynamic, the most engaging, the most fun. Mischief offers up a relief from the serious, stodgy poetry of Mercy and suggests that a reflexive allegiance to Mercy is unnecessary and laughable. Mischief's looser poetry and demystified mock-Latin language are designed to draw the audience away from Mercy, to make the audience lose interest in Mercy and all his requirements, rules, and recommendations precisely by making them seem like requirements, rules, and recommendations, rather than normative and natural ways of being, talking, and relating to others. Mischief performs a debunking vernacularity in the play, one that shows the fungibility and plasticity of Mercy's notionally high and mighty Latinity. If Mercy is Latinity, Mischief is a kind of vernacularity that challenges and colonizes Latinity itself—as if to suggest that Latin is, itself, subject to vernacularization, subject to being dragged from the reaches of the church and into the mess of everyday life.

Predictably, Mercy is far from thrilled with Mischief's discursive behavior, and he attempts to hold his linguistic and poetic ground. Even in the face of Mischief's three henchmen—Nought, New Guise (or "Guyse"), and Nowadays—each of whom joins in the fun of tampering with and diminishing Mercy's Latinity, Mercy tries to keep his language tidy, proper, and Latinate: "Mercy ys my name by denomynacyon/ I conseyve ye hae but a lytyll favour in my communicacyon" (*M*, 122–23). This effort to insist on a serious and Latinate tone merely provokes the henchmen further, who respond first by debunking the high seriousness of what Mercy's doing by physicalizing it—"Ey, ey! Yowr body ys full of Englysch Laten!" (*M*, 124)—and then by inviting Mercy to render a couplet of scatological English lines, "I have etun a dyschfull of curdys/ Ande I have schetun yowr mouth full with turdys" (131–32), into Latin: "Now opyn yowr sachell wyth Laten wordys/ Ande sey me this in clerycall manere!" (133–34). First, this challenge simply undermines the sanctity of Mercy's Latin, registering that Latin operates in part by leveraging the kind of authority that comes with elitism and rarefaction: Mercy's Latin is depicted not as something public but rather as something sequestered away in a "sachell," and his mode of speech is referred to as "clerycall." But more than that, in this invitation to translate scatological English into Latin, the three malefactors remind viewers that Latin, too, contains its own scatological vocabulary, that it is not just the spiritual language of God and of the Bible but is indeed perfectly capable of containing all the gritty nastiness of the vernacular.[9] Latin is not innately morally or spiritually special; it is simply another mode of speaking, subject to the same debaucheries and degradations as any other language. To drive home the point, they later shout, "osculare fundamentum," or "kiss my ass" (*M*, 142).[10] Thus, whereas *Wisdom* uses French and slang as inset vernaculars to convey embedded levels of debauchery, thus implicitly acknowledging that *some* language might be above the immoral fray of sin and dissipation, the malefactors in *Mankind* register that Latin and English are equally susceptible to profanity and to the evacuation of sacred meaning. No language is safe from Mischief. Therefore, no language can be a true refuge for Mankind.

Amplifying this dynamic, when New Guise, Nowadays, and Nought begin to torment Mankind, Mankind has already busied himself with his spade, and so the three malefactors turn to address the audience in a scatological song that they call a "Crestmes" song.[11]

> NOUGHT: Now I prey all the yemandry that ys here
> To synge wyth us wyth a mery chere:
> Yt ys wretyn wyth a coll, yt ys wretyn wyth a cole,
> NEW GYSE AND NOWADAYS: Yt ys wretyn wyth a colle, yt ys wretyn wyth a colle,
> NOUGHT: He that schytyth wyth hys hoyll, he that schytyth wyth hys hoyll,
> NG AND N: He that schytyth wyth hys hoyll, he that schytyth wyth hys hoyll,
> NOUGHT: But he wyppe hys ars clen, but he wyppe hys ars clen,
> NG AND N: But he wype hys ars clen, but he wype hys ars clen,
> NOUGHT: On hys breche yt shall be sen, on hys breche yt shall be sen,
> NG AND N: On hys breche yt shall be sen, on hys breche yt shall be sen.
> *Cantant Omnes*. Holyke, holyke, holyke! Holyke, holyke, holyke!
>
> (*M*, 333–43)

In its call-and-response structure, as well as its six-time repetition of the word "holyke," a pun on "holy" and "hole-like" or perhaps even "hole-lick," the song parodies the Sanctus and spoofs more generally the call-and-response worship of church liturgy. Nought's invitation to all the "yemandry" present to sing along with him signals a scene of performance in which the members of the audience would have participated in this scatological profanation of the liturgy, and would have done so "wyth a mery chere."[12] Thus, even before the three malefactors attempt to corrupt Mankind, they have already succeeded in corrupting the audience members, drawing them into the universe where all language and all Christian ritual are subject to profanation and debasement. As a result, the members of the audience go into the coming attempts to corrupt Mankind already alerted to their own vulnerability, their own susceptibility to seduction by frivolities. The problem is that this susceptibility to frivolities, this vulnerability to sin and to the undermining of Mercy, is pleasurable: Mischief and the Worldlings are fun, funny, unpredictable, and engaging. For that reason, the admonitory dynamic that could exist in this play instead registers as a playful one—we are glad to sing along with Mischief and his cronies.

In contradistinction to the audience's easy seduction into mirthful scatology, Mankind initially proves resistant to the temptations and tauntings of Nought, New Guise, and Nowadays. Part of the reason for his resistance, from a poetics standpoint, is that he starts out with the same kind of discourse and the same tidily managed verse as we encountered with Mercy; he is, in effect, metrically and lexically inoculated against the ill of sin.

> Of the erth and of the cley we have owr propagacyon.
> By the provydens of Gode thus be we deryvatt,
> To whos mercy I recomende this holl congrygacyon:
> I hope onto hys blysse ye be all predestynatt.
>
> Every man for hys degré I trust shall be partycypatt,
> Yf we wyll mortyfye owr carnall condycyon
> Ande owr voluntarye dysyres, that ever be perverscyonatt,
> To renounce them and yelde us under Godys provycon.
>
> (*M*, 186–93)

Like Mercy, Mankind deploys a markedly Latinate lexicon, extremely tidy versification, a pastoral toggling between first person singular and plural, and a general tone of somber devotion. Mankind seems safely fortified by Mercy's poetics, made aurally distinct from the mock-Latin, scatological vernacular of Mischief and the Worldlings. As a physical, material correlative to his remaining tied to Mercy's poetry, when the Worldlings attempt to push him toward sin, Mankind remains steadfastly devoted to his physical labor. In fact, he quickly repurposes his spade as a weapon with which to combat his foes, beating them about the face and body and thereby literalizing how labor protects one from temptation.

Mankind's combatting of the tempters quickly turns away from physical slapstick to become more linguistic. Mankind pontificates to the fallen three troublemakers, "Yyt this instrument, soverens, ys not made to defende./ Davide seyth, '*Nec in hasta nec in gladio salvat Dominus*,'" citing the Bible as proof that not only swords and spears can be used as weapons against sin (*M*, 396–97). In response to this sobering and serious thought, however, Nought mimics Mankind's utterance, saying, "No, mary, I beschrew yow, yt ys in *spadibus*" (*M*, 398). On the one hand, Nought here simply parodies Mankind's reliance on biblical Latin for his justification, creating a mock-Latin word in his response. But on the other hand, what Nought is saying is literally true: Mankind used a spade, rather than sword or spear, to vanquish him. In demetaphorizing and deallegorizing Mankind's rejoinder, Nought pulls the tone of the interaction into the real and messy world of physicality and social interactions, rather than letting the audience's attention be drawn up toward God. In a manner analogous to the Christmas song's insistence on the porosity between what is "holy" and what is "hole-like," the Worldlings' responses to Mankind's buffets force viewers to be aware of how thin the boundary is that separates transcendent, spiritual, and holy ideas from base, physical, and earthly ones. Their responses do so by forcing Latin and English into strange and uncomfortable proximities with each other, proximities that produce comedy.

PARTICIPATING IN SHIT AND NOTHINGNESS: THE SEDUCTIONS OF TITIVILLUS

That blurring of sacred and profane entails more direct audience participation when the three Worldlings take up a collection to summon the devil Titivillus. On the extradiegetic level of semiprofessional performance, the collection pot serves to defray the costs of the production; if the audience wishes to see the denouement, they must act as patrons.[13] As New Guise puts it, "We shall gather mony onto,/ Ellys ther shall no man hym se" (*M*, 457–58). But simultaneously, the sending around of a collection pot evokes the collecting of tithes—in effect paying for the salvation that comes with participation in a Christian community. Titivillus himself underscores this second meaning, darkly, when he finally appears, saying, "*Ego sum dominancium dominus*" (*M*, 475). Stepping sacrilegiously into the role of God himself as "lord of lords," Titivillus reminds the audience of the morally discomfiting fact that they just paid not for their salvation, not for the privilege of participating in God's body through communion, as they would by contributing their tithes, but instead for the dubious privilege of witnessing the appearance of a devil. This mock-ecclesiastical scene of audience participation reminds the audience members that they are, quite literally, responsible for summoning sin, for summoning temptation, and indeed for summoning the devil into their own midst. Participation in the drama inaugurates participation in sacrilege, scatology, and sin. How is that possibly a good thing? Why is the play ushering its viewers into damnation by literalizing and, indeed, monetizing their complicity with the malefactors of the play?

To answer these questions, we have to zero in on the precise nature of the sin in question. On the surface, it seems to be the same sin that so bedevils Langland's spiritual and social landscape in *Piers Plowman*—namely, the sin of sloth.[14] Titivillus's main goal is to get Mankind to quit his virtuous labor, to stop tilling the fields in which he works away so diligently at first. To activate Mankind's inner tendency toward sloth, Titivillus makes his labor harder—placing a wooden board under the field he tills, stealing his grain, and taking his spade away from him. But, in spite of all of this, Mankind chooses to begin to pray, assigning his field "for my kyrke" (*M*, 552). Titivillus responds by changing tactics to appeal to a sense more basic than Mankind's innate tendency toward sloth: rather than making Mankind's labor yet harder, he appeals to the basest possible parts of Mankind—his desire to urinate, defecate, and sleep. Nature, as Titivillus puts it, "compellys" (*M*, 560) him. When Mankind is thrown into sensible consciousness of his lowest, basest, most bodily self, he goes to sleep, and Titivillus whispers in his ear that Mercy—until now Mankind's access to salvation—has been convicted of crimes and hanged. Believing Mercy to be not only dead but also a condemned sinner, Mankind loses his resolve to be virtuous, and he rapidly becomes the plaything of Titivillus, Mischief, and the Worldlings.

This arc of temptation suggests that it is not just sloth that lures Mankind away from his salvific labors and makes him vulnerable to Titivillus's whisperings. Instead, it is, first and foremost, his basic bodily needs; it is the fact of his inescapably profane human nature. Second, it is the belief that Mercy is no longer watching him, guiding him, witnessing his choices. Believing himself to be in a world without Mercy, Mankind sins.[15] Taking the allegorical form of the play seriously, believing oneself to be in a world without Mercy means believing oneself to be beyond God's gracious forgiveness, to be beyond salvation itself. It means to be in a state of despair.[16] Mankind's sin, the sin that tears him away from salvific labor, is the sin of despair, represented by the play as the necessarily deluded belief that Mercy is both dead and disgraced.[17] Mankind is led to this desperate state by the simple fact of his acquiescing to his bodily needs: to shit, to piss, and to sleep. He is led to despair by being, in a word, human.

Retroactively, this revelation of Mankind's intrinsic, human vulnerability to despair sheds light on the earlier scenes of the play and on how the audience was invited to participate in them. Through his mocking interactions with Mercy, Mischief made Mercy's claims to sanctity and sacrality seem empty, just artifacts of Mercy's high-flown, Latinate diction. Through his systematic debasement of Mercy's language, Mischief made Mercy seem an inkhorn ecclesiarch, alienated from the real experiences of everyday people, rather than the pure force of divine forgiveness that Mercy truly is. Mischief made Mercy seem ridiculous. When the Worldlings came along, singing their shit-strewn Christmas carol, they made Mercy seem ridiculous again. Titivillus's success in moving Mankind to despair by forcing him to reckon with the scatology of human life is in fact precedented by Mischief and the Worldlings' urging the audience to a parallel state of despair—the belief in the meaninglessness and laughability of Mercy—through a programmatic debasement of language's formality, order, and Latinity.

Given the conspicuous grotesqueness of *Mankind*'s vernacular humor, it is tempting to classify that humor as carnivalesque.[18] But this classification would be somewhat misleading, and it would obscure what is contemplatively powerful about the play. For Bakhtin, the carnivalesque humor of the Middle Ages is free, radical, and ruthless, designed to send up the high seriousness of official religious culture quite mercilessly.[19] Carnivalesque laughter is politically resistant, contrary to orthodoxy, and in strong opposition to institutions of religious power.[20] Carnivalesque humor is regenerative, implying a resurgence of life, a reaffirmation of the body, and a return of fertility, fecundity, and productivity.[21] It is neither moralistic, nor meditative; instead, it is parodic and animated by abuse, billingsgate, and profanity.[22] As such, it ushers in what Bakhtin characterizes as a "second life," a life separate from the primary life of participation in political and religious institutions, a place of escape, a place of mirth.[23] The carnivalesque is a dynamic of radical, total, unreconstructed social liberation; it is life-affirming, community-reaffirming, and beyond the law.[24]

A difficulty with applying Bakhtin's theory to late Middle English drama is that it is overly binaristic: for him, public performance is necessarily either institutional (he refers to the liturgy in this context) or resistant (festivals, the carnivalesque.)[25] But the laughter that *Mankind* invites is somewhere in between the two extreme poles. Although it is a grotesque play, and although it does spoof aspects of the liturgy and critique the putative authoritativeness of Latin itself, the play's contemplative mechanics are far closer to reform than they are to firebrand radicalism:[26] as will become clear, they reaffirm the need for Mercy in the world, they insist on the social and religious importance of equity, they affirm the role of sin in the process of salvation, and they hammer home the centrality of worldly labor to the accumulation of spiritual virtue. The sinful, vernacular humor in these plays is not the fecund, countercultural, "second life" that Bakhtin describes; instead, it stages contemplation of the radical vulnerability of the self to sin and misstep en route to a deeper understanding of God's mercy.

Instead of being Bakhtinian, then, I would argue that the comedy in this play is more in line with Stanley Fish's theories about *Paradise Lost,* though with a twist. Fish contends that *Paradise Lost* is designed to make God the Father and God the Son rebarbative, alienating, cold, and unpleasant,[27] while making Satan charming, compelling, engaging, and relatable. The point of this is to force readers to experience and then reckon with their own innate proclivities toward sin, as well as their own sense of alienation from the true majesty and excellence of God. Once readers experience and reckon with these inclinations, they are "surprised by sin," or, to be more precise, surprised and shamed by their own tendency toward sin.[28] This dynamic of surprise and shame then creates the conditions for regret and for the reformation of mind, heart, and spirit that is Milton's ultimate goal.[29] Milton harasses his reader in order to save him.[30] The comedy in *Mankind* works similarly: by making Mercy inkhorn and stodgy, while making Mischief and the Worldlings hilarious and fun, the play invites its audience into sin, en route to redemption.

There are two important differences between the workings of *Paradise Lost* and those of *Mankind.* First, in *Mankind,* being drawn into sin is not the final stop before redemption, as it is in *Paradise Lost.* Instead, *Mankind* takes us one step further, into despair. Thus, when Mercy returns, and the play, through Mankind's redemption, stages the possibility of merciful salvation for all mankind, the audience is brought back from a farther verge even than in *Paradise Lost*: here, in our identification with Mankind, we are not merely sinners but, indeed, sinners who have despaired of our own salvageability. Whereas Milton's surprising his readers by sin is geared to make them understand their own sinfulness and to recoil from it, *Mankind*'s surprising of its audience members by despair is designed to make them understand the true depths to which they can fall and the salvific capaciousness of Mercy in the wake of that fall. The second difference is one of register: the surprised-by-sin dynamic in *Mankind* hinges on low-style, vernacular comedy, whereas the surprised-by-sin dynamic in *Paradise Lost* hinges on the high-style, rhetorical elegance and polish of Satan. In being low-style and comedic, *Mankind* relies not on its malefactors' ability to use English masterfully and perfectly but instead on its malefactors' ability to manipulate and distort it, to use it disfluently.

The activation of despair by disfluent usage of English gains momentum in the play's trial scene, in which Mischief and the Worldlings adjudicate Mankind's readiness to be Mischief's lackey. During the trial, Nought takes notes, and he produces an official court document for Mischief. The document reads, "*Blottybus in blottis/ Blottorum blottibus istis*" (*M*, 680–81). In a hybridizing linguistic joke similar to Mischief's own much earlier reminder that "*corn servit bredibus,*" the trial scene insists yet more stridently than any scene to this point that language itself is fundamentally vulnerable to debasement, as it also was in the Joseph play and *Wisdom*. But now, that debasement is taken to an extreme of the evacuation of referential meaning.[31] Here, not only is the formal grammar of Latin nouns being spoofed, but the English word through which the spoofing happens is the word *blot*, denoting an erasure or an illegibility. Anchoring this dynamic of erasure or illegibility, Mischief continues to read the bill, noting it originates in the regnal year of "*Edwardi nullateni,*" "*anno regni regis nulli*"—the nothingth year of King Edward the Zeroth.[32] The mishmash vernacular of this play leaves very little of either English or Latin standing.

Titivillus's investment in blotting and annihilating language has, however, a yet darker and far more directly intersubjective counterpart, consisting of his reliance on calling out the names of local denizens. Taking the dynamic of *Wisdom*'s calling out of "Jenet N" to a new level of specificity and menace, Titivillus names the local people whom the Worldlings should tap for assistance in the seduction of Mankind. He names "William Fyde," and then the Worldlings name "Master Huntyngton of Sauston," "Wylliam Thurlay of Hauston," "Pycharde of Trumpyngton," "Wyllyham Baker of Waltom," "Rycharde Bollman of Gayton," and "Wyllyam Patryke of Massyngham." They all agree that they shall "spare" "Master Woode of Fullburn," who is a "*noli me tangere,*" and "Master Alyngton of Botysam" and "Hamonde of Soffeham," because the Worldlings are afraid of their legal power (*M*, 503–16). The individual people and place-names listed here seem to refer to actual historical figures and towns in the East Midlands, bringing eerily home to the audience their own social proximity to the staged drama before them.[33] After all, the help that Titivillus and the Worldlings seek is financial support; the people they plan to tap are thus cast not only as coconspirators but also as victims who fall prey to sinful temptation themselves. In this scene, then, Titivillus reminds his audience—by recourse to naming specific members of local communities—that by giving in to the Titivillian predilection for scatology and for the debasement of language, they are, themselves, sinners who contribute to the debauchery of Mankind. Titivillus stages contemplation of a world in which stable meaning can be blotted and annihilated but in which, eerily, local proper names retain their specificity and referentiality.

This is a crucial moment for the participatory dynamics in the play. Up until now, it has been possible and even probable to laugh at Mankind, to enjoy the malefactions of the Worldlings, Mischief, and Titivillus, to laugh at the nothings and blottings and shit. But now, with this conspicuous reminder of the interpenetration of the world of the play and the world of the audience, the proverbial rug is jerked out from under our feet: we can no longer participate in the verbal fun of the bad guys without being aware that we are becoming one of them, that we are vulnerable to their seductions, and that this vulnerability—if not guarded against—will play out badly for us. This is the surprised-by-sin apogee of this play, making us suddenly uncomfortably aware that our laughter and pleasure have put us in the dangerous position of rooting against Mercy, rooting against the salvation of Mankind, and thus rooting against providence itself. Thus, Titivillus's role is not simply that of a tempter, it is also that of an enforcer, or even whistleblower: he reminds all present that they accede to living in a world rife with political corruption, a world in which the powerful few invite, in effect, despair and malefaction into the larger social realm. The calling out of the specific complicit men and our own complicity with them signals that the play has ambitions not only to reform the soul for better contemplative participation but also to reform the social world.

The nature of these reforms is clarified when Mercy returns, only to find that Mankind has fallen prey to the temptations of the Worldlings. This discovery that "Mankynde ys so flexybull" (*M*, 741) leaves Mercy devastated. Mercy calls Mankind mutable and odious (*M*, 747), but the most revealing charge that Mercy lays on him is to call him "Man onkynde" (742). Through this vernacular wordplay on "Mankynde," Mercy suggests that everything Mankind—whether the individual sinner or the polis—has been doing is, in some way, against his fundamental nature, against his "kynde." Mercy is labeling all of the scatology, debauchery, and revelry of the play "onkynde" and suggesting that Mankind's path back to righteousness will involve jettisoning all this unnaturalness in order to return to his own true nature, his "kynde" as a pious, laboring, obedient servant of God.

But that jettisoning will not prove so easy. Finally seeking Mankind directly, Mercy calls out, "Mankynde, *ubi es?*" (*M*, 774). This phrase echoes God's question to the newly fallen Adam (Gen. 3:9) and, in so doing, reminds the audience that Mankind's transgression—indeed, every act of sin—echoes and reenacts original sin. This echo, then, reminds the audience members that Mankind is, in fact, mankind, and includes all of them, as inheritors and reenactors of original sin. To Mercy's poignantly resonant question, New Guise responds with a spastic "hic, hyc, hic, hic, hic, hic, hic, hic!" (*M*, 775). By converting the Latin word for "here" into yet another base bodily function—the hiccup—New Guise tries to nudge Mankind and the audience again back into the body and into humor, and away from any more spiritual contemplations they might have been tempted to undertake in the wake of Mercy's "ubi es." If we do not attend, with all our might and at all times, to the things of God, we will inevitably be dragged down into the dross, dung, disorder, and despair of a purely physical existence, an "onkynde" existence without salvation, without even the hope of divine mercy.[34]

Rendering that despair yet more comprehensible for the audience, immediately after this mockery of the mass, Mankind seeks to commit suicide: "A roppe, a rope, a rope! I am not worthy" (*M*, 800). After Mercy attempts to reassure him that he (Mercy) is still available, Mankind clings to his desperation, making increasingly clear and specific the psychological logic that underpins despair: "The egall justice of God wyll not permytte such a synfull wrech/ To be revyvyd and restoryd again; yt were impossibyll" (*M*, 831–82). This final assertion, that it would be "impossible" for God to revive and restore Mankind again is the core cognitive belief that makes despair qualify as a sin: it is a belief that God's power is limited, that something—namely, merciful forgiveness—lies beyond his volition, beyond his scope, beyond his infinite justice. Mankind's error is to believe that he cannot be pardoned—that divine Mercy cannot reach him any longer.

CONTEMPLATING MERCY: WHAT LIES BEYOND TURDS AND BLOTS

The play stages the falseness of that belief not through Mankind but rather through Mercy, and specifically through how Mercy himself responds to Mankind's "onkynde" transgressions.

> My mynde ys dyspersyde, my body trymmelyth as the aspen leffe.
> The terys shuld trekyll down by my chekys, were not yowr reverrence.

> Yt were to me solace, the cruell vysytacyon of deth.
> Wythout rude behaver I kan not expresse this inconvenyens.
> Wepynge, sythynge, and sobbynge were my suffycyens.
> All naturall nutriment to me as caren ys odybull.
> My inwarde afflixcyon yeldyth me tedyouse unto yowr presens.
> I kan not bere yt evynly that Mankynde ys so flexybull.
>
> (*M*, 734–41)

In this passage, Mercy, too, seems to feel a certain kind of despair. He speaks of the "dispersal" of his mind, the "trembling" of his body. He laments that death would constitute a welcome relief from his suffering; this lamentation resonates with Mankind's own impulse toward self-destruction in the wake of his transgressions. Bearing that resonance out, he rejects food that would sustain his body, as "natural" nutrition becomes as hateful to him as dead flesh. And eventually, when he identifies his problem as "my inwarde afflixyon," he claims this sickness of mind and body as his own, though caused my Mankind's "flexybull" nature. In this play, Mercy suffers, Mercy trembles, Mercy is vulnerable; this is not an untouchable, impregnable Mercy, not a Mercy that hovers above the world in the searing light of divine equanimity, but rather a strikingly vulnerable and human one. This is a Mercy whose baseline mental and physical state reflect those of Mankind—this is an empathic Mercy. In fact, this is a Mercy who empathizes with Mankind to such an extent that he allows himself to suffer along with Mankind. This is, simply put, a Christic, incarnational form of Mercy. The wish for death as an escape from pain, after all, though it does resonate with Mankind, also resonates with Christ on the cross, with the kind of agony whose relief is expressed in the *consumatus est*. By depicting Mercy as at once resonant with Mankind and with Christ, the play stages a likeness between Mankind and Christ, with Mercy as the stuff that both joins Mankind to Christ and separates them from each other.

A strong association between Mercy and Christ is not, in itself, remarkable, nor is the idea that Mercy would act as a kind of intercessor between man and God: in the traditional and common narrative trope of the Four Daughters of God, Christ is associated with Mercy and Peace, while God the Father is associated with Justice and Righteousness. What is striking, however, is the way that Mercy talks: his staging of his own imbrication in Mankind's inner torture, in his vulnerability, in his suffering. Contemporary vernacular depictions of the Four Daughters of God, such as Langland devises in *Piers Plowman* or in cycle dramas, do not expend much energy showing Mercy's own suffering and vulnerability.[35] Here, the *Mankind*-playwright wants his audience to feel not only Mankind's despair but also Mercy's investment and involvement in that despair. Everyone in this play is tarred with the brush of despair, even Mercy himself. And in this way, too, the play's staging of sin and despair part ways with what Fish identifies in *Paradise Lost*; *Mankind*'s ostensibly unflappable, formal, unrelatable protagonist (Mercy) is shown to be something that Milton's Father and Son never are—namely, weak, fearful, and vulnerable. *Mankind* thus registers the bidirectional kind of participation that contemplative theorists like Augustine describe: just as Mankind gets to participate in Mercy, Mercy gets to (or perhaps it is more accurate to say has to) participate in mankind.

The revelation of Mercy's involvement in Mankind ushers in the contemplative apotheosis of the play. After dragging Mankind, Mercy, and the audience into the "onkynde" muck of the Worldlings and the despair that comes with it, the play's final move is to insist, through Mercy, that "Trowthe may not so cruelly procede in hys streyt argument/ But that Mercy shall rewle the mater wythowte contraversye" (*M*, 839–40). However strict the "truth" of the law, the rule of Mercy shall come out on top. This is a world in which the temptation literally to talk shit is overwhelming. Mankind finds itself drawn to the baser side of life; it fails to keep its attention trained on the transformative and merciful meaning of the words of the mass. But, as Mercy reminds in his closing quatrain, addressed directly to the "sofereyns" in the audience:

> Mankend ys wrechyd, he hath sufficient prove.
> Therefore God grant yow all *per suam misericordiam*
> That ye may be pleyferys wyth the angellys above
> And have to your porcyon *vitam eternam.*
>
> (*M*, 911–14)

In Mercy's view, eternal life is man's "porcyon," his inheritance, his fate. Thus, *Mankind*, although bound and determined to make us feel the grossness of our bodies, our minds, our language, and our desires, is, in the end, an optimistic play. It is a play that envisions not just the possibility of reforming the soul but the certainty that reform is efficacious, that the soul can attain mercy for its inevitably "onkynde" ways if only it truly seeks that mercy.

This optimism about reform extends to the political world as well. Going back to the play's earlier interest in the social world, as embodied in the list of local bigwigs whom Titivillus and the Worldlings name, when Mankind initially turns toward Titivillus and his compatriots, giving himself over as a servant of Mischief, he does so in a specific kind of legal setting. When the Worldlings strip Mankind of his overcoat, he is told he will get "a fresch jakett after the new gyse" (*M*, 676)—that is, he will be indoctrinated into the livery and service of Mischief and his Worldlings. Then, when Mankind vows himself to be Mischief's man, vowing, "I wyll, ser," to each of Mischief's mandates to uphold disorder and disobey morality, it becomes clear that this scene asks us to imagine a manorial court, at which Mankind vows to become the serf of the manor lord.[36] Crucially, however, when Mercy reappears, the legal discourse in the play shifts toward the language of equity.[37] Mercy cries out that Mary must have "pety and compassyon" (*M*, 756) on Mankind; he urges that mercy should "excede justice" and that "equyté" should "prevayll" (758, 759). To be sure, pity and compassion are gifts traditionally associated with Mary, and Mercy does, repeatedly, call out to Mary for her support, but they are also terms that appear frequently in legal documents pertaining to the ideology of the royal courts of equity, which are intended to represent the king's compassionate and merciful consciousness, and, indeed, to act as an equitable corrective to the strict letter of the law.[38] In this scene, then, the play asks viewers to imagine at once a world in which corrupted local interests have taken hold, reducing the freedom of all mankind and a world in which the higher seats of power—such as the royal courts of equity—remain an avenue open for redress and reform. And indeed, in the late English Middle Ages, the courts of equity operated in precisely this way, overturning falsely prosecuted cases as well as militating against the severe local justice of manorial courts in numerous other types of cases. The play, then, imagines a world of profound corruption, a world in which the rites and rituals of justice have been woefully perverted, but in that very imagining, it simultaneously imagines a world of mercy, not only originating with God but, indeed, also originating with man and with the political institutions of mankind.

The invocation of the ideology of equity law in the play, however, does more than simply assert the need for justice and mercy in the material world of man. It also analogically points up a crucial aspect of the play's contemplative theology. The law of equity is designed as a corrective to error, to misapplication of the law. It is a remedial kind of justice, not designed to get things right from the outset—indeed, criminal and common law cases cannot originate in courts of equity but can only end up there through an appeals process—but instead to fix things after they are broken. Applying this idea to the contemplative theology at work in the play, what the play's emphasis on equity suggests is that sin is necessary for mercy to have a real effect.

Sin is necessary for salvation; the play is staging the logic of the felix culpa, but it goes further, to suggest that sin is necessary not just for salvation but also for *contemplation* to take place.

This idea of sin's necessity both to salvation and to contemplation is not unique to the play, being articulated prominently in at least three other major Middle English works of theology. One is Walter Hilton's *Scale of Perfection,* in which Hilton insists that the image of sin in the soul must be broken down before the soul can be reformed in the image of God.[39] Implicit in this idea of reform, of course, is the very idea that is implicit in the logic of equity: something has to be de-formed before it can be re-formed. Hilton's is not a world of easy grace; it is a world of suffering through sins, recognizing them as part of the process of perfection. A second is *The Cloud of Unknowing.* In one of his more imaginative passages, the *Cloud*-author urges readers to gaze deep into themselves, to see what they find there:

> & forthi that ever the whiles thou levyst in this wrechid liif, thee behoveth alweys fele in som partye this foule stynkyng lump of synne, as it were onyd & congelid with the substaunce of thi beyng, therfore schalt thou chaungabely mene thees two wordes—*synne* & *God*: with this general knowyng: that and thou haddest God, then schuldest thou lacke synne, & mightest thou lacke synne, then schuldest thou have God. (*CU*, 40.79, 13–19)

What we find "congelid" to the core of our being is not a luminous halo of goodness but a "foule stynkyng lump of synne." That sin, the *Cloud*-author is careful to point out, is not good in itself, but it "behoveth" the would-be contemplative to feel that lump of sin, to grope and wrestle with it, to experience it. Indeed, as I mentioned earlier, he offers up "synne" as an alternate monosyllabic word on which to pray atomically, in addition to "God" and "love." Wrestling with sin, grappling with one's own fundamentally sinful nature, contemplating sin itself enables one to let go of one's sin, and move toward God. The third vernacular contemplative work that emphasizes the necessity of sin is Julian of Norwich's *A Revelation of Love,* which insists that sin is "behovely," or beneficial, to the contemplative (*Rev.*, 209.27.10). What Julian seems to mean by this is precisely what the *Mankind*-playwright seems to be getting at in his play—namely, that sin is an opportunity for mercy and therefore for a renewed closeness with God. Indeed, the play's broader scatology even seems to echo Julian's claim that God loves us even in the moment of our "nescessery," that is "downe to us to the lowest parte of oure nede."[40] He loves in mankind, that is, the very nature that "compellys" Mankind to leave his salvific labor, the very nature that leads him straight into the arms of the

Worldlings, and thence into despair. He loves in mankind, according to Julian, mankind's vulnerability, his grossness, his closeness to shit. The play's efforts to induce its audience to participate in despair—believing that Mercy is laughably inefficacious and that language itself is meaningless—are central to its logic of participatory contemplation. Mercy must be traduced and overthrown by Mischief, by mockery, sin, defecation, and nihilism, if mercy itself is to have any real significance in the world. As it is in Julian's *Revelation*, in *Mankind*, sin is "behovely."

In exporting its "behovely" participation in sin to its viewers, the play relies not on a careful exposition of how sin works, nor even on an imagistic representation of the foul stinking lump of sin in the human soul such as the *Cloud* contains. Instead, the play relies on the infectiously participatory powers of laughter. The derisive mock Latinity of the play, the scatology, the parodic Christmas song, the "blott" passage, and the nihilistic recording of the zeroth year of Edward the nothingth are all designed to prompt the audience into an awareness of the constructedness and artificiality of language itself—its "unkindness." These comedic stagings of the unkindness of language urge the audience to experience the futility of language's effort to signify stably and formally. The play's comedic dispersal of significative stability then fuels the play's participatory despair, and that despair, in turn, leads to the play's staging of the return of Mercy.

Because of its heavy reliance on clashes between English words and Latin forms and the calling out of proper names, the play's linguistic comedy pervasively registers the salience of the Middle English vernacular as a language for staging participatory contemplation on sin, despair, and mercy. Englished Latin and Latinized English make Mercy seem ridiculous, make compassion and forgiveness feel unnatural. The calling out of specific, local proper names makes the audience members aware of their inescapable entrapment in the dynamics of sin and despair that the play stages. English and its frictions with Latin drive the audience, both individually and as a group, to a participatory contemplation of their own attraction to sin and their own desperate involvement in it. Thus, like *The Cloud of Unknowing*, *A Revelation of Love*, *Piers Plowman*, *Mary*, and *Wisdom*, *Mankind*'s particular brand of participatory contemplation embodies a rationale for vernacular composition that is centered on the participatory workings of dramatic comedy that are possible in English and in English's "onkynde" relationship with Latinity.

Mankind's reliance on the familiarity and, at the same time, unkindness of English has its own fascinating culmination, in the final scenes of the play. Just before Mankind leaves Mercy alone on stage to bid farewell to the audience, Mercy addresses Mankind thus:

> MERCY: Mankend, ye were oblivyows of my doctrine monytorye.
> I seyd before, Titivillus wold asay yow a bronte.
> Beware fro hensforth of hys fablys delusory.
> The proverbe seyth, "*Jacula prestita minus ledunt.*"
>
> Ye have thre adversaryis and he ys mayster of hem all:
> That ys to sey, the Devell, the World, the Flesch and the Fell.
> The New Gyse, Nowadayis, Nowgth, the World we may hem call;
> And propyrly Titivillus syngnyfyth the fend of helle;
>
> The Flesch, that ys the unclene concupissens of your body.
> These be your thre gostly enmyis, in whom ye have put your confidens.
> Thei browt yow to Myscheffe to conclude your temporall glory,
> As yt hath be schewyd before this worscheppyll audiens.
>
> Remembyr how redy I was to help yow; fro swheche I was not dangerus;
> Wherfore, goode sunne, absteyne fro syn evermore after this.
> Ye may both save and spyll yowr sowle that ys so precyus.
> *Libere welle, libere nolle* God may not deny iwys.
>
> Beware of Titivillus wyth his net and of all enmys will,
> Of your synfull delectacion that grevyth your gostly substans.
> Your body ys your enmy; let hym not have hys wyll.
> Take your leve whan ye wyll. God send yow good persverans!
>
> (*M*, 879–98)

What we see in Mercy's final address to Mankind is that Mercy's own vernacular has shifted: rather than being aggressively and relentlessly Latinate, the discourse here is dominated by recognizably English words. The rhyme words are no longer exclusively (or even primarily) the *-yfye* and *-cyon* words but, instead, "bronte," "all," "Fell," "call," "helle," "body," "glory," "dangerus," "this," "iwys," and "wyll"—they are almost all simple, quotidian, English words. To be sure, Mercy is still inclined to cite Latin proverbial discourse, but, by and large, his tone and register are now far more quotidian, familiar, and plain than they were at his initial appearance in the play. No longer a churchy, inkhorn pedant, Mercy now seems like a regular, relatable person. Mercy has been touched by Mankind's sin, despair, and vulnerability, and his relationship to language reflects it. In Mercy's discursive and registral malleability, the play helps its audience experience the importance and even value of daily, simple, English speech in making contemplation possible.

Mercy needed to be brought down to earth in order for Mankind truly to connect with him.

Even so, the play hastens to remind its audience, after Mankind departs the stage, that Mercy is still, in the end, Mercy. His last twelve lines overflow with the very Latinity he seemed to discard in his final conversation with Mankind:

> Wyrschepyll sofereyns, I have do my propirté:
> Mankynd ys deliveryd by my faverall patrocynye.
> God preserve hym fro all wyckyd captivité
> And send hym grace hys sensuall condicions to mortifye!
>
> Now for Hys love that for us receyvyd hys humanité,
> Serge your condicyons wyth dew examinacion.
> Thynke and remembyr the world ys but a vanité,
> As yt ys provyd daly by diverse transmutacyon.
>
> Mankend ys wrechyd, he hath sufficyent prove.
> Therefore God grant yow all *per suam misericordiam*
> That ye may be pleyferys wyth the angellys above
> And have to your porcyon *vitam eternam. Amen!*
>
> (*M*, 903–14)

Having demonstrated his capacity to dial down his Latinity in an effort to relate to Mankind, Mercy's final lesson—to the audience—is that they should not *need* him to do that. People should be able to see in Mercy's seeming churchiness and inflexibility his constancy, his eternal and unchanging availability to them. The weakness, the vulnerability, and even the panic that Mercy exhibited during Mankind's fall into sin and despair did not signal Mercy's derogation, invalidation, or even reduction. Quite the contrary, *Mankind* is a play that uses carefully deployed English to stage Mercy's susceptibility as an index of his infinite availability, his ability to forgive even despair. As is true of Christ, Mercy's ability to fall into human suffering merely reaffirms and shores up his power, his divinity, and his claim on our contemplative attention. And the play stages this paradoxical nature of Mercy as both decisively human and decisively divine through the unkind kindliness of English.

CONCLUSION

Staging Contemplation in the Vernacular

In addition to contributing new attention to the problems of vernacularity, participation, and collectivity that are formally staged in the Middle English literature of contemplation, this book has contested a long-standing, implicit critical maxim that "contemplative" texts ought not be studied (or taught) alongside "dramatic" works. Although medieval plays are recognized as religious and devotional, they are not typically considered as or even alongside more traditionally "contemplative" works. One reason for this traditional segregating of devotional dramatic works from other contemplative ones is, of course, the issue of audience. Plays are notionally written for performance in front of a large and probably diverse group. Contemplative prose works, by contrast—those works such as *The Cloud of Unknowing*, *The Form of Living*, *A Revelation of Love*, and *The Mirrour of the Blessed Lyf of Jesu Christ*, all of which have appeared in this book—are assumed to have been written for a single devotional reader at a time.[1] But, as Jessica Brantley has demonstrated, medieval devotional texts, putatively written for single readers, are often performed and integrated into group life in a way that is, in a word, dramatic. Vice versa, Brantley has shown that medieval dramatic texts are often used for private devotion.[2] Then, as Michael Sargent has proven, *Wisdom* owes a good deal to Walter Hilton's prose devotional work *The Scale of Perfection*, itself ostensibly written for a single reader at a time; likewise, the N-Town cycle borrows from Nicholas Love's *Mirrour of the Blessed Lyf of Jesu Christ*.[3] Teresa Coletti's study of the Digby *Mary Magdalene* play has shown that that work, too, draws on the devotional writings of Walter Hilton.[4] Clearly, the imagined difference in audience is not robust enough to sustain a radical, fundamental divide between dramas and prose works of contemplation—at least, not in the minds of medieval playwrights and users of devotional texts.

Staging Contemplation has taken the genre-rethinking work of Brantley, Sargent, and Coletti in a different direction, and the difference has, in broadest terms, been one of methodology. Brantley's argument hinges primarily on manuscript studies, Sargent's on source studies, and Coletti's on hagiographic studies. *Staging Contemplation* has focused on the poetic modes and devices by which Middle English contemplative works perform the contemplations that they describe. It has suggested, that is, that the homologies between plays and other contemplative writings go deeper than established thematic borrowings or citations, extending down to the fine detail of how literary and dramatic form and contemplative theology interpenetrate each other in the transmission of contemplative modes of knowing to a Middle English audience. I hope to have shown that all of these works' investments in the experiential rendering of man's participation in God create in them a through line not just of theological ideas but, indeed, of local formal and stylistic practice, which underpins the larger-scale paraphrases, citations, and other borrowings in the texts. In essence, I hope to have, through my analysis of the participatory phenomenon of contemplation, shed light on the poetry of late Middle English drama as *poetry*.

Moreover, I hope to have contributed to research on medieval literature more broadly by revealing the centrality of the Middle English language to the formal staging of contemplation. All of the works I have studied manifest how the vernacular brings with it a host of formal resources for staging participatory contemplation, whether the vernacular work in question is prose, poetry, or drama. English grammar, English syntax, English semantics, English rhythms, and the friction that English creates when brought into disfluent conversation with Latin: all of these are sensory resources that contemplative literary works of the fourteenth and fifteenth centuries play with, en route to the staging of a participatory experience of contemplation. English is not just a language or set of practices but an aggregate of sensory expectations—expectations that can be gratified or, more often, exploited in a way that draws audiences into participatory states of contemplation. The English vernacular is the foundational form for contemplative participation.

One lingering difference between drama and other modes of contemplative literature, as I emphasized in my last three chapters, is that the dramatic works stage participatory contemplation in a more complete and more audacious way than the other works do. Julian insists that her book does not fully "perform" the work it describes. The *Cloud*-author teaches atomic prayer not because he expects reading about it to be a satisfactory enactment of contemplation but instead because he expects it to be a portal into a larger and far more ongoing practice of contemplative prayer in one's own private life. *Piers Plowman* edges closer to a fuller kind of participation, with its semiallegorical main character Will functioning as a proxy for the reader's own will and ushering that reader through various states of contemplative unrest and indecision on the way to a growing understanding of likeness as a core principle of contemplative experience. But even *Piers* does not offer the completion, perfection, or full performance of contemplation—that much becomes clear when Conscience goes wandering off into the sunset at the end, if it had not been clear enough already from the poem's tortuous movements and narrative switchbacks. Like the *Revelation* and the *Cloud*, *Piers* stages the kinds of sensory experiences one might expect to have during the actual work of contemplation, so that the literary work functions as a portal into or preparation for the ongoing practice of contemplation in daily life. In the dramas, however, the nature of participatory contemplation becomes more concretely and fully participatory: one's friends and neighbors are playing roles; characters onstage interact with members of the audience both physically and verbally; the audience is urged to enter into cognitive states in parallel with those of the actors before them. Through all of these forms of audience engagement, play audiences are reminded that the action onstage is not purely onstage; it is an externalization of the dramas that go on already in their own souls. They are made to feel, that is, *implicated* in the events onstage, true participants in them.

Another, related difference between the dramas and the nondramatic contemplative works is that the earlier works I examined in this book—*The Cloud of Unknowing*, *The Form of Living*, *A Revelation of Love*, *Piers Plowman*, and the *Mirrour of the Blessed Lyf of Jesu Christ*—avail themselves of the sensory properties of vernacular forms primarily in local poetic, prosodic, lexical, or grammatical effects. The *Cloud* uses monosyllabic words and monosyllabic rhythms to create a sensory reflex of the experience of the contemplative approach to God that it describes. The *Revelation* devises prosodic meditations (the "I it am" passage) as well as grammatical ones (the modal verb Trinity) to meditate on the nature of the relationship between man and God. Richard Rolle's works, including his *Form of Living*, rely on alliteration, rhythm, and other forms of poetic patterning. *Piers* mines complex paronomastic words—"kynde" being the most important, most pervasive, and most metacritical—as well as complexly interwoven code-switching passages between

Latin and English. Love's *Mirrour,* in spite of its expressed commitment to "symple" prose, includes passages of extremely wrought prosody. The dramatic works I have studied leverage the sensibility of the vernacular through many formal methods analogous to those we find in the nondramatic works, including code-switching, puns, rhythms and rhymes, and acrostics. But there is a vernacular form that is disproportionately represented in the dramatic mode, and not in nondramatic ones. As I have described, the play of Joseph in the N-Town cycle devises a strange series of punning misunderstandings by Joseph concerning his own fitness to be Mary's husband. *Wisdom* makes its viewers hear the moral peril of engaging with Satan as the jocular and near-simultaneous introduction of French and slang into the play. Analogously, *Mankind* drags viewers through the lexical gutters, combining the high-style Latinate language of Mercy with the low-style vulgarities of the Worldlings and Titivillus. The code-switching that these plays rely on—be it purple puns in English, interlinguistic punning between Latin and English, the introduction of slang, or the introduction of profanity—has a signal and overarching effect, an effect that helps explain why drama proves such a flexible form of vernacular contemplative literature. That effect is comedy.

Dramatic comedy enables contemplation of a different sort than we see in prose works or in *Piers Plowman*. It enables, first, a more flexible and provocative orientation toward contemplation than other literary modes, because it stages doubts and misunderstandings in marginal as well as major characters, only later to encapsulate and neutralize them. In *Wisdom,* however plausibly orthodox Lucifer's readings of the Bible may seem for a fleeting moment, the audience still knows that, since it's Lucifer talking, he must necessarily be wrong. The threat his slant exegesis poses is quickly plowed under the audience's realization that his supervening, transhistorical maleficence preemptively invalidates his status as biblical interpreter. The flickering menace of a truly seductive Luciferian hermeneutics is offered up only to be quickly contained. In the N-Town plays, the evocation of Joseph's "whande" forces the audience to think seriously, concretely, and physically, for a second, about the siring of Jesus; Joseph's paronomastic and dunderheaded obsessing over his phallus makes clear that that thought always already has its orthodox answer in the Virgin Birth—Joseph himself is manifestly too goofy, too buffoonish, and too impotent to have impregnated Mary.

Amplifying these diegetic elements of comedy, the players' intermittent interactions with the audience enable a telegraphing of comedic tone not only from the play to the viewers but also among the viewers; in *Mankind,* watching one's neighbors laugh at Titivillus, or even be named by him as a coconspirator in the attempt to corrupt Mankind, creates a dynamic in which individual viewers feel vulnerable to the action onstage not only as vulnerable individuals but also as a vulnerable and interimplicated Christian collectivity. The staging of contemplation helps audiences experience not just the relation of their own individual souls to God but also the relation of their souls as a community to sin. In that experience, the dramatic staging of contemplation helps audience members not only remember their true essences as participants in the divine but also register that that participation in the divine is concomitant with their participation in the social world. Part of drama's contribution to the practice of contemplation, then, is to make it well and truly collective, social, and intersubjective. Thus, the dramas of the fifteenth century both respond to and extend the ambitions of Chichele-era socioreligious reforms: they invite not just the spiritual elite but whole, diverse communities to be coparticipants in contemplation as part of their broader civic life. In so doing, they reinforce what Langland formally enacts in *Piers Plowman*—namely, that the life of participatory contemplation and the life of active participation in the social world are and *should be* one life.

Notes

INTRODUCTION

1. I also treat Nicholas Love's *Mirrour of the Blessed Lyf of Jesu Christ*—admittedly a translation of the *Meditationes Vitae Christi,* but a translation that takes significant liberties—and some of Richard Rolle's works, though they are not primary foci.

2. This is true not only in the study of medieval literature but also ongoingly in the practice and theorization of contemplation in the modern day. See John Corson, "Contemplation and Contemplatives," *Life of the Spirit* 4 (1950): 318–22.

3. *The Cloud of Unknowing, The Scale of Perfection,* and *The Form of Living* are Middle English examples of this pattern.

4. Samuel Fanous and Vincent Gillespie, eds., *Cambridge Companion to Medieval English Mysticism* (Cambridge: Cambridge University Press, 2011), 292 (glossary definition).

5. Ibid.

6. Vincent Gillespie registers this in his pluralization of the "practice" of contemplative prayer: "changes and extensions in popular devotional practice and taste are marked by a growing curiosity for meditative and contemplative prayer *practices* in the contexts of their own homes and parishes." Vincent Gillespie, "1412–1534: Culture and History," in Fanous and Gillespie, *Cambridge Companion to Medieval English Mysticism,* 178; italics mine.

7. Vincent Gillespie also classifies this play, along with several others in the fifteenth century, as contemplative, and notes the name of Contemplacio as part of his justification. See ibid.

8. See Augustine, *De Trinitate,* bk. 9, ch. 12, in *Patrologia Latina,* ed. Jacques-Paul Migne, vol. 42, http://pld.chadwyck.com/all/fulltext?ALL=Y&WARN=N&PRINT=YES&ALL=Y&warn=N&ACTION=byid&ID=Z400051707&FILE=../session/1508957468_25119&PRINT=yes (Migne-edited *Patrologia Latina* hereafter cited in notes as *PL*). For an analysis of how the idea of man's being created in the image of God works for Paul, see Bernard McGinn, *Three Treatises on Man* (Collegeville, MN: Cistercian Publications, 1977), 4–5.

9. David H. May, "Paul's Understanding of Faith as Participation," *Paul and His Theology* (Boston: Brill, 2006), 45–76.

10. See David C. Schindler, "What's the Difference? On the Metaphysics of Participation in a Christian Context," *Saint Anselm Journal* 3 (2005): 1–27. According to Schindler, for Plato, participation is what makes it possible for many different individual objects to all be a "chair," or to participate in chairness. Elaborating from this essential theory, according to Thomas Aquinas, people have being because they participate in the first and only true being, which is God (Schindler, "What's the Difference?" 20). As Sister M. Annice puts it, Aquinas's *Commentary on the Sentences*

indicates that something that participates has "something which exists properly and perfectly in another thing." Annice, "Historical Sketch of the Theory of Participation," *New Scholasticism* 26 (1952): 49–79, at 50. Tracing his belief in participation to Plato, Annice goes on to argue that "For Plato, the 'absolute' is the separated 'idea,' the form existing extra-mentally as such, and this is it that constitutes the world of permanency and the absolute norm. The 'ideas' are primary, most real, and existing in their own right" (51). As McGinn puts it, "the most important effect of Greek thought on early Christian anthropology was the adoption of the Platonic understanding of 'image' (*eikon*) as the central anthropological concept." McGinn, *Three Treatises on Man*, 4.

11. Augustine's *De Trinitate* states it thus: "There would be no mutable goods, unless there were the immutable good. Thus, when you hear of this good thing and that good thing, which can also in other ways be said not good, if you can put aside those things which are good by participation in the good, to see that good in itself by the participation in which other things are good; because when you hear of this or that good, you understand also the Good itself: if thus you can take away these things to see the Good in itself, you will perceive God." [Nulla essent mutabilia bona, nisi esset incommutabile bonum. Cum itaque audis bonum hoc et bonum illud, quae possunt alias dici etiam non bona, si potueris sine illis quae participatione boni bona sunt, perspicere ipsum bonum cujus participatione bona sunt; simul enim et ipsum intelligis, cum audis hoc aut illud bonum: si ergo potueris illis detractis per se ipsum perspicere bonum, perspexeris Deum.] From *De Trinitate*, bk. 8, ch. 3, *PL*; translation mine.

12. "Omne quod bonum est boni participatione bonum." Boethius, *Boethii: Philosophiae Consolatio*, in *Corpus Christianorum*, Series Latina, vol. 94, ed. Ludwig Bieler (Turnhout, Belgium: Brepols, 1957), bk. 3, prose 11, sentence 8.

13. Per Augustine in *De Trinitate:* "For our enlightening is our participation in the Word, that is, in that life which is the light of men. But for this participation we were outright unable, and we were less than equal to it, due to the foulness of our sins. Therefore, we had to be cleansed. Moreover, the cleansing of the wicked and of the proud is the Just One's blood, the humbling of God: in order that we might contemplate God . . . we are by nature men, we are by sin not righteous. For that reason, God was made a just man, and he interceded with God on behalf of sinful man. For the sinner is not aligned with righteousness. Man is aligned with man. By conjoining himself with our likeness by his humanity, he expunged the dissimilarity of our wickedness: and made participant in our mortality, he made us participant in his divinity." [Illuminatio quippe nostra participatio Verbi est, illius scilicet vitae quae lux est hominum. Huic autem participationi prorsus inhabiles, et minus idonei eramus, propter immunditiam peccatorum. Mundandi ergo eramus. Porro iniquorum et superborum una mundatio est sanguis justi, et humilitas Dei: ut ad contemplandum Deum quod natura non sumus . . . homines natura sumus, justi peccato non sumus. Deus itaque factus homo justus, intercessit Deo pro homine peccatore. Non enim congruit peccator justo, sed congruit homini homo. Adjungens ergo nobis similitudinem humanitatis suae, abstulit dissimilitudinem iniquitatis nostrae: et factus particeps mortalitatis nostrae, fecit nos participes divinitatis suae.] (bk. 4, ch. 2, para. 4, in *PL*).

14. Pseudo-Bernard's enormously influential *Meditationes piissimae*, for instance, picks up on Augustine's formulation of the mental trinity as an image of God. According to him, "Our mind thus is made in his image and it is in that that we are able to participate in him." [Mens siquidem nostra eo ipso ejus imago est quo ejus capax est ejusque particeps esse potest.] Pseudo-Bernard, *Meditationes*, in *Sancti Bernardi Opera omnia* (Paris, 1839), vol. 2, ch. 1, pt. 2.

15. According to Nicholas Watson, the joint doctrines of the human mind's being created in the image of the divine one and of God's having taken on the mantle of flesh as Jesus are the cornerstones of contemplative literature: "The first doctrine is that each individual human soul is made in the Trinitarian image of God, mirroring the divine likeness; and the belief that God has, in turn, chosen to be made in the image of the human, entering the order of creation in the incarnate Christ, that 'scandal to the Jews and folly to the Gentiles' (1 Corinthians 1:23)." Nicholas Watson, introduction to Fanous and Gillespie, *Cambridge Companion to Medieval English Mysticism*, 2.

16. Julian of Norwich, *The Writings of Julian of Norwich: A Vision Showed to a Devout Woman and a Revelation of Love,* ed. Nicholas Watson and Jacqueline Jenkins (Philadelphia: University of Pennsylvania Press, 2006), *Rev.*, 379.86. 1–3. All further citations, both from the *Vision* (abbreviated as *Vis.*) and the *Revelation* (*Rev.*) will be drawn from this source and will follow Watson and Jenkins's citation convention: page number, followed by chapter number, followed by line numbers.

17. Indeed, the contemplative is expected to continue on from her readings to immerse herself in prayer to God, as a continuance of the work begun in the encounter with Julian's vision, as Jessica Brantley has suggested. See Jessica Brantley, *Reading in the Wilderness: Private Devotion and Public Performance in Late Medieval England* (Chicago: University of Chicago Press, 2008), 18. Patricia Dailey construes the assertion that the work is not yet "performid" as a gesture toward an "earthly afterlife in the addressee's promised body." Patricia Dailey, *Promised Bodies: Time, Language, and Corporeality in Medieval Women's Mystical Texts* (New York: Columbia University Press, 2013), 170.

18. See Jennifer Herdt, *Putting on Virtue: The Legacy of the Splendid Vices* (Chicago: University of Chicago Press, 2008).

19. See Shannon Gayk, *Image, Text, and Religious Reform in Fifteenth-Century England* (Cambridge: Cambridge University Press, 2010), 8. For Gayk, "affective piety and images crafted to encourage emotional response had moved to the center of late medieval devotional practice" (9).

20. Gail McMurray Gibson, *The Theater of Devotion: East Anglian Drama and Society in the Late Middle Ages* (Chicago: University of Chicago Press, 1989), 10.

21. Sarah McNamer, "The Origins of the *Meditationes vitae Christi*," *Speculum* 84 (2009): 905–55, at 905–6, 912.

22. See Nicholas Watson, *Richard Rolle and the Invention of Authority* (Cambridge: Cambridge University Press, 1991).

23. Nicholas Watson has nominated affectivity as, in some ways, the defining dynamic of medieval contemplative writings: "affectivity . . . marks medieval contemplative writings as medieval." See Watson, introduction to Fanous and Gillespie, *Cambridge Companion to Medieval English Mysticism*, 18.

24. James Simpson, "From Reason to Affective Knowledge," *Medium Aevum* 55 (1986): 1–23.

25. Indeed, Aristotle says that knowledge does not exist outside of perception. See Aristotle, *Posterior Analytics*, trans. G. R. G. Mure (Oxford: Clarendon, 1928), bk. 2, pt. 19. As Bruce Holsinger has pointed out, contemporary linguists and philosophers have circled back to this notion, so that "all conceptual systems, philosophical or otherwise, are both grounded in and shaped by sensory and motor systems, and thus that concepts can be formed only through and within the body." Bruce Holsinger, *Music, Body, and Desire in Medieval Culture: Hildegard of Bingen to Chaucer* (Stanford, CA: Stanford University Press, 2001), 12.

26. This notion is far from unusual in late antiquity and the Middle Ages, during which times sensation was seen as the first step on a ladder of human cognition which culminated in intellectual understanding. For a brilliant treatment of this issue, see Robert Pasnau, *Theories of Cognition in the Later Middle Ages* (Cambridge: Cambridge University Press, 1997), at 126.

27. For an elegant treatment of the cognitive ladder that begins with sensation and ends with intellection, see Elaine Scarry, "The Well-Rounded Sphere: The Metaphysical Structure of the *Consolation of Philosophy*," in *Essays in the Numerical Criticism of Medieval Literature*, ed. Carolyn Eckhardt (Lewiston, NY: Bucknell University Press, 1980), 95–96.

28. See Sarah Beckwith, *Signifying God: Social Relation and Symbolic Act in the York Corpus Christi Plays* (Chicago: University of Chicago Press, 2001), esp. 42–55. See also her earlier work "Rituals, Church, and Theatre," in *Culture and History: 1350–1600, English Communities, Identities, and Writing*, ed. David Aers (Detroit: Wayne State University Press, 1992), at 65, 89, 102.

29. Brantley, *Reading in the Wilderness*, 1–26, 269–90.

30. Michelle Karnes, *Imagination, Meditation and Cognition in the Middle Ages* (Chicago: University of Chicago Press, 2011).

31. Denise Despres, "Sacramentals and Ghostly Sights," *Religion and Literature* 42 (2010): 101–2.

32. Suzannah Biernoff, *Sight and Embodiment in the Middle Ages* (New York: Palgrave, 2002), 63.

33. Barbara Newman, "What Did It Mean to Say, 'I Saw'?: The Clash between Theory and Practice in Medieval Visionary Culture," *Speculum* 80 (2005): 1–43, esp. 5, 14–15. She notes that the experience of the visual, in her texts, was ultimately designed to catapult contemplatives into a higher, imageless form of understanding (16).

34. Ian Johnson's research has pointed in this direction, arguing for a "theological vernacular" as a hermeneutic complement to "vernacular theology." Johnson suggests that English boasts a "resourcefulness and flexibility" that enables it to remix and refigure various theological genres for consumption by a vernacular readership. See Ian Johnson, "Vernacular Theology/Theological Vernacular," in *After Arundel: Religious Writing in Fifteenth-Century England*, ed. Vincent Gillespie and Kantik Ghosh (Turnhout, Belgium: Brepols, 2011), 83. The flexibility of English enables theological texts of the fifteenth century to create multiple simultaneous meanings in themselves, thus courting heterodoxy while plausibly seeming orthodox, Johnson observes (87).

35. There is a considerable critical literature emerging on "disfluency," which is what native speakers experience when the rules and norms they expect are violated. See S. M. Laham, P. Koval, and Adam Alter, "The Name-Pronunciation Effect: Why People Like Mr. Smith More Than Mr. Colquhoun," *Journal of Experimental Social Psychology* 48 (2012): 752–56; L. M. Reder and G. W. Kusbit, "Locus of the Moses Illusion: Imperfect Encoding, Retrieval, or Match?" *Journal of Memory and Language* 30 (1991): 385–406; M.S. McGlone and J. Tofighbakhsh, "Birds of a Feather Flock Conjointly (?): Rhyme as Reason in Aphorisms," *Psychological Science* 11 (2001): 424–28; H. Song and N. Schwarz, "If It's Difficult to Pronounce, It Must Be Risky," *Psychological Science* 20 (2009): 135–138; H. Song and N. Schwarz, "Fluency and the Detection of Misleading Questions: Low Processing Fluency Attenuates the Moses Illusion," *Social Cognition* 26 (2008): 791–99. Recent studies have shown that "disfluent" reading situations can produce better cognitive understanding than more normative ones, precisely because the aberrant usage activates a reader's attention. See A. L. Alter et al., "Overcoming Intuition: Metacognitive Difficulty Activates Analytic Reasoning," *Journal of Experimental Psychology: General* 136 (2007): 569–76; C. Diemand-Yauman, D. M. Oppenheimer, and E. B. Vaughn, "Fortune Favors the Bold (and the Italicized): Effects of Disfluency on Educational Outcomes," *Cognition* 118 (2009): 111–15. Also see Adam Alter, "Benefits of Cognitive Disfluency," *Current Directions in Psychological Science* 22 (2013): 437–42.

36. This idea affirms what Niklaus Largier sees at work in medieval mysticism more broadly: "The movement through which this is reached can be characterized as a de-naturalization of the senses by artificial means—the techniques of prayer—and a re-naturalization, a return to the intensity of sensory and emotional experience of the world, in form of a sensory experience which is constructed with the help of these artificial means." Niklaus Largier, "Inner Senses–Outer Senses: The Practice of Emotions in Medieval Mysticism," in *Codierungen von Emotionen im Mittelalter*, ed. C. Stephen Jaeger and Ingrid Kasten (Berlin: Walter de Gruyter, 2003), 3–15, at 5.

37. See Vincent Gillespie, "Vernacular Theology," in *Middle English*, ed. Paul Strohm (Oxford: Oxford University Press, 2007), 411 and 413.

38. See Marian Davis, "Nicholas Love and the N-Town Cycle" (PhD diss. Auburn University, 1979), 26, for a treatment of the pervasiveness of vernacular devotional practices and writings in late medieval England. See also W. A. Pantin, who notes that the fourteenth century's burst of vernacular writings enabled lay people "to take a more intelligent, educated, active, and, so to speak, professional part in the life of the church. Thus laymen were enabled and encouraged to attempt the practice of contemplative prayer." W. A. Pantin, *English Church in the Fourteenth Century* (Cambridge: Cambridge University Press, 1955), 253.

39. Bernard McGinn, *The Flowering of Mysticism: Men and Women in the New Mysticism: 1200–1350* (New York: Crossroad Publishing, 1998), 30.

40. See Nicholas Watson, "Censorship and Cultural Change in Late Medieval England: Vernacular Theology, the Oxford Translation Debate, and Arundel's Constitutions of 1409," *Speculum* 70 (1995): 822–35.

41. Andrew Cole has shown that Wycliffism and Lollardy, in the English Middle Ages, neither were nor even meant the same thing to many people but were instead diverse and varied forms of religious experimentalism. See Andrew Cole, *Literature and Heresy in the Age of Chaucer* (Cambridge: Cambridge University Press, 2008), 73. Wycliffism is associated, for many people and poets (including Langland and Chaucer) with certain intellectual and literary stances, Cole explains (80–99, 186), but is not, prima facie, the same as Lollardy, which, at least for Langland, more often signals laziness and nonwork than any specific academic heresy.

42. Anne Hudson, *Premature Reformation: Wycliffite Texts and Lollard Heresy* (Oxford: Oxford University Press, 1988), 69. Indicating the lack of success of the Blackfriars prohibitions, William of Rymington in 1383 explicitly and directly blamed Wycliffe's writings for some of the more violent risings in the Peasants' Rebellion, Hudson notes (68).

43. Kathryn Kerby-Fulton, "Prophecy and Suspicion," *Speculum* 75 (2000): 318–41, 319n3.

44. Kerby-Fulton notes that, in *Chastising of God's Children*, women's mystical writings were particularly targeted as sources of potentially dangerous religious knowledge (ibid., 319).

45. Jeremy Catto notes that the Carthusians seem to have played a significant role in translating and popularizing contemplative writings. See Jeremy Catto, "1349–1412, Culture and History," in Fanous and Gillespie, *Cambridge Companion to Medieval English Mysticism*, 126.

46. Paul Patterson, "The Book and Religious Practice in Late Medieval England," *Religion and Literature* 37, no. 2 (2005): 1–8, at 3. See also Hudson, *Premature Reformation*, 103.

47. Hudson, *Premature Reformation*, 82.

48. See Cole, *Literature and Heresy*, xvi. Indeed, in Cole's view, it was precisely the public denunciations, such as that made by the Blackfriars Council, that made Wycliffism and Lollardy popularly recognizable as available cultural forms of dissent (9–10).

49. England is not the only geographic area in which a formal study of the rise of the vernacular as the language of theology might be undertaken. Examining the role of the formal features of literary language in prompting or shaping the rise of the German vernacular as the language of theology has prompted Sara Poor to argue that "the key to vernacular mysticism is the language itself." Sara Poor, *Mechthild of Magdeburg and Her Book: Gender and the Making of Textual Authority* (Philadelphia: University of Pennsylvania Press, 2004), 18.

50. Barry Windeatt, "1412–1534: Texts," in Fanous and Gillespie, *Cambridge Companion to Medieval English Mysticism*, 195.

51. Gillespie, "Chichele's Church," in Gillespie and Ghosh, *After Arundel*, 13. Gillespie also notes, however, that the Wycliffites, in the long run, ended up having a much greater impact on the writing of English religious texts than did Arundel himself (21).

52. Gillespie notes that the atrophy of innovatory English religious writing is not total; he advocates for reading numerous noncontemplative, not even usually "religious" writings—such as Lydgate's *Troy Book*—as designed to respond to and rework Lollard principles and commitments. For him, Hoccleve, Langland, Digby MS poets, and other writers demonstrate an interest in making a new, Latinized, aureate English that would serve to reach a wider public without activating concerns about Lollardy, since Lollard style was known for its simplicity and lack of aureation. Gillespie, "Chichele's Church," 33–35.

53. Michael Sargent, Teresa Coletti, and Jessica Brantley have each shown how productive it can be to consider dramatic works alongside other types of devotional literature: Sargent has noted the direct and shaping influence of devotional prose works on certain medieval dramas; Coletti has demonstrated the existence of a Magdalenian devotional genre, encompassing many types

of literature, including drama alongside hagiography; Brantley has brilliantly analyzed a single manuscript to show how false it is to separate the world of medieval literature into performed and nonperformed texts in the first place. I will return to their arguments in my conclusion. See Michael Sargent, "Mystical Writings and Dramatic Texts in Late Medieval England," *Religion and Literature* 37, no. 2 (2005): 77–78; Teresa Coletti, *Mary Magdalene and the Drama of Saints* (Philadelphia: University of Pennsylvania Press, 2004), throughout; Brantley, *Reading in the Wilderness,* 1–26, 269–90.

54. See in particular James Simpson, *The Oxford English Literary History*, vol. 2, *1350–1547: Reform and Cultural Revolution* (Oxford: Oxford University Press, 2002), 1–4. See also Gillespie, "1412–1534: Culture and History," 165.

55. Gillespie, "1412–1534: Culture and History," 168, 170, 173.

56. Ibid., 177.

57. See Jeremy Catto, "After Arundel: The Opening or the Closing of the English Mind," in Gillespie and Ghosh, *After Arundel*, 44–45, 49–50.

58. Gillespie, "1412–1534: Culture and History," 185; Windeatt, "1412–1534: Texts," 210.

59. See Anonymous, *Tretise on Miracles Pleyinge*, ed. Clifford Davidson (Kalamazoo, MI: Medieval Institute Publications, 1993), 93, 94. Lawrence Clopper has dismissed this reading of the *Tretise,* saying the text is not written in condemnation of plays but simply of the "bourding" and derision that sometimes occur in priestly *ludi* (plays). As I will elaborate on in my fourth chapter, I think that Clopper is right to point to the anxiety about "bourding" in the *Tretise*, but, given the strong tendency in dramas to veer precisely in that direction, I still believe the *Tretise* was written to condemn dramas more broadly than Clopper allows. See Lawrence Clopper, "*Miracula* and the *Tretise of Miraclis Pleyinge*," *Speculum* 76 (1990): 878–905.

60. Anonymous, *Tretise*, 111–12.

61. Ibid., 103.

62. Beckwith, "Rituals, Church, and Theatre," 67.

63. Hudson, *Premature Reformation*, 56, 304, 307.

64. As Lawrence Clopper has pointed out, the *Tretise* condemns dramatic enactment of Christ's life or the lives of saints when such enactment misappropriates sacred events in a manner conducive instead to sin and misdeed. See Clopper, "*Miracula* and *Tretise*," 895. But Clopper's larger argument contends that the *Tretise* is not so much concerned with prohibiting vernacular religious drama as it is with prohibiting paganizing spoofs. Much of the reason for this claim is that the *Tretise* seems to object to mockery (901), not to real, sustained religious fervor, such as the religious dramas of the period often invite; as Clopper puts it, the treatise "emphasizes behavior that involves 'bourding and pleyinge'" (901). My own view is that the *Tretise* actually *does* seek to condemn religious drama—and indeed all extraliturgical dramatic presentations of religious material—in part because, through its artifice and image making, religious drama almost invariably tends, at some point, to swerve precisely and pointedly into "bourding and pleyinge," as I shall explain in the coming chapters.

65. James Simpson has shown that some degree of anxiety about imagery and its devotional uses was present even in orthodox writings during the fifteenth century. See James Simpson, "Orthodoxy's Image Trouble," in Gillespie and Ghosh, *After Arundel*, 91–93. Even so, the Constitutions of 1409, by condemning the Lollard focus on the dangers of imagery, indelibly associated Lollardy with that idea, and associated orthodoxy with a relatively high degree of acceptance of imagery.

66. V. A. Kolve, *The Play Called Corpus Christi* (Stanford, CA: Stanford University Press, 1966), 130–31, 143, 145–74, esp. 171–74.

67. Ibid., 171–72, 173.

68. As Seeta Chaganti points out, there exists an "ill fit between contemporary performance studies and medieval studies." Seeta Chaganti, "The *Platea* Pre- and Postmodern: A Landscape of Medieval Performance," *Exemplaria* 25 (2013): 252–64, at 252.

69. See A. P. Rossiter, *English Drama from Early Times to the Elizabethans: Its Background, Origins, and Developments* (London: Hutchinson University Press, 1966), 107; Arnold Williams, *The Drama of Medieval England* (Ann Arbor: University of Michigan Press, 1961), 156; Lawrence Clopper, "*Mankind* and its Audience," *Comparative Drama* 8 (1974–75): 347–55; Marshall, "'O ye Soverens that Sytt and Ye Brothern that Stonde Ryght Wppe': Addressing the Audiences of *Mankind*." *European Medieval Drama* 1 (1997): 189–202; Tom Pettitt, "*Mankind:* an English Fastnachspiel?" in *Festive Drama: Papers from the Sixth Triennial Colloquium of the International Society for the Study of Medieval Theatre Lancaster, 13–19 July, 1989*, ed. Meg Twycross (Cambridge: Brewer, 1996), 190–202, at 191.

70. This approach reflects Donnalee Dox's assertion about medieval "textuality" and "performance"—namely, that the distinction between those two categories does not really obtain in the late Middle Ages. See Donnalee Dox, *The Idea of Theater in Latin Christian Thought* (Ann Arbor: University of Michigan Press, 2004), 5.

71. To cite just a few examples, Kathy Eden's brilliant work on Greek tragedy relies on the theories of spectatorship put forth by Aristotle: Kathy Eden, *Poetic and Legal Fiction in the Aristotelian Tradition* (Princeton, NJ: Princeton University Press, 1986); Joseph Harris's equally brilliant work relies on early modern theorists of drama and spectatorship: Joseph Harris, *Inventing the Spectator: Subjectivity and the Theatrical Experience in Early Modern France* (Oxford: Oxford University Press, 2014). The only work decisively in this genre in medieval England is the aforementioned *Tretise on Miraclis Pleyinge*, which I will come back to much later.

72. Joseph Harris asserts, "The 'spectator' invoked in dramatic theory, then, is always to some extent a composite or hypothetical construct that can helpfully be distinguished from what Michele Aaron calls the 'viewer'—'the live, breathing, actual audience member, coming from a specific socio-historical context.'" Harris, *Inventing the Spectator*, 13.

73. Joseph Harris notes that early modern literature and, in Harris's view, especially drama, was generally composed for a mixed and various audience. See Harris, *Inventing the Spectator*, 8.

74. Allison Hobgood, *Passionate Playgoers in Early Modern England* (Cambridge: Cambridge University Press, 2014), 2.

75. Jeremy Catto notes the increasing openness of contemplation not just to monastics, but also to the laity in the late English Middle Ages. See Catto, "1349–1412, Culture and History," 122–23.

76. Eamon Duffy, *The Stripping of the Altars: Traditional Religion in England, 1400–1580* (New Haven, CT: Yale University Press, 1992), 2, 3, 7, 93, 131–54.

77. For Duffy, the liturgy is the core experience of worship for medieval people, lay and clerical alike. See ibid., 2–5, 11, 25–29, 91.

78. Watson, introduction to *Cambridge Companion to Medieval English Mysticism*, 11.

CHAPTER 1

1. Analyses of prose style were prominent in studies of the first half of the twentieth century. See George Philip Krapp, *The Rise of Early English Literary Prose* (Oxford: Oxford University Press, 1915); R. W. Chambers, ed., *On the Continuity of English Prose from Alfred to More and His School* (London: Oxford University Press, EETS, 1932); R. M. Wilson, "On the Continuity of English Prose," in *Mélanges de linguistique et de philologie Fernand Mossé in memoriam* (Paris: Didier, 1959), 486–94. See also Phyllis Hodgson, introduction to *The Cloud of Unknowing and the Book of Privy Counselling* (London: Oxford University Press, 1944), EETS, o.s., 218; Helen Gardner, "Walter Hilton and the Authorship of the *Cloud of Unknowing*," *Review of English Studies* 9 (1933): 129–47. In more recent works, see J. A. Burrow, "Fantasy and Language in *The Cloud of Unknowing*," *Essays in Criticism* 27 (1977): 283–98; Janel Mueller, *The Native Tongue and the Word* (Chicago: University of Chicago Press, 1985), 72–74.

Turning toward theological analyses, for an overview of the *Cloud* in context of the English mystical tradition, see David Knowles, *The English Mystical Tradition* (New York: Harper and Brothers, 1961); Bernard McGinn, "Love, Knowledge, and Mystical Union in Western Christianity," *Church History* 56 (1987): 7–24; Bernard McGinn, "The Changing Shape of Late Medieval Mysticism," *Church History* 65 (1996): 197–219, at 199; Louis Dupré, "The Christian Experience of Mystical Union," *Journal of Religion* 69 (1989): 1–13, at 1; Owen C. Thomas, "Interiority and Christian Spirituality," *Journal of Religion* 80 (2000): 41–60. For an extended overview and critique of the classification of the work as part of the mystical or devotional "traditions," see Nicholas Watson, "The Middle English Mystics," in *The Cambridge History of Medieval English Literature*, ed. David Wallace (Cambridge: Cambridge University Press, 1998). For Victorine influences on the *Cloud*, see Alastair Minnis, "The Sources of the *Cloud of Unknowing*: A Reconsideration," in *Medieval Mysticism in England*, ed. Marion Glasscoe (Exeter: Short Run, 1982), 63–73. To situate the *Cloud* among other "vernacular theological" writings, see Watson, "Censorship and Cultural Change," 831–32 (see intro., n. 40).

2. A few studies have begun the work of demonstrating how the stylistics of the *Cloud* reinforce its theological messages, though in most cases, these works focus on the relationship between apophatic theology and "negative" language. See Rosemary Ann Lees, *The Negative Language of the Dionysian School of Mystical Theology: An Approach to the* "Cloud of Unknowing" (Salzburg: Institut für Anglistik und Amerikanistik, 1983); Tarjei Park, *Selfhood and 'Gostly Menyng' in Some Middle English Texts* (Lewiston, NY: Edwin Mellen Press, 2002), at xi, 120; Cheryl Taylor, "Paradox upon Paradox: Using and Abusing Language in *The Cloud of Unknowing* and Related Texts," *Parergon* 22, no. 2 (2005): 31–51; Carmel Bendon Davis, *Mysticism and Space: Space and Spatiality in the Works of Richard Rolle, The Cloud of Unknowing-author, and Julian of Norwich* (Washington, DC: Catholic University of America Press, 2008), 177–212.

3. Anonymous, *The Cloud of Unknowing and the Book of Privy Counselling*, ed. Phyllis Hodgson, EETS, o.s., 218 (Oxford: Oxford University Press, 1943–44), ch. 3, p. 17, lines 4–5 (hereafter cited as *CU*, with chapter, page, and line numbers). I normalize Hodgson's orthography, converting *v* to *u* and *u* to *v* according to modern English spellings, rendering thorn as *th*, and yogh as *gh* or *y*.

4. William Langland also uses "grope" to talk about how one seeks to know God. Describing how Christ "took Thomas by the hand and taughte hym to grope/ and feele with hise fyngres his flesshliche herte." William Langland, *Piers Plowman: A Parallel-Text Edition of the A, B, C and Z Versions*, ed. A. V. C. Schmidt (New York: Longman, 1995), B text, passus 19, lines 170–71 (hereafter cited as *PP*, with text version letter, passus number, and line numbers).

5. "Groping" also occurs in the *Book of Privy Counselling*, the sequel to the *Cloud*: "right is the desire of the soule as groping & steppyng is of the body; & bothe ben groping & steppyng blynde werkes of the body" (in *CU*, p. 165, lines 6–8). "Naked feeling" is discussed there on pages 147 and 155.

6. Alastair Minnis usefully situates the *Cloud*-author's "love" in context of the Victorine "principalis affectio." See Minnis, "Sources of *Cloud*," 63–73. For additional instances of "nakid entente," see *CU*, 3.17.2; 24.58.15–16; 34.70.21.

7. In the *Cloud*-author's view, true spiritual practice is an immersion into "a darknes" that prevents one from seeing God "cleerly by light of understanding in thi reson" (*CU*, 3.17.2, 4–5).

8. Hodgson notes that prayer is the "main theme" of the *Cloud*. See *CU*, p. lviii.

9. "Anni tui omnes simul stant, quoniam stant, nec euntes a uenientibus excluduntur, quia non transeunt: isti autem nostri omnes erunt, cum omnes non erunt. anni tui dies unus, et dies tuus non cotidie, sed hodie, quia hodiernus tuus non cedit crastino; neque enim succedit hesterno. Hodiernus tuus aeternitas." Augustine, *Confessionum libri tredecim*, in *Corpus Christianorum*, Series Latina, vol. 27, ed. L. Verheijen (Turnhout, Belgium: Brepols, 1981), bk. 11, cap 13, line 19 (hereafter cited as *Confessions*, with book, cap, and line numbers). My translations throughout.

10. "Nocturnis enim et diurnis horis omnibus uiginti quattuor expletur, quarum prima ceteras futuras habet, nouissima praeteritas, aliqua uero interiectarum ante se praeteritas, post se futuras. et ipsa una hora fugitiuis particulis agitur: quidquid eius auolauit, praeteritum est, quidquid ei restat, futurum. si quid intellegitur temporis, quod in nullas iam uel minutissimas momentorum partes diuidi possit, id solum est, quod praesens dicatur; quod tamen ita raptim a futuro in praeteritum transuolat, ut nulla morula extendatur. nam si extenditur, diuiditur in praeteritum et futurum: praesens autem nullum habet spatium." Augustine, *Confessions,* 11.15.41.

[A day] contains twenty-four hours, of night and of day, of which the first has the rest as futures, and the most recent has the rest as pasts, and truly any thrown in between has those before it as past and those that come after as future. And that one hour itself is done in fleeting fractions: what of it has flown away, is past, what remains, future. If anything can be understood of time, which can in no way now be divided even into the most minute parts of moments, it alone is what present is; but still, this flies so rapidly from future to past, so that it can at all be extended by delay. For if it is extended, it is then divided into past and future. But the present has no extension whatsoever.

11. "Longum carmen est, nam tot uersibus contexitur; longi uersus, nam tot pedibus constant; longi pedes, nam tot syllabis tenduntur; longa syllaba est, nam dupla est ad breuem . . . Deus creator omnium: uersus iste octo syllabarum breuibus et longis alternat syllabis: quattuor itaque breues, prima, tertia, quinta, septima, simplae sunt ad quattuor longas, secundam, quartam, sextam, octauam. hae singulae ad illas singulas duplum habent temporis; pronuntio et renuntio, et ita est, quantum sentitur sensu manifesto. quantum sensus manifestus est, breui syllaba longam metior eamque sentio habere bis tantum." Augustine, *Confessions,* 11.26.9; 11.27.26.

12. "Sed neque ita comprehenditur certa mensura temporis, quandoquidem fieri potest, ut ampliore spatio temporis personet uersus brevior, si productius pronuntietur, quam longior, si correptius. Ita carmen, ita pes, ita syllaba." Augustine, *Confessions,* 11.26.16.

13. "Inde mihi uisum est nihil esse aliud tempus quam distentionem: sed cuius rei, nescio, et mirum, si non ipsius animi." Augustine, *Confessions,* 11.26.17.

14. "Uocas itaque nos ad intellegendum uerbum, deum apud te deum, quod sempiterne dicitur et eo sempiterne dicuntur omnia . . . alioquin iam tempus et mutatio, et non uera aeternitas nec uera immortalitas . . . non ergo quidquam uerbi tui cedit atque succedit, quoniam uere immortale atque aeternum est." Augustine, *Confessions,* 11.7.1, 3, 10.

15. As Dailey puts it, Augustine wonders how a person can know God, "given God's being outside the measure of time and space?" (*Promised Bodies,* 27–28, see also 31.)

16. Focusing on *De Trinitate,* Patricia Dailey has said, "Because the human being is both like and unlike God, made in God's image but unlike God in its mode of dwelling in time and space, Augustine is faced with the question of how to reconcile the body's existence in a temporal and changeable medium with the unchangeable and eternal nature of its creator" (31).

17. "Minimum autem omnium, et quod nulla ratione dividi queat tempus, atomum Graece, hoc est, indivisibile sive insectibile, nominant." Bede, *De temporum ratione,* in *PL,* vol. 90, cap. 3. For an overview of atomic theories in the Middle Ages between Bede's time and the fourteenth century, see Bernhardt Pabst, *Atomtheorien des lateinischen Mittelalters* (Darmstadt: Wissenschaftliche Buchgesellschaft, 1994).

18. For specific analyses of the fourteenth-century English philosophers who were interested in measurement of quantities as atomic, see Edith Sylla, "Medieval Quantifications of Qualities: The Merton School," *Archive for History of Exact Sciences* 8 (1971): 7–39. For a continuation of this analysis, which extends the exploration of atomic theory into more intangible realms—realms not just physical but also theological—see especially John Murdoch, "From Social into Intellectual Factors: An Aspect of the Unitary Character of Late Medieval Learning," in *The Cultural Context of Medieval Learning,* ed. John Murdoch and Edith Sylla (Boston: Springer, 1975), 271–348, esp. at 287 and the following pages.

19. *Accord,* in this context, signifies "harmony," a likeness, as between sounds in music, and thus, an "affinity" between two things: *Middle English Dictionary* (*MED*), s.v. "accord," 6, https://quod.lib.umich.edu/cgi/m/mec/med-idx?size=First+100&type=headword&q1=accord&rgxp=constrained. In its derived adjectival form, *accordable,* the term means "consonant," "harmonious," and "fitting": *MED,* s.v. "accordable."

20. The *Cloud*-author understands "meaning" and "intention" as interchangeable concepts; he makes this interchangeability plain when he says to his readers, "mene God love that maad thee, & bought thee," in which "mene" clearly signifies "intend," or "will." The semantic equivalence of *mean* with "intend" is standard in late Middle English. See *MED,* s.v. "menen," 1, 2.

21. "grammaticis potius quam calculatoribus visibile est: quibus cum versum per verba, verba per pedes, pedes per syllabas, syllabas per tempora dividant, et longae quidem duo tempora, unum brevi tribuant, ultra in quod dividant non habentibus, hoc atomum nuncupari complacuit." Bede, *De temporum ratione,* cap. 3.

22. "quia omnis syllaba aut brevis est, et tempus recipit unum, quod atomum metrici vocant." See Bede, "De syllaba," in *De arte metrica,* in *P,* vol. 90, cap. 2.

23. *Oxford English Dictionary* (*OED*), s.v. "mete," 1, 5; *MED,* s.v. "meten," 1, 2.

24. "Aeternitas igitur est interminabilis uitae tota simul et perfecta possessio." Boethius, *Philosophiae Consolatio,* bk. 5, prose 6, sentence 4 (see intro., n. 12).

25. "Hunc enim uitae immobilis praesentarium statum infinitus ille temporalium rerum motus imitatur, cumque eum effingere atque aequare non possit, ex immobilitate deficit in motum, ex simplicitate praesentiae decrescit in infinitam futuri ac praeteriti quantitatem." (Thus, this infinite motion of temporal things imitates the ever-present state of unchanging life; since, however, it cannot imitate or equal this, it falls from immutability into change, and falls away from the simplicity of presence into an infinite quantity of future and past.) Boethius, *Philosophiae Consolatio,* bk. 5, prose 6, sentence 12.

26. "et cum totam pariter uitae suae plenitudinem nequeat possidere, hoc ipso quod aliquo modo numquam esse desinit illud quod implere atque exprimere non potest aliquatenus uidetur aemulari alligans se ad qualemcunque praesentiam huius exigui uoluscrisque momenti, quae, quoniam manentis illius praesentiae quamdam gestat imaginem, quibuscunque contigerit id praestat ut esse uideantur." Boethius, *Philosophiae Consolatio,* bk. 5, prose 6, sentence 12.

27. See also *CU,* 37.73.7–11: "I maad no force, thof thou haddest now-on-dayes none other meditacions of thin owne wrechidnes, ne of the goodnes of God—I mene yif thou fele thee thus steryd by grace & by counseyl—bot soche as thou mayst haue inthis worde SYNNE & in this worde GOD, or in soche other, whiche as the list."

28. Robert Myles focuses on the *Cloud*-author's preference for short words in the *Cloud*-author's later work, the *Book of Privy Counselling,* as a means by which the *Cloud*-author creates a feeling of presence in his readers through a meditation on the word *is.* See Robert Myles, "'This Litil Worde "Is'": The Existential Metaphysics of the *Cloud* Author," *Florilegium* 8 (1986): 140–68.

29. See Phyllis Hodgson, "*A Ladder of Foure Ronges by the Whiche Men mowe wele clyme to Heven*: A Study of the Prose Style of a Middle English Translation," *Modern Language Review* 44 (1949): 465–75. See also Margery M. Morgan, "A Talking of the Love of God and the Continuity of Stylistic Tradition in Middle English Prose Meditations," *Review of English Studies* 3 (1952): 97–116.

30. Admittedly, there are disyllables in these passages—"betir," "apon," "bitwix," and "steryng." Although the *Cloud*-author seeks to embody atomic accord in his atomic style, he does not seek to do so at the expense of clarity. For that reason, he admits disyllabic words into his monosyllabic chains.

31. For an analysis of exclamatory and phatic language in the *Cloud* as an index of its informality, see Mueller, *Native Tongue,* 73.

32. Ruth Nisse notes the *Cloud*-author's distaste for sensory engagement as well, primarily because of the risk of "confusing body and spirit." See Nisse, *Defining Acts: Drama and the Politics of*

Interpretation in Late Medieval England (Notre Dame: Notre Dame University Press, 2005), 54–55, quotation at 63.

33. Addressing the disparity between the *Cloud*-author's style and his expressed attitude toward sensation, Alastair Minnis has suggested that the *Cloud* permits levels of sense-experience in writing that it will not admit in the doing of spiritual work. Indeed, as Minnis has elegantly shown, the *Cloud*-author's distaste for "imagination" in the work of devotion is not matched by a rejection of imagery in his writing. See Alastair Minnis, "Affection and Imagination in *The Cloud of Unknowing* and Hilton's *Scale of Perfection*," *Traditio* 39 (1983): 323–66. Although this analysis of imagination and imagery in the *Cloud* is undoubtedly right—the *Cloud*-author uses imagery in his writing that he would outright condemn in spiritual practice—there remains more to account for in his attitude toward sense-experience in the work of the spirit.

34. Jeremy Catto notes that the *Cloud* seeks to chasten the overflowing and unregulated emotionality of writings typical of Richard Rolle. Catto, "1349–1412, Culture and History," 113 (see intro., n. 45). Catto goes on to note that Rolle and his correctors inaugurate a new and recognizable genre of writing in Middle English; namely, Middle English contemplative writing (114).

35. The most compelling analysis of how Rolle's writing style is designed to encapsulate the feeling of spiritual devotion that he describes is Nicholas Watson's, in which Watson argues that the sensory effects of song, which map onto the highest stage of spiritual development, called *canor*, are the organizing principles behind Rolle's style. See Watson, *Richard Rolle* (see intro., n. 22). For another treatment of Rolle's stylistic practices, and particularly of his alliteration, see Richard Rolle, *The Contra amatores mundi of Richard Rolle of Hampole*, ed. and trans. Paul F. Theiner (Berkeley: University of California Press, 1968). Theiner notes in his introduction that alliteration is conspicuous throughout Rolle's writings, although noting it is nowhere as "dense" as in his Latin *Melos amoris*. "One of the devices which has been most consistently observed in both the Latin and English writings is alliteration. While no other work approaches the *Melos Amoris* in density of alliterative words" (Theiner, introduction to Rolle, *Contra*, 32).

36. Watson, *Richard Rolle*, 170.

37. Ibid., 178.

38. "And ymang other affeccions & sanges, thou (may in thi) langyng syng this in thi hert til thi lorde Ihesu, (when) thou covaytes hys comyng and thi gangyng." Richard Rolle, *Form of Living*, in *The English Writings of Richard Rolle, Hermit of Hampole*, ed. Hope Emily Allen (Oxford: Oxford University Press, 1963), 107, 92–95. For critical treatments of the songfulness of Rolle's prose, see especially Gabriel Liegey, "Carmen Prosaicum," *Medieval Studies* 19 (1957): 26–28.

39. Rolle, *Form of Living*, 107, 1–10.

40. Richard Rolle, *Ego dormio*, in Allen, *English Writings*, 69, 257–262.

41. Latinate manuals on prose stylistics, from which the *Cloud*-author may well have drawn in composing his vernacular work, often associate poetry with falseness, and prose with truth. Thomas of Capua, a prominent dictaminist, observes that prose, because unconstrained to fit a particular meter, leaves its author freer to express himself: "Prose is said to come from the Greek 'proson,' which means in Latin 'long,' because in prose you may wander off farther and wider or, as much as you please, be more restrained" (Prosaicum dicitur a proson grece, quod latine significant longum, quia in prosa licet alicui longius et latius aut quantumlibet castigatius evagari). Thomas von Capua, *Die ars dictandi des Thomas von Capua*, ed. Emmy Heller (Heidelberg: Carl Winters Universitätsbuchhandlung, 1929), 14. Another dictaminist, Bernard of Silvester, goes farther, outright condemning meter as a debasement of meaning: "Prose publishing of a letter is a type of writing, different from metrical rules, proceeding in a long and congruous continuity. . . . Prose, as Bede says in *The Art of Meter*, is continuous speech unbound by metrical rule, because it should not be mutilated by metrical quantity" (Prosaicum dictamen est litteralis edicio, a lege metrice differens, longa congruaque continuatione procedens. . . . Prosa, ut ait Beda in Arte Metrica, est longa oratio a lege metri soluta, quia extra metricam non debet quantitatem mutilari). Bernard of Silvester,

"Il *'Dictamen'* di Bernardo Silvestre," in *Rivista Critica della Storia Filosofia, Testi e Documenti* 20 (1965): 202. For Bernard, as, I believe, for the *Cloud*-author, the difference between metrical and prosaic writing has become an ethic: since prose is not "mutilated" by meter, it becomes a privileged form for creating sensible effects, but without debasing its own meaning in that process.

42. The association between the formal regularity of meter and falseness, to which I have suggested the *Cloud*-author is sensitive, is not uniquely his, even among vernacular writers. Studying historiographies of thirteenth-century France, Gabrielle Spiegel finds that vernacular historiographers become increasingly suspicious of the power of meter to bear truth, saying, "No one is able to recite a chanson de geste without lying, there where the verse determines that the words be ordered and cut to fit the rhyme" (Nus hom ne puet chancon de geste dire que il ne menta la ou li vers define aus mos drecier et a tailler la rime). Cited in Omer Jodogne, "La Personnalité de l'Ecrivain d'öil," in *L'Humanisme médiéval dans les Littératures Romanes du XIIe au XIVe siècle*, ed. Anthime Fourrier (Paris: Klincksieck, 1964), 95, cited again in Gabrielle Spiegel, "Forging the Past: The Language of Historical Truth in the Middle Ages," *History Teacher* 17 (1984): 267–288, at 272. In Spiegel's own words in her book, "Finding the poet's search for rhyme and measure to be incompatible with the historian's pursuit of truth and need for exactitude of narration, laymen increasingly sought to satisfy their curiosity about the past in new ways." Those "new ways" are prose chronicles. See Gabrielle Spiegel, *Romancing the Past: The Rise of Vernacular Prose Historiography in Thirteenth-Century France* (Berkeley: University of California Press, 1995), 2.

43. *Book of Privey Counselling*, in *CU*, p. 137, lines 6–11.

44. Ibid., pp. 138–139, lines 28–29, 1–5.

45. "Sed quoniam plurimus tibi affectuum tumultus incubuit diuersumque te dolor ira maeror distrahunt, uti nunc mentis es, nondum te ualidiora remedia contingunt. Itaque lenioribus paulisper utemur, ut quae in tumorem perturbationibus influentibus induruerunt ad acrioris uim medicaminis recipiendam tactu blandiore mollescant." Boethius, *Philosophiae Consolatio*, bk. 1, prose 5, sentence 11–12.

46. Charles Lock notes that criticism on the *Cloud* has suggested "tentatively and on tenuous ground" that the motive behind vernacularity is that the *Cloud*-author intends it for a female audience. But Lock himself assesses the level of erudition that suffuses the work to be inconsistent with its having been written in English for reasons of promoting access. He suggests that the *Cloud*-author chooses English, instead, to mine it for its etymological particularities. See Charles Lock, "The Cloud of Unknowing: Apophatic Discourse and Vernacular Anxieties," in *Text and Voice: The Rhetoric of Authority in the Middle Ages*, ed. Marianne Børch (Odense: University of Southern Denmark Press, 2004.)

47. Interestingly, the history of the dissemination of the work registers the centrality of English to its contents. The *Cloud* is translated into Latin during the fifteenth century. In this Latin translation, the passage on monosyllabic prayer in chapter 7 becomes, "Ut ergo verbum istud non ignores, tale sit quale est hoc: DEUS siue AMOR, aut eis consimile, que Anglice loquendo vna sillaba exprimi possunt, de quibus id assumas quod melius tibi placet." See Anonymous, *The Latin Versions of* The Cloud of Unknowing, *Nubes ignorandi, MS. Bodley 856* (Analecta Cartusiana 119:1), ed. John Clark (New York: Edwin Mellen Press, 1999), 37, 4–7. Evidently, readers are intended to use English in the actual work of their prayer, even though they may be reading the description of that prayer in Latin.

48. This evident intent that spiritual practice take place in Middle English is, actually, another point on which the *Cloud*-author and Richard Rolle differ. Rolle's alliterative forms obtain in his Latinate writings and the prayers they contain as much as they do in his Middle English devotional writings. Perhaps the most striking instance of Rolle's incantatory style, indeed, occurs in *Orationes ad honorem nominis Ihesu*. This work is alliterative throughout, though Rolle starts with relatively little alliteration and gradually works himself up into an alliterative lather, so that by the end, he is in full Rollean alliterative ecstasy: "O dulcis Domine, qui diligis devotos, quantum tibi

teneor qui te ipsum tradidisti, ut me tuearis a tantis tormentis et servum susciperes, dimisso dolore, ad dulcissimum diligendum! O pie Ihesu, quam penaliter percuciebaris! Pectus meum pietas tue passionis penetret, et sagittet me sanguis quem sudasti. Memoria misericordie tue in mentis mee medullas migret, et funditur ferar a febribus funeris vulnerum tuorum virtute . . . O Trinitas, sine termino tene me in tranquillitate, et non tradas temptatori thronum tuum." Richard Rolle, *Emendatio vitae and Orationes ad honorem nominis Ihesu*, ed. Nicholas Watson (Toronto: Medieval Latin Texts, 1995), 83. Apparently, for Rolle, unlike the *Cloud*-author, the formal embodiment of spiritual practice—what Watson elegantly calls "canor"—in language can take place as easily in Latin as it can in English. But for the *Cloud*-author, English is valuable specifically for its formal properties and for how they differ from Latin's.

CHAPTER 2

1. Margery refers in her own book to a meeting she had with Julian: "And than sche was bodyn be owyr Lord for to gon to an ankres in the same cyté whych hyte Dame Jelyan. And so sche dede and schewyd hir the grace that God put in hir sowle of compunccyon, contricyon, swetnesse and devocyon, compassyon wyth holy meditacyon and hy contemplacyon, and ful many holy spechys and dalyawns that owyr Lord spak to hir sowle, and many wondirful revelacyons whech sche schewyd to the ankres to wetyn yf ther wer any deceyte in hem, for the ankres was expert in swech thyngys and good cownsel cowd gevyn. The ankres, heryng the mervelyows goodnes of owyr Lord, hyly thankyd God wyth al hir hert for hys visitacyon, cownselyng this creatur to be obedyent to the wyl of owyr Lord God and fulfyllyn wyth al hir mygthys whatevyr he put in hir sowle yf it wer not ageyn the worshep of God and profyte of hir evyn cristen, for, yf it wer, than it wer nowt the mevyng of a good spyryte but rathyr of an evyl spyrit." See Margery Kempe, *The Book of Margery Kempe*, ed. Lynn Staley (Kalamazoo: METS, 1996), lines 954–65.

2. Liz Herbert McAvoy, introduction to *A Companion to Julian of Norwich*, ed. Liz Herbert McAvoy (Cambridge: Brewer, 2008), 4. See also E. A. Jones, "Anchoritic Aspects of Julian of Norwich," in McAvoy, *Companion to Julian of Norwich*, 77.

3. G. Gibson, *Theater of Devotion*, 1 (see intro., n.20). Indeed, at this time, Norwich is second only to London in size and wealth among towns in England (19).

4. Ibid., 21.

5. Sarah McNamer writes about the Pseudo-Bonaventurian *Meditationes Vitae Christi* as a key text for inspiring affective identification with Christ and Mary. See McNamer, "Origins of *Meditationes Vitae Christi*," 905–6 (see intro., n.21).

6. Ibid., 912. See also Roger Ellis and Samuel Fanous, "1349–1412: Texts," in Fanous and Gillespie, *Cambridge Companion to Medieval English Mysticism*, 156 (see intro., n. 4).

7. McNamer, "Origins of *Meditationes Vitae Christi*," 918, 941.

8. For an analysis of imagery in the most heavily illustrated surviving manuscript of the *Meditationes*, see H. Flora's analysis of Paris Bibliothèque Nationale Ms. ital. 115, made near Pisa in the first half of the fourteenth century for Franciscan nuns. Flora argues that this manuscript was used in performative affective devotional practices. See H. Flora, *The Devout Belief of the Imagination: The Paris 'Meditationes Vitae Christi' and Female Franciscan Spirituality in Trecento Italy* (Turnhout, Belgium: Brepols, 2009). The *Meditationes*'s style of devotion, centering on affect, image, compassion, and imitation, became so popular that some scholars have argued that Margery Kempe's intensely affective devotion to Christ, however excessive it may seem to modern readers and even to medieval people not from Margery's native East Anglia, was in fact consistent with the impassioned devotional trends of the period. See Raymond Powell, "Margery Kempe: An Exemplar of Late Medieval Piety," *Catholic Historical Review* 89 (2003): 1–23. See also G. Gibson, *Theater of Devotion*, 48–49, 50.

9. McAvoy, *Companion to Julian of Norwich*, 7, 9. For more details on the "incarnational aesthetic" of East Anglia, see again G. Gibson, *Theater of Devotion*, 1 and following.

10. See *Vis.*, 69.4.21–23 (for explanation of abbreviated citations of Julian's writings, see intro., n. 16). For a discussion of Marian theology in East Anglia, see my fourth chapter on the N-Town *Mary* plays, likely written in or near Bury St. Edmunds in East Anglia.

11. See Ellis and Fanous, "1349–1412: Texts," 140.

12. Santha Bhattacharji, "Independence of Thought in Julian of Norwich," *Word and Spirit* 11 (1989): 79–92.

13. Andrew Sprung, "'We nevyr shall come out of hym': Enclosure and Immanence in Julian of Norwich's *Book of Showings*," *Mystics Quarterly* 19 (1993): 47–62.

14. For an extended treatment of Julian's bodiliness, see Elizabeth Robertson, "Medieval Medical Views of Women and Female Spirituality in the *Ancrene Wisse* and Julian of Norwich's *Showings*," in *Feminist Approaches to the Body in Medieval Literature*, ed. Linda Lomperis and Sarah Stanbury (Philadelphia: University of Pennsylvania Press, 1993), 142–67.

15. M. L. del Mastro, "Juliana of Norwich: Parable of the Lord and Servant: Radical Orthodoxy," *Mystics Quarterly* 14 (1988): 84–93; and Janet Grayson, "The Eschatological Adam's Kirtle," *Mystics Quarterly* 11 (1985): 153–60.

16. Kari Børresen, "Christ notre mère, la Théologie de Julienne de Norwich," *Mitteilungen und Forschungsbeitrage der Cusanus-Gesellschaft* 13 (1978): 320–29; Ritamarie Bradley, "The Motherhood Theme in Julian of Norwich," *14th-Century English Mystics Newsletter* 2 (1976): 25–30; Jennifer P. Heimmel, *"God Is Our Mother": Julian of Norwich and the Medieval Image of Christian Feminine Divinity* (Salzburg: Institut für Anglistik und Amerikanistik, Universität Salzburg, 1982); Sarah McNamer, "The Exploratory Image: God as Mother in Julian of Norwich's *Revelations of Divine Love*," *Mystics Quarterly* 15 (1989): 21–28.

17. Brant Pelphrey, *Love Was His Meaning: The Theology and Mysticism of Julian of Norwich*, Salzburg Studies in English Literature 92 (Salzburg: Institut für Anglistik und Amerikanistik, Universität Salzburg, 1982).

18. As per the Athanasian Creed, "For there is one Person of the Father, another of the Son, and another of the Holy Ghost.But the Godhead of the Father, of the Son, and of the Holy Ghost, is all one, the Glory equal, the Majesty co-eternal. Such as the Father is, such is the Son, and such is the Holy Ghost. The Father uncreate, the Son uncreate, and the Holy Ghost uncreate. The Father incomprehensible, the Son incomprehensible, and the Holy Ghost incomprehensible. The Father eternal, the Son eternal, and the Holy Ghost eternal.And yet they are not three eternals, but one eternal" (Alia est enim persona Patris alia Filii, alia Spiritus Sancti:Sed Patris, et Fili, et Spiritus Sancti una est divinitas, aequalis gloria, coeterna maiestas.Qualis Pater, talis Filius, talis Spiritus Sanctus. Increatus Pater, increatus Filius, increatus Spiritus Sanctus.Immensus Pater, immensus Filius, immensus Spiritus Sanctus.Aeternus Pater, aeternus Filius, aeternus Spiritus Sanctus. Et tamen non tres aeterni, sed unus aeternus). From *Fordham University Medieval Sourcebook*, http://www.fordham.edu/halsall/source/quicumque.asp.

19. Julian's work has been seen as theologically sophisticated since it was "rediscovered" in the seventeenth century. See Julian of Norwich, *A Book of Showings*, ed. James Colledge and Edmund Walsh (Toronto: PIMS, 1978), 10–14. For analyses of Julian's writing in historical context, see Frances Beer, *Women and Mystical Experience in the Middle Ages* (Woodbridge: Boydell, 1992), 132. See also Nicholas Watson, introduction to Julian of Norwich, *Writings of Julian of Norwich* (see intro., n. 16). The most thorough study of Julian's process of revising her vision from short to long version is Denise Baker, *Julian's Shewings: From Vision to Book* (Princeton, NJ: Princeton University Press, 1993). For an analysis of the rhetorical particularities of Julian's writings, see "Appendix: Rhetorical Figures Employed by Julian," in *Book of Showings*, 735–48. For an analysis of Julian's authorial self-positioning, see Felicity Riddy, "Julian of Norwich and Self-Textualization" in *Editing Women*, ed. Anne M. Hutchinson (Toronto: University of Toronto Press, 1998), 101–24; and

Lynn Staley, "The Trope of the Scribe and the Question of Literary Authority in the Works of Julian of Norwich and Margery Kempe," *Speculum* 66 (1991): 820–38. For readings of how Julian read, internalized, and responded to earlier works as provocations for her own, see Sandra McEntire, "The Likeness of God," in *Julian of Norwich: A Book of Essays*, ed. Sandra McEntire (New York: Garland, 1998), 3–35; Felicity Riddy, "Women Talking about the Things of God," in *Women and Literature in Britain, 1100–1500*, ed. Carol Meale (Cambridge: Cambridge University Press, 1993), 112; and Christopher Abbott, *Julian of Norwich: Autobiography and Theology* (London: Boydell and Brewer, 1999), 105–139. For an analysis of the styles and poetics of Julian's writings, see Ena Jenkins, "Julian's *Revelation of Love*: A Web of Metaphor," and Elizabeth Robertson, "Julian of Norwich's 'Modernist' Style and the Creation of Audience," both in *Companion to Julian of Norwich*, ed. Liz Hebert McAvoy (Cambridge: Brewer, 2008), 181–91 and 139–53.

20. For readings of Julian in literary and cultural context, the works of Nicholas Watson have been particularly illuminating. See Nicholas Watson, "The Trinitarian Hermeneutic in Julian of Norwich's *Revelation of Love*," in McEntire, *Julian of Norwich*, 61–90; "Censorship and Cultural Change" (see intro., n. 40); and "The Composition of Julian of Norwich's *Revelation of Love*," *Speculum* 68 (1993): 637–83. See also Watson, "Middle English Mystics," 539–65 (see ch. 1, n. 1). As he puts it in the lattermost essay, "That Hilton, Julian and the *Cloud*-author are the contemporaries of Chaucer, Langland, and the makers of the Wycliffite Bible—not to mention of a long series of socio-political convulsions—has been acknowledged, but not fully integrated into our picture of medieval English literature" (Watson, "Middle English Mystics," 540). Vincent Gillespie also notes Julian's sophistication and learnedness, saying, "The advanced and highly sophisticated vernacular theology of Julian of Norwich . . . derives much of its pliability and playful responsiveness to key issues . . . from her virtuoso command of the full range of contemporary didactic and devotional vernacular writing. . . . She is the master of multiple discourses, capable of alluding to and pastiching various contemporary styles of religious and philosophical writing, without ever allowing any of them to become dominant or specifying. Her text is a vast echo chamber of allusion and imitation" (Gillespie, "Vernacular Theology," 403 [see intro., n. 37]).

21. Nicholas Watson's magnificent analysis of Rolle's alliterative stylistics, both in Latin and in English, remains the most useful point of origin for the criticism on these vernacular treatises of contemplation and devotion. See Watson, *Richard Rolle*, 171–92 (see intro., n. 22).

22. *Vis.*, p. 63, heading, lines 3–4.

23. She recurs to this formulation of Jesus's "saying full comfortabely" that he may, can, shall, and will make all things well in the long version of her text (*Rev*, 217.31.2–10).

24. "Omne quod bonum est boni participatione bonum." Boethius, *Philosophiae Consolatio*, bk. 3, prose 11, sentence 8 (see intro., n. 12).

25. Charles Lock also notes this expository difference between Julian's writings and those of other "mystical" or "vernacular theological" writers in the period. See Lock, "Apophatic Discourse," 213 (see ch. 1, n. 46).

26. As will become clear in what follows, the specific *consolatio* with which Julian's work resonates most loudly is Boethius's *Consolatio Philosophiae*. Archival proof of Julian's having known the *Consolatio* directly is lacking: we do not know, based on manuscript evidence or Julian's direct mention of "Boethius," that she read his work, although we do know that a copy of the *Consolatio* circulated in Norwich during the late Middle Ages, and likely during her lifetime. As Norman Tanner points out, there was at least one copy of Boethius's *Consolatio* being passed between owners in Norwich in the late Middle Ages; it is thus plausible that his work would have come to Julian's attention in book form. See Norman Tanner, *The Church in Late Medieval Norwich 1370–1532* (Toronto: PIMS, 1984), 329–30. This should not be surprising: the *Consolatio* was one of the most frequently copied and widely circulated literary works throughout the High and Late Middle Ages, and it was a frequent part of classical curriculum as well as, evidently, part of vernacular literary

culture. On the pedagogical role of the *Consolatio* in medieval schools, see Margaret Gibson, "Boethius in the Carolingian Schools," *Transactions of the Royal Historical Society* 32 (1982): 43–56. The proliferation of copies of the *Consolatio* in Latin and the concomitant proliferation of glosses and commentaries on it in the ninth through thirteenth centuries further attest to its popularity as part of a liberal arts curriculum. For details on these copies and commentaries, see the introduction to Pierre Courcelle, *La Consolation de Philosophie dans la tradition littéraire* (Paris: Études Augustiniennes, 1967). In view of these cultural and literary contexts, the *Consolatio* was in wide enough circulation that it is plausible that Julian would have been aware of it.

27. *Vis.*, 63, heading, line 3; *Rev.*, 139.5.3; 161.10.55; 217.31.2. Furthermore, Julian uses the term *comfort* more than seventy times throughout her works, to signal the feeling she derives from her visions and seeks to impart to readers.

28. "Manet etiam spectator desuper cunctorum praescius deus uisionisque ejus praesens semper aeternitas cum nostrorum actuum futura qualitate concurrit bonis praemia, malis supplicia dispensans. Nec frustra sunt in deo positae spes precesque; quae cum rectae sunt, inefficaces esse non possunt. Auersamini igitur uitia, colite uirtutes, ad rectas spes animum subleuate, humiles preces in excelsa porrigite. Magna uobis est, si dissimulare non uultis, necessitas indicta probitatis, cum ante oculos agitis judicis cuncta cernentis." Boethius, *Philosophiae Consolatio*, bk. 5, pr. 6, sentences 45–48.

29. For "endeless" or "endelesslye," see *Vis.*, 101.18.17–18. For "sekerlye," *Vis.*, 101.18.19.

30. See *OED*, s.v. "word" 2a, "utterance."

31. For Julian, this eternal and changeless love is the "endelesse comforth" of God (*Vis.*, 101.18.19). When she, at the very end, characterizes God's intent toward mankind, she again deploys the vocabulary of eternity, saying, "God will ever that we be sekere in lufe" (*Vis.*, 119.25.32).

32. Glasscoe also notes the centrality of eternity to Julian's argument and suggests that Julian and the *Cloud*-author have a certain relationship to each other in their mutual valuation of time, and of the idea that God keeps mankind safe in time. See Marion Glasscoe, *Medieval English Mystics: Games of Faith* (New York: Longman, 1993), 264.

33. For further treatment of the "evere" passage, see ibid., 237.

34. "Or that he made us, he loved us" (*Rev.*, 295.53.30).

35. See Glasscoe, *Medieval English Mystics*, 264. As Elisabeth A. Andersen has noted, in her treatment of Mechthild of Magdeburg's visionary revelations, Boethius was one of the most important touchstones for theorizing the eternity of God throughout the Middle Ages, especially for religious women. See Elisabeth A. Andersen, *The Voices of Mechthild of Magdeburg* (Bern: Peter Lang, 2000), 220 and 224.

36. Nicholas Watson has identified Julian's message of universal salvation as typical of vernacular theology in late fourteenth-century England. See Nicholas Watson, "Visions of Inclusion: Universal Salvation and Vernacular Theology," *Journal of Medieval and Early Modern Studies* 27 (1997): 145–87.

37. See also Cynthea Masson, "The Point of Coincidence" in McEntire, *Julian of Norwich*, 167.

38. Ibid.

39. "ad aeternitatem tempus, ad punctum medium circulus, ita est fati series mobilis ad prouidentiae stabilem simplicitatem." Boethius, *Philosophiae Consolatio*, bk. 4, prose 6, sentence 17.

40. "Haec actus etiam fortunasque hominum indissolubili causarum conexione constringit." Boethius, *Philosophiae Consolatio*, bk. 4, prose 6, sentence 19.

41. Editors Edmund Colledge and James Walsh have noted Julian's use of Boethius in her articulation of these ideas. See Julian of Norwich, *Book of Showings*, 337–39nn10, 18, 20, 21, 36, 39.

42. As Watson's edition notes, another version of the *Revelation* at this point reads instead, "Nor nathinge es done be happe ne be aventure, botte be the endeles forluke of the widsome of God" (*Rev.*, 163.11.11).

43. Boethius, *Philosophiae Consolatio*, bk. 5, prose 1, sentence 14.

44. Moreover, as Colledge and Walsh note, her lexical choices here resemble Chaucer's in his Middle English *Boece*. Like Julian, Chaucer describes the perception of "chance" and "happe" as contingent upon "unforseyn" causes and "unwar" human blindness: "forsothe it nis nat of naught, for it hath his propre causes, of whiche causes the cours unforseyn and unwar semeth to han makid hap." Geoffrey Chaucer, *Boece*, in *The Riverside Chaucer*, ed. Larry D. Benson (Boston: Houghton Mifflin, 1987), bk. 5, prose 1, 74–6. For a list of the similarities between Julian's third revelation and *Boece*, see again Julian of Norwich, *Book of Showings*, 337–39nn.

45. "ordo namque fatalis ex prouidentiae simplicitate procedit"; ". . . ita deus prouidentia quidem singulariter stabiliterque facienda disponit." Boethius, *Philosophiae Consolatio*, bk. 4, prose 6, sentences 11 and 12.

46. Reflecting this spontaneity and naturalness, Marion Glasscoe describes Julian's style as "speech-like." Marion Glasscoe, introduction to *Julian of Norwich, A Revelation of Love*, ed. Marion Glasscoe (Exeter: University of Exeter Press, 1986), xv–xvi.

47. Cristina Cervone notes that Julian's poetics tend to produce "timelessness and placelessness," particularly in the parable of the master and servant. See Cristina Maria Cervone, *Poetics of the Incarnation: Middle English Writing and the Leap of Love* (Philadelphia: University of Pennsylvania Press, 2013), 138–55.

48. Cervone also notes that Julian is interested in "the importance of time in human perception," particularly in her analysis of the lord and servant parable (ibid., 142).

49. Ruth Caspar gives attention to the modal verb passages in Julian's text, albeit focusing on them thematically rather than for their syntactic and formal effect. See Ruth Caspar, "'All Shall Be Well': Prototypical Symbols of Hope," *Journal of the History of Ideas* 42 (1981): 139–50.

50. "Sed prius mens in se ipsa consideranda est antequam sit particeps Dei, et in ea reperienda est imago ejus. Diximus enim eam etsi amissa Dei participatione obsoletam atque deformem, Dei tamen imaginem permanere. Eo quippe ipso imago ejus est, quo ejus capax est, ejusque particeps esse potest; quod tam magnum bonum, nisi per hoc quod imago ejus est, non potest. Ecce ergo mens meminit sui, intelligit se, diligit se: hoc si cernimus, cernimus trinitatem; nondum quidem Deum, sed jam imaginem Dei." Augustine, *De Trinitate*, bk. 14, ch. 8, 11 (see intro., n. 9).

51. Patricia Dailey has also emphasized the presence of Augustinian Trinitarian logic in the *Revelation*, focusing on the master-servant parable and Julian's emphasis on "substance" and "sensualite" as figures for inner and outer personhood. See Dailey, *Promised Bodies*, 161–66 (see intro., n. 17).

52. God is eternal, existing outside of time; the world exists in time but will never end, and is thus perpetual. As Boethius explains in his final prose, "Thus, if we want to place fit labels on things, following Plato, we can say truly that God is eternal, the world, perpetual" (Itaque si digna rebus nomina uelimus imponere, Platonem sequentes deum quidem aeternum, mundum uero dicamus esse perpetuum). Boethius, *Philosophiae Consolatio*, bk. 5, prose 6, sentence 14.

53. This understanding of Jesus's participation in the world as perpetual is not unique to Julian; Meister Eckhart reminds readers that "the Father gives his Son birth without ceasing." In *Meister Eckhart: The Essential Sermons, Commentaries, Treatises, and Defense, German Works*, Sermon 6, ed. Edmund Colledge and Bernard McGinn (New York: Paulist Press, 1981), 188.

54. Several scholars have recently come to question her assertion that she is unlearned. Jeremy Catto notes that Julian's "remarkable learning, of a generally monastic kind, and her familiarity with rhetorical colours, also throw light on what the life of a recluse could achieve, free from secular cares yet unburdened by the demands of a community" (Catto, "1349–1412, Culture and history," 123; see intro., n. 45). He later says, "Julian of Norwich, whose sex precluded her from sharing the university experience, was clearly familiar with a rich literature in Latin and had some rhetorical training" (127).

55. This turn toward a theoretically unlimited community of Christian contemplative faithful bodies forth the turn that Nicholas Watson and others see in late medieval contemplative literature

more broadly. As he puts it, "While Christian contemplative thought and practice has its own pronouncedly elitist tendencies—tendencies that were only ever partly translated out of their original social register into that of the spiritual—the late-medieval idea that everyone should, in some sense, participate in contemplation has deep roots" (Watson, introduction to Fanous and Gillespie, *Cambridge Companion to Medieval English Mysticism*, 12; see intro., n. 14).

CHAPTER 3

1. *The Cloud of Unknowing* does briefly address the active life, though mainly to dismiss it as a concern separate from or at least preliminary to the *Cloud*'s own theory of spiritual practice. See *CU*, prologue, p. 2, lines 2, 7–8, 24; prologue, p. 3, line 1 (see ch. 1, n. 3).

2. Boethius's *Consolation of Philosophy*, for instance, reveals that the pi embroidered on Philosophy's dress, which denotes "practica" and which later medieval writers construe as the active life, is positioned lower than the theta, which denotes "theorica" and which comes to signal the life of contemplation (Boethius, *Philosophiae Consolatio*, bk. 1, prose 1, sentence 4). For a treatment of when and how practica and theorica come to signal active and contemplative life, see Ian Johnson, "Making the *Consolatio* in Middle English," in *A Companion to Boethius in the Middle Ages*, ed. Noel Harold Kaylor and Philip Edward Philips (Leiden: Brill, 2012), 418–19.

3. Gregory the Great recognizes that such an "oscillation is necessary" between active and contemplative lives. See Bernard McGinn, *The Growth of Mysticism* (New York: Crossroad Publishing, 1994), 74–79, at 75.

4. "The Victorines insist that the final goal of the life of faith is not the contemplative enjoyment of God in itself, 'but consists in taking on Christ, and therefore returning from ecstasy to loving service of neighbor.'" Steven Chase, *Contemplation and Compassion* (Maryknoll, NY: Orbis Books, 2003), 13.

5. As Nicholas Watson notes, "Originally, the *vita mixta* of bishops and abbots was exceptional. From the twelfth century on, however, some contemplative orders—the canons and, later, the friars—began to engage publicly in active ministries, increasing numbers of laypeople undertook contemplative programmes, and the hierarchic relation between the contemplative and the active was challenged by those who regarded preaching as an activity as important as prayer. . . . In the late Middle Ages . . . the adjective *contemplative* slowly followed its noun into renewed identification with an inner state . . . as the association between the term *vita contemplativa* and professional monasticism weakened in parallel with what may have been an ideological weakening of the monastic movement itself." See Watson, introduction to Fanous and Gillespie, *Cambridge Companion to Medieval English Mysticism*, 13 (see intro., n. 14). Moreover, as Jeremy Catto notes, contemplative practice in this period escapes "from the structured world of religious houses and reclusories where spiritual advice from the learned was available through personal instruction, into a larger literary world in which texts were scrutinized, licensed, and proliferated systematically for the edification of a sophisticated and independent-minded laity." See Catto, "1349–1412, Culture and history," 114 (see intro., n. 45).

6. As Nevill Coghill suggested, in the mid-twentieth century, the focus on salvation and contemplation in *Piers* is an emergent property of Langland's revision of his A-text into his B-text. See Nevill Coghill, *The Pardon of Piers Plowman* (London: British Academy Proceedings, 1945), 38. For this reason, I omit the A-text entirely from my discussion. However, the parallel-text version of *Piers Plowman* that I cite parenthetically in text does include some A-text references (see ch. 1, n. 14).

7. H. W. Wells, in point of fact, argued that the three "Dos" whom Will seeks—Do-well, Do-bet, and Do-best—are Langland's representations of the well-lived active life, the contemplative life, and the mixed life, respectively. Indeed, Wells went so far as to contend that the fundamental

structure of the poem is indebted to Langland's ongoing meditation on the hierarchy of active, contemplative, and mixed life, and, indeed, that Langland's conclusion is to valorize the mixed life clearly and decisively above the other two, in the tradition of Aquinas, Gregory, and the Victorines. H. W. Wells, "The Philosophy of Piers Plowman," *PMLA* 53 (1938): 340–44. S. S. Hussey suggests that Langland's privileging of the mixed life over the contemplative life goes farther in praising the mixed life than do other Middle English treatments of the issue. Hussey, "Langland, Hilton, and the Three Lives," *Review of English Studies* 7 (1956): 136–37.

8. Mark Miller, "Sin and Structure in *Piers Plowman:* On the Medieval Split Subject," *MLQ* 76 (2015): 201–24, at 215–17.

9. In insisting on the centrality of *Piers*'s formal operations to its contemplative functioning, my work reaches back to the *Piers* studies of the 1960s through the early 1990s, when scholars began to argue for the poem's *poetic* merits, diverting a then long-standing scholarly focus on how it fit into theological and political history. Scholars began to assert the innate and immutable literary merits of the poem, and they asserted them on the basis of the poem's formal functionality and construction. Elizabeth Salter, for instance, insisted that the artistic construction of the poem—its allegorical workings, its alliterations, and its sermonic structure—were of primary interest in studying the poem. In her words, "a reading of *Piers Plowman* which neglects the fact that this is essentially a work of art, a product of the creative imagination, is seriously restricted." See Salter, *Piers Plowman, an Introduction* (Cambridge, MA: Harvard University Press, 1962), 7. She later says, "No one has ever denied the interest of *Piers Plowman,* but only recently has it been defended wholeheartedly for artistic merits" (12). In these studies and others like them, scholars registered that the formal properties of the poem were intimately connected to its thematic investments. Salter asserts that, "more than any other medieval poet, [Langland] feels himself to be committed to the rarest of all purposes, and like the mystics, his art is inseparable from his vision" (63). But for Salter, Langland's art is just plain better than the art of the contemporary mystics: "Hilton *tells* of the process; Langland *shows* it to us in action" (88, italics original). These studies, moreover, manifested the New Critical turn in medieval studies; as such, they tended to focus not on formal qualities per se but, rather, on how those qualities succeeded or failed in producing something like objective, transhistorical literary value in the work. Though it will, like these much earlier studies, focus on the sensory properties of the poem, my study will be less interested in establishing categories like "literary value" or "literary success" than in seeking to understand, in the context of medieval cultural history and of insular contemplative writing in particular, why certain sensory properties and formal elements might have been selected and cultivated in *Piers Plowman.*

10. See Anne Middleton, "The Audience and Public of *Piers Plowman,*" in *Middle English Alliterative Poetry,* ed. David Lawton (Cambridge: Brewer, 1982), 101–23, at 114–16.

11. Maureen Quilligan, *The Language of Allegory* (Ithaca, NY: Cornell University Press, 1979), 33.

12. *MED,* s.v. "kennen," 1a, 1b. *OED,* s.v. "ken," v. 2a, 3b.

13. The wordplay that this particular term will make possible for Langland has been noted and analyzed by Mary Clemente Davlin, who argues, indeed, that wordplay is perhaps the cardinal formal device of the poem and is designed to draw the reader deep into its theological problems and controversies by creating enigmas in language that beg to be pored over—wordplay, that is, demands active participation in the poem. As she puts it, "Not only particular words and passages, but the poem as a whole demands the reader's participating in completing, discovering, or creating its meaning. The demands which *Piers* makes upon its readers are extreme, and we play a game, work a puzzle, enter a competition with the poet when we study it." See Mary Clemente Davlin, *A Game of Heuene: Word Play and Meaning in Piers Plowman B* (Cambridge: Brewer, 1989), 3, 111.

14. *OED,* s.v. "kind," n. I: 1a, 3, 4a, 5, 6, 7, 8, 9; II: 10, 13a.

15. *MED,* s.v. "kindeli," adv. 1, 2, 3, 4. Hugh White has noted that "one of the reasons why the *kynde* can function so importantly for Langland is that *kynde* and related terms have a great semantic richness. Nature is one of the more polysemous words in Modern English, and it can be argued

that Middle English *kynde* was even more so, since its field included not only the idea of nature but also the idea of kindness, which modern nature terms do not cover." See Hugh White, *Nature and Salvation in Piers Plowman* (Cambridge: Brewer, 1988), 1. White devotes a chapter to the phrase "kynde knowynge" in Langland, arguing that, in this phrase, "kynde" means "true" or "proper," not just "natural" (44–45, 47, 53). See also C. S. Lewis, *Studies in Words* (Cambridge: Cambridge University Press, 1960), 26–33.

16. Michelle Karnes has suggested that "kynde knowyng" is Langland's way of categorizing one of the two major types of knowledge, according to Thomistic epistemologies: natural knowing, derived from sensation and intellection. The other type, revelatory knowledge, is not encompassed by "kynde knowynge." See Michelle Karnes, "Will's Imagination in *Piers Plowman*," *Journal of English and Germanic Philology* 108 (2009): 27–58. Similarly, Nicolette Zeeman understands "kynde" to denote "nature," and "kyndeliche" to denote "naturally," so she sees "kynde knowynge" as "natural knowledge." See Nicolette Zeeman, *Piers Plowman and the Medieval Discourse of Desire* (Cambridge: Cambridge University Press, 2006), 3, 7, 20. In her analysis of "kynde" knowing in opposition with "clergie," Zeeman understands "kynde knowynge" as "natural knowledge," and clergie as "revealed" knowledge (201). More recently, Cristina Maria Cervone has defined Langland's "kynde knowynge" as "innate understanding, particularly as noted in a person without clerical training, where that lack of learnedness may make the individual and especially attractive or likely recipient of grace." See Cervone, *Poetics of the Incarnation*, 114 (see ch. 2, n. 47). Rebecca Davis contends that "kynde" for Langland signals nature as an "exemplarist" discourse, form, and reality, with which the dreaming Will can and must compare himself in order to gain greater understanding of himself and his relation to Truth. See Rebecca Davis, "'Save Man Alone': Human Exceptionality in *Piers Plowman* and the Exemplarist Tradition," in *Medieval Latin and Middle English Literature: Essays in Honor of Jill Mann*, ed. Christopher Cannon and Maura Nolan (London: Brewer, 2011), 41–64.

17. James Simpson has argued that Langland's main cognitive drive is less for "natural knowledge" or "innate knowledge" in the poem than it is for an affective kind of knowledge. This mode of knowing is deeply tied to the formal structure of the poem, at the level of the poem's rhetorical organization and *modus tractandi*. See James Simpson, "From Reason to Affective Knowledge" (see intro., n. 24).

18. For a paradigmatic treatment of semantic correlation's being registered alliteratively in English, see Anne Middleton, "Aelfric's Answerable Style: The Rhetoric of the Alliterative Prose," *Studies in Medieval Culture* (1973): 83–91. For a treatment of this poetic phenomenon in the poem more broadly, see Bernard F. Huppé, "Petrus id est Christus: Word Play in Piers Plowman, the B-Text," *ELH* 17 (1950): 163–90. Huppé argues that Langland uses sound (particularly alliteration, assonance, consonance) to emphasize and underscore word meanings and relationships between words, both within English and between English and Latin (164, 169).

19. Mary Carruthers also identifies this concept as central to the poem's logic and theology. For her, "the word *kynde* means 'nature,' yet it always carries the idea of innate or inherent being. . . . Thus to understand *kyndely* would be to understand a thing in its essential being. . . . But the phrase 'kynde knowyng' also means to understand something according to one's own nature or essential being." Mary Carruthers, *The Search for St. Truth: A Study of Meaning in Piers Plowman* (Evanston, IL: Northwestern University Press, 1973), 82.

20. Schmidt's commentary on this passage defines "kynde knowynge" as "natural, instinctive knowledge or understanding." He goes on to note that this concept is often interpreted as a vernacular rendering of "synderesis," "ratio naturalis," "sapientia," or "notitia intuitive." See A. V. C. Schmidt, *Piers Plowman*, vol. 2, p. 486. The phrasing "kynde knowynge" recurs five additional times, at B.1.163; B.5.538; B.10.217; B.15.2; and B.15.49.

21. In this analysis, I will use the B-text as my base, turning to the C-text toward the end of the chapter.

22. According to Karnes, Thought, Wit, and the other preimaginative cognitive faculties are engaged with precisely to be dispelled, ultimately in preference to imagination as a far more powerful meditative tool. See Karnes, *Imagination, Meditation and Cognition*, 179 (see intro., n. 30). According to Zeeman, the poem's "reiterative experiences of failure, rebuke, and loss," which often take place in the poem's staging of epistemological processes, are what allow the poem to achieve "its most powerful and uncompromising locations of desire" (Zeeman, *Piers Plowman and Medieval Discourse*, 18, 19–22). Kruger also notes the "problems of epistemology" that this section of the poem enacts and notes the reciprocal recognition between Thought and Will himself, arguing that "in focusing attention on Will's self, the action of the third dream thus raises an epistemological question: how can will arrive at self-knowledge?" See Steven Kruger, "Mirrors and the Trajectory of Vision in *Piers Plowman*," *Speculum* 66 (1991): 74–95, at 75–76. Mary Carruthers has argued that one of the fundamental organizing principles of the poem is Will's cognitive development (Carruthers, *Search for St. Truth*). In James Simpson's formulation, "movement in the poem is produced out of epistemological or cognitive limitations: Will needs to move toward Study, to govern his untutored and exuberant 'wit,' just as he must move on from Study to learn Dowel from deeper Scriptural sources of knowledge" (Simpson, "From Reason to Affective Knowledge," 2).

23. As Emily Steiner puts it, "this section of the poem is less about formal education and its discontents than it is about forms of learning and their limits." Emily Steiner, *Reading Piers Plowman* (Cambridge: Cambridge University Press, 2013), 99.

24. As Robert Pasnau and Elaine Scarry have both set out, medieval writers were well aware of the Aristotelian hierarchy of modes of knowing, with the sensory normally at the bottom of a ladder that then ascended to imagination, reason, and eventually intellection. Langland seems here to be inverting that hierarchy, or at least repositioning sensation higher up the ladder. See Pasnau, *Theories of Cognition*, 126 (see intro., n. 26). For a more detailed treatment of the relation of physical sensation to intellectual knowing, see Scarry, "Well-Rounded Sphere," 95–96 (see intro., n. 27).

25. As Pierre Courcelle's *Connais-toi Toi-même* reveals, the contemplative tradition, from Plato through the Middle Ages, identifies self-knowledge as a core facet of gaining contemplative understanding. Indeed, self-knowledge is taken as the primary obligation in the effort to come to know oneself as the image of God. Pierre Courcelle, *Connais-toi Toi-même: De Socrate à St. Bernard* (Paris: Etudes Augustiniennes, 1974), 115, 117, 121, 131, 132. For Platonic and Neoplatonic writers, Courcelle notes, "Si nous revenons à notre propre Coeur, nous trouverons Dieu, qui est au fond. Mais si, faute de rentrer en soi, on ne se trouve pas soi-même, *a fortiori* l'on ne peut trouver Dieu. Car rien ne sert de chercher au-dehors do soi le Dieu du Coeur. En réalité, c'est ce Dieu qui, en nous parlant et en nous illuminant, nous fait connaître à nous-même [If we return to our proper heart, we will find God, who is at the bottom. But if, absent a reentry into oneself, we do not find ourselves, *a fortiori* we cannot find God. Because it serves no point to search outside of the self for the God of the heart. In reality, it's this God who, in speaking to us and illuminating us, makes us know ourselves]" (137).

26. Mary Carruthers identifies this as the core problem Will faces. See Carruthers, *Search for St. Truth*, 115–118, 128.

27. Karnes notes the dangers and inadequacies of Thought as a representative of "kynde" or natural knowing, pointing out that Will must go beyond him if he is to attain any true understanding of God. See Karnes, "Will's Imagination," 38–39.

28. See also Kruger, "Mirrors," 76, 78–79; Steiner, *Reading Piers Plowman*, 97.

29. In this insistence, the poem makes contact with Cistercian psychology, such as that of William of St. Thierry, who emphasizes that Christ requires self-knowledge as a corequisite of spiritual contemplation. See William of St. Thierry, *The Nature of the Body and the Soul*, in *Three Treatises on Man*, ed. Bernard McGinn (Kalamazoo, MI: Cistercian Publications, 1977), 103. See also the anonymous *Treatise on the Spirit and the Soul* in the same collection, 181.

30. See Middleton, "Aelfric's Answerable Style," 88.

31. Masha Raskolnikov notes that "to get to the poem's end . . . Will must engage figures that are increasingly *like* him in their nature." Raskolnikov, *Body against Soul: Gender and Sowlehele in Middle English Allegory* (Columbus: Ohio State University Press, 2008), 188.

32. See also Susan Deskis and Thomas Hill, "'The longe man ys seld wys': Proverbial Characterization and Langland's Long Will," *Yearbook of Langland Studies* 18 (2004): 73–79, at 73.

33. Thus, the poem's alliterative doublet and the paronomasia that it creates bear out Bloomfield's claim about the logic of medieval personification allegory; namely, that medieval personification allegory assumes that a personification is what it does. Therefore, Will "wills." See Morton Bloomfield, "A Grammatical Approach to Medieval Personification Allegory," *Modern Philology* 60 (1963): 165.

34. In Carruthers's phrasing, "It is a poem of searching, the record of a mental wandering to find a way to the soul's native country" (Carruthers, *Search for St. Truth*, 25).

35. Joseph Wittig has demonstrated that *Meditationes piissimae* had a significant impact on the construction of passus 9–12 in the B-text, the "inward journey" of Will into the facets of his own mind. According to Wittig, the *Meditationes* helped organize the poem's focus on self-knowledge as the goal of these passus. See Joseph Wittig, "*Piers Plowman* B, Passus IX-XII: Elements in the Design of the Inward Journey," *Traditio* 28 (1972): 211–80.

36. In arguing for a progressive reading of the poem, in which earlier efforts at gaining understanding are exhausted in favor of later, and ultimately more successful, models, my readings correspond with those of James Simpson, although I believe that *Piers* never jettisons reason per se in favor of affect but instead moves readers toward an increasingly participatory and increasingly integrated model of cognitive knowledge. See Simpson, "From Reason to Affective Knowledge," 1–23.

37. This passage also encodes William Langland's own authorial signature. For a reading of Langland's own "authorial evanescence," see Anne Middleton, "William Langland's 'Kynde Name': Authorial Signature and Social Identity in Late Fourteenth-Century England," in *Literary Practice and Social Change in Britain, 1380–1530*, ed. Lee Patterson (Berkeley: University of California Press, 1990), 15–82, at 18.

38. 1 Corinthians 13:12: "Videmus nunc per speculum in ænigmate: tunc autem facie ad faciem. Nunc cognosco ex parte: tunc autem cognoscam sicut et cognitus sum" (For now we see through a glass, darkly; but then face to face: now I know in part; but then shall I know even as also I am known). Nicolette Zeeman agrees that Langland's "Will" is designed to reflect and embody Augustinian notions of will, though she branches out from the *De Trinitate* also to includes theories of will that appear in the *Confessions* and elsewhere. See Zeeman, *Piers Plowman and Medieval Discourse*, 68–72.

39. As James Simpson puts it, "It is this idea [that Will can only know charity through "wil oone"], indeed, which shapes the most profound parts of the poem, from Passus XV onward, in which Will, as the human will, seeks a more direct and experiential knowledge of God" (Simpson, "From Reason to Affective Knowledge," 7).

40. As Carruthers puts it of the quest for kynde knowing, "In searching for 'kynde knowing,' of Dowel, Will is also seeking himself and seeking God—though the key to the proper understanding of the others lies within himself" (*Search for St. Truth*, 83).

41. Emily Steiner also points out the radical multiplicity of this moment. Petrus, she says, signifies not just Piers himself, but also, "both Christ's apostle, St. Peter, to whom Christ entrusted the Church, and Piers's alter ego as Christ" (Steiner, *Reading Piers Plowman*, 161).

42. For a treatment of medieval connections of the Trinity with marriage and how Langland's poem modifies and reinvents them, see M. Teresa Tavormina, "Kindly Similitude: Langland's Matrimonial Trinity," in *Modern Philology* 80 (1982): 117–28. As she notes, although this association was by no means standard in medieval theological works, it was also not unheard of, despite its being condemned by Augustine himself in *De Trinitate* (117).

43. As Steiner notes, trinitarianism is "a foundational theology for *Piers Plowman*" (*Reading Piers Plowman*, 189). Steiner goes on to perform an elegant reading of the useful explanatory powers of the marriage analogy for the Trinity, noting in particular its affective power (194–96).

44. Lawrence Clopper has argued for the salience of Trinitarian exemplarity in the poem—what he calls the "trifunctional image"—with particular focus on how Langland uses trifunctional images to capture and comment on the nature and structure of the social world. See Lawrence Clopper, *Songes of Rechelesnesse*: *Langland and the Franciscans* (Ann Arbor: University of Michigan Press, 1997), 149–60.

45. Tavormina suggests that Langland arrogates increasing importance and legitimacy to marriage over the course of his revisions of his poem. See M. Teresa Tavormina, *Kindly Similitude: Marriage and Family in Piers Plowman* (Cambridge: Brewer, 1995). For her, marriage is a "kindly similitude" of God himself—a natural figure for him—"that reflects and transmits a divine exemplar of community" (i).

46. It is this kind of awkward ontological overlapping that gives Augustine such anxiety in the *De Trinitate*. See *De Trinitate*, bk. 9, ch. 9, 16.

47. Tavormina, *Kindly Similitude*, 140–47.

48. This problem of hierarchy had bedeviled the poem's earlier attempts to figure the Trinity via its incomplete treatments of Do-Well, Do-Better, and Do-Best, often construed in scholarship as personifications of the active life, the contemplative life, and the mixed life. Nevill Coghill argued that this Trinity of Dos "became the thought on which the whole revision [into the B-text] was moulded; once more, there was an equation of Trinities" (*Pardon of Piers*, 54), but this argument does not register that the Dos are a highly theologically unorthodox kind of Trinity, since even *grammatically* they bespeak comparison and superiority. Langland's meditation on the nature and role of contemplation and action in human life will unfurl along less hierarchical lines.

49. See also Steiner, *Reading Piers Plowman*, 196–97.

50. For an argument that Langland has a strong theological bias toward Augustine in general, in particular for his theorizing about desire, see Zeeman, *Piers Plowman and Medieval Discourse*, 30–31. In activating this Augustinian theory, Langland is also undoubtedly thinking with Pseudo-Bernard's *Meditationes piissimae*, which, as Joseph Wittig has shown, is a crucial source for the poem (Wittig, "Inward Journey," 211–80).

51. See Courcelle, *Connais-toi Toi-même*, 149.

52. See Carruthers, *Search for St. Truth*, 16–17.

53. In this assertion, my argument reinforces Andrew Cole's reading of the Tree of Charity as, among other things, a meditation on the social order that reaffirms the centrality of work to living a good life in a Christian community. See Andrew Cole, "Trifunctionality and the Tree of Charity," *ELH* 61 (1995): 1–27. For Cole, the Tree of Charity picks up the tripartite social order that had been evoked in the half acre and reworks it to amplify and nuance the feudal labor crisis that had been staged in the earlier scene. As Cole puts it, "Langland's project of writing, as theologically centered as it may be, always feels the imperatives of history itself, always betrays them" (17). To my mind, as I will explain shortly, Langland's historical imperatives, particularly as they concern normative labor practices, are *coincident with* much of his theological interest.

54. In comparing *Piers* with one of its sources, the *Meditationes piissimae*, Joseph Wittig noted that however much *caritas* in the poem may be aimed at contemplation, it must "nevertheless express itself in action" ("Inward Journey," 225).

55. In this emphasis on "kynde" knowing as self-knowing that is also the knowing of others en route to a knowing of God, *Piers* echoes the Cluniac tradition, which construes the knowing of the self as a knowing of others: "Chez les Clunisiens aussi, le *connais-toi toi-même* est en faveur. Pierre de Celles (1183) flétrit l'homme qui ne se connaît pas et le compare à un aveugle. Il l'exhorte à se connaître, au moins en observant autrui [According to the Cluniacs also, the "know yourself" is in favor. Peter Cellensis (1183) criticizes the man who does not know himself and compares him

with a blind man. He exhorts this man to know himself, at least by observing others]" (Courcelle, *Connais-toi Toi-même*, 278).

56. This notion resonates with Kate Crassons's argument about need and poverty in the poem; namely, "that misrecognizing one's own need affects others" and that the poem seeks to train readers to understand their own material needs and obligations as linked up with those of other people. See Kate Crassons, *Claims of Poverty* (Notre Dame, IN: University of Notre Dame Press, 2010), 29.

57. The idea of "kyndely" labor as natural or virtuous social activity directed toward one's fellow Christians corresponds with Andrew Galloway's arguments about Langland's Samaritan. For Galloway, "The Samaritan's notion of 'kyndenesse' sacralizes an ethos of secular social cohesion, a community figuratively warmed and illumined by its shared knowledge as much as its common goods . . . and including within Langland's Whitmanesque surveillance both 'werkmen' and 'ye wise men that with the world deleth.'" Andrew Galloway, "The Making of a Social Ethic in Late-Medieval England: From Gratitudo to 'Kyndenesse,'" *Journal of the History of Ideas* 55 (1994): 365–83, at 382.

58. This reading of *Piers*'s retheorizing of the mixed life dovetails with the current tendency to examine Langland's attitudes toward labor, work, and social responsibility as the focus of his poem. Indeed, perhaps the single most powerful current in Langland studies since the late twentieth century has been to assert that *Piers Plowman* is a social poem, thoroughly imbricated with contemporary socioeconomic and especially labor issues of the late fourteenth century. See Steven Justice, *Writing and Rebellion* (Berkeley: University of California Press, 1994), 102–39; see also Steven Justice, "Authorial Work and Literary Ideology," in *Written Work: Langland, Labor, and Authorship*, ed. Justice and Kathryn Kerby-Fulton (Philadelphia: University of Pennsylvania Press, 1997), 1–12. According to many of these studies, Langland's primary ethical focus is not so much on abstract matters of spiritual contemplation but instead on the hard and fast realities of how being a good Christian Englishman demanded a certain level of labor and social engagement. See Anne Middleton, "Acts of Vagrancy: The C Version 'Autobiography' and the Statute of 1388," in Justice and Kerby-Fulton, *Written Work*, 208–317; Ralph Hanna, "Will's Work," in Justice and Kerby-Fulton, *Written Work*, 23–66; Eleanor Johnson, "The Poetics of Waste," *PMLA* 127 (2012): 460–76; J. A. Burrow, "Wasting Time, Wasting Words in *Piers Plowman* B and C," *Yearbook of Langland Studies* 17 (2003): 191–202. *Staging Contemplation* reaffirms that these emphases on labor and social justice are absolutely warranted, but it simultaneously insists that these very emphases on prosocial, active labor in the temporal world come into their sharpest focus in the poem when viewed in consideration of the poem's organizing commitments to divine contemplation and to its relation to the active life.

59. For a useful overview on the scholarship on the poem's allegoresis, see Lawrence M. Clopper, "Langland and Allegory: A Proposition," *Yearbook of Langland Studies* 15 (2001): 35–42. See also Mary Carruthers, "Allegory without the Teeth: Some Reflections on Figural Language in *Piers Plowman*," *Yearbook of Langland Studies* 19 (2005): 27–43. For her, Langland's allegorical personifications rely on obscuring their own meanings, forcing meditative attitudes from readers, but then clarify themselves, bringing readers back into more straightforward understanding and facilitating memory (29).

60. For treatments of the English vernacular as the "kynde" or natural tongue, see Fiona Somerset and Nicholas Watson, "Preface: On 'Vernacular,'" and Nicholas Watson, "Introduction: On Solomon's Tablets," in *The Vulgar Tongue: Medieval and Postmedieval Vernacularity*, ed. Nicholas Watson and Fiona Somerset (College Park: Pennsylvania State University Press, 2003), ix, 1, 7.

61. See Watson, "Introduction: On Solomon's Tablets," 10.

62. For instance, see the Latin insertion between passus 1, lines 32 and 33; between passus 3, lines 241 and 242, at 249; between passus 5, lines 284 and 285, lines 487 and 488, lines 509 and 510, and lines 602 and 603; between passus 6, lines 75 and 76, lines 81 and 82. Perhaps the instance of poetic slippage between Latin and English that is most germane to this point, however, comes in the prologue of the B-text, when an angel appears and immediately "speke in Latyn" (B

prologue, 129). The Latin block the angel speaks is versified, but it does not follow the alliterative pattern of the English that surrounds it. Interestingly, the angel is not the only figure present who speaks Latin; the learned man, whom Langland calls "a gloton of wordes" (B prologue, 139) responds to the Angel in Latin as well, as does the assembled "commune," indicating that the Angel's language is comprehensible to people living in the quotidian world, despite its not being fully integrated metrically into Langland's poetic scheme.

63. "Dicitur Deus. Non enim revera in strepitu istarum duarum syllabarum ipse cognoscitur, sed tamen omnes latinae linguae scios, cum aures eorum sonus iste tetigerit, movet ad cogitandam excellentissimam quamdam immortalemque naturam." Augustine, *De Doctrina Christiana*, bk. 1, ch. 6, in *PL*, vol. 34.

64. David Aers comes to a parallel conclusion in his assessment of Langland's investment in the sacrament of the altar. He argues that "splitting off the spiritual from social and material practices, sacramental theology from ethics, and individual spirituality from the community's forms of life" is a wrongheaded way to engage with *Piers Plowman*. See David Aers, *Sanctifying Signs* (Notre Dame, IN: University of Notre Dame Press, 2004), 34.

65. Jeremy Catto notes that in broader society, even those worldly people who undertook contemplation often ended up in monastic houses: "It is salutary nevertheless to remember that however much the doubts and anxieties of the professional world may have been the starting point for many who set out on the difficult stages of a contemplative life, monastic houses following a regular rule tended to be where they came to rest" (Catto, "1349–1412, Culture and History," 123).

66. For an excellent treatment of how the C-text in particular handles the categories of poverty and need, see Crassons, *Claims of Poverty*, 21–88. David Aers notes that in C, Patience (a largely spiritual virtue) is entirely dependent on the Active Life of labor, though Patience himself tends to forget that fact (*Sanctifying Signs*, 124–25).

67. Middleton, "Acts of Vagrancy," 208–317; Burrow, "Wasting Time, Wasting Words," 191–202.

68. See again Middleton, "Acts of Vagrancy," 210–16.

69. Burrow, "Wasting Time, Wasting Words." See also E. Johnson, "Poetics of Waste."

70. C. David Benson and Lynne Blanchfield, *The Manuscripts of* Piers Plowman: *The B-Version* (Cambridge: Brewer, 1997), 33, 41, 45, 51, 57, 61, 65, 69, 72, 78, 83, 87, 93, 99, 103, 108.

71. William Skeat, *Parallel Extracts from Forty-Five Manuscripts of* Piers Plowman (London: Trubner, 1885), 4–5.

72. Lawton associates this stridency about labor with a correlated negative attitude toward the established clergy and then associates both with the ideological coalescence of Lollardy. D. A. Lawton, "Lollardy and the *Piers Plowman* Tradition," *Modern Language Review* 76 (1981): 780–93. Indeed, both Mike Rodman Jones and Sarah Kelen have demonstrated that this *Piers* tradition continues well into the early modern period, appearing in a wide range of editions and adaptations, most of which are radical in their politics and theology. See Mike Rodman Jones, *Radical Pastoral, 1381–1594: Appropriation and the Writing of Religious Controversy* (London: Ashgate, 2010); and Sarah Kelen, *Langland's Early Modern Identities* (New York: Palgrave, 2007). Barbara Johnson suggests that *Piers* becomes a central Protestant text precisely due to its figuring of Piers the plowman as a "moral exemplar" for the social importance of agricultural labor. Barbara Johnson, *Reading* Piers Plowman *and* The Pilgrim's Progress: *Reception and the Protestant Reader* (Carbondale: Southern Illinois University Press, 1992), 72.

73. The manuscript information is culled from LALME, searching among the East Anglian counties for *Piers* manuscripts. Ruth Nisse has argued strongly for the influence of the *Piers Plowman* tradition on the "Wakefield Master" play. See Nisse, *Defining Acts*, 82, 84, 88 (see ch. 1, n. 32).

Ralph Hanna has demonstrated that there was, in the fifteenth-century, a "trickledown" of alliterative poetry in Eastern England, suggesting that it was not simply in the West that the form had cultural currency. See Ralph Hanna, "The Scribe of Huntington HM 114," *Studies in Bibliography* 42 (1989): 120–33, at 123.

74. Beckwith, *Signifying God*, 25 (see intro., n. 28). In her account, "The endemic fissures and tensions in late medieval urban life, between the mercantile oligarchy and an artisanate that it increasingly sought to delimit by repressive labor legislation, could all be assuaged by the sense of wholeness and participation both represented but more crucially generated by the composite, sacral, and unified body of Christ" (26).

75. Ibid., 53.

76. Williams, *Drama of Medieval England* (see intro., n. 69). Toward the end of the tenth century, there emerges a resurrection (Easter) play in England (10–11). Other than the Easter play, the earliest European drama is the Nativity play (21), which, like the Easter play, seems to be attached to the mass. These early liturgical dramas also include other episodes, such as the Virgin in the Temple (30) or the raising of Lazarus (30). All these liturgical plays were composed before 1200 (37).

77. Robert Mannyng, *Handlyng Synne*, ed. Frederick Furnivall (London: EETS, Keegan Paul, 1901), lines 4640–4662.

78. According to Williams's analysis, between about 1200 and 1300, the transition from clergy to laity, from church to public, begins (*Drama of Medieval England*, 38), so that, by 1303, Robert Mannyng can tolerate miracles being performed in church, but not performed in public (49).

79. See Theodore K. Lerud, *Memory, Images, and the English Corpus Christi Drama* (New York: Palgrave, 2008), 67. For a study of how dramatic scenes within the church evolved, with a focus on the scenes that I think might most have informed the composing of *Piers*, see Karl Young, *The Drama of the Medieval Church*, vol. 1 (Oxford: Clarendon Press, 1933), 201–13, 492–539.

80. Vincent Gillespie also notes the central role of dramatic literature in carrying contemplative writing into the fifteenth and sixteenth centuries, zeroing in on *Wisdom*: "In the play *Wisdom who is Christ*, which bristles with locations from the heartland of London legal life, and uses contemplative and para-mystical materials from Hilton and Suso, it is Lucifer himself who acts as a persuasive advocate in favour of laymen pursuing the mixed life of action and contemplation, perhaps reflecting official concerns at the potential abuse of such spiritual ambition." Gillespie, "1412–1534: Culture and History," 178–79 (see intro., n. 6).

81. Barry Windeatt's treatment of the contemplative texts that exist in the fifteenth and early sixteenth centuries, for instance, while compendious, excludes dramatic works, focusing instead on compilations, reworkings, and translations. Windeatt, "1412–1534: Texts," 207 (see intro., n. 50).

My argument about the social importance of morality plays corroborates Ineke Murakami's thesis, which is that "moral drama, through protracted and intense engagement with socioeconomic changes at a formative period in England's early modernity (late fifteenth century to early seventeenth), developed as a public forum—soliciting and honing the judicative skills of emergent, politically active publics and counterpublics. . . . Moral drama was from its inception a medium for social commentary, and a space to rehearse critical public reflection—its form both facilitating and shaped by this vital social function." Ineke Murakami, *Moral Play and Counterpublic: Transformations in Moral Drama, 1465–1599* (New York: Routledge, 2011), 3.

CHAPTER 4

1. Throughout this chapter, I will treat the *Mary Plays* from the N-Town cycle as a unit. My reason for doing so is that these plays seem to have been created as such by a redactor at a particular point in the larger cycle's complex compilation history. As Marian Davis, who sees the N-Town cycle overall as more unified than do most scholars, points out, the work is inescapably a pastiche ("Nicholas Love and the N-Town Cycle," 53 [see intro., n. 38]), but the Mary plays constitute "a self-contained unit" (54) within them. The critical tradition of reading the Mary plays as, in effect, a coherent play within a larger and more varied cycle of plays gets perhaps its most compelling

articulation in the work of Alan Fletcher, who suggests that the Mary plays are probably the work of a single scribe. See Alan J. Fletcher, "The Design of the N-Town Play of Mary's Conception," *Modern Philology*, 79 (1981): 166–73. Peter Meredith has also suggested that the Marian sequence may indeed be the work of a single playwright. See Peter Meredith, "Establishing an Expositor's Role: Contemplacio and the N.Town Manuscript," in *The Narrator, the Expositor, and the Prompter in European Medieval Theatre* (Turnhout, Belgium: Brepols, 2007), 289–306. Ruth Nisse likewise treats the Marian sequence as a single work by a single author. See Nisse, *Defining Acts*, 65–67 (see ch. 1, n. 32). I will, however, also include the play about Joseph's doubts in my analysis, though that is not part of what Meredith refers to as the *Mary Play*. The play of Joseph's doubts is likely a later addition, but its dynamics are germane to my analysis of the Mary sequence proper.

2. Penny Granger, *The N-Town Play* (Cambridge: Brewer, 2009), 39, 60.

3. Martin Stevens, "Dramatic Setting of the Wakefield Cycle," *PMLA* 81 (1966): 193–98, at 193–94. See also Peter Meredith's edition, in which he argues that the Mary sequence should be considered as a unified dramatic work and that the N-Town plays are not a cycle drama but are instead a collection of compiled dramatic works. Peter Meredith, ed., *The Mary Play: From the N.Town Manuscript*, (Exeter: Exeter University Press, 1997), 1–22; all further citations from the *Mary* hereafter cited as *MP* with line numbers. Teresa Coletti reminds us that N-Town was probably played in a large, fixed play place, or platea, with a heaven scaffold and several different other sites for particular locations, such as Anna's house, Elizabeth's house, and the temple. Teresa Coletti, "Devotional Iconography in the N-Town Marian Plays," *Comparative Drama* 11 (1977): 22–44, at 23. See also Glynne Wickham, who asserts that N-Town was undoubtedly written for a fixed stage. Glynne Wickham, *Early English Stages, 1300–1660* (London: Routledge, 1959), 156. More recently, James Stokes has noted that playing places in and near East Anglia probably included churches as well as markets, streets, houses, and common greens. The Marian plays, in his view, seem likely to have been played in churchyards on set stages. James Stokes, "The Lost Playing Places of Lincolnshire," *Comparative Drama* 37 (2003): 275–295, at 285.

4. G. Gibson, *Theater of Devotion*, 117–123, 127 (see intro., n. 20).

5. Coletti talks about Mary's compassionate and intercessory relationship with man, and how she acts as an impartial advocate for him before God (Coletti, "Devotional Iconography," 37).

6. As Rachel Fulton has shown, the immense increase in Marian worship throughout Europe between 850 and 1200 hinges on *imitatio Mariae* as the linchpin of affective and empathetic devotion to Christ and Mary. See Rachel Fulton, *From Judgment to Passion: Devotion to Christ and the Virgin Mary, 800–1200* (New York: Columbia University Press, 2002), 3, 215–40.

7. According to Fulton, affective identification with the suffering Mary produced, for imitants, an avenue for increased identification with the agonized Christ (*From Judgment to Passion*, 197, 200, 204, 224). As she puts it, "the story . . . is . . . one of empathy. It is a story of the effort to identify empathetically with the God who so emptied himself as to become incarnate from a human woman and to die a humiliating death. It is a story of art, literature, and liturgy through which medieval Christians attempted their mimesis of Christ and Mary's compassionate and bodily pain" (3). This compassionate identification with Mary in particular seems to have been geared, particularly for female imitants, toward a compassion for all humans, a sense of "consolation and fellowship" (232). This sense of fellowship, as will become clear, is crucial to the theological functionality of the *Mary* plays. Amy Neff also elegantly discusses this kind of devotion, popular from the thirteenth century onward, in her analysis of visual images of the Swoon of Mary at the death of Christ. According to Neff, beginning in the early thirteenth century, images of Mary at the foot of Christ often depict her body collapsing from sorrow, and, in this image, "compassion for Mary and imitation of Mary's sufferings were encouraged as powerful tools of devotional practice." Amy Neff, "The Pain of Compassio: Mary's Labor at the Foot of the Cross," *Art Bulletin* 80 (1998): 254–73, at 254.

8. In Gail McMurray Gibson's phrasing, "Divinity comes to rest in Mary, who is image and sign of the Word-bearer" (*Theater of Devotion*, 139).

9. Ibid., 16.

10. The most complete work on the indebtedness of the *Mary* plays to Love's *Mirrour* remains Marian Davis's "Nicholas Love."

11. G. Gibson, *Theater of Devotion*, 137–38.

12. Ibid., 1. This focus on the incarnation exists throughout late medieval Europe. As Cristina Maria Cervone has argued, many late medieval English writers "turned to the hypostatic union—the conjoining of divinity and humanity in the person of Jesus Christ—as a lens through which to examine the nature of God and, conversely, to explore God's relationship to humanity" (*Poetics of the Incarnation*, 1–2 [see ch. 2, n. 47]).

13. G. Gibson, *Theater of Devotion*, 137.

14. Coletti, "Devotional Iconography," 22.

15. Martin Stevens, *Four Middle English Mystery Cycles* (Princeton, NJ: Princeton University Press, 1987), 234.

16. As Jaroslav Pelikan notes, "The most important intellectual struggle of the first five centuries of Christian history—indeed the most important intellectual struggle in all of Christian history—took place in response to the question of whether the divine in Jesus Christ was identical with God the Creator. For the answer to that challenge, too, was Mary, defined now as Theotokos and Mother of God. . . . As herself a creature, she was as well the one through whom the Logos Creator had united himself to a created human being." Jaroslav Pelikan, *Mary through the Centuries: Her Place in the History of Culture* (New Haven, CT: Yale University Press, 1998), 48, 51. Barbara Newman notes that there exists a robust tradition in Marian hymnody of exploring the paradox that Mary was the mother of her own father and daughter of her own son from the eleventh century onward. Barbara Newman, *God and the Goddesses: Vision, Poetry, and Belief in the Middle Ages* (Philadelphia: University of Pennsylvania Press, 2005), 250. As Newman points out, the German poet Heinrich von Meissen's *Marienleich* explicates Maria-Sapientia's eternal relationship with God, "Here, Mary becomes explicitly divine: she is God's partner and parent, and he hers; both alike are Father and Mother" (252). By the fifteenth century, according to Newman, Mary "represents humankind's point of entry into an intimate, familial union with the Divine . . . like Christ, she too could model both 'divinity' and 'humanity' in her own way" (259–61).

17. For an extended treatment of Mary as mediatrix in the Middle Ages, see Pelikan, *Mary through the Ages*, 125–33.

18. As Gibson puts it, "Mary of Nazareth had been chosen God's bride and God's mother; her body had enclosed divinity, had given Godhead a human form and likeness" (*Theater of Devotion*, 157).

19. Substantiating the shaping influence of Love's work on the plays, scholars have shown that the seven *Mary* plays in N-Town that are not in other play cycles are all precedented in Love's *Mirrour* (M. Davis, "Nicholas Love," 55). Love's emphasis on Mary becomes, thus, the N-Town plays' emphases on Mary, Davis explains (60), both reflecting the trend toward "affective piety" that typifies Marian devotion in the fifteenth century in England (60, 62). See Sargent, "Mystical Writings," 81–83 (see intro., n. 53). See also Patricia Forrest, "The Role of the Expositor Contemplacio in the Saint Anne's Day Plays of the Hegge Cycle," *Mediaeval Studies* 28 (1966): 60–76.

20. It is known that Love was familiar with the English translation of Henry Suso's *Orologium*, and likely also with the *Ancrene Riwle* and the works of Walter Hilton. See Elizabeth (Zeeman) Salter, "Nicholas Love: A Fifteenth-Century Translator," *Review of English Studies* 6 (1955): 115.

21. Nicholas Love, *Mirrour of the Blessed Lyf of Jesu Christ* (Oxford: Clarendon, 1908), 8.

22. Ibid.

23. Salter, "Fifteenth-Century Translator," 118. Indeed, many scholars take as read that Love's comments about access fully account for his Englishing of Bonaventure's *Meditationes*—that access was the sole motivation behind his translation. See, e.g., M. Davis, "Nicholas Love," 39, 43, 48.

24. Love, *Mirrour*, 8.

25. See also Nicholas Watson, "Conceptions of the Word: The Mother Tongue and the Incarnation of God," *New Medieval Literatures* 1 (1997): 85–124, at 93–98.

26. Watson has suggested, indeed, that Love's attitude toward the vernacular is that it is bodily, emotional, accessible, and simple; therefore, it is an optimal vehicle for incarnational meditation, for meditation on Jesus (ibid., 93–98, 104).

27. In this associative claim for the value of the vernacular, Love aligns his project with the earlier Middle English *Speculum Vitae* (c. 1350), which calls English, as Watson has noted, "oure kynde langage." See Nicholas Watson, "The Politics of Middle English," in *The Idea of the Vernacular*, ed. Jocelyn Wogan-Brown et al. (University Park: Penn State University Press, 1999), 337. See also Watson's introduction, with Fiona Somerset, and his essay in *Vulgar Tongue*, ix, 1, 7 (see ch. 3, n. 60).

28. Love, *Mirrour*, 9.

29. In this vein, Watson has argued, "to write about Christ's human, rather than divine, nature and reflect on its meaning for the religious life was hence almost by definition to theorize about the status of the 'mother tongue,' the English vernacular" ("Conceptions of the Word," 93).

30. In so doing, Watson casts Love's vernacular text as designed to forestall some of the intellectual ambition of Wycliffite projects of translation, to suggest that "symple" people ought to keep their gazes trained somewhat closer to earth than to the heavens (ibid., 94–98).

31. Ibid., 100.

32. Along similar lines, Ian Johnson has suggested that "Love draws on the productive capacities of English language and culture to enable (empower) his audience as meditators and sensitized readers of the Sacred Humanity for their own very considerable benefit. To translate the *Meditationes Vitae Christi* into English is to provide it with new vernacular life" (*Middle English Life of Christ*, 31).

33. This democratizing potential is what Watson claims for *Pore Caitif*'s use of the vernacular ("Conceptions of the Word," 108).

34. M. Davis, "Nicholas Love," 43.

35. See I. Johnson, *Middle English Life of Christ*, 140.

36. Love, *Mirrour*, 36.

37. See Elizabeth (Zeeman) Salter, *Nicholas Love's "Myrrour of the Blessed Lyf of Jesu Christ,"* Analecta Cartusiana 10 (Salzburg: Universität Salzburg, 1974), 263.

38. As Ian Johnson has noted, this poem is a "loosened" vernacularization of a Latin poem that poem reads:

> Ave Maria virgo mitissima
> Digna angelica salutacione
> Gracia plena Mater castissima
> In tui prolis iocunda generacione
> Dominus tecum, fide firmissima
> In tui filii gloriosa resurrecione
> Benedicta tu in mulieribus spe certissima
> In eius admiranda assencione
> Et benedictus fructus ventris tui Jesus
> Caratitate [*sic*] plenissima te coronans in celesti habitacione
> Esto nobis auxiliatrix
> In omni angustia et temptacione. Amen.

See I. Johnson, *Middle English Life of Christ*, 141.

39. This reading bears out Michelle Karnes' contention that, "Love does not simply translate the content of the MVC, as his [own] comments suggest he will. He makes systematic alterations that belie his claims about the inherent simplicity of the content of the MVC and complicate his equation of gospel meditations with lay spirituality" (*Imagination*, 215).

40. Focusing on the Marian "miracle tales," Claire Waters has recently called attention to Mary's unique and, in some ways, uniquely disruptive relation to human temporality. "Her whole relationship to time, moreover, makes a mockery of the linear temporality on which the study of history usually rests. Virgin mother, daughter of her son, she disrupts the normative genealogies that undergird normative temporality; her disruption of logical causality and her problematic temporal status created doctrinal controversy in the early Church, whose resolution vindicated her exemption from the supposedly linear progression of time and contributed to the Virgin's emerging cult." Claire Waters, "A Miracle of History: The Conqueror, the Virgin, and 'Del Harpur a Roucestre,'" *New Medieval Literatures* 12 (2010): 47–68.

41. See also Teresa Coletti, "Purity and Danger: the Paradox of Mary's Body and the En-gendering of the Infancy Narrative in the English Mystery Cycles," in *Feminist Approaches to the Body in Medieval Literature*, ed. Linda Lomperis and Sarah Stanbury (Philadelphia: University of Pennsylvania Press, 1993), 65–95. According to Coletti, "The central Christian mystery that God had become man through a human mother who remained a virgin after his conception and birth furnished a dramatic situation that was theatrically complex, theologically sensitive, and socially resonant" (65).

42. For a treatment of Contemplacio as an "expositor" figure, who implicitly gives authority to the claim that the Marian sequence of plays was, at some earlier moment in the N-Town manuscript's compilation, a single and unified piece, see Meredith, "Establishing an Expositor's Role," 289–306.

43. Marian Davis argues that "Contemplacio functions as a chorus, preparing the audience for the plays they are about to see, settling them into a properly religious state of mind, and commenting on the significance of the scenes they witness." Although Davis has suggested that the name Contemplacio may have been inspired by Nicholas Love's marginal markings of "contemplacio" in the *Mirrour*, which come when Love "wishes to emphasize a point or scene for meditation," in the *Mary*, the figure Contemplacio functions decidedly as what Gail McMurray Gibson calls an "expositor" for the plays. See M. Davis, "Nicholas Love," 62, 3–4.

44. According to Douglas Sugano, "Another noteworthy feature of this group of Mary plays is the figure of Contemplacio, who serves as a kind of wise counselor/narrator with his insightful meditations/mediations that both pace and advance the action of the plot and, at the same time, engage the spirit of Christian culture as it contemplates the events unfolding before the very eyes and ears of the audience. His role in these plays is so pronounced that these Marian plays are sometimes referred to as 'The Contemplacio Group.'" Douglas Sugano, "Note for the *Mary Play*," *N-Town Plays*, ed. Douglas Sugano (Kalamazoo, MI: TEAMS, 2007), 355. Gibson also notes the centrality of contemplation to the play's theology; see G. Gibson, *Theater of Devotion*, 135.

45. Indeed, Seeta Chaganti has shown that the material stagecraft of the plays and the included stage directions urge viewers to understand Mary's body as, in effect, a reliquary, an "object of enshrinement," which is physically placed "in templo" during the play. *Contemplation* literally means, "with the temple," "being in the temple," or a "going into the temple." Thus Mary's body serves, in the play, as a de facto reliquary, and her physical movement into the temple signals the activity that the audience is meant to enact toward her: contemplation. Seeta Chaganti, *The Medieval Poetics of the Reliquary: Enshrinement, Inscription, Performance* (New York: Palgrave, 2008), 76, 81–84.

46. In his commentary on Luke, Walafrid Strabo notes not just that Mary is pregnant with Jesus but that she "carried the Lord": "Mary is praised because she carried the Lord" (Hic Maria laudatur quae Dominum portavit). Walafrid Strabo, *Evangelium Secundum Lucam*, ch. 11, verse 27, col. 0291C, in *PL*, vol. 114. Or, in Gail McMurray Gibson's words, "Mary by her acceptance of the angel's words becomes the new Ark of the Covenant, bearing within her sides not the tablets of the Law, but the Holy of Holies of the new order—the incarnate body of God's son" (*Theater of Devotion*, 144).

47. This intense deictic language recalls a similar stylistic dynamic in the York plays, as noted by Sarah Beckwith, in which the York plays call the audience's attention to the way in which bibli-

cal history—although past in real time—is nevertheless ongoing in the spiritual lives of the audience. See Beckwith, *Signifying God,* xvi, 26, 32, 38–39, 72, 100–103 (see intro., n. 28).

48. V.A. Kolve describes how the overlay of biblical time on historical (which is to say, contemporary medieval English) time constitutes one of the major theological drives of cycle dramas, and he notes that much of this overlay is rendered linguistically, through what he terms "verbal contemporaneity" (*Play Called Corpus Christi,* 106 [see intro., n. 6]). The cycle dramas, in Kolve's view, stage biblical time as theologically coterminous with all other times (108).

49. As Kolve phrases it in his discussion of Corpus Christi dramas as a mode, "the past was played as an image of present time" (ibid., 110).

50. See Peter Meredith, introduction, to Meredith, *Mary Play,* p. 12.

51. Beckwith, Kolve, and others who study the York plays have noted the theological significance of having the audience recognize that, at all moments in the contemporary life of medieval urban England, Christ is symbolically copresent with and indeed embodied by the people of a town. See especially Beckwith's account of how the economic life of urban York is registered in the casting and enactment of the York plays (*Signifying God,* 42–55).

52. Beckwith, *Signifying God,* 39.

53. The play sequence's focus on Mary's mother, Anne, is uncommon for late medieval dramas, and it suggests that the plays were likely composed, at least in part, to celebrate her contribution to the Christian narrative.

54. This is a dramatic version of the "crowded now" that Carolyn Dinshaw talks about in her treatment of Margery Kempe, insisting on "what Chakrabarty calls an 'irreducible plurality in our own experiences of historicity.'" See Carolyn Dinshaw, *How Soon Is Now? Medieval Texts, Amateur Readers, and the Queerness of Time* (Durham, NC: Duke University Press, 2012), 104.

55. The collectivity and inclusivity of this participatory contemplation would have been reified demographically if Catherine Sanok's argument is correct that women were likely cast as the actors in these particular Marian plays. Without question, there is a robust tradition of female performance of feminine sanctity in the Marian and virgin martyr plays more broadly, and there is no reason to assume the N-Town's *Mary* would not have been among them. If such were the case, the *Mary* would promote participatory contemplation in social demographic that, with the exception of anchorites and nuns, is traditionally excluded from the higher ranks of spiritual experience: women. In staging Mary's life, her pregnancy, and her mind-boggling ability to hold the eternal God, in the form of Jesus, in her womb, as a play *of women,* the *Mary* plays would make plain that mothers, wives, and women in general could do the work of contemplation and could participate in its public, shared, and participatory staging. The Marian sequence, then, would visually, tangibly, sensorily render the idea that all people could share in this staged, collective contemplation. The Marian sequence shows that contemplation, that is, can be intersubjective and relational, rather than individual or monadic, in ways that cross traditional social boundaries such as gender. Sanok argues that the N-Town *Mary* plays are likely associated with the religious guild of Saint Anne in Lincoln, so that they may well have been performed by women. See Catherine Sanok, *Her Life Historical: Exemplarity and Female Saints' Lives in Late Medieval England* (Philadelphia: University of Pennsylvania Press, 2007), 160, 164. See also note 58, which describes the scholarship on young girls who might have played Mary in various medieval dramatic contexts.

56. According to Pelikan, in the late Middle Ages, traits and powers traditionally ascribed exclusively to Christ were transferred also onto Mary, so that "Mary was 'the repository of all the books of the Old Testament and of the Gospels, all of which she knew completely.'" Jaroslav Pelikan, *The Christian Tradition: A History of the Development of Doctrine,* vol. 4, *Reformation of Church Dogma, 1300–1700* (Chicago: University of Chicago Press, 1985), 40–41.

57. Walafrid Strabo's commentary on Mary's pregnancy puts it thus: "Not only is Mary to be praised, because she carried the Word of God in her uterus, but she is the most blessed, because she honored the precepts of God in her works" (Non solum laudanda Maria, quia Verbum Dei portavit

in utero, sed maxime beata est, quia praecepta Dei servavit in opere). Strabo, *Evangelium Secundum Lucam*, Commentary on verse 28.

58. See Lynette R. Muir, "Playing God in Medieval Europe," in *The Stage as Mirror: Civic Theatre in Late Medieval Europe*, ed. Alan E. Knight (London: Brewer, 1997), 29. Indeed, Philippe's play (1370s) may have been a source or at least a cultural precedent, for the N-Town *Mary* sequence's "Presentation" play. According to Karl Young's massive study, Philippe's Feast Day of the Presentation of the Virgin (November 21) included singing, processing to the altar, a fleet of representational actors from Mary's life, two stages, and Mary, onstage throughout the play, surrounded by candles and eventually releasing a dove from her hands. Karl Young, *Drama of the Medieval Church*, vol. 2 (Oxford: Clarendon Press, 1933), 225, 242–43, 244, 227. As Young points out, Philippe further instructs that the young, female impersonator of Mary should pay "reverent attention" throughout the liturgical service (244).

59. Popular hymns in the Middle Ages such as the Salve Regina bear witness to the centrality of Mary's role as advocate. The hymn is sung, "Salve, Regina, mater misericordiae; vita, dulcedo et spes nostra, salve. Ad te clamamus exsules filii Hevae. Ad te suspiramus gementes et flentes in hac lacrimarum valle. Eia ergo, *advocata nostra*, illos tuos misericordes oculos ad nos converte. Et Iesum, benedictum fructum ventris tui, nobis post hoc exsilium ostende. O clemens, o pia, o dulcis Virgo Maria [Hail, Queen, mother of mercy; hail, our life, sweetness, and hope. To you we cry out, we banished children of Eve. To you we sigh, mourning and weeping in this valley of tears. Thus a sigh, *our advocate*, turn those merciful eyes toward us. And show us Jesus, blessed fruit of your womb, after our exile. O clement one, O pious one, O sweet Virgin Mary]" (italics mine).

60. Chaganti reads the acrostic as a particularly important moment, both formally and theologically, for the plays as well: "An angel appears and makes an acrostic of Mary's name, associating identifying concepts with each of its letters. . . . In spelling out the name, the angel's utterance reaches toward enclosure and completion, with the enunciation of Mary's name preceding and following the articulation of each of its letters" (*Medieval Poetics of the Reliquary*, 93).

61. For more on this trope in the larger context of English literary history, see Robert W. Hanning, "From Eva and Ave to Eglentyne and Alisoun: Chaucer's Insight into the Roles Women Play," *Signs* 2 (1977): 580–99.

62. This scene, too, resonates with the liturgical dramas of the Feast of the Presentation of the Virgin, as codified by Philippe de Mezières. In Philippe's liturgical drama, as Young notes, Mary and Elizabeth perform the Magnificat together, both in Latin, with Elizabeth doing some glossing in Latin on Mary's singing, her brief verses of salutation being added to the Vulgate (*Drama of the Medieval Church*, 248).

63. Nicholas Watson has shown how vernacularization provided an important formal realization of Jesus's incarnation in time and in a human body; English comes to figure "Christ's human, rather than divine nature" ("Conceptions of the Word," 93). Watson later notes that "the Latin language" is associated with "the divinity of Christ" (95) in many late Middle English devotional texts (see also 109). This is not remotely to say that the vernacular is demoted, vis-à-vis Latin, as a possible language of theology: quite the contrary, as Watson shows, the vernacular becomes a form for "radical" (122) theology, and is, for some texts "preferable to Latin" (123).

64. Watson notes that "Latin can pose as a reconstituted version of Adamic language because of its lucidity, its distance from ordinary speakers, and the way it had to be acquired through formal study aided by grace . . . the Latin language is closer to heaven than the vernacular" (introduction to *Vulgar Tongue*, 10).

65. See David Townsend, "The Current Questions and Future Prospects of Medieval Latin Studies," in *Oxford Handbook of Medieval Latin Literature* (Oxford: Oxford University Press, 2012), 15–19. For a treatment of the relativity of "English" and "Latin" in John Gower's *Confessio amantis*, see also Eleanor Johnson, *Practicing Literary Theory in the Middle Ages* (Chicago: University of Chicago Press, 2013), 190–93.

66. As Nisse notes, "Elizabeth's English *Magnificat* is more a free 'adaptation' than a translation" (*Defining Acts*, 73 [see ch. 1, n. 66]).

67. See Fletcher, "Design of N-Town Play," 168; E. K. Chambers, *Medieval Stage* (London: Oxford University Press, 1903), ii, 126–27.

68. For a brilliant analysis of the spoofing of Joseph's sexuality in the Mérode Tryptic, see Louise O. Vasvari, "Joseph on the Margin: The Mérode Tryptic and the Medieval Spectacle," *Mediaevalia* 18 (1995): 163–89. In Vasvari's account, Joseph's drilling of a wooden board—depicted in the tryptic—serves ironically to highlight his sexual impotence and cuckoldry.

69. A later contributor to the N-Town play cycle registered the comedic presentation of Joseph and amplified it greatly by the introduction of the play "Joseph's Doubts." Since it is a separate work from the other *Mary* plays that surround it, I will not treat it as part of the Marian contemplative set, except as evidence that the early readings of Joseph's character in the broader Marian plays were comedic ones; those readings play out in later additions to the cycle that are, if anything, more aggressively comedic than the earlier ones. Kolve notes the pervasive comedy surrounding Joseph in the traditional Corpus Christi plays about Joseph's doubts, yet further notes that the laughter we experience at Joseph never penetrates to our perception of Mary: she is kept pristine, "like a green island in a turbulent and dirty sea" (*Play Called Corpus Christi*, 138–39).

CHAPTER 5

1. F. P. Wilson, *The English Drama: 1485–1585* (Oxford: Clarendon, 1968), 5. Gail McMurray Gibson has suggested that the play may have been written slightly later, in 1469, for performance at the Benedictine Abbey of Bury St. Edmunds. See Gail McMurray Gibson, "The Play of *Wisdom* and the Abbey of St. Edmund," *Comparative Drama* 19 (1985): 117–35, at 126, 130.

2. Anonymous, *Two Moral Interludes: Pride of Life and Wisdom*, ed. David Klausner (Kalamazoo, MI: Medieval Institute Publications, 2008), lines 93–94 (hereafter cited as *W* for *Wisdom*, with line numbers).

3. David Bevington argues that *Wisdom* works by visualizing metaphors from the Bible and that the vocabulary of image and likeness is one that Walter Hilton, a primary source for the play, also stresses. In Bevington's view, the dominant metaphor in the play is one of contrasting foul with fair images, as in the fair costumes of Anima and Wisdom early on and the foul costumes of Lucifer and Anima later. David Bevington, "Blake and Whytt, Fowll and Fayer: Stage Picture in *Wisdom Who is Christ*," *Comparative Drama* 19 (1985): 136–50.

4. Though, in the Vulgate, the line reads "*speciosior* sole," not "specialior."

5. There is a theological distinction to be made between "likenesses" and "images," or between "imago" and "similitudo"—namely, that the image of God in man is fundamental and inalienable, whereas the likeness to God is one that is improved or damaged based on one's degree of virtue or sin. This distinction would undoubtedly not have been lost on any in the audience who might have been highly educated in theology, but would, I think, almost certainly have been lost on the average audience member, and is it not a distinction the play does anything with going forward, suggesting, to me, that the play was not written exclusively for a theologically sophisticated audience.

6. The spelling of "Understondynge" is inconsistent in the play, sometimes "Undyrstondynge" and sometimes "Understondynge."

7. Cf. 1 Corinthians 13:12: "For now we see through a glass, darkly; but then face to face: now I know in part; but then shall I know even as also I am known" (Videmus nunc per speculum in enigmate: tunc autem facie ad faciem. Nunc cognosco ex parte: tunc autem cognoscam sicut et cognitus sum).

8. Reasonable and in currency: indeed, this is the kind of logic used by Hilton in the *Mixed Life* in justifying the importance of taking care of one's worldly responsibilities in spite of one's larger

devotion to the contemplative life. See Walter Hilton, *Walter Hilton's* Mixed Life *Edited from Lambeth Palace MS 472*, ed. S. J. Ogilvie-Thompson (Salzburg: Institut für Anglistik und Amerikanistik, 1986), 35, 394–404. Many scholars have noted the close theological relationship between *Wisdom* and Walter Hilton's writings more broadly. Michael Sargent and Ruth Nisse have produced the most recent and most thorough treatments of the play's affiliations with Hilton. See Sargent, "Mystical Writings," 83–88 (see intro., n. 53); and Nisse, *Defining Acts*, 127–42 (see ch. 1, n. 32). Clifford Davidson also notes the reliance of *Wisdom* on Hilton's writings. See Clifford Davidson, *Visualizing the Moral Life: Medieval Iconography and the Macro Morality Plays* (New York: AMS Press, 1989), 88, 83, 93, 109.

9. Nisse sees Lucifer's distortionary readings of this tradition of Christ as a follower of the mixed life specifically as directed toward sovereigns and aristocrats, not toward common people (*Defining Acts*, 139).

10. Nisse points out Lucifer's heavy and manipulative reliance on Hilton's writings: "Lucifer, apparently armed here only with Hilton's collected writings and his own psychological acuity, is as much spin-doctor as seducer" (ibid., 140).

11. As Richard Rastall notes, "Considering the use of processional plainsong in scenes 1 and 4, we should probably understand part-music to belong to the forces of evil: in other words, it represents *evil* mirth. . . . Will sings treble, Understanding the mean (i.e. the middle voice), and Mind the tenor (the lowest voice.)" Richard Rastall, *Minstrels Playing: Music in Early English Religious Drama* (Cambridge: Brewer, 2001), 456.

12. The play's registering of moral decay through musical proliferation resonates with Bruce Holsinger's demonstration that polyphony was closely associated with sodomy and sexual dissipation. See Holsinger, *Music, Body, and Desire*, 137–87, esp. 138, 140, 157 (see intro., n. 25).

13. In Davenport's reading, Mind has become "Maintenance," Understanding has become "Perjury," and Will has become "Lechery." W. A. Davenport, *Fifteenth-Century English Drama: The Early Moral Plays and their Literary Relations* (London: Brewer, 1982), 87–88.

14. As Robert Mullaly notes, moralists referred to caroles as "les processions au deable"—processions to the devil. See Robert Mullaly, *The Carole: A Study of a Medieval Dance* (Surrey, UK: Ashgate, 2011), 33. As Walter Salmen notes, despite the wide and wild popularity of caroles and other round dances, "there was no lack of impediments, prohibitions, and condemnations. St. Augustine's dictum 'chorea est circulus, cuius centrum est diabolus' (the dance is a circle, the center of which is the Devil) lived on . . . Both the established Church and various sects objected to dancing, regarding it as the Devil's own festivity." Walter Salmen, "Dances and Dance Music, c. 1300–1530," in *Music as Concept and Practice in the Late Middle Ages*, ed. Reinhard Strohm and Bonnie J. Blackburn (Oxford: Oxford University Press, 2001), 163.

Robert Mannyng's telling of the tale of the "Cursed Dancers of Colbeck" nicely encapsulates this anxiety: according to Mannyng's version of the tale, a group of dancers refused a priest's warning that they should leave off their round dance and return to church to hear mass. As a result of their refusal, the priest curses them, and God makes them dance in a circle, unstopping, for an entire year. The tale thus registers both the priestly resistance to dance as an acceptable form of pastime and registers the moral and physical dangers of dance to the dancers themselves. See Mannyng, *Handlyng Synne*, 1901, lines 9017–9209 (see ch. 3, n. 77).

15. See Christopher Page, *The Owl and the Nightingale: Musical Life and Ideas in France, 1100–1300* (London: Dent, 1989), 14–15.

16. Mullaly, *Carole*, 31–32, 34–38.

17. Marshall notes that this turn to dance would have been quite striking, since the play, to this point, has largely been kinetically static. See John Marshall, "Marginal Staging Marks in the Macro Manuscript of *Wisdom*," *Medieval English Theatre* 7 (1985): 77–81, at 80.

18. As Salmen notes, round dances often required bagpipers and minstrels as accompaniment in the late Middle Ages ("Dances and Dance Music," 175–76).

19. Indeed, there is evidence that medieval people specifically viewed public carole dances as occasions on which women might find husbands. "Special clothes, floral garlands in the hair, the generous application of striking facial cosmetics—these and other such details recorded in the sermon literature suggest that *caroles* could function as a marriage market in which young girls of marriageable age could be shown to potential suitors" (Page, *Owl and Nightingale*, 15).

20. Ibid., 113–17, 121–25, at 123.

21. Rastall, *Minstrels Playing*, 464.

22. What can I give back to the Lord for all he has given to me? I will take the cup of salvation and call upon the name of the Lord.

23. Ibid.

24. Indeed, where caroles were often condemned as irreligious, there was a robust tradition of ritual motion in and around churches, which was viewed as entirely appropriate devotional practice. As Salmen notes, "Dance customs in and around churches ranged from the devout bending of the knee, devotional gestures of prayer, processional steps, and the circumambulation of places of worship, to the dancing accompaniment of sequences and tropes, and round dances about the Christmas crib or around the altar" ("Dances and Dance Music," 166). Processional steps, enacted to liturgical tropes, are precisely what Wisdom returns the play to upon his arrival.

25. Opposing this scholarly contention, Nisse argues that *Wisdom* was written for an aristocratic audience and was designed specifically as a caution against misrule by a lordly person (*Defining Acts*, 129, 131).

26. Robert Potter has argued that morality plays originate in sermonic traditions—a claim which may account for the play's emphasis on collectivity and communality. See Robert Potter, *The English Morality Play: Origins, History, and Influence of a Dramatic Tradition* (New York: Routledge, 1975).

27. In this insistence, *Wisdom* also echoes the *Glossa Ordinaria*'s reading of the Song of Songs: according to the *Glossa*, the Song must be understood, in the end, as advocating the active life. See Suzanne LaVere, "From Contemplation to Action: The Role of the Active Life in the *Glossa ordinaria* on the Song of Songs," *Speculum* 82 (2007): 54–69.

28. Thus, late medieval drama, too, bears out Nicholas Watson's assertion that contemplative literature is not entirely colonized by affective traditions of piety but retains some of its philosophical and intellectual heft throughout the Middle Ages. See Watson, introduction to Fanous and Gillespie, *Cambridge Companion to Medieval English Mysticism*, 18 (see intro., n. 14). Michelle Karnes also emphasizes the intimate and ongoing relationship between medieval philosophy and devotional texts. See Karnes, *Imagination, Meditation, and Cognition*, 11, 14, 16–17 (see intro., n. 30).

29. Thence Davidson's assertion that the end of the play reaffirms contemplation is true, but not the whole story (*Visualizing the Moral Life*, 111). Indeed, Chester Scoville's suggestion, that medieval playwrights were ultimately concerned with uniting the "community of the audience in its desire for holy living," seems more apropos, though he is speaking of cycle dramas. See Chester Scoville, *Saints and the Audience in Medieval Biblical Drama* (Toronto: University of Toronto Press, 2004), 7.

30. Davenport, *Fifteenth-Century English Drama*, 80, 90–91.

31. Milla Cozart Riggio, "The Staging of Wisdom," in *The Wisdom Symposium*, ed. Milla Cozart Riggio (New York: AMS Press, 1986), 10, 14–15.

32. Gail McMurray Gibson, "The Play of *Wisdom* and the Abbey of St. Edmund," in Riggio, *Wisdom Symposium*, 39–66, esp. 48. Arnold Williams contends that, whether monastic or lay, the play was clearly designed for an educated audience (*Drama of Medieval England*, 157).

33. As Teresa Coletti puts it, Wisdom "articulate[s] the self-understandings of a prosperous society in which economic ambitions and religious values could both conflict with and affirm each other" (Coletti, *Drama of Saints*, 38 [see intro., n. 53]).

34. According to Claire Sponsler, speaking of three other morality plays, "In their emphasis on sin and salvation, these three moralities drive home a definition of individual behavior in which

the body is carefully controlled for the ends of proper labor and acceptable consumption. By ritually exorcising antisocial tendencies—whether represented in the body of the discontented worker, the rebellious youth, or the wanton woman—these moralities work at the behest of the existing social order." Claire Sponsler, *Drama and Resistance* (Minneapolis: University of Minnesota Press, 1997), 102.

35. Bertolt Brecht famously says that the breaking of the fourth wall is a central formal mode of creating the *Verfremdungseffekt*, or "alienation effect," by which the audience is forced to realize they are watching a play, a created, nonnatural object. This breaking of the fourth wall, he notes, is particularly common in Chinese theater, but he advocates for its increasing inclusion in twentieth-century European theater as well. See Bertolt Brecht, "Alienation Effects in Chinese Acting," in *Brecht on Theatre: The Development of an Aesthetic*, trans. John Willett (London: Methuen, 1964), 91–92. Because of this breaking of the fourth wall, "the audience can no longer have the illusion of being the unseen spectator at an event which is really taking place" (92). Brecht further says that the breaking of the fourth wall is "of course necessary" to undermine the idea that "the stage action is taking place in reality and without an audience" (Bertolt Brecht, "Short Description of a New Technique of Acting which Produces an Alienation Effect," in *Brecht on Theatre*, 136).

36. Milla Cozart Riggio, "Masqueing the Moral Expositor," in Butterworth, *Narrator, Expositor, and Prompter*, 163 (see ch. 4, n. 1). Indeed, about medieval drama more broadly, Jerome Bush has argued, "the *platea* is unlocalized, nonarchitectural, and nonrepresentational space.... [It] is constituted by, rather than constructed on, a natural setting or a permanent structure: the village green or the city square. It is part of both the audience's everyday life and the play's staging." See Jerome Bush, "The Resources of Locus and Platea Staging: The Digby Mary Magdalene," *Studies in Philology* 86 (1989): 139.

37. Beckwith, *Signifying God*, xv–xvi (see intro., n. 28).

38. For a further elaboration on the way the "invisible wall" must be taken to work in medieval contexts, see Hans-Jürgen Diller, "Theatrical Pragmatics: The Actor-Audience Relationship from the Mystery Cycles to the Early Tudor Dramas," *Comparative Drama* 23 (1989): 156–65, at 157.

39. Donald Baker suggests that the boy "may have been a novice or a village youth." See Donald C. Baker, "Is Wisdom a 'Professional' Play?" in Riggio, *Wisdom Symposium*, 67–86, at 85.

40. See G. Gibson, *Theater of Devotion*, 108–113, 124, 128, 174 (see intro., n. 20).

41. Milton McC. Gatch, "Mysticism and Satire in the Morality of *Wisdom*," *Philological Quarterly* 53 (1974): 342–46.

42. Stanley Fish describes this as a core dynamic of *Paradise Lost*, in which a reader is led to sympathize with the wrong ideas and agents, only to be brought up short and corrected by the text. Stanley Fish, *Surprised by Sin: The Reader in* Paradise Lost (London: Macmillan, 1997), 1–12.

CHAPTER 6

1. Arnold Williams goes farther, calling the play the "least learned" of the morality plays (*Drama of Medieval England*, 155 [see intro., n. 69]). Hardin Craig notes that the play is degenerate because of its relentless appeals to the audience's vulgarity. Hardin Craig, *English Religious Drama* (Oxford: Clarendon, 1967), 350. E. K. Chambers rejects out of hand the notion that the play could have been written for any didactic purpose. E. K. Chambers, *English Literature at the Close of the Middle Ages*, (Oxford: Clarendon, 1945), 61–62.

2. In claiming the centrality of the scatological humor of the play to its overall plot and contemplative ideation, I disagree sharply with early scholarship that read the humor as meaningless vulgarity, such as that of Louis B. Wright, who argued that the play's comedy was "irrelevant and unrelated to the dramatic needs of the play." Louis B. Wright, "Variety-Show Clownery on the Pre-Restoration Stage," *Anglia* 52 (1928): 51.

3. See also Clopper, "*Mankind* and its Audience," 352 (see intro., n. 69). Clopper notes that the laughter of the play is clearly designed to align viewers with the sinful parties of the play.

4. Here and throughout, I will refer to the TEAMS edition of this play: Anonymous, *Mankind*, ed. Kathleen Ashley and Gerard NeCastro (Kalamazoo, MI: Medieval Institute Publications, 2010), hereafter cited as *M*, with line number.

5. Referring to Mercy's opening salvos as a "sermon," Rainer Pineas notes that morality plays in general seek "to teach their audiences the means to salvation." Rainer Pineas, "The English Morality Play as a Weapon of Religious Controversy," *Studies in English Literature, 1500–1900* 2 (1962): 157–80, at 159, 157.

6. Kathleen Ashley, in her introduction to the TEAMS edition of *Mankind* (see n. 4), points out that *Piers* made the rural laborer a recognizable sign of political resistance in the late fourteenth century and suggests that Mankind's own identity as that very type of laborer may affiliate the play with the ideologies of the poem.

7. John Watkins sees this attitude toward Latinity as radically and importantly opposed to what is found in other morality plays, such as the much earlier *Castle of Perseverance*. In *Castle*, Latin possesses a "seeming timelessness" that shows scorn for "everyday life," while in *Mankind*, the vices "not only reject Mercy's Latinity but ridicule it." John Watkins, "The Allegorical Theatre: Moralities, Interludes, and Protestant Drama," in *Cambridge History of Medieval English Literature*, ed. David Wallace (Cambridge: Cambridge University Press, 1999), 771.

8. In Watkins's view, the conflict between Latin and English is one of the main drivers of the action of the play: "*Mankind* . . . becomes a metadrama about the respective social valences of clerkly Latin and vulgarizing English" (ibid., 771).

9. Kathy Cawsey characterizes the play's use of Latin as "transgressive," noting that the humor of the play revolves around the usage of bad Latin. Kathy Cawsey, "Tutivillus and the Kyrkchaterars: Strategies of Control in the Middle Ages," *Studies in Philology* 102 (2005): 434–51, at 449.

10. Pineas suggests that the usage of Latin—the language of the divine service—for obscenity would have immediately marked its user as being of the party of the devil ("Morality Play as Weapon of Controversy," 162).

11. Pamela King suggests that the play was written for performance sometime between Christmas and Lent, given the mention of the Christmas song, on the one hand, and the play's intermittent citations of Job, which are part of the Ash Wednesday liturgy, on the other. Pamela King, "Morality Plays," in *The Cambridge Companion to Medieval English Theatre*, ed. Richard Beadle (Cambridge: Cambridge University Press, 2006), 250.

12. See also Stanton B. Garner, "Theatricality in 'Mankind' and 'Everyman,'" *Studies in Philology* 84 (1987): 272–85, at 279–80.

13. Diller, "Theatrical Pragmatics," 162 (see ch. 5, n. 38). David Bevington has argued that this scene offers evidence for this playing having been the first or one of the first plays performed by professional, traveling troupes in England. David Bevington, *From Mankind to Marlowe: Growth of Structure in the Popular Drama of Tudor England* (Cambridge, MA: Harvard University Press, 1965), 8–25.

14. Indeed, the sin of sloth is often read as the core moral challenge of the play (Watkins, "Allegorical Theatre," 772). See also Siegfried Wenzel, *The Sin of Sloth: Accedia in Medieval Thought and Literature* (Chapel Hill: University of North Carolina Press, 1967), 148–54.

15. In treating Mercy as its literal meaning, the abstract quality of divine forgiveness as manifest in the world, I follow Sarah Beckwith. Beckwith insists, against a mountain of scholarship that reads Mercy as a priest or a friar of some sort, that Mercy must be taken seriously as *mercy*, in all its particularity, as the force that constitutes the divine office of forgiveness in each of its individual realizations. Sarah Beckwith, "Language Goes on Holiday: English Allegorical Drama and the Virtue Tradition," *JMEMS* (2012): 112.

16. As Beckwith notes, despair is treated as a subspecies of sloth in medieval penitential manuals (ibid., 111).

17. Ibid., 111–12.

18. Indeed, many scholars of the play who focus on its humor do indeed characterize it this way. In particular, Anthony Gash identifies the humor of the play as carnivalesque and designed to spoof Lenten self-denial. See Gash, "Carnival against Lent: The Ambivalence of Medieval Drama," in *Medieval Literature: Criticism, Ideology, and History*, ed. David Aers (Brighton, UK: Harvester Press, 1986), 74–98.

19. Mikhail Bahktin, *Rabelais and His World* (Bloomington: Indiana University Press, 1984), 7, 33, 70.

20. For a different perspective on the carnivalesque in which it *is* compatible with these plays, see Kathleen Biddick, "Genders, Bodies, Borders: Technologies of the Visible," *Speculum* 68 (1993): 389–418, at 409; see also Margaret Owens, *Stages of Dismemberment: The Fragmented Body in Late Medieval and Early Modern Drama* (Newark: University of Delaware Press, 2005), 67–68.

21. Bakhtin, *Rabelais and His World*, 148, 317.

22. Ibid., 15–17, 167.

23. Ibid., 9, 11, 19, 26, 75, 154.

24. Ibid., 5, 7, 34, 71

25. Martha Bayless makes this point in her study of Latin medieval parody. She shows that "Medieval Latin parody confounds the polarity between the official and unofficial cultures: these carnivalesque texts, many lampooning religious forms and ideas, were written by and for members of what has been considered the bastion of medieval seriousness, the Church." Martha Bayless, *Parody in the Middle Ages* (Ann Arbor: University of Michigan Press, 1996), 2. For further elaborations of the difficulties in applying Bakhtin's theory to Latin parody, see ibid., 179–81.

26. Beckwith has suggested that the play embodies a "reformist orthodoxy" ("Language Goes on Holiday," 120).

27. Even divine logic is discomfiting in the poem, being too precise, too concise, and too acutely aimed at the reader, as a participant in the fall from grace (Fish, *Surprised by Sin*, 81–82 [see ch. 5, n. 42]).

28. "In the pattern I discern in the poem, the reader is continually surprised by sin and in shame, 'sore displeased with himself,' his heart 'riseth against it'" (ibid., 44).

29. Fish says, "The reader who falls before the lure of Satanic rhetoric displays again the weakness of Adam, and his inability to avoid repeating that fall throughout indicates the extent to which Adam's lapse has made the reassertion of right seem impossible. Rhetoric is thus simultaneously the site of the reader's infirmity and the means by which he is brought first to self-knowledge, and then to contrition, and finally, perhaps, to grace and everlasting bliss" (ibid., 38).

30. Fish refers to Milton has having a "programme of reader harassment" Stanley Fish, *Surprised by Sin* (London: Macmillan, 1997), 4.

31. Cawsey views this moment of the destruction of language as a sign of the play's larger investment in critiquing the judicial system via its use of bad Latin ("Tutivillus and the Kyrkchaterars," 450).

32. Sarah Peverley has suggested that this moment in the play may refer to the exile of Edward IV, who, because exiled, truly was the king of nothing. See Peverley, "Political Consciousness and the Literary Mind in Late Medieval England: Men 'Brought up of Nought' in Vale, Hardyng, Mankind, and Mallory," *Studies in Philology* 105 (2008): 1–29, at 19.

33. See Ashley and NeCastro's note to *M*, 505.

34. Sarah Beckwith has suggested that New Guise's nonsensical hiccupping mocks Mercy's sincere searching for mankind by undermining the transformative words of the mass: "The very capacity of language to denote is being called into question here. Titivillus has turned Mankind's prayers to piss and shit; here New Guise's words answers [*sic*] Mercy's heartfelt search parodying the central words of the Mass ('Hoc est corpus meum') in a semi-nonsensical hiccough" ("Language goes on Holiday," 113).

35. When Mercy explains the significance of Christ's crucifixion to Truth, she simply says, "Sith this barn was ybore ben thritti wynter passed,/ Which deide and deeth tholed this day aboute mydday—/And that is cause of this clips that closeth now the sonne,/ In menynge that man shal fro merknesse be drawe/ The while this light and this leme shal Lucifer ablende./ For patriarkes and prophetes han preched herof often—/ That man shal man save thorugh a maydenes helpe,/ And that was tynt thorugh tree, tree shal it wynne,/ And that Deeth down broughte, deeth shal releve." (*PP*, B.18.133–41). Langland's Mercy is matter-of-fact, dispassionate, and informative, not at all the horrified, panicked, empathic Mercy of *Mankind.*

36. On this scene as a dark representation of a manorial court, see W. Nicholas Knight, "Equity and Mercy in English Law and Drama (1405–1641)," *Comparative Drama* 6 (1972): 51–67, at 55.

37. See ibid., 55–56.

38. And indeed, the equity court did function this way, even in the years immediately preceding the probable composition of *Mankind* in around 1470. The Chancellor in 1467 judged in favor of an appellant plaintiff who was ignorant of the law in his previous trial, saying that only God can judge foolish men. See George Burton Adams, "The Continuity of English Equity," *Yale Law Review* 26 (1916): 562, cited in Knight, "Equity and Mercy," 53.

39. Hilton's *Scale of Perfection* is a late fourteenth century work. See Walter Hilton, *Scale of Perfection*, ed. Thomas Bestul (Kalamazoo, MI: TEAMS, 2000), bk. 2, ch.1, 14–30; ch. 5, 209–27.

40. "A man goyth vppe ryght and the soule of his body is sparyd, as a purse fulle feyer. And whan it is tyme of his nescessery, it is openyde and sparyde ayen fulle honestly. And that it is he that doyth this it is schewed ther wher he seyth, he comyth downe to vs to the lowest parte of oure nede" (*Rev.*, 143.6.30, 32–33).

CONCLUSION

1. Rolle's *Form of Living* (see ch. 1, n. 38), the *Cloud*-author's *Cloud of Unknowing* (see ch. 1, n. 3), and Walter Hilton's *Scale of Perfection* (see ch. 6, n. 39) are all written as if addressed to a single, specific reader.

2. See Brantley, *Reading in the Wilderness*, 1–26, 269–290 (see intro., n. 17).

3. Sargent, "Mystical Writings," 77–78 (see intro., n. 53).

4. Coletti, *Drama of Saints*, 103 (see intro., n. 53).

Bibliography

Abbott, Christopher. *Julian of Norwich: Autobiography and Theology.* London: Boydell and Brewer, 1999.

Adams, George Burton. "The Continuity of English Equity." *Yale Law Review* 26 (1916): 550–63.

Aers, David. *Sanctifying Signs: Making Christian Tradition in Late Medieval England.* Notre Dame, IN: University of Notre Dame Press, 2004.

Alter, Adam L. "Benefits of Cognitive Disfluency." *Current Directions in Psychological Science* 22 (2013): 437–42.

Alter, A[dam] L., D. M. Oppenheimer, N. Epley, and R. N. Eyre. "Overcoming Intuition: Metacognitive Difficulty Activates Analytic Reasoning." *Journal of Experimental Psychology: General* 136 (2007): 569–76.

Andersen, Elisabeth A. *The Voices of Mechthild of Magdeburg.* Bern: Peter Lang, 2000.

Annice, Sister M. "Historical Sketch of the Theory of Participation." *New Scholasticism* 26 (1952): 49–79.

Anonymous. *The Cloud of Unknowing and the Book of Privy Counselling.* Ed. Phyllis Hodgson, EETS, o.s., 218. Oxford: Oxford University Press, 1943–44.

Anonymous. *The Latin Versions of* The Cloud of Unknowing, *Nubes ignorandi, MS. Bodley 856.* Analecta Cartusiana 119:1, ed. John Clark. New York: Edwin Mellen Press, 1999.

Anonymous. *Mankind.* Ed. Kathleen Ashley and Gerard NeCastro. Kalamazoo, MI: Medieval Institute Publications, 2010.

Anonymous. *Tretise on Miraclis Pleyinge.* Ed. Clifford Davidson. Kalamazoo, MI: Medieval Institute Publications, 1993.

Anonymous. *Two Moral Interludes: Pride of Life and Wisdom.* Ed. David Klausner. Kalamazoo, MI: Medieval Institute Publications, 2008.

Aristotle. *Posterior Analytics.* Trans. G. R. G. Mure. Oxford: Clarendon, 1928.

Augustine. *Confessionum libri tredecim.* In *Corpus Christianorum,* Series Latina, vol. 27. Ed. L. Verheijen. Turnhout, Belgium: Brepols, 1981.

———. *De Doctrina Christiana.* In Migne, *Patrologia Latina,* vol. 34.

———. *De Trinitate.* In Migne, *Patrologia Latina,* vol. 42.

Bahktin, Mikhail. *Rabelais and His World.* Bloomington: Indiana University Press, 1984.

Baker, Denise. *Julian's Shewings: From Vision to Book.* Princeton, NJ: Princeton University Press, 1993.

Baker, Donald C. "Is Wisdom a 'Professional' Play?" in Riggio, *Wisdom Symposium*, 67–86.

Bayless, Martha. *Parody in the Middle Ages.* Ann Arbor: University of Michigan Press, 1996.

Beckwith, Sarah. "Language Goes on Holiday: English Allegorical Drama and the Virtue Tradition," *JMEMS* (2012): 107–30.

———. "Rituals, Church, and Theatre." In *Culture and History: 1350–1600, English Communities, Identities, and Writing*, ed. David Aers. Detroit: Wayne State University Press, 1992.

———. *Signifying God: Social Relation and Symbolic Act in the York Corpus Christi Plays.* Chicago: University of Chicago Press, 2001.

Bede. "De syllaba," in *De arte metrica.* In Migne, *Patrologia Latina*, vol. 90.

———. *De temporum ratione.* In Migne, *Patrologia Latina*, vol. 90.

Beer, Frances. *Women and Mystical Experience in the Middle Ages.* Woodbridge: Boydell, 1992.

Benson, David C., and Lynne Blanchfield. *The Manuscripts of* Piers Plowman: *The B-Version.* Cambridge: Brewer, 1997.

Bernard of Silvester. "Il *'Dictamen'* di Bernardo Silvestre." *Rivista Critica della Storia Filosofia, Testi e Documenti* 20 (1965): 182–230.

Bevington, David. "Blake and Whytt, Fowll and Fayer: Stage Picture in *Wisdom Who is Christ.*" *Comparative Drama* 19 (1985): 136–50.

———. *From Mankind to Marlowe: Growth of Structure in the Popular Drama of Tudor England.* Cambridge, MA: Harvard University Press, 1965.

Bhattacharji, Santha. "Independence of Thought in Julian of Norwich." *Word and Spirit* 11 (1989): 79–92.

Biddick, Kathleen. "Genders, Bodies, Borders: Technologies of the Visible." *Speculum* 68 (1993): 389–418.

Biernoff, Suzannah. *Sight and Embodiment in the Middle Ages.* New York: Palgrave, 2002.

Bloomfield, Morton. "A Grammatical Approach to Medieval Personification Allegory." *Modern Philology* 60 (1963): 161–71.

Boethius. *Boethii: Philosophiae Consolatio.* In *Corpus Christianorum*, Series Latina, vol. 94, ed. Ludwig Bieler. Turnhout, Belgium: Brepols, 1957.

Børresen, Kari. "Christ notre mère, la Théologie de Julienne de Norwich." *Mitteilungen und Forschungsbeitrage der Cusanus-Gesellschaft* 13 (1978): 320–29.

Bradley, Ritamarie. "The Motherhood Theme in Julian of Norwich." *14th-Century English Mystics Newsletter* 2, no. 4 (1976): 25–30.

Brantley, Jessica. *Reading in the Wilderness: Private Devotion and Public Performance in Late Medieval England.* Chicago: University of Chicago Press, 2008.

Brecht, Bertolt. "Alienation Effects in Chinese Acting" and "Short Description of a New Technique of Acting which Produces an Alienation Effect." In *Brecht on Theatre: The Development of an Aesthetic*, trans. John Willett. London: Methuen, 1964.

Burrow, J. A. "Fantasy and Language in *The Cloud of Unknowing.*" *Essays in Criticism* 27 (1977): 283–98.

———. "Wasting Time, Wasting Words in *Piers Plowman* B and C." *Yearbook of Langland Studies* 17 (2003): 191–202.

Bush, Jerome. "The Resources of Locus and Platea Staging: The Digby Mary Magdalene." *Studies in Philology* 86 (1989): 139–65.

Butterworth, Philip, ed. *The Narrator, the Expositor, and the Prompter in European Medieval Theatre.* Turnhout, Belgium: Brepols, 2007.

Carruthers, Mary. "Allegory without the Teeth: Some Reflections on Figural Language in *Piers Plowman.*" *Yearbook of Langland Studies* 19 (2005): 27–43.

———. *The Search for St. Truth: A Study of Meaning in Piers Plowman.* Evanston, IL: Northwestern University Press, 1973.

Caspar, Ruth. "'All Shall Be Well': Prototypical Symbols of Hope." *Journal of the History of Ideas* 42 (1981): 139–50.

Catto, Jeremy. "After Arundel: The Opening or the Closing of the English Mind." In Gillespie and Ghosh, *After Arundel*, 43–54.

———. "1349–1412, Culture and History." In Fanous and Gillespie, *Cambridge Companion to Medieval English Mysticism*, 113–132.

Cawsey, Kathy. "Tutivillus and the Kyrkchaterars: Strategies of Control in the Middle Ages." *Studies in Philology* 102 (2005): 434–51.

Cervone, Cristina Maria. *Poetics of the Incarnation: Middle English Writing and the Leap of Love*. Philadelphia: University of Pennsylvania Press, 2013.

Chaganti, Seeta. *The Medieval Poetics of the Reliquary: Enshrinement, Inscription, Performance*. New York: Palgrave, 2008.

———. "The *Platea* Pre- and Postmodern: A Landscape of Medieval Performance." *Exemplaria* 25 (2013): 252–64.

Chambers, E. K. *English Literature at the Close of the Middle Ages*. Oxford: Clarendon, 1945.

———. *Medieval Stage*. London: Oxford University Press, 1903.

Chambers, R. W., ed. *On the Continuity of English Prose from Alfred to More and His School*. London: Oxford University Press, EETS, 1932.

Chase, Steven. *Contemplation and Compassion*. Maryknoll, NY: Orbis Books, 2003.

Chaucer, Geoffrey. *Boece*. In *The Riverside Chaucer*, ed. Larry D. Benson. Boston: Houghton Mifflin, 1987.

Clopper, Lawrence. "Langland and Allegory: A Proposition." *Yearbook of Langland Studies* 15 (2001): 35–42.

———. "*Mankind* and its Audience." *Comparative Drama* 8 (1974–75): 347–55.

———. "*Miracula* and the *Tretise of Miraclis Pleyinge*." *Speculum* 76 (1990): 878–905.

———. *Songes of Rechelesnesse: Langland and the Franciscans*. Ann Arbor: University of Michigan Press, 1997.

Coghill, Nevill. *The Pardon of Piers Plowman*. London: British Academy Proceedings, 1945.

Cole, Andrew. *Literature and Heresy in the Age of Chaucer*. Cambridge: Cambridge University Press, 2008.

———. "Trifunctionality and the Tree of Charity." *English Literary History* 61 (1995): 1–27.

Coletti, Teresa. "Devotional Iconography in the N-Town Marian Plays." *Comparative Drama* 11 (1977): 22–44.

———. *Mary Magdalene and the Drama of Saints*. Philadelphia: University of Pennsylvania Press, 2004.

———. "Purity and Danger: The Paradox of Mary's Body and the En-gendering of the Infancy Narrative in the English Mystery Cycles." In *Feminist Approaches to the Body in Medieval Literature*, ed. Linda Lomperis and Sarah Stanbury, 65–95. Philadelphia: University of Pennsylvania Press, 1993.

Corson, John. "Contemplation and Contemplatives." *Life of the Spirit* 4 (1950): 318–22.

Courcelle, Pierre. *Connais-toi Toi-même: De Socrate à St. Bernard*. Paris: Études Augustiniennes, 1974.

———. *La Consolation de Philosophie dans la tradition littéraire*. Paris: Études Augustiniennes,1967.

Craig, Hardin. *English Religious Drama in the Middle Ages*. Oxford: Clarendon, 1960.

Crassons, Kate. *Claims of Poverty: Literature, Culture, and Ideology in Late Medieval England*. Notre Dame, IN: University of Notre Dame Press, 2010.

Dailey, Patricia. *Promised Bodies: Time, Language, and Corporeality in Medieval Women's Mystical Texts*. New York: Columbia University Press, 2013.

Davenport, W. A. *Fifteenth-Century English Drama: The Early Moral Plays and Their Literary Relations*. London: Brewer, 1982.

Davidson, Clifford. *Visualizing the Moral Life: Medieval Iconography and the Macro Morality Plays*. New York: AMS Press, 1989.

Davis, Carmel Bendon. *Mysticism and Space: Space and Spatiality in the Works of Richard Rolle, The Cloud of Unknowing-author, and Julian of Norwich*. Washington, DC: Catholic University of America Press, 2008.

Davis, Marian. "Nicholas Love and the N-Town Cycle." PhD diss., Auburn University, 1979.

Davis, Rebecca. "'Save Man Alone': Human Exceptionality in *Piers Plowman* and the Exemplarist Tradition." In *Medieval Latin and Middle English Literature: Essays in Honor of Jill Mann*, ed. Christopher Cannon and Maura Nolan, 41–64. London: Brewer, 2011.

Davlin, Mary Clemente. *A Game of Heuene: Word Play and Meaning in Piers Plowman B*. Cambridge: Brewer, 1989.

del Mastro, M. L. "Juliana of Norwich: Parable of the Lord and Servant; Radical Orthodoxy." *Mystics Quarterly* 14 (1988): 84–93.

Deskis, Susan, and Thomas Hill. "'The longe man ys seld wys': Proverbial Characterization and Langland's Long Will." *Yearbook of Langland Studies* 18 (2004): 73–79.

Despres, Denise. "Sacramentals and Ghostly Sights." *Religion and Literature* 42 (2010): 101–10.

Diemand-Yauman, C., D. M. Oppenheimer, and E. B. Vaughn. "Fortune Favors the Bold (and the Italicized): Effects of Disfluency on Educational Outcomes." *Cognition* 118 (2009): 111–15.

Diller, Hans-Jürgen. "Theatrical Pragmatics: The Actor-Audience Relationship from the Mystery Cycles to the Early Tudor Dramas." *Comparative Drama* 23 (1989): 156–65.

Dinshaw, Carolyn. *How Soon Is Now? Medieval Texts, Amateur Readers, and the Queerness of Time*. Durham, NC: Duke University Press, 2012.

Dox, Donnalee. *The Idea of Theater in Latin Christian Thought*. Ann Arbor: University of Michigan Press, 2004.

Duffy, Eamon. *The Stripping of the Altars: Traditional Religion in England, 1400–1580*. New Haven, CT: Yale University Press, 1992.

Dupré, Louis. "The Christian Experience of Mystical Union." *Journal of Religion* 69 (1989): 1–13.

Eckhart, Meister. "The Father Gives His Son Birth without Ceasing." In *Meister Eckhart: The Essential Sermons, Commentaries, Treatises, and Defense, German Works*, Sermon 6, ed. Edmund Colledge and Bernard McGinn. New York: Paulist Press, 1981.

Eden, Kathy. *Poetic and Legal Fiction in the Aristotelian Tradition*. Princeton, NJ: Princeton University Press, 1986.

Ellis, Roger, and Samuel Fanous, "1349–1412: Texts," in Fanous and Gillespie, *Cambridge Companion to Medieval English Mysticism*.

Fanous, Samuel, and Vincent Gillespie, eds. *Cambridge Companion to Medieval English Mysticism*. Cambridge: Cambridge University Press, 2011.

Fish, Stanley. *Surprised by Sin: The Reader in* Paradise Lost. London: Macmillan, 1997.

Fletcher, Alan J. "The Design of the N-Town Play of Mary's Conception." *Modern Philology* 79 (1981): 166–73.

Flora, H. *The Devout Belief of the Imagination: The Paris 'Meditationes Vitae Christi' and Female Franciscan Spirituality in Trecento Italy*. Turnhout, Belgium: Brepols, 2009.

Forrest, Patricia. "The Role of the Expositor Contemplacio in the Saint Anne's Day Plays of the Hegge Cycle." *Mediaeval Studies* 28 (1966): 60–76.

Fulton, Rachel. *From Judgment to Passion: Devotion to Christ and the Virgin Mary, 800–1200*. New York: Columbia University Press, 2002.

Galloway, Andrew. "The Making of a Social Ethic in Late-Medieval England: From Gratitudo to 'Kyndenesse.'" *Journal of the History of Ideas* 55 (1994): 365–83.

Gardner, Helen. "Walter Hilton and the Authorship of the *Cloud of Unknowing*." *Review of English Studies* 9 (1933): 129–47.

Garner, Stanton B. "Theatricality in 'Mankind' and 'Everyman.'" *Studies in Philology* 84 (1987): 272–85.

Gash, Anthony. "Carnival against Lent: The Ambivalence of Medieval Drama." In *Medieval Literature: Criticism, Ideology, and History*, ed. David Aers, 74–98. Brighton, UK: Harvester Press, 1986.

Gatch, Milton McC. "Mysticism and Satire in the Morality of *Wisdom*." *Philological Quarterly* 53 (1974): 342–62.

Gayk, Shannon. *Image, Text, and Religious Reform in Fifteenth-Century England*. Cambridge: Cambridge University Press, 2010.

Gibson, Gail McMurray. "The Play of Wisdom and the Abbey of St. Edmund." *Comparative Drama* 19 (1985): 117–35.

———. "The Play of *Wisdom* and the Abbey of St. Edmund." In Riggio, *Wisdom Symposium*, 39–66.

———. *The Theater of Devotion: East Anglian Drama and Society in the Late Middle Ages*. Chicago: University of Chicago Press, 1989.

Gibson, Margaret. "Boethius in the Carolingian Schools." *Transactions of the Royal Historical Society* 32 (1982): 43–56.

Gillespie, Vincent. "Chichele's Church." In Gillespie and Ghosh, *After Arundel*, 3–42.

———. "1412–1534: Culture and History." In Fanous and Gillespie, *Cambridge Companion to Medieval English Mysticism*, 163–94.

———. "Vernacular Theology." In *Middle English*, ed. Paul Strohm, 401–19. Oxford: Oxford University Press, 2007.

Gillespie, Vincent, and Kantik Ghosh, eds. *After Arundel: Religious Writing in Fifteenth-Century England*. Turnhout, Belgium: Brepols, 2011.

Glasscoe, Marion. Introduction to *Julian of Norwich, A Revelation of Love*, ed. Marion Glasscoe, vii–xviii. Exeter, UK: University of Exeter Press, 1986.

———. *Medieval English Mystics: Games of Faith*. New York: Longman, 1993.

Granger, Penny. *The N-Town Play: Drama and Liturgy in Medieval East Anglia*. Cambridge: Brewer, 2009.

Grayson, Janet. "The Eschatological Adam's Kirtle." *Mystics Quarterly* 11 (1985): 153–60.

Hanna, Ralph. "The Scribe of Huntington HM 114." *Studies in Bibliography* 42 (1989): 120–33.

———. "Will's Work." In Justice and Kerby-Fulton, *Written Work*, 23–66.

Hanning, Robert W. "From Eva and Ave to Eglentyne and Alisoun: Chaucer's Insight into the Roles Women Play." *Signs* 2 (1977): 580–99.

Harris, Joseph. *Inventing the Spectator: Subjectivity and the Theatrical Experience in Early Modern France*. Oxford: Oxford University Press, 2014.

Heimmel, Jennifer P. *"God Is Our Mother": Julian of Norwich and the Medieval Image of Christian Feminine Divinity*. Salzburg: Institut für Anglistik und Amerikanistik, Universität Salzburg, 1982.

Herdt, Jennifer. *Putting on Virtue: The Legacy of the Splendid Vices*. Chicago: University of Chicago Press, 2008.

Hilton, Walter. *Scale of Perfection*. Ed. Thomas Bestul. Kalamazoo, MI: TEAMS, 2000.

———. *Walter Hilton's* Mixed Life *Edited from Lambeth Palace MS 472*. Ed. S. J. Ogilvie-Thompson. Salzburg: Institut für Anglistik und Amerikanistik, 1986.

Hobgood, Allison. *Passionate Playgoers in Early Modern England*. Cambridge: Cambridge University Press, 2014.

Hodgson, Phyllis. Introduction to *The Cloud of Unknowing and the Book of Privy Counselling*. EETS, o.s., 218. London: Oxford University Press, 1944.

———. "*A Ladder of Foure Ronges by the Whiche Men mowe wele clyme to Heven*: A Study of the Prose Style of a Middle English Translation." *Modern Language Review* 44 (1949): 465–75.

Holsinger, Bruce. *Music, Body, and Desire in Medieval Culture: Hildegard of Bingen to Chaucer*. Stanford, CA: Stanford University Press, 2001.

Hudson, Anne. *Premature Reformation: Wycliffite Texts and Lollard Heresy*. Oxford: Oxford University Press, 1988.

Huppé, Bernard F. "Petrus id est Christus: Word Play in Piers Plowman, the B-Text." *English Literary History* 17 (1950): 163–90.

Hussey, S. S. "Langland, Hilton, and the Three Lives," *Review of English Studies* 7 (1956): 132–50.

Jenkins, Ena. "Julian's *Revelation of Love:* A Web of Metaphor." In McAvoy, *Companion to Julian of Norwich*, 181–91.

Jodogne, Omer. "La Personnalité de l'Ecrivain d' öil." In *L'Humanisme Médiéval dans les Littératures Romanes du XIIe au XIVe siècle*, ed. Anthime Fourrier. Paris: Klincksieck, 1964.

Johnson, Barbara. *Reading* Piers Plowman *and* The Pilgrim's Progress: *Reception and the Protestant Reader*. Carbondale: Southern Illinois University Press, 1992.

Johnson, Eleanor. "Feeling Time, Will, and Words in the *Cloud of Unknowing*." *Journal of Medieval and Early Modern Studies* 41 (2011): 345–68.

———. "The Poetics of Waste." *PMLA* 127 (2012): 460–76.

———. *Practicing Literary Theory in the Middle Ages*. Chicago: University of Chicago Press, 2013.

Johnson, Ian. "Making the *Consolatio* in Middle English." In *A Companion to Boethius in the Middle Ages*, ed. Noel Harold Kaylor and Philip Edward Philips, 413–46. Leiden: Brill, 2012.

———. *The Middle English Life of Christ: Academic Discourse, Translation, and Vernacular Theology*. Turnhout, Belgium: Brepols, 2013.

———. "Vernacular Theology/Theological Vernacular." In Gillespie and Ghosh, *After Arundel*, 73–90.

Jones, E. A. "Anchoritic Aspects of Julian of Norwich." In McAvoy, *Companion to Julian of Norwich*, 75–87.

Jones, Mike Rodman. *Radical Pastoral, 1381–1594: Appropriation and the Writing of Religious Controversy*. London: Ashgate, 2010.

Julian of Norwich. *A Book of Showings*. Ed. James Colledge and Edmund Walsh. Toronto: PIMS, 1978.

———. *The Writings of Julian of Norwich: A Vision Showed to a Devout Woman and a Revelation of Love*. Ed. Nicholas Watson and Jacqueline Jenkins. Philadelphia: University of Pennsylvania Press, 2006.

Justice, Steven. "Authorial Work and Literary Ideology." In Justice and Kerby-Fulton, *Written Work*, 1–12.

———. *Writing and Rebellion*. Berkeley: University of California Press, 1994.

Justice, Steven, and Kathryn Kerby-Fulton, eds. *Written Work: Langland, Labor, and Authorship*. Philadelphia: University of Pennsylvania Press, 1997.

Karnes, Michelle. *Imagination, Meditation and Cognition in the Middle Ages*. Chicago: University of Chicago Press, 2011.

———. "Will's Imagination in *Piers Plowman*." *Journal of English and Germanic Philology* 108 (2009): 27–58.

Kelen, Sarah. *Langland's Early Modern Identities*. New York: Palgrave, 2007.

Kempe, Margery. *The Book of Margery Kempe*. Ed. Lynn Staley. Kalamazoo, MI: TEAMS, 1996.

Kerby-Fulton, Kathryn. "Prophecy and Suspicion." *Speculum* 75 (2000): 318–41.

King, Pamela. "Morality Plays." In *The Cambridge Companion to Medieval English Theatre*, ed. Richard Beadle, 240–64. Cambridge: Cambridge University Press, 1994.

Knight, W. Nicholas. "Equity and Mercy in English Law and Drama (1405–1641)." *Comparative Drama* 6 (1972): 51–67.

Knowles, David. *The English Mystical Tradition.* New York: Harper and Brothers, 1961.

Kolve, V. A. *The Play Called Corpus Christi*. Stanford, CA: Stanford University Press, 1966.

Krapp, George Philip. *The Rise of Early English Literary Prose*. Oxford: Oxford University Press, 1915.

Kruger, Steven. "Mirrors and the Trajectory of Vision in *Piers Plowman*." *Speculum* 66 (1991): 74–95.

Laham, S. M., P. Koval, and Adam Alter. "The Name-Pronunciation Effect: Why People Like Mr. Smith more than Mr. Colquhoun." *Journal of Experimental Social Psychology* 48 (2012): 752–56.

Langland, William. *Piers Plowman: A Parallel-Text Edition of the A, B, C and Z Versions*. Ed. A. V. C. Schmidt. 2 vols. New York: Longman, 1995.

Largier, Niklaus. "Inner Senses-Outer Senses: The Practice of Emotions in Medieval Mysticism." In *Codierungen von Emotionen im Mittelalter*, ed. C. Stephen Jaeger and Ingrid Kasten, 3–15. Berlin: Walter de Gruyter, 2003.

LaVere, Suzanne. "From Contemplation to Action: The Role of the Active Life in the *Glossa ordinaria* on the Song of Songs." *Speculum* 82 (2007): 54–69.

Lawton, D. A. "Lollardy and the *Piers Plowman* Tradition." *Modern Language Review* 76 (1981): 780–93.

Lees, Rosemary Ann. *The Negative Language of the Dionysian School of Mystical Theology: An Approach to the* "Cloud of Unknowing." Salzburg: Institut für Anglistik und Amerikanistik, 1983.

Lerud, Theodore K. *Memory, Images, and the English Corpus Christi Drama*. New York: Palgrave, 2008.

Lewis, C. S. *Studies in Words*. Cambridge: Cambridge University Press, 1960.

Liegey, Gabriel. "Carmen Prosaicum." *Medieval Studies* 19 (1957): 15–36.

Lock, Charles. "The Cloud of Unknowing: Apophatic Discourse and Vernacular Anxieties." In *Text and Voice: The Rhetoric of Authority in the Middle Ages*, ed. Marianne Børch. Odense: University of Southern Denmark Press, 2004.

Love, Nicholas. *Mirrour of the Blessed Lyf of Jesu Christ*. Ed. Lawrence F. Powell. Oxford: Clarendon, 1908.

Mannyng, Robert. *Handlyng Synne*. Ed. Frederick Furnivall. London: EETS, Keegan Paul, 1901.

Marshall, John. "Marginal Staging Marks in the Macro Manuscript of *Wisdom*." *Medieval English Theatre* 7 (1985): 77–81.

———. "'O ye Soverens that Sytt and Ye Brothern that Stonde Ryght Wppe': Addressing the Audiences of *Mankind*." *European Medieval Drama* 1 (1997): 189–202.

Masson, Cynthea. "The Point of Coincidence: Rhetoric and the Apophatic in Julian of Norwich's *Shewings*." In McEntire, *Julian of Norwich*, 153–81.

May, David H. "Paul's Understanding of Faith as Participation." In *Paul and His Theology*, ed. Stanley E. Porter, 45–76. Boston: Brill, 2006.

McAvoy, Liz Herbert, ed. *A Companion to Julian of Norwich*. Cambridge: Brewer, 2008.

McAvoy, Liz Herbert. Introduction to McAvoy, *Companion to Julian of Norwich*, 1–16.

McEntire, Sandra, ed. *Julian of Norwich: A Book of Essays*. New York: Garland, 1998.

McEntire, Sandra. "The Likeness of God." In McEntire, *Julian of Norwich*, 3–35.

McGinn, Bernard. "The Changing Shape of Late Medieval Mysticism." *Church History* 65 (1996): 197–219.

———. *The Flowering of Mysticism: Men and Women in the New Mysticism: 1200–1350*. New York: Crossroad Publishing, 1998.

———. *The Growth of Mysticism*. New York: Crossroad Publishing, 1994.

———. "Love, Knowledge, and Mystical Union in Western Christianity." *Church History* 56 (1987): 7–24.

———. *Three Treatises on Man: A Cistercian Anthropology*. Collegeville, MN: Cistercian Publications, 1977. Distributed by Liturgical Press.

McGlone, M. S., and J. Tofighbakhsh. "Birds of a Feather Flock Conjointly (?): Rhyme as Reason in Aphorisms." *Psychological Science* 11 (2001): 424–28.

McNamer, Sarah. "The Exploratory Image: God as Mother in Julian of Norwich's *Revelations of Divine Love*." *Mystics Quarterly* 15 (1989): 21–28.

———. "The Origins of the *Meditationes vitae Christi*." *Speculum* 84 (2009): 905–55.

Meredith, Peter. "Establishing an Expositor's Role: Contemplacio and the N.Town Manuscript." In Butterworth, *Narrator, Expositor, and Prompter*, 289–306.

———, ed. *The Mary Play: From the N-Town Manuscript*. Rev. 2nd ed. Exeter Medieval Texts and Studies. Liverpool: Liverpool University Press, 1997.

Middleton, Anne. "Acts of Vagrancy: The C Version 'Autobiography' and the Statute of 1388." In Justice and Kerby-Fulton, *Written Work*, 208–317.

———. "Aelfric's Answerable Style: The Rhetoric of the Alliterative Prose." *Studies in Medieval Culture* 4 (1973): 83–91.

———. "The Audience and Public of *Piers Plowman*." In *Middle English Alliterative Poetry*, ed. David Lawton, 101–23. Cambridge: Brewer, 1982.

———. "William Langland's 'Kynde Name': Authorial Signature and Social Identity in Late Fourteenth-Century England." In *Literary Practice and Social Change in Britain, 1380–1530*, ed. Lee Patterson, 15–82. Berkeley: University of California Press, 1990.

Miller, Mark. "Sin and Structure in *Piers Plowman*: On the Medieval Split Subject." *Modern Language Quarterly* 76 (2015): 201–24.

Migne, Jacques-Paul. *Patrologia Latina*. 221 vols. Paris: Garnier, 1841–1865. http://pld.chadwyck.com/all/fulltext?ALL=Y&WARN=N&PRINT=YES&ALL=Y&warn=N&ACTION=byid&ID=Z400051707&FILE=../session/1508957468_25119&PRINT=yes.

Minnis, Alastair. "Affection and Imagination in *The Cloud of Unknowing* and Hilton's *Scale of Perfection*." *Traditio* 39 (1983): 323–66.

———. "The Sources of the Cloud of Unknowing: A Reconsideration." In *Medieval Mysticism in England*, ed. Marion Glasscoe, 63–73. Exeter: Short Run, 1982.

Morgan, Margery M. "A Talking of the Love of God and the Continuity of Stylistic Tradition in Middle English Prose Meditations." *Review of English Studies* 3 (1952): 97–116.

Mueller, Janel. *The Native Tongue and the Word*. Chicago: University of Chicago Press, 1985.

Muir, Lynette R. "Playing God in Medieval Europe." In *The Stage as Mirror: Civic Theatre in Late Medieval Europe*, ed. Alan E. Knight, 25–50. London: Brewer, 1997.

Mullaly, Robert. *The Carole: A Study of a Medieval Dance*. Surrey, UK: Ashgate, 2011.

Murakami, Ineke. *Moral Play and Counterpublic: Transformations in Moral Drama, 1465–1599*. New York: Routledge, 2011.

Murdoch, John. "From Social into Intellectual Factors: An Aspect of the Unitary Character of Late Medieval Learning." In *The Cultural Context of Medieval Learning: Proceedings of the First International Colloquium on Philosophy, Science, and Theology in the Middle Ages—September 1973*, ed. John Emery Murdoch and Edith Dudley Sylla, 271–348. Boston: Springer, 1975.

Myles, Robert. ""This Litil Worde 'Is'": The Existential Metaphysics of the *Cloud* Author." *Florilegium* 8 (1986): 140–68.

Neff, Amy. "The Pain of Compassio: Mary's Labor at the Foot of the Cross." *Art Bulletin* 80 (1998): 254–73.

Newman, Barbara. *God and the Goddesses: Vision, Poetry, and Belief in the Middle Ages*. Philadelphia: University of Pennsylvania Press, 2005.

———. "What Did It Mean to Say, 'I Saw'?: The Clash between Theory and Practice in Medieval Visionary Culture." *Speculum* 80 (2005): 1–43.

Nisse, Ruth. *Defining Acts: Drama and the Politics of Interpretation in Late Medieval England*. Notre Dame, IN: Notre Dame University Press, 2005.

Owens, Margaret. *Stages of Dismemberment: The Fragmented Body in Late Medieval and Early Modern Drama*. Newark: University of Delaware Press, 2005.

Pabst, Bernhardt. *Atomtheorien des lateinischen Mittelalters*. Darmstadt, Ger.: Wissenschaftliche Buchgesellschaft, 1994.

Page, Christopher. *The Owl and the Nightingale: Musical Life and Ideas in France, 1100–1300*. London: Dent, 1989.

Pantin, W. A. *English Church in the Fourteenth Century*. Cambridge: Cambridge University Press, 1955.

Park, Tarjei. *Selfhood and 'Gostly Menyng' in Some Middle English Texts*. Lewiston, NY: Edwin Mellen Press, 2002.

Pasnau, Robert. *Theories of Cognition in the Later Middle Ages.* Cambridge: Cambridge University Press, 1997.

Patterson, Paul. "The Book and Religious Practice in Late Medieval England." *Religion and Literature* 37, no. 2 (2005): 1–8.

Pelikan, Jaroslav. *The Christian Tradition: A History of the Development of Doctrine.* Vol. 4, *Reformation of Church Dogma, 1300–1700.* Chicago: University of Chicago Press, 1985.

———. *Mary through the Centuries: Her Place in the History of Culture.* New Haven, CT: Yale University Press, 1998.

Pelphrey, Brant. *Love Was His Meaning: The Theology and Mysticism of Julian of Norwich.* Salzburg Studies in English Literature 92. Salzburg: Institut für Anglistik und Amerikanistik, Universität Salzburg, 1982.

Pettitt, Tom. "*Mankind:* An English Fastnachspiel?" In *Festive Drama: Papers from the Sixth Triennial Colloquium of the International Society for the Study of Medieval Theatre Lancaster, 13–19 July, 1989,* ed. Meg Twycross, 190–202. Cambridge: Brewer, 1996.

Peverley, Sarah. "Political Consciousness and the Literary Mind in Late Medieval England: Men 'Brought up of Nought' in Vale, Hardyng, Mankind, and Mallory." *Studies in Philology* 105 (2008): 1–29.

Pineas, Rainer. "The English Morality Play as a Weapon of Religious Controversy." *Studies in English Literature, 1500–1900* 2 (1962): 157–80.

Poor, Sara. *Mechthild of Magdeburg and Her Book: Gender and the Making of Textual Authority.* Philadelphia: University of Pennsylvania Press, 2004.

Potter, Robert. *The English Morality Play: Origins, History, and Influence of a Dramatic Tradition.* New York: Routledge, 1975.

Powell, Raymond. "Margery Kempe: An Exemplar of Late Medieval Piety." *Catholic Historical Review* 89 (2003): 1–23.

Pseudo-Bernard. *Meditationes.* In *Sancti Bernardi Opera omnia.* Paris, 1839.

Quilligan, Maureen. *The Language of Allegory: Defining the Genre.* Ithaca, NY: Cornell University Press, 1979.

Raskolnikov, Masha. *Body against Soul: Gender and Sowlehele in Middle English Allegory.* Columbus: Ohio State University Press, 2008.

Rastall, Richard. *Minstrels Playing: Music in Early English Religious Drama.* Cambridge: Brewer, 2001.

Reder, L. M., and G. W. Kusbit. "Locus of the Moses Illusion: Imperfect Encoding, Retrieval, or Match?" *Journal of Memory and Language* 30 (1991): 385–406.

Riddy, Felicity. "Julian of Norwich and Self-Textualization." In *Editing Women,* ed. Anne M. Hutchinson, 101–24. Toronto: University of Toronto Press, 1998.

———. "Women Talking about the Things of God: A Late Medieval Sub-Culture." In *Women and Literature in Britain, 1100–1500,* ed. Carol Meale, 104–27. Cambridge: Cambridge University Press, 1993.

Riggio, Milla Cozart. "Masqueing the Moral Expositor." In Butterworth, *Narrator, Expositor, and Prompter,* 161–89.

———. "The Staging of Wisdom." In *Wisdom Symposium,* 1–17.

———, ed. *The Wisdom Symposium: Papers from the Trinity College Medieval Festival.* New York: AMS Press, 1986.

Robertson, Elizabeth. "Julian of Norwich's 'Modernist' Style and the Creation of Audience." In McAvoy, *Companion to Julian of Norwich,* 139–53.

———. "Medieval Medical Views of Women and Female Spirituality in the *Ancrene Wisse* and Julian of Norwich's *Showings.*" In *Feminist Approaches to the Body in Medieval Literature,* ed. Linda Lomperis and Sarah Stanbury. Philadelphia: University of Pennsylvania Press, 1993.

Rolle, Richard. *The Contra amatores mundi of Richard Rolle of Hampole.* Ed. and trans. Paul F. Theiner. Berkeley: University of California Press, 1968.

———. *Ego Dormio* and *Form of Living*. In *The English Writings of Richard Rolle, Hermit of Hampole*, ed. Hope Emily Allen. Oxford: Oxford University Press, 1963.

———. *Emendatio vitae and Orationes ad honorem nominis Ihesu*. Ed. Nicholas Watson. Toronto: Medieval Latin Texts, 1995.

Rossiter, A. P. *English Drama from Early Times to the Elizabethans: Its Background, Origins, and Developments*. London: Hutchinson University Press, 1966.

Salmen, Walter. "Dances and Dance Music, c. 1300–1530." In *Music as Concept and Practice in the Late Middle Ages*, ed. Reinhard Strohm and Bonnie J. Blackburn, 162–90. Oxford: Oxford University Press, 2001.

Salter, Elizabeth (Zeeman). "Nicholas Love: A Fifteenth-Century Translator." *Review of English Studies* 6 (1955): 113–27.

———. *Nicholas Love's "Myrrour of the Blessed Lyf of Jesu Christ."* Analecta Cartusiana 10. Salzburg: Universität Salzburg, 1974.

———. *Piers Plowman, an Introduction*. Cambridge, MA: Harvard University Press, 1962.

Sanok, Catherine. *Her Life Historical: Exemplarity and Female Saints' Lives in Late Medieval England*. Philadelphia: University of Pennsylvania Press, 2007.

Sargent, Michael. "Mystical Writings and Dramatic Texts in Late Medieval England." *Religion and Literature* 37, no. 2 (2005): 77–98.

Scarry, Elaine. "The Well-Rounded Sphere: The Metaphysical Structure of the *Consolation of Philosophy*." In *Essays in the Numerical Criticism of Medieval Literature*, ed. Carolyn Eckhardt, 99–103. Lewiston, NY: Bucknell University Press, 1980.

Schindler, David C. "What's the Difference? On the Metaphysics of Participation in a Christian Context." *Saint Anselm Journal* 3 (2005): 1–27.

Scoville, Chester. *Saints and the Audience in Medieval Biblical Drama*. Toronto: University of Toronto Press, 2004.

Simpson, James. "From Reason to Affective Knowledge: Modes of Thought and Poetic Form in *Piers Plowman*." *Medium Aevum* 55 (1986): 1–23.

———. "Orthodoxy's Image Trouble." In Gillespie and Ghosh, *After Arundel*, 91–114.

———. *The Oxford English Literary History*. Vol. 2, *1350–1547: Reform and Cultural Revolution*. Oxford: Oxford University Press, 2002.

Skeat, William. *Parallel Extracts from Forty-Five Manuscripts of* Piers Plowman. London: Trubner, 1885.

Somerset, Fiona, and Nicholas Watson. "Preface: On 'Vernacular.'" In Watson and Somerset, *Vulgar Tongue*, ix–xiii.

Song, H., and N. Schwarz. "Fluency and the Detection of Misleading Questions: Low Processing Fluency Attenuates the Moses Illusion." *Social Cognition* 26 (2008): 791–99.

———. "If It's Difficult to Pronounce, It Must Be Risky." *Psychological Science* 20 (2009): 135–38.

Spiegel, Gabrielle. "Forging the Past: The Language of Historical Truth in the Middle Ages." *History Teacher* 17 (1984): 267–88.

———. *Romancing the Past: The Rise of Vernacular Prose Historiography in Thirteenth-Century France*. Berkeley: University of California Press, 1995.

Sponsler, Claire. *Drama and Resistance*. Minneapolis: University of Minnesota Press, 1997.

Sprung, Andrew. "'We nevyr shall come out of hym': Enclosure and Immanence in Julian of Norwich's *Book of Showings*." *Mystics Quarterly* 19 (1993): 47–62.

Staley, Lynn. "The Trope of the Scribe and the Question of Literary Authority in the Works of Julian of Norwich and Margery Kempe." *Speculum* 66 (1991): 820–38.

Steiner, Emily. *Reading Piers Plowman*. Cambridge: Cambridge University Press, 2013.

Stevens, Martin. "Dramatic Setting of the Wakefield Cycle." *PMLA* 81 (1966): 193–98.

———. *Four Middle English Mystery Cycles*. Princeton, NJ: Princeton University Press, 1987.

Stokes, James. "The Lost Playing Places of Lincolnshire." *Comparative Drama* 37 (2003): 275–95.

Strabo, Walafrid. *Evangelium Secundum Lucam.* In Migne, *Patrologia Latina*, vol. 114.

Sugano, Douglas. "Note for the *Mary Play.*" In *N-Town Plays*, ed. Douglas Sugano, 355–56. Kalamazoo, MI: TEAMS, 2007.

Sylla, Edith. "Medieval Quantifications of Qualities: The Merton School." *Archive for History of Exact Sciences* 8 (1971): 7–39.

Tanner, Norman. *The Church in Late Medieval Norwich 1370–1532.* Toronto: PIMS, 1984.

Tavormina, M. Teresa. "Kindly Similitude: Langland's Matrimonial Trinity." In *Modern Philology* 80 (1982): 117–28.

———. *Kindly Similitude: Marriage and Family in Piers Plowman.* Cambridge: Brewer, 1995.

Taylor, Cheryl. "Paradox upon Paradox: Using and Abusing Language in *The Cloud of Unknowing* and Related Texts." *Parergon* 22, no. 2 (2005): 31–51.

Thomas, Owen C. "Interiority and Christian Spirituality." *Journal of Religion* 80 (2000): 41–60.

Thomas von Capua. *Die ars dictandi des Thomas von Capua.* Ed. Emmy Heller. Heidelberg: Carl Winters Universitätsbuchhandlung, 1929.

Townsend, David. "The Current Questions and Future Prospects of Medieval Latin Studies." In *Oxford Handbook of Medieval Latin Literature*, 15–19. Oxford: Oxford University Press, 2012.

Vasvari, Louise O. "Joseph on the Margin: The Mérode Tryptic and the Medieval Spectacle." *Mediaevalia* 18 (1995): 163–89.

Waters, Claire. "A Miracle of History: The Conqueror, the Virgin, and Del harper a Roucestre." *New Medieval Literatures* 12 (2010): 47–68.

Watkins, John. "The Allegorical Theatre: Moralities, Interludes, and Protestant Drama." In *Cambridge History of Medieval English Literature*, ed. David Wallace, 767–92. Cambridge: Cambridge University Press, 1999.

Watson, Nicholas. "Censorship and Cultural Change in Late Medieval England: Vernacular Theology, the Oxford Translation Debate, and Arundel's Constitutions of 1409." *Speculum* 70 (1995): 822–64.

———. "The Composition of Julian of Norwich's *Revelation of Love.*" *Speculum* 68 (1993): 637–83.

———. "Conceptions of the Word: The Mother Tongue and the Incarnation of God." *New Medieval Literatures* 1 (1997): 85–124.

———. "Introduction: On Solomon's Tablets." In Watson and Somerset, *Vulgar Tongue*, 1–14.

———. Introduction to Fanous and Gillespie, *Cambridge Companion to Medieval English Mysticism*, 1–28.

———. "The Middle English Mystics." In *The Cambridge History of Medieval English Literature*, ed. David Wallace. Cambridge: Cambridge University Press, 1998.

———. "The Politics of Middle English." In *The Idea of the Vernacular*, ed. Jocelyn Wogan-Brown, Nicholas Watson, Andrew Taylor, and Ruth Evans, 331–51. University Park: Penn State University Press, 1999.

———. *Richard Rolle and the Invention of Authority.* Cambridge: Cambridge University Press, 1991.

———. "The Trinitarian Hermeneutic in Julian of Norwich's *Revelation of Love.*" In McEntire, *Julian of Norwich*, 61–90.

———. "Visions of Inclusion: Universal Salvation and Vernacular Theology." *Journal of Medieval and Early Modern Studies* 27 (1997): 145–87.

Watson, Nicholas, and Fiona Somerset, eds. *The Vulgar Tongue: Medieval and Postmedieval Vernacularity.* College Park: Pennsylvania State University Press, 2003.

Wells, H. W. "The Philosophy of Piers Plowman." *PMLA* 53 (1938): 339–49.

Wenzel, Siegfried. *The Sin of Sloth: Accedia in Medieval Thought and Literature.* Chapel Hill: University of North Carolina Press, 1967.

White, Hugh. *Nature and Salvation in Piers Plowman.* Cambridge: Brewer, 1988.

Wickham, Glynne. *Early English Stages, 1300–1660: Plays and their Makers to 1576.* London: Routledge, 1959.

William of St. Thierry. *The Nature of the Body and the Soul* and *Treatise on the Spirit and the Soul.* In *Three Treatises on Man,* ed. Bernard McGinn. Kalamazoo, MI: Cistercian Publications, 1977.

Williams, Arnold. *The Drama of Medieval England.* Ann Arbor: University of Michigan Press, 1961.

Wilson, F. P. *The English Drama: 1485–1585.* Oxford: Clarendon, 1968.

Wilson, R. M. "On the Continuity of English Prose." In *Mélanges de linguistique et de philologie Fernand Mossé in memoriam,* 486–94. Paris: Didier, 1959.

Windeatt, Barry. "1412–1534: Texts." In Fanous and Gillespie, *Cambridge Companion to Medieval English Mysticism,* 195–224.

Wittig, Joseph. "*Piers Plowman* B, Passus IX-XII: Elements in the Design of the Inward Journey." *Traditio* 28 (1972): 211–80.

Wright, Louis B. "Variety-Show Clownery on the Pre-Restoration Stage." *Anglia* 52 (1928): 51–68.

Young, Karl. *The Drama of the Medieval Church.* 2 vols. Oxford: Clarendon Press, 1933.

Zeeman, Nicolette. *Piers Plowman and the Medieval Discourse of Desire.* Cambridge: Cambridge University Press, 2006.

Index